RESTORATION
REVOLUTION
REACTION

Economics and Politics in Germany

1815-1871

By THEODORE S. HAMEROW

PRINCETON, NEW JERSEY
PRINCETON UNIVERSITY PRESS

Copyright © 1958 by Princeton University Press

L. C. Card 58-7117

ISBN 0-691-00755-1 (paperback edn.)

ISBN 0-691-05146-1 (hardcover edn.)

First PRINCETON PAPERBACK Edition, 1966

Second Printing, 1967

Third Printing, 1970

Fourth Printing, 1972

Sixth Hardcover Printing, 1972

Printed in the United States of America
by Princeton University Press, Princeton, New Jersey

To M. L. H.

PREFACE

MY INTEREST in Germany arose out of the Second World War. Those who lived through that terrible conflict will remember the sense of excitement which accompanied the news of invasions and campaigns on distant continents. And they will also recall the battle of words in which countless books and magazines described to a curious America an enemy nation which within the lifetime of a single generation had recovered from political disaster to achieve political domination. No state had ever come so close to the mastery of Europe, no state was ever forced to such a calamitous surrender. Its rise began less than a century ago, when a land of pleasant landscapes and romantic ruins boldly transformed its economy, reorganized its political system, and constructed a military machine of unrivaled efficiency. But, unable to satisfy its civic aspirations within the liberal tradition, it came to place increasing reliance on will-o'-the-wisp autocratic principles which led it deeper and deeper into a morass of authoritarianism to catastrophe. To study German history is to witness the unfolding of a national tragedy, a tragedy of a people stumbling mesmerized into the abyss.

The revolutionary events of 1848 attracted my special attention. For here Central Europe was exposed to influences and forces long familiar to western states. Here the ideals of freedom and unity inspired a political movement which briefly overcame the tradition of conservatism. And here liberalism suffered a defeat from which it never recovered. As Mr. A.J.P. Taylor puts it, "German history reached its turning-point and failed to turn." Yet how differently things might have turned out had Heinrich von Gagern become the architect of German unity instead of Otto von Bismarck. Would a parliamentary system of government have embraced so blindly a policy of blood and iron? Would democratic statesmen have taken the fatal road to Sarajevo? Would a public opinion nurtured on freedom have tolerated the Third Reich? The failure of the Revolution strengthened ideas and practices which led Europe to the holocaust. The penalty for the mistakes of 1848 was paid not in 1849, but in 1918, in 1933, and in 1945.

An examination of the causes and results of the Revolution thus seemed to me an important undertaking. But once I came to grips with it, I began to discover unexpected difficulties. First of all, I soon realized that an understanding of the political events of 1848 involved an investigation of the economic and social forces which drove the masses of Germany to insurrection. Secondly, these economic and social forces themselves could be properly evaluated only in the light of developments originating in the Restoration and culminating in the German Empire. It became apparent that the Revolution was the expression not only of ideological forces like nationalism and liberalism, but also of deep-seated popular dissatisfactions engendered by the transition from agrarian manorialism to industrial capitalism. Indeed, throughout the first half of the nineteenth century politics in Central Europe were profoundly affected by a painful social adjustment to new economic conditions. While parliamentarians and businessmen fought the policies of princes and landowners, the lower classes were engaged in a life-and-death struggle against the consequences of industrialization. And their influence on the direction of national growth was of paramount importance.

My purpose is to analyze that influence. The stirring political events of the years between Metternich and Bismarck are familiar in story and history. But outside the palaces and the legislatures, outside the universities and the government offices stretched overcrowded fields and teeming slums where the masses earned their daily bread. For the uprooted guildsman, the unemployed journeyman, the lackland peasant, and the agricultural laborer the conflict between liberal and conservative, between nationalist and particularist was of little

interest. Their major concern was the endless fight for survival, and in ideology they looked only for relief from want.
During the Restoration they pleaded their cause before established authority. Then, embittered by thirty years of disappointment, they turned to parliamentarianism. And at last,
after bourgeois constitutionalists had failed them, they threw
their support to a patriarchal legitimism of social welfare.
Their efforts to ward off economic disaster had a vital effect
on political life for more than fifty years, until the final triumph of the Industrial Revolution destroyed the precapitalistic world of independent artisans and small farmers.

I have tried to re-create that world. The task, difficult at
best, would have been altogether impossible without the generous assistance of libraries and archives which admitted me
to their collections. In Europe I received unstinted help from
the personnel of the *Bayerische Staatsbibliothek*, the *Bayer-
isches Hauptstaatsarchiv*, and the *Stadtarchiv* in Munich, the
Stadtarchiv in Frankfurt am Main, and the *Bibliothek der
Justus Liebig Hochschule*, formerly the *Universitäts-Biblio-
thek* in Giessen. In this country I found materials of great
value in the New York Public Library and the Library of
Congress. The Library of the Association of the Bar of the
City of New York permitted me to examine its extensive collection of statute books of the states of Germany. The libraries
of Harvard, Yale, and Columbia Universities courteously
gave me access to useful data. And I am under special obligation to the Library of the University of Illinois, not only for
allowing me to use its considerable resources, but also for
obtaining for me rare publications from other institutions.

My debt to friends and counselors is equally great. Professor John H. Wuorinen of Columbia University initiated
me into the study of German history. Professor Harry R.
Rudin of Yale University first pointed out to me the need to
investigate the economic background of the events of 1848.
Dr. Karl Demeter, formerly of the *Bundesarchiv* in Frank-

furt am Main, took a kind interest in my work, helped me locate important materials, and placed at my disposal the records of the German Handicraft and Artisan Congress. My colleagues at the University of Illinois, Professors J. Leonard Bates, C. Ernest Dawn, Charles E. Nowell, John B. Sirich, and Chester G. Starr, cheerfully faced the chore of reading the manuscript and made constructive suggestions for its betterment.

Finally, I want to express particular gratitude to Professor Hajo Holborn of Yale University. Patient and understanding, he encouraged, advised, reproved, improved, criticized, and sympathized tirelessly. My sincerest thanks to him.

THEODORE S. HAMEROW

Urbana, Illinois
January 1958

CONTENTS

PART ONE

RESTORATION

Ich frage, wem ist's wohl bekannt,
Wer sah vor 20 Jahren
Den übermüthigen Fabrikant
In Staatskarossen fahren?

Wer traf wohl da Hauslehrer an
Bei einem Fabrikanten.
In Livreen Kutscher angethan,
Domestiken, Gouvernanten?

SONG OF THE SILESIAN WEAVERS (1844)

1

THE ORIGINS OF INDUSTRIALISM

"Wealth and speed are the things the world admires and for which all men strive," wrote Goethe on June 6, 1825, to the musician Karl Zelter. "Railways, express mails, steamboats, and all possible means of communication are what the educated world seeks. . . . Actually this is the century of clever minds, of practical men who grasp things easily, who are endowed with a certain facility, and who feel their own superiority to the multitude, but who lack talent for the most exalted tasks. Let us as far as possible retain the ideals in which we were raised. We and perhaps a few others will be the last representatives of an era which will not soon return."[1]

The great poet was in his seventy-sixth year. From Weimar's Olympian heights he was contemplating the Germany of the early nineteenth century, so different from the Germany he had known in his youth. Then it had been a country of picturesque castles and metaphysical philosophers. The Holy Roman Empire of the Ottos and the Hohenstaufens had still been in existence, though reduced to a venerable relic and the favorite battleground of the Great Powers. The enlightened despotism of the age had still maintained the corporate foundations of civic life, for its ideal had been the society of equilibrium of the Middle Ages, but refined, rationalized, perfected. Political relationships between benevolent princes and obedient subjects, traditional economic institutions like the trade guild and the entailed estate, social distinctions between nobleman and commoner—all were designed to support a condition of stability. One could still enjoy in those days the pleasant provincialism of a people removed from the main currents of European life.

The eighteenth-century world, however, had gone down before the French Revolution. The sovereign people had defeated the sovereign kings; an aristocracy of talent had supplanted an aristocracy of birth. In Germany the Holy Roman Empire was replaced first by the Confederation of the Rhine and then by the German Confederation. The imperial baronies, counties, abbeys, and cities were absorbed by the kingdoms, grand duchies, and duchies. Servitudes were abolished, class distinctions were eliminated, written constitutions appeared, the subject of the king became the citizen of the state, and the economy of stability was superseded by an economy of competition. In the course of twenty-five years a way of life which had endured for centuries came to an end.

The peace settlement arranged in Vienna in 1815 sought to re-establish the equipoise which Europe had known before 1789, but its success was superficial. The restored dynasties, unable to control the new social forces of the nineteenth century, maintained themselves in power only through the constant exercise of repression. Yet what they were trying to impose from above by legislation the silent forces of economic development were undermining from below. The gulf between the system of government and the condition of society grew wider and deeper, until a violent revolutionary upheaval brought a realignment of political forces on the Continent.

The conflict between an old governmental order and the new social forces created by the Industrial Revolution dominated the German scene between 1815 and 1848. The great reform movement accompanying the national uprising against French oppression had come to an end by 1819. The promise of constitutional government implicit in Article XIII of the Act of Confederation was honored only by the southern states and by some of the secondary governments of the north. The economic liberation of the Prussian peasantry begun by Stein and Hardenberg was restricted after 1815 at the behest of the landed aristocracy. And the Diet of the Confederation meeting in Frankfurt am Main remained essentially an assembly of diplomats representing sovereign countries rather than a federal parliament speaking for a united people.

At the very moment of the triumph of conservatism, however, the factory system began to destroy the social basis of its policies. The nineteenth century witnessed the remarkable revival of German economic might which paralleled and facilitated the growth of German political power. The industrialization of Central Europe originated in the period of the Restoration; and, while Germany did not assume a position of economic leadership in Europe until after 1871, the foundations of its hegemony were laid in the years preceding the revolution.

Weaving and mining were the fields where a significant mechanization of production first occurred. In the linen trade the process of industrialization was particularly rapid, but factories were also established for the manufacture of cotton, wool, and silk cloth. Metallurgy grew, especially the output of iron and copper. Between 1825 and 1850 the production of pig iron increased fivefold and the output of coal tripled. In the decade 1840-50 the horsepower available to industry expanded almost 500 per cent. In 1827, in Essen, Alfred Krupp started to build what was to become one of the great industrial empires of the world. Ten years later August Borsig founded his famous machine works in Berlin. And shortly thereafter Europe began to hear the names of Matthias Stinnes, Franz Haniel, Karl Henschel, and Reinhard Mannesmann, names which became increasingly familiar as the century advanced.[2]

Even in this early stage of the factory system industry displayed the tendency toward economic concentration characteristic of a capitalistic age. Especially in textile manufacture the large enterprise was steadily absorbing the small marginal producer. While in 1837, for example, there were 3,345 Prussian spinneries with 345,894 spindles, twelve years later the number of spindles was 420,415 and of spinneries 1,787, an average increase of more than 100 per cent in spindles per spinnery.[3]

The great centers of early industrialism were Saxony and the Rhineland. In the former a trend toward large-scale production, apparent as early as the end of the eighteenth century, was strengthened by the Continental system, and the famous textile mills of Rhenish cities like Krefeld and Aachen traced their origins to Huguenot refugees from France who had brought their skill and experience to western Germany. By the time of the founding of the Zollverein, however, the factory system was also spreading to such southern towns as Mannheim, Ludwigshafen, Esslingen, Augsburg, and Nürnberg. Westphalia and Silesia were entering a period of growth as producers of coal and yarn, while Berlin in the east had already become an important center for the manufacture of machinery and cloth.[4]

Changes in the organization of production led directly to readjustment in the financial structure of Central Europe. In 1800 Germany had only 5 joint-stock companies; in 1825 there were 25 in the Hohenzollern possessions alone; and by 1850 the number had risen to more than 100. Between 1834 and 1848 Prussian investors spent almost 60,000,000 marks to help develop the heavy industry of the country, and by the middle of the century their purchases of shares in railway lines amounted to more than 450,000,000 marks. On the eve of the Revolution even rural Bavaria, seized by the speculative fever, was busily floating loans and building factories.[5]

Yet the funds with which the public was providing industry through subscription to stocks and bonds were insufficient to meet the demands of a growing economy. Although the great financial need of Central Europe was an expanded and flexible credit structure, a tradition of bureaucratic conservatism made its creation difficult. In places of authority, among royal ministers and governmental experts, there was a profound distrust of paper money. Only with extreme reluctance did a few states finally countenance the creation of a small number of banks of issue. In 1834 King Ludwig I of Bavaria authorized the establishment of such an institution in Munich, Saxony followed this example in 1838, and in 1846 the Royal Bank in Berlin was reorganized as the Prussian Bank with a limited power of issue.[6]

An even more serious obstacle to economic growth was the multiplicity of monetary systems and commercial codes, for the legal basis of financial activity reflected the political weakness of the German Confederation. Each of the members was free to coin its own money, to promulgate its own business laws, and to maintain its own weights and measures. Although Article XIX of the Act of Confederation called on the states to consult regarding matters affecting interstate commerce, only two measures were adopted before 1848 to implement this provision. A Zollverein convention in Dresden in 1838 established a fixed ratio among the values of the various coinage systems without, however, reducing their number. And in 1847 a conference of the governments of Germany which met in Leipzig drafted a common code governing the use of bills of exchange, although four more years were to elapse before it was adopted by all the lands.[7]

Of the revolutionary changes in transportation and communication accompanying industrialization the most important was the railroad. The first line, completed in December 1835, ran a distance of seven kilometers from Nürnberg to Fürth. Only fifteen years later a network of rails costing 800,000,000 marks linked the industries of central Germany with the great northern ports, and a traveler could go from Berlin to Cologne by train in less than half the time formerly required by the stagecoach. As late as 1830 the industrialist Friedrich Harkort had complained that the Westphalian iron industry could not develop because the coal and iron lay seventy-five kilometers apart. By 1850 the German railway system, the largest on the Continent, had cut the cost of shipping a ton of coal one kilometer from forty pfennigs to less than thirteen. It made possible the increasing exchange of goods, the rise of new industries, and the reduction of price differentials between the various regions of Central Europe. As for its political implications, the young poet Karl Beck sang them in verses which made up by enthusiasm what they lacked in lyricism:

> For these rails are bridal bracelets,
> Wedding rings of purest gold;
> States like lovers will exchange them,
> And the marriage-tie will hold.[8]

The operation of railways was at first almost exclusively in the hands of private companies, for the rulers of Germany viewed all innovation with suspicion. King Frederick William III of Prussia announced that he did not see that it made a great deal of difference whether one arrived in Potsdam a few hours sooner or later. Postmaster General Karl von Nagler grumbled that while every day empty stagecoaches traveled across the country, people were now insisting upon trains, of all things. The Prussian law of November 3, 1838, which gave the state authority to regulate the construction of future lines, audit their books, supervise their administration, and acquire them by purchase after thirty years, was typical in its distrust of steam transportation. The Rhenish industrialist David Hansemann expressed an opinion widely held in business circles, when he warned the government that its hostile attitude would frighten investors away from railroad enterprises.[9]

After 1840 official opposition to the principle of state ownership of railways began to disappear, especially after the Belgian experiment in a publicly-owned railroad system proved a success. In states like Baden, Brunswick, Württemberg, and Oldenburg the governments soon gained virtually complete control over the rail networks. In others such as Bavaria,

Saxony, and Hesse-Kassel a mixed system prevailed, with both public and private lines in operation. And then there were lands like Prussia, Hesse-Darmstadt, and Mecklenburg-Schwerin where private ownership was the rule until after 1848. This diversity in methods of railway operation imposed on the shipper, groaning beneath the burden of an assortment of customs duties, the additional task of dealing with a bewildering variety of state licenses, business regulations, freight rates, and contractual procedures. A railroad congress meeting in Hamburg in 1847 called for the creation of a central authority to supervise and regulate the entire national transportation system, but the Diet of the Confederation ignored the demand. It raised too many embarrassing economic questions and implied criticism of existing political institutions.[10]

The steamboat was another important achievement of the revolution in transportation. While the first vessels propelled by steam appeared on the Rhine and the Elbe as early as 1818, it was not before 1830 that their full effect was felt. The volume of goods moving on the Rhine more than doubled between 1836 and 1846, and the Main River Steamship Company of Würzburg tripled its freight volume between 1843 and 1847. Many entrepreneurs like Matthias Stinnes, Franz Haniel, and Ludolf Camphausen, after making their fortunes in mining or manufacture, turned to steam shipping and soon superseded the sailing vessels owned by independent proprietors.[11]

Thousands of freighters, sailors, and artisans paid with their livelihood for the progress of German shipping. Their plight moved even their bitterest competitors. In 1840 Ludolf Camphausen wrote to his brother Otto: "The shippers, while they exaggerate greatly, are for the time being in a truly pitiable state, and I find it difficult not to allow myself to be driven by sympathy to the adoption of false measures for their relief. The interesting experiences which we have thus far had have demonstrated beyond a doubt that the new sys-

tem will expand rapidly and will produce a complete transformation in shipping on the Rhine."[12]

The steamship, however, had to cope with problems more
serious than the protests of hungry boatmen. River traffic
was still subject to tolls levied nominally for the maintenance
of installations essential to safe navigation, but used in practice to enrich the treasuries of the riverain governments. The
worst offenders were the smaller states. Their sources of revenue were limited, and so they found in the taxation of commerce moving within their borders a painless method of increasing their income. States like Hanover and Mecklenburg-
Schwerin situated along the lower Elbe were able to extort
tribute from goods shipped to Saxony or Bohemia farther
upstream. Commerce on the Rhine was likewise subject to a
variety of taxes, even after restrictions on free navigation
were removed by the convention of March 31, 1831. Business
therefore tended to depend more heavily on railways, and
Central Europe was deprived of the benefits of cheap transportation which its waterways could have provided.[13]

The rulers of Germany, while slow to satisfy the needs
arising out of industrial growth, were not entirely indifferent
to them. The projects of political improvement advanced by
the followers of Stein during the struggle against France
were largely abandoned under the Restoration. In the field
of tariff legislation, however, the liberal influence remained
important, and its most impressive achievement was the Zollverein. The statesmen chiefly responsible for the creation of
the customs union, Friedrich von Motz and Karl Maassen,
were reformist in their policies and middle-class in their sympathies. By their efforts the Prussian state established an expanding market for manufactured goods which gave it a new
economic importance, although Austria continued to dominate
the German Confederation through political influence over
the secondary governments.

When on April 20, 1819, the Commercial and Industrial

Union, an organization of merchants and manufacturers in the central and southern states, petitioned the Diet of the Confederation for tariff reform, it voiced the economic philosophy of an important section of the middle class: "Reasonable freedom is the condition of all human physical and spiritual development. Just as the human spirit is abased by restrictions on the exchange of ideas, so the welfare of peoples is restrained by chains which are imposed on production and the exchange of material goods. Only when they establish among themselves general, free, unrestricted commerce, will the nations of the earth reach the highest level of physical well-being."[14] The diplomats in Frankfurt refused to accept the views expounded in the memorial, but fifteen years later the Zollverein did succeed in creating "general, free, unrestricted commerce" among most of the German lands.

The considerations behind the formation of the Zollverein, however, were not exclusively economic. Many contemporary observers recognized the political implications of a customs union led by Prussia. A memorandum of June 11, 1831, prepared by Metternich for the consideration of Emperor Francis I is a tribute to the Austrian chancellor's powers of perception. Three years before the creation of the tariff association he prophesied that a community of commercial interest in the north must lead to a community of political interest, thereby weakening the Habsburg position in Germany. Prussian statesmen similarly realized that a customs union from which Austria was excluded could play an important role in a future struggle for supremacy in Central Europe. While economic and political motives were thus intertwined in the negotiations leading to the Zollverein, their ultimate outcome was an institution whose importance for German industrial growth cannot be overstated.[15]

As soon as the Zollverein was established, its founders began to wrestle with the tariff problem. They were men deeply influenced by the teachings of economic liberalism, and so at first the import duties of the Zollverein remained below those of most states of Western Europe. But the free-trade ideas dominant in Germany were soon under attack from important industrial circles suffering the effects of English, Belgian, and French competition. Before long both sides of the question had managed to enlist the support of powerful interests. In one camp were the bankers and merchants of the north, favorable to a high volume of foreign trade and therefore opposed to protectionism. Their most valuable allies were the conservative landowners of the east who, having found rich markets for their grain abroad, trembled at the mere thought of an international tariff war. Opposed to them were the industrialists of the south and west, the millowners and financiers of the Rhineland, Saxony, Silesia, Bavaria, Baden, and Württemberg.[16]

The prophet of protectionism was Friedrich List, a man whose lifework was one impassioned plea for a politically directed industrial policy. Economic growth, he maintained, cannot be entrusted to the enlightened self-interest of the individual in search of mere personal gain. The need of the national state must be its guide: "History demonstrates that restrictions [on commerce] are not the invention of speculative minds, but are rather the natural consequences of conflicts of interest and of the striving of nations for independence or for overwhelming power. They are the natural consequences of national rivalry and of wars, and they can disappear only when this conflict of national interests disappears, that is, through the union of nations under the rule of law."[17] In the meantime, Germany should foster manufacture by protecting it against the competition of foreign states, because for Central Europe the price of free trade was political weakness.

The import of List's theories was clear. Industrialism had found a spokesman capable of expressing its demands for protection in universal terms. It now became the task of trade organizations, chambers of commerce, and associations of manufacturers to persuade kings and bureaucrats of the folly of low tariffs. After 1827 the diet of the Rhine Province petitioned the Prussian government time and again for protective duties. In the Forties the Aachen chamber of commerce went on record in favor of a high tariff policy, at least until all nations should agree on a common system of free trade. Some industrialists like Friedrich Harkort and the Stumm family fought for the exclusion of British iron. Others such as Gustav Mevissen and Friedrich Diergardt warned against the importation of foreign textiles. The governments of Württemberg and Baden defended the cause of protectionism at the Zollverein conferences after 1836. And in 1845 even the Cologne chamber of commerce, hitherto free-trade in its economic outlook, joined its sister organizations throughout the Rhineland in advocating protection for the cotton and linen trades.[18]

The champions of free trade were slower to organize, but by 1848 they too had managed to bring their views before the nation. Their leader was John Prince Smith, a Prussianized Englishman settled in Berlin, who in 1847 helped found the Free-Trade Association to preach the principles of Manchesterism. He found favor among influential northern newspapers like the *Bremer Handelsblatt* and the *Börsennachrichten von der Ostsee*, and even some western and southern newspapers like the *Germania* of Heidelberg and the *Kölnische Zeitung* gave their support to the theories of laissez faire. The corn laws in England were repealed in 1846, and the following year Richard Cobden of the Anti-Corn Law League visited Germany. These developments drew public attention to the tariff problem, winning new prestige for the opponents of protective duties. In 1847 they founded in Hamburg the weekly journal *Deutscher Freihandel*, which promptly engaged in a bitter polemic with the protectionist press.[19]

The authorities commissioned to establish the tariff rates of the Zollverein found themselves subjected to petitions,

arguments, and pleas emanating from the rival camps. Ulti-
mately they decided to steer a middle course between the
two extremes, with the result that neither party was satisfied.
The free traders were dismayed to note that after 1843 the
Zollverein began to follow a policy of moderate protectionism, while the protectionists considered the new tariffs utterly
inadequate in view of the dangers threatening industry.

The duties imposed on the importation of raw iron in 1844
and on textiles in 1846 were far from prohibitive, but they
were enough to discourage the north from joining the customs union. In the Mecklenburgs, Holstein, Lübeck, Oldenburg, and Hanover tariffs of more than two per cent were
considered exorbitant. The mercantile interests of these states
were not indifferent to the economic advantages which membership in the Zollverein would bring them, but they hesitated lest their welfare be sacrificed to the clamor for protection.
The new tariff policy introduced in the Forties convinced
them that their fears were justified and postponed their entry
into the customs union until after the Revolution. The Zollverein was thus deprived of valuable outlets to the North
Sea and the Baltic. Its frontiers were 8,200 kilometers long,
but only 971 were on the sea. Even this limited seaboard in
Pomerania and Prussia was a natural outlet only for the eastern provinces along the Oder and the Vistula. The commerce
of western and central Germany as far east as Berlin continued to depend on rivers like the Elbe, the Weser, and the
Rhine, where it was subject to transit dues levied by states
outside the Zollverein.[20]

An even more unfortunate consequence of the refusal of
the northern governments to join the Zollverein was the lack
of a common German trade policy. The customs union was
in a position to negotiate commercial treaties advantageous
to its members, for its area and population were so large that
it did not have to sell its favors cheaply. It was able to conclude favorable agreements with Holland in 1839, Turkey

in 1840, Belgium in 1844, Sardinia in 1845, and the Kingdom of the Two Sicilies in 1847. In 1841 it won an important victory when the convention of commerce and navigation signed by Prussia and England in 1824 was extended to the other participants in the Zollverein. The penalty for political and economic disunity, however, was paid by the states of the north whose small size and dependence on international trade made them vulnerable to foreign pressure. At the time of the formation of the customs union the shipping of Hamburg, Bremen, and Lübeck was suffering discriminatory treatment at the hands of England, France, Spain, Portugal, and Holland. And while after 1830 the Hanseatic cities succeeded in negotiating treaties ending the worst abuses against their merchant service, in return they had to grant virtually free entry to the ships and goods of the western nations.[21]

During the Forties, Mayor Johann Smidt and Senator Arnold Duckwitz of Bremen sought to create a navigation and commercial union between the Zollverein and the other members of the German Confederation without establishing uniformity in tariff rates. They approached Prussia and Hanover, but the negotiations never advanced beyond preliminary conversations. For one thing, the Prussian government was more interested in incorporating the Hanseatic cities into the Zollverein than in facilitating their independence from it. Secondly, England hastily made a strenuous effort to cultivate closer relations with the northern states and prevent them from gravitating to the customs union. On April 4, 1844, it concluded a trade convention with Oldenburg, and on May 1, 1844, the Mecklenburgs signed a similar pact which the British negotiator Colonel G. Lloyd Hodges expected to keep them out of the Prussian tariff system. The most significant success of English diplomacy, however, came on July 22, 1844, with the conclusion of a commercial agreement with Hanover effectively precluding its adhesion to the Zollverein before 1854. Finally, the United States negotiated treaties

with Hanover in 1846 and with Oldenburg and Mecklenburg-Schwerin in 1847 by which the latter definitely committed themselves to a low tariff policy.[22]

The truth is that the Zollverein, great as its achievements
were, could not solve the problems created by political particularism and economic discord. Transportation and communication, business and industry, commerce and shipping,
banking and finance, all suffered from the absence of an effective central governmental authority. August Hoffmann von
Fallersleben, the author of *Deutschland, Deutschland über
Alles,* saw in the Prussian customs union the germ of such an
authority and apostrophized it in his verse:

> Leather, salmon, eels and matches,
> Cows and madder, paper, shears,
> Ham and cheese and boats and vetches,
> Wool and soap and yarns and beers;
>
> Gingerbread and rags and fennels,
> Nuts, tobacco, glasses, flax,
> Leather, salt, lard, dolls and funnels,
> Radish, rope, rep, whisky, wax;
>
> Articles of home consumption,
> All our thanks are due to you!
> You have wrought without presumption
> What no intellect could do;
>
> You have made the German Nation
> Stand united, hand in hand,
> More than the Confederation
> Ever did for Fatherland.[23]

But not all shared his enthusiasm. The *Düsseldorfer Zeitung* of September 3, 1843, voiced the bitter complaint of
thousands of businessmen thwarted by an outmoded system
of government:

Thus we have instead of one Germany, thirty-eight German states, an equal number of governments, almost the same number of courts, as many representative bodies, thirty-eight distinct legal codes and administrations, embassies, and consulates. What an enormous saving it would be, if all of that were taken care of by one central government. . . . Yet far worse than the present waste of money is the fact that in these thirty-eight states prevail as many separate interests which injure and destroy each other down to the last detail of daily intercourse. No post can be hurried, no mailing charge reduced without special conventions, no railway can be planned without each seeking to keep it in his own state as long as possible.[24]

The Industrial Revolution, which had given rise to a new aristocracy of wealth grumbling about the political and economic inadequacy of the established order, had also created a new urban working class. The factory was attracting the landless peasant and unemployed artisan to the city, destroying their connections with village life and transforming them into a rootless proletariat. The serf or journeyman who had once occupied a position of subservience vis-à-vis the landlord or the shopowner now found himself a member of an emancipated labor force. He was free in the sense that the conditions of his work were dictated not by the prescriptions of law or custom but by the fluctuations of supply and demand in the open market. And since he was unable to satisfy his economic needs within the framework of older corporate associations of tradesmen, he abandoned the guild system and sought to fix his terms of employment through a process of individual negotiation.

The growth of an industrial working class in Germany was considerably slower than in England or France. Around the middle of the nineteenth century the number of factory workers in Prussia was reported as less than 700,000, about 4 per cent of the population. Bavaria had 93,000 mill hands among 4,500,000 inhabitants. Baden, with a population of 1,300,000, employed 17,000 persons in its plants. And these estimates were maximal, for many of the enterprises officially classified as factories were only outsize artisan shops. All in all, factory workers were probably no more than 33 per cent of all non-agricultural workers, although through efficient organization and mechanical power the mill was able to produce a disproportionately high percentage of the total manufacturing output of Central Europe.[25]

The wages received by the factory employee reflected on a modest scale the industrial boom of the Restoration. While the handicraftsman was losing ground in his struggle against the machine, the industrial worker was enjoying a period of full employment and rising income from 1815 until the great depression of the middle Forties. The demand for his services remained high, while restrictions on the movement of population within Central Europe made it difficult for manufacturers to import cheap labor from backward regions. A shrewd English observer, Thomas C. Banfield, noted that the Rhenish industrialist did not have the advantage of a swollen supply of workingmen on which the British millowner could draw. Although the standard of living of the German factory hand was anything but high, it was far superior to that of his fellows laboring in the fields or in the shops.[26]

Yet he too had to face abuses arising out of the circumstances of his employment. The working day was long, from twelve to eighteen hours, and wages were frequently reduced through the imposition of fines by millowners and through the use of the truck system of payment. The latter practice was especially resented, for manufacturers tended to inflate the value of the goods they gave their employees in lieu of cash. Finally, the growing employment of women and children reduced the demand for adult male labor. By the middle of the century some 32,000 children under the age of fifteen were employed in the factories of Prussia, about 5 per cent of all factory workers in the kingdom. Before the adoption of remedial legislation these unfortunate youngsters toiled twelve, fourteen, sixteen hours a day under brutalizing and unhealthy conditions, without recreation or schooling.[27]

Still, social evils did not escape criticism. Bureaucrats, economists, provincial diets, even a few enlightened industrialists petitioned the authorities for legal action to eliminate the truck system and regulate the employment of children. It was a concern for the military efficiency of the state, however, which finally brought about the promulgation of the first child labor law. In 1828 General Heinrich von Horn informed the Prussian government that the factory districts of the west were no longer able to meet their annual quotas of recruits, because the early employment of children in mills had impaired the physical fitness of the population. The report alarmed King Frederick William III, who ordered the cabinet to study the problem and prepare measures for dealing with it. The outcome was the cabinet order of April 6, 1839, prohibiting the employment in manufacturing establishments of children under nine and restricting the working day of those under sixteen to ten hours. Thereby Prussia became the first state on the Continent to follow the English example in adopting factory legislation. Bavaria and Baden published similar measures on January 15 and March 4, 1840, but efforts to improve the position of the industrial working class by government action stopped there. They were not resumed until the Revolution.[28]

The economic growth of Central Europe led also to a remarkable increase in population. Advances in medical science and public sanitation lowered the death rate among adults and reduced the incidence of infant mortality. Thirty years of uninterrupted peace and a steady industrial expansion encouraged marriages and births. And the end of serfdom and the establishment of a free rural economy modernized agricultural production, created a demand for farm labor, and increased the food supply. Between 1815 and 1845 the population of Germany grew 38 per cent, rising from 25,000,000 to 34,500,000. While the thinly-populated agrarian regions of the north and east were able to absorb the increase without great difficulty, in the west and south a serious problem of overpopulation arose. There the sudden demographic expansion had an important effect on every aspect of economic life, providing a labor supply for the factory system, creating land hunger among the peasantry, intensifying the crisis in artisan trades, and driving the masses to large-scale emigration.[29]

Moreover, the equilibrium between city and country which had been established in the eighteenth century was now upset, for as a result of internal migration industrial centers began to grow far more rapidly than the nation as a whole. Surplus population was leaving the village for urban communities, where opportunities for employment and advancement were greater. In Berlin in the period 1837-44 births exceeded deaths by only 15,453, but the number of inhabitants rose 101,130. During the years 1840-44 the city population of Saxony expanded 8.48 per cent, while the countryside increased 4.25 per cent. Although at the time of the Revolution two out of three Germans still lived on the land, the difference in size between the rural and the urban population was rapidly diminishing.[30]

For Central Europe the early years of industrialism were thus a period of difficult adaptation to new conditions. A sleepy land of noblemen and peasants was miraculously turning into a bustling nation of entrepreneurs and workingmen, experiencing the strains of far-reaching economic and social change. Within the lifetime of one generation Germany was forced to accept new forms of production, new methods of transportation, new social classes, new civic ideals, new demographic pressures. It proved too much for a bewildered people. The masses in their agitation began to mutter, complain, threaten, and finally they rose in open revolt against the effects of technological progress.

2

THE DECLINE OF THE HANDICRAFT
SYSTEM

THE advance of industrialism meant ruin for the artisan class and for that form of economic and social organization which it had created, the corporate guild. To the casual observer the Restoration was a period of tranquil stability, interrupted here and there by short-lived manifestations of political discontent, but essentially devoted to hard work, material progress, and middle-class morality. Yet beneath the surface there was a struggle between the new dynamic of industrial capitalism and an old way of life built about the concept of economic equilibrium. The logic of historical development was on the side of the factory, but its triumph was bought with the sacrifice of the guildsman whose livelihood depended on a precapitalistic mode of production.

The handicraft system had made possible an organization of manufacture suitable to a static communal order. It was designed to meet the needs of a stable population, to maintain an unchanging standard of living, to supply a market local in scope. As for the structure and outlook of artisan guilds, they reflected the pastoral economic world in which they had matured. They sought to regulate output in such a way as to assure an adequate supply of goods for the consumer and a fair return for the producer. Endowed by the state with quasi-legal powers, they sought to prescribe methods of manufacture, prices and wages, terms of employment, and standards of workmanship. Their ultimate goal was the achievement of a social justice appropriate to a rural polity composed of autonomous corporate interests. The advantages inherent in mechanical efficiency and competitive individualism were renounced for the sake of security and order.

During the eighteenth century, however, guilds began to decline in those countries most directly affected by the early Industrial Revolution. As new methods of finance, production, and trade developed, the functions of handicraft organizations lost their significance, and the state began to remove restrictions on the free development of economic initiative. In Western Europe the transition from a handicraft to a mechanized method of manufacture was more gradual and the process of social adjustment to the factory system less difficult than in Central Europe. For whereas by 1789 the guilds of England and France had lost much of their economic importance, in the Holy Roman Empire they still enjoyed full possession of their ancient rights. It was the French Revolution which opened a new era in the development of Germany by violently thrusting upon it the tenets of liberalism, nationalism, and industrial freedom.

In 1791 the National Assembly of France removed all restrictions on admission to a craft and outlawed trade associations seeking to regulate the wages and hours of labor. The Napoleonic regime continued to uphold the laissez-faire principle in manufacture, extending it to all territories annexed to the empire. The first region of Germany to feel the effects of liberal economic legislation was therefore the left bank of the Rhine, which was under French rule after 1793. As Bonaparte gained mastery over northern Germany, guilds were also abolished in Hanover, Oldenburg, and the Hanseatic cities. Finally, between 1808 and 1810 the Kingdom of Westphalia and the Grand Duchy of Berg removed the legal obstacles to the free exercise of a trade.[1]

The states of central and southern Germany, although not immediately subject to foreign control, were impressed with the example of French economic policy. Napoleon, who dominated their diplomatic affairs through the Confederation of the Rhine, encouraged them to follow his precedent in domestic legislation as well. Thus in Bavaria the leading minister Count Maximilian von Montgelas, influenced by the teachings of enlightened despotism, pursued a course calculated to concentrate political and economic power in the hands of the state. In a series of industrial measures promulgated between 1799 and 1815 he reduced the prerogatives of the guilds by restricting their right to license tradesmen. The Thuringian principalities too began to transfer jurisdiction in economic questions from guild courts to government authorities, and in 1811 Duke Karl August of Saxe-Weimar, "Augustus and Maecenas" to Goethe's generation, undertook a revision of guild statutes in order to encourage a freer exchange of goods within his small realm.[2]

The most far-reaching economic changes, however, were introduced in Prussia. The Treaty of Tilsit had reduced the proud kingdom of Frederick the Great to the rank of a third-rate power. Deprived of half its territory and population, forced to endure foreign occupation, its army reduced to impotence, its treasury drained by an indemnity, the Prussian state after 1807 was in a condition of such complete collapse that recovery seemed impossible. Yet during this very time of national degradation a group of exceptionally gifted political and military leaders undertook to revolutionize the country from above. Learning the lessons of the French Revolution and adapting them to German conditions, they sought to endow their nation with a moral purpose worthy of the allegiance of a free citizenry. To achieve this purpose they introduced in swift succession several thoroughgoing reforms: the abolition of serfdom, the establishment of municipal self-government, the adoption of general conscription, and the relaxation of industrial regulation.

While in general agreement that the government must encourage individual initiative, they differed in their attitudes toward guild organizations. The greatest of the reformers, Baron Karl vom Stein, favored a modification in the structure of corporate associations, but he was resolutely opposed to their abolition. Admitting that they made difficult the development of an efficient system of manufacture, he yet recognized the ethical value of the principles on which they were built. To him the state was more than a conglomeration of factories and farms organized for the production of industrial goods and raw materials. It was also an instrumentality for the spiritual growth of its subjects in which trade guilds could exercise an important moral influence.[3]

Most Prussian statesmen, however, did not share his sentiments. The ministry of Karl von Altenstein and Alexander von Dohna formed in 1808 was of the opinion that industry ought to develop naturally without let or hindrance by the government. And Karl von Hardenberg, chancellor from 1810 to 1822, was bitter in his opposition to handicraft corporations. Outlining his views before a representative assembly in Berlin in 1811, he emphasized that the citizen must be able to exercise his talents freely, so that achievement in every walk of life could find its proper reward. While not referring specifically to guilds, he nevertheless saw in them an obstacle to the establishment of the system of free competition which he favored. His assumption of office as the chief counselor of Frederick William III meant the end of corporate regulation of industrial production.[4]

The first blow fell on November 2, 1810. On that day the Prussian government promulgated a decree effectively destroying the coercive powers of artisan organizations. It was officially described as a tax edict, and its preface emphasized the need to increase the sources of state revenue. Yet while it is true that the financial demands of the French occupation could be met only through additional taxation, the measure dealt not only with financial problems, but also with the question of economic regulation. After imposing a new tax on persons engaged in trade and manufacture, it provided that payment of the fee and evidence of sound character were the only requirements for admission to employment. Having met them, the citizen could engage in several occupations simultaneously in defiance of guild statutes. Thereafter control over the practice of a calling was to be exercised only locally by police ordinance for the purpose of maintaining general order.

Even this restriction came to an end a year later. The law of September 7, 1811, reduced the competence of police authorities in the regulation of economic affairs and deprived artisan corporations of the last vestiges of power. Membership in a guild became entirely voluntary and ceased to confer special privileges. Participants could dissolve their association by majority vote or withdraw from it individually through resignation. Moreover, the government reserved the right to order the abolition of any trade organization whose existence was incompatible with the welfare of the state. Prussia thus destroyed the system of corporate direction of industrial production which had come into conflict with the principle of the free development of individual capacity. Out of the unrestrained interaction of competing talents the reformers hoped to create a spirit of independence which would arm their country for the struggle against the foreign oppressor.[5]

The great national uprising began early in 1813 and achieved its goal eight months later with the defeat of Napoleon at Leipzig and the withdrawal of his troops across the Rhine. Yet the very success of the foreign policy which the reformers were advocating made possible the frustration of their domestic program. The end of the threat from abroad released the rulers of Germany from the pressures which had driven them to adopt liberal measures. They now tended to favor the views advanced by the landed aristocracy which had won new prestige by its military contributions to the War of Liberation. After the Congress of Vienna they little by little suppressed the patriotic movement in the universities, suspended projects for constitutional reform, abandoned plans for the introduction of local self-government, and forced the retirement of the reformers themselves. Conservative influences were also felt in industrial life, for economic individualism no less than political liberalism had come with the hated foreigners and found its justification in theories of social egalitarianism. Statesmen hostile to everything which smacked of the French Revolution began to look with suspicion on the doctrines of freedom of enterprise.

The reaction against economic liberalism was most thoroughgoing in the smaller principalities of the north. By 1830 the governments of Hesse-Kassel, Hanover, and Oldenburg had reintroduced guild organizations in their lands, for in these rural states industrial freedom had been imposed by the fiat of French administrators without regard to local conditions. There were no textile mills or iron foundries to support a movement for the abolition of artisan corporations, and laissez faire meant little in a country of peasants and handicraftsmen. Other states of the seaboard like the Mecklenburgs, Hamburg, and Lübeck, which had been under French authority only briefly, never had made a serious attempt to suppress corporate organizations, and hence the fall of Napoleon had little effect on their economic policy. Indeed, until the eve of the Revolution the north remained a stronghold of guild authority.[8]

In the south and west the Restoration at first was also able to slow the progress of industrial freedom, but within a few years after the Congress of Vienna guilds found themselves once more forced to retreat before the factory system. The Duchy of Nassau, which had already attracted public attention in 1814 by becoming the first German state to promulgate a constitution after the collapse of the Confederation of the Rhine, was the pioneer in the reintroduction of a laissez-faire economic policy. On May 15, 1819, a new industrial law abolished the rights and privileges of guilds and permitted every citizen to practice his chosen occupation without restriction. Its provisions went even beyond those of the

Prussian decrees of 1810 and 1811, and the economic legislation of Nassau remained the most liberal in Central Europe
until after 1848.[7]

The government of Bavaria moved with greater caution.
After 1815 two systems of industrial law prevailed in the
Wittelsbach possessions. The Palatinate on the left bank of
the Rhine had fallen under French control after 1793, and
for the next twenty years it continued to enjoy economic
freedom. Upon its return to Bavarian rule by the Treaty of
Vienna it was permitted to retain the liberal industrial measures which had been introduced by the previous regime, thus
remaining free of corporate control. The heart of the Bavarian state, however, lay east of the Rhine, and there handicraft associations were still influential, although their privileges had been reduced through the efforts of the Montgelas
ministry. A new law promulgated on September 11, 1825,
provided for a further relaxation of trade regulation by taking the power to limit admission to an occupation out of the
hands of the guild system and vesting it in the bureaucracy.
The latter could still require proof of professional skill and
financial responsibility, but it was far more favorable toward
economic competition than corporate organizations. The measure was particularly generous in its treatment of factory owners, freeing them from many restrictions on the employment
of labor and the use of machinery. It enabled Bavaria to
steer a middle course between the policy of strict artisan
regulation prevalent in the north and the complete industrial
freedom recently established in Nassau.[8]

Hesse-Darmstadt, where the liberalization of economic institutions had been introduced during the Napoleonic period,
also continued to whittle away the powers of artisan corporations. In many parts of the grand duchy guild membership
ceased to be a prerequisite for the practice of a trade, while
by the law of June 16, 1827, the government removed geo-
graphic restrictions on the sale of industrial goods and per-

mitted the handicraftsman to dispose of his wares in markets located anywhere in the state. Finally, in the Thirties trade associations lost their quasi-judicial status, and jurisdiction over industrial disputes was transferred to the ordinary courts.[9]

In near-by Württemberg the laws of April 22, 1828, and August 5, 1836, prepared the way for a rapid expansion of industrialism. Factories were exempted from guild regulations governing manufacture, and their operation was made subject only to concessions granted by the government. For most other branches of nonagricultural production the principle of corporate control remained in force, but even here a few of the most restrictive practices were modified.[10]

In the decade preceding the Revolution industrial freedom invaded central Germany and even spread northward to the citadels of corporate privilege. In Saxony the guilds defended themselves for a time against the attacks of liberalism, but on October 9, 1840, a new law facilitated the establishment of manufacturing enterprises, freed a number of occupations from corporate control, and encouraged a greater exchange of goods.[11]

A few years later Prussia introduced a consistent application of liberal industrial principles throughout the kingdom. The earlier economic legislation promulgated by Hardenberg was enforced only in the provinces retained by the Hohenzollerns after 1807 under the Treaty of Tilsit, while the regions acquired in 1815 were permitted to maintain the manufacturing practices current before their annexation. Thus the two western provinces, Westphalia and the Rhine Province, continued to maintain the extensive industrial freedom which French rule had introduced, while the new acquisitions in the east, Upper and Lower Lusatia, the Province of Saxony, New Hither Pomerania, and Posen, remained subject to traditional guild control. Eventually, however, the government decided that the lack of uniformity in industrial law must in the long run hinder a balanced development of the national economy.

It therefore appointed a commission in 1835 to consider the adoption of a single code of manufacture for the entire state, and invited provincial estates and provincial administrators to submit their views. The outcome of these efforts was the statute of January 17, 1845.

The new measure extended the liberal economic principles of the laws of 1810 and 1811 to all the provinces of Prussia. It abolished the monopolistic and coercive rights of guilds, depriving them of the power to grant industrial concessions and ending the exclusive trade privileges of towns. Corporate organizations of tradesmen survived only as voluntary associations of a benevolent character engaged in the maintenance of benefit funds and savings accounts, the management of charitable activities for the widows and orphans of deceased members, and the supervision of the education of apprentices. In special branches of industry and under special local conditions restrictions could still be imposed on the free exercise of a trade, but police authorities rather than artisan corporations were to apply them. The government attempted to sweeten the bitter pill for trade organizations by stipulating that in some forty handicraft occupations the right to employ apprentices was contingent on guild membership. Yet the essential purpose of the law remained the establishment of a uniform system of economic freedom through the abolition of the authority hitherto exercised by artisan corporations.[12]

Hanover was the last state to abandon the guild system prior to the Revolution. In 1846 the ministry submitted to the legislature the draft of a new industrial law. The diet discussed, amended, and approved the measure, which was then promulgated on August 1, 1847. Although it did not establish complete freedom of manufacture, it liberalized economic practices and reduced the prerogatives of guilds. Anticipating violent opposition in artisan circles, the government postponed the effectiveness of the decree until July 1, 1848, and hoped that the transition to a laissez-faire policy would thereby be facilitated. But its solicitude did not alter the fact that industrial liberalism had won a major victory in the agricultural north.[13]

For the artisan of Germany these were years of crisis, years when government, technology, and fate all seemed to conspire to encompass his ruin. With wealth and law increasingly on the side of the factory, he faced insurmountable odds in the struggle for economic survival. Yet he doggedly resisted the growth of industrialism through his guilds and associations, in pamphlets and newspapers, and by appeals to influential personages and organizations. Occasionally he employed violence to halt the construction of a new factory or prevent the enforcement of a new decree. At times he was able to enlist the aid of conservative statesmen and humanitarian reformers ready to defy prevailing fashions in economic theory. There was the scientist Karl Winkelblech, for example, who wrote on social problems under the pseudonym Karl Marlo, advocating the corporate organization of labor and deploring the consequences of industrial individualism. The handicraftsman himself, however, had to bear the brunt of the fight, and his petitions to government authorities are the most eloquent statements of his plight.

In the session of the Bavarian legislature of 1827-28 twenty-three memorials from guild organizations were submitted to the lower chamber, all complaining of economic privation, all urging revision of the industrial law of September 11, 1825. Typical was a "Representation and Plea of All Presiding Officers of the Handicraft Organizations of the University City of Erlangen Dealing with the Crowded State of Industry in General," which opened with a vivid description of the economic hardships confronting the urban workingman:

> The presiding officers of the so-called tax-exempt crafts of the city of Erlangen propose by this petition to present a picture of the overcrowding of those engaged in industry

in this city, for out of 9,000 inhabitants there are 1,200 practicing a craft. These, in view of the proximity of the cities of Nürnberg, Fürth, and Bamberg, must depend very heavily on local demand. Because of this overcrowded condition we have an increase in destitution and complete impoverishment, which are in turn further aggravated by the creation of new master artisans which the industrial law facilitates. This is especially so because of another development, namely, the fact that a person who in one town has been proven by examination to be incompetent will be recognized as adequately trained in another.[14]

The disastrous effects of industrial freedom were the theme of almost every address presented by the guilds of Bavaria to the government. Rising prices, exorbitant rents, declining standards of workmanship, all were ascribed to the relaxation of corporate controls over production. Even in the Palatinate, where for a generation industry had developed freely, the handicraftsman began to demand the reimposition of restrictions on competition. Artisan agitation won the interest of conservative members of the diet and led to several attempts to modify the economic legislation of 1825. Prince Ludwig Oettingen-Wallerstein who became minister of the interior in 1831 was also in sympathy with the views of trade organizations and favored measures to relieve their distress. Yet the advocates of economic freedom were influential enough to repel all attacks on the factory, and the artisan was left alone to face ruin through industrialization.[15]

The Prussian handicraftsman, whose government had been even more liberal in its industrial legislation, pressed his campaign against economic freedom with still greater determination. He was aided, moreover, by municipal officials and provincial authorities who had to deal directly with the social dislocation created by the growth of capitalism. On December 31, 1810, only a few weeks after the promulgation of the first of Hardenberg's decrees against guilds, the commissioners of Königsberg submitted to the government a statement warning against the disruptive effects of the new law and predicting a decline in the prosperity of their city. A memorandum prepared in 1818 by one of the Berlin municipal councilors informed King Frederick William III that the experience of recent years demonstrated that industrial freedom led to a deterioration in standards of workmanship and encouraged speculation and irresponsibility among artisans. And some twenty years later a report of the commissioners of the capital city, describing the decay of handicraft trades, the decrease of tax receipts, and the rise in bankruptcy proceedings, pointed to the rapid growth of annual expenditures for municipal poor relief from 312,411 marks in 1821 to 1,120,590 marks in 1838.[16]

The campaign against industrial freedom also attracted considerable support in the western half of the kingdom where the factory system had made the greatest advances. After 1820 there developed among the artisans of the Rhineland a strong sentiment for a return to the good old days of corporate regulation. It affected not only the smaller towns and villages, but large cities like Cologne as well. Even provincial deliberative bodies felt its influence, and the diet of the Rhine Province petitioned the king in 1826 and in 1833 for legislative action to combat the harmful effects of economic anarchy. After 1840, however, the effectiveness of handicraft organizations in the Rhineland declined with the increase in wealth and prestige of the industrial bourgeoise.[17]

The artisan crisis did not spare those states which were trying to swim against the current of economic liberalism. In the Thuringian principalities, for example, guilds still retained considerable powers, but there too the handicraftsman felt the pressure of growing competition. Especially after 1833, when Thuringia joined the Zollverein, the small trades had to cope with a flood of Prussian manufactured articles

produced under a system of industrial freedom. The tradesmen of Frankfurt am Main also faced glutted markets, falling profits, and cheap goods from Prussia which began to pour
into their city after it entered the customs union in 1836. A
petition which they submitted to the municipal senate in 1845
warned that the further growth of the factory would soon
reduce them to the alternative of seeking employment as mill
hands or begging in the streets. In Baden the Heidelberg
association of handicraftsmen urged the adoption of measures
restraining industrial freedom in order to prevent the ruin of
the artisan. Yet it was all in vain, for the rulers of Central
Europe were increasingly ready to sacrifice the guild system
for the economic advantages of industrialism.[18]

There was nothing for the artisan to do except continue
pleading and warning. On occasion his threats led to outbursts
of violence, but as remedies for economic ills these proved no
more effective than petitions and remonstrances. They did,
however, testify to the desperate situation of the urban masses,
foreboding the great uprising of handicraftsmen in the spring
of 1848. Thus the accession of Hesse-Kassel to the Zollverein
in 1831 led to an open conflict in Hanau between the populace and the military. The new tariff arrangements meant
that the Hessian worker, already hard pressed in the struggle against the factory system of his native state, would have
to face the additional competition of freely imported Prussian
goods. Early in January 1832 armed mobs began to attack
toll houses and to threaten customs officials, the visible sym-
bols of the detested Zollverein. The disorders, enjoying considerable sympathy in neighboring Frankfurt, spread rapidly
along the southern frontier of the electorate and raged un-
checked for a few days. Only with the arrival of troops did
the rioting come to an end, although a week later Baron
Paul von Handel, Austrian minister resident in Frankfurt,
reported to Metternich not without satisfaction: "In the
neighborhood of Hanau things are for the moment peaceful

once again, but fire glows beneath the ashes. And since un-fortunately the new toll and excise arrangements and the Prussian system of indirect taxation are not an imaginary but a real calamity for these states, the first mild shock from without may become the occasion of a great disaster."[19]

About six months after the riots in Hesse-Kassel unrest swept the Palatinate. The slogans of popular sovereignty and national unity raised by the leaders of the democratic move-ment at the Hambach Festival of May 1832 found a favor-able reception in a region predisposed toward radicalism by heavy taxation, rising prices, hard times for the artisan, and poor harvests for the peasant. The Diet of the Confederation, however, acted promptly in the face of this danger. Its resolu-tions of July 5 suspended the right of assembly and freedom of the press, while the government of Bavaria hastened to ar-rest or exile the more important members of the republican opposition. Yet economic discontent could not be so easily suppressed, and for almost a year there were outbreaks of violence along the Rhine. Unruly mobs plundered food shops, abused unpopular officials, defied tax collectors, and engaged in encounters with troops. The disorder did not subside until 1833, when a rich harvest and a reduction in taxes brought better times.[20]

The most tragic of the artisan uprisings which preceded the Revolution was the insurrection of the Silesian villagers im-mortalized in Gerhart Hauptmann's *Die Weber*. To thou-sands of families in the Eulengebirge dependent on the pro-duction of linen for their livelihood the nineteenth century brought ruin. As cotton goods became popular, as markets for German fabrics in Spain and Russia shrank, as English yarns invaded the Continent, the demand for linen cloth declined disastrously. And with earnings in the textile trade falling, labor conditions deteriorated and unemployment mounted. To make matters worse, unscrupulous middlemen like the firm of Zwanziger Brothers in Peterswaldau proceeded to profit from the crisis by reducing the prices paid weavers for their wares to the barest minimum. An economic depression aggravated by exploitation finally precipitated a revolt.

The uprising broke out among the starving villages on June 4, 1844. Lacking clear objectives and intelligent leadership, it was more of a mass hunger riot than a purposeful political movement. The participants, about five thousand in number, destroyed the homes of manufacturers, attacked factories, looted wine cellars, and sacked fashionable residences. In some cases, however, wealthy citizens were able to buy immunity for themselves and their property in return for a small sum of money or a prompt distribution of food. Their hunger satisfied, the weavers adopted a more temperate attitude. But just as disorder began to subside, troops supported by artillery arrived at the scene, and the revolt was put down in blood. The final act was played out in Breslau, where the ringleaders were tried and sentenced to lashings and long terms of imprisonment.[21]

Artisan riots were obvious symptoms of the decay of the handicraft system, but within the trade guild itself there was even more convincing evidence that all was not well with the small independent shop owner. For corporate craft associations were ceasing to reward hard work and professional skill with advancement to employer status. While the increase in artisans kept step with the general rise in inhabitants, the expansion was largely in the ranks of employees, of journeymen and apprentices. The numbers of master tradesmen grew at a much smaller rate than the population as a whole, a plain indication that economic opportunity had contracted and that the guild structure had lost its resilience.[22]

Thus at the same time that industrial liberalism was facilitating admission to artisan occupations, those able to profit from the new economic freedom were becoming fewer. The average handicraftsman lacked equipment and capital, and he lacked faith in his own future. Still, in complaining about the overcrowding of trade he was mistaking effect for cause, for it was not the relative increase in workers but the decline in the demand for their labor which was so drastic. The fundamental source of the crisis which the artisan faced was the factory, the factory which took away his markets, reduced his income, threw him out of work.

By the Forties the disintegration of the handicraft system was far advanced. Of 2,812 shoemakers in Berlin only 407 had an income high enough to be liable for the trade tax, and among master joiners no more than 640 out of 1,088 were subject to it. In Elberfeld-Barmen, where almost half of the 1,100 shoemakers suffered from unemployment, there were barely 32 who paid the fee. Between 1821-25 and 1841-45 per capita consumption of meat in Hamburg declined by 20 per cent. Everywhere the income of the artisan fell, hours of labor increased, and work became scarce, as one master after another was forced to dismiss his journeymen to keep his own head above water.

Conditions among factory workers, on the other hand, were good. Those employed by manufacturers of industrial equipment like the Egells machine plant or the Borsig locomotive works enjoyed steady work and high wages, profiting from the continuing boom in railway construction. Even in the textile mills a skilled hand could earn as much as ten marks a week, when in Westphalia a linen weaver toiling at home received less than two. Industrial workers had become the aristocrats of labor, while the once proud handicraftsman was sinking to the level of a propertyless, rootless proletarian.[23]

Yet in the early nineteenth century the guild retained one important asset, superior numbers. Factories employed only about a third of all laborers engaged in nonagricultural production, while the great majority practiced a handicraft occupation and worked in a master tradesman's shop. About 1850 even in economically advanced Prussia 9.12 per cent of the population continued to find a source of livelihood in artisan establishments and only 4.08 per cent in industrial plants. In Nassau the percentages were 3.65 and 1.79, in Hesse-Darmstadt 5.99 and 3.05, in Hesse-Kassel 4.81 and 3.04, in Bavaria 4.55 and 3.95. As for the rural states of the north where the factory was still a rarity—in Hanover, Oldenburg, Schleswig-Holstein, and the Mecklenburgs—the numerical preponderance of the independent handicraftsman in all fields of manufacture was even greater.[24]

The growth of industrialism, therefore, presented a serious threat to the social equilibrium of Central Europe, for it undermined the way of life of millions still dependent on a precapitalistic organization of production. The rulers of Germany, impressed with the economic and military advantages offered by the factory system, overlooked the disruptive tendencies which came in its wake. Familiar with the guild traditions of conservatism and orderliness, they remained blind to the cumulative effects of years of suffering on the lower classes. And so the artisan, having exhausted all peaceful means of influencing the course of government policy, driven to despair by the prospect of economic annihilation, broke at last with established authority and sought salvation in a new political order.

THE AGRARIAN PROBLEM

WHEN the storm broke in the spring of 1848 the agrarian problem was still of paramount importance for the economic life of Central Europe. At the time of the Congress of Vienna 80 per cent of the inhabitants of the German Confederation lived on the land, while thirty years later two out of three Germans could still be found in the village. Despite the steady progress of the factory system, almost every state retained its rural character until after the middle of the century. The only exceptions were Hamburg, Bremen, Lübeck, and Frankfurt, the four municipal republics whose territories hardly extended beyond their city walls, and Saxony, where a flourishing industry and commerce employed more than half of the entire labor force. The rest was the country of the peasant tilling the fields, grumbling about servile dues, and awaiting the day when the land would be his.[1]

The agrarian problem involved first of all the personal status of a servile agricultural working class tied to the soil by law and tradition. The question of the legal position of the peasantry assumed importance in the eighteenth century, as serfdom ceased to be financially profitable or morally acceptable. To begin with, the physiocratic theories and social teachings of the era of benevolent despotism began to condemn human bondage as economically and ethically unjustifiable. Then the experiences of the French Revolution and of the Industrial Revolution lent strength to the movement for the abolition of servitude. By 1848 the liberation of the serf and his transformation into an independent peasant struggling for a livelihood in a free economy had become an essential aspect of the growth of German agriculture.

Secondly, a change in the personal relationships binding the peasant to the land and subjecting him to the aristocrat necessitated a change in the economic relationships prevalent under manorialism. The entire complex of servile dues, labor obligations, financial fees, and feudal prerogatives was so inextricably bound up in the institution of serfdom that the end of one led ineluctably to a redefinition of the other. What is more, the liberation of the peasant raised the question of ultimate ownership of the soil in which both serf and noble had property rights. The attempt to translate corporate concepts of possession derived from the Middle Ages into contractual rights characteristic of an age of capitalism meant that the system of dual proprietorship of the land had to be abolished and the conflicting claims of the joint owners settled. This process of adjustment was the most delicate of the issues created by the liberation of the peasant, for on its outcome depended the direction in which rural life in Central Europe would develop after its emergence from feudalism.

Finally, the agrarian problem arose out of the need for a more rational approach to the cultivation of the soil. In the course of the eighteenth century farming had begun to play a new role in the economy of the Continent, as the demands of the local market ceased to determine the output of agriculture. The desire for financial profit inspired a mode of tillage which actively imitated the example of industrial capitalism. The emphasis on an increased yield and a more intensive exploitation of the soil encouraged the adoption of farming methods designed to raise the productive capacity of the countryside. Even before 1815 the open-field system was disappearing, the peasant's scattered parcels of land were becoming compact farms, village common lands were being partitioned and cultivated, and progressive landowners were turning with growing enthusiasm to crop specialization. Then came important scientific discoveries in organic chemistry and veterinary medicine which strengthened the trend toward a modernization of agriculture, encouraging the transition of the rural economy from a subsistence to a profit basis.

Three distinct forms of agricultural organization developed in Germany after the Middle Ages, each with its unique system of land distribution and cultivation. The south and west became the country of undersized farms held by the peasantry under a system of hereditary or lifetime tenure. Although here and there the aristocrat practiced agriculture on a large scale, he was as a rule not a gentleman-farmer but a landlord deriving his wealth from dues levied upon the countryman. In the Rhineland, in Thuringia, and in the states south of the Main the rustic performed labor services on the noble estate and paid a wide variety of fees for the right to till the soil which had once belonged to him. The burden of manorial charges, moreover, grew heavier as population expanded in the eighteenth century, and since primogeniture had never become an accepted principle in this region, the peasant divided and subdivided his holding among his heirs to the point at which efficient management of it became impossible. Overpopulation was at the root of the difficulties which the rural masses were experiencing, but manorial exploitation aggravated what would under the best of circumstances have been a serious problem.[2]

The Elbe was the traditional boundary between the small holdings of the west and the great estates of the east. Since the sixteenth century the sandy plain which extends along the southern shore of the Baltic had brought rich profits to Dutch shippers and German landowners supplying rye and wheat for the grain markets of the West. The international demand for agricultural goods encouraged the growth of latifundia and the creation of a class of noble proprietors actively participating in the cultivation of the land. The average Junker of East Prussia or Pomerania lived on his estates and supervised his serfs, shunning the glories and pleasures of the court. Although in the years of benevolent despotism his king finally persuaded him to enter the royal service as an officer or a bureaucrat, usually his first love was still farming.

The nobleman's industriousness was the peasant's undoing. The aristocrat of western Germany was content to let the rustic keep his parcel of land as long as he paid manorial dues, but the Junker must consolidate, he must expand, he must absorb the holdings of the villager. And since he needed a cheap source of labor to operate his estates, the independent farmer had to be reduced to serfdom. The economic decline of the rural population therefore paralleled a decline in its personal status from freeman to bondsman. Where a powerful monarchy arose as in Prussia the rulers attempted to protect the peasantry against the extravagant demands of the nobility. In the aristocratic oligarchies of the north, however, nothing could save the countryman. In Swedish Pomerania a peasant was sold for the first time in 1723, and before long Junkers were blithely paying off their gambling debts in serfs. On the lands of the Mecklenburg aristocracy, where 12,000 peasants had lived in 1628, there were fewer than 2,000 at the end of the eighteenth century. The nobleman of the eastern latifundia was growing wealthy through the impoverishment of the villager.[3]

Between the Elbe and the Weser lay a region where the transition from an independent peasant agriculture to a system of landed estates had not reached its ultimate stage. In Schleswig-Holstein, Hanover, Oldenburg, and East Friesland could be found a class of prosperous farmer proprietors, free in their persons and unencumbered in their holdings. While latifundia were not uncommon, they were unable to expand at the expense of the villager, who held his land under advantageous terms of tenure and enjoyed the protection of the state. Furthermore, since local economic conditions were not favorable to large-scale agricultural production, there was little inducement for the great landowner to extend his possessions. Indeed, in the eighteenth century some noblemen like Count Rantzau auf Aschberg and Count Holck auf Eckhof began to divide their estates into small farms for hereditary tenants. Nowhere in Central Europe did the rural population enjoy a more advanced status than in the northwest, although even there manorial dues and land hunger were giving rise to dissatisfaction among the rustics.[4]

Before the French Revolution agrarian reform was primarily the work of enlightened rulers who desired to maintain social equilibrium, who feared aristocratic ambition, or who felt a sincere concern for the welfare of their subjects. Yet the power of the nobility was so firmly entrenched that only in the southwest could the well-intentioned monarch do more than better the lot of the crown peasants. There serfdom was not a flourishing institution, and most noblemen were rentiers rather than entrepreneurs. The humanitarian ideals of the Age of Enlightenment which influenced the policies of many German statesmen found their most ardent champion in Margrave Karl Friedrich of Baden. This remarkable prince labored to abolish serfdom, to commute manorial obligations to money rents, and to transform hereditary tenants into free proprietors. An avid student of the agricultural methods of other nations, he urged the countryside to improve the breeding of cattle, to make effective use of pasture land, and to raise the quality of grain. While the results of his efforts to create an independent peasantry were disappointing, his program of rural improvement was observed with considerable interest by the other rulers of the Holy Roman Empire, some of whom even began to imitate cautiously the example of the benevolent margrave.[5]

In the states along the North Sea the crown made little effort to drive the nobleman to reform. It preferred to show the way, hoping that sooner or later he would learn to accept a new agricultural order. In Hanover the bureaucracy worked hard to end servile obligations on government lands and replace them with money payments. This modest goal was finally attained in the last decade of the eighteenth century, but most of the landowners preferred not to tamper with traditional forms of manorial dues. And even the crown peasants continued to nurse grievances, for while they now paid their obligations in coin instead of produce, they still had no opportunity to obtain the land as their private property.

The rulers of Schleswig-Holstein were somewhat more generous, for between 1765 and 1787 the state serfs obtained not only personal freedom but unencumbered proprietorship as well. A decree of 1763, moreover, provided for the division of crown domains into parcels to be leased to individual peasants on hereditary tenure, and soon afterward the obligation to perform labor services on the estates of the monarch came to an end. By the time of the French Revolution the government was preparing to extend reform legislation to the possessions of the aristocracy. In 1788 Denmark abolished serfdom within the kingdom, and the prince regent who later became King Frederick VI sought to extend emancipation to the duchies as well. Some noblemen who recognized the handwriting on the wall even hastened to anticipate him by liberating their serfs and strengthening the economic position of the peasant farm. As the century drew to a close, the northwestern states were slowly moving in the direction of rural emancipation.[6]

Agrarian reform was least advanced where it was most needed. The peasants in the east were victims of an exploitation harsher than in the north or south, yet they were precisely those to whom the state offered the smallest measure of protection. It was to be expected that in Swedish Pomerania and in the Mecklenburgs the nobility would successfully resist all attempts to reduce its prerogatives, but even the energetic rulers of Prussia wielding a power which was in theory absolute could do little to free the serf or better his lot. Frederick William I attempted to oppose Junker greed by decreeing in 1739 that no farmer could be evicted from his holding without good cause, and his more illustrious son repeated the injunction against peasant expropriation in 1749.

Then came the Seven Years' War, and Frederick the Great could no longer afford to alienate an aristocracy whose support was essential for victory. It was therefore not before 1764 that he turned again to the task of stabilizing agrarian conditions once and for all. His goal was the establishment of a just equilibrium between the demands of the nobility and the needs of the peasantry, so that each class could enjoy the undisturbed possession of a property commensurate with its position in the community. Under the new law 1756 became the base year for the division of land between aristocrat and serf, the conditions which prevailed on that date were made permanent, and changes in ownership rights occurring after it were declared invalid. The peasant was given neither freedom from serfdom nor relief from manorialism, but he did gain a sense of personal security and economic stability. The decree of 1764, expressing the corporate view of society still accepted in the Age of Enlightenment, continued to govern agrarian relations in Prussia until the nineteenth century.[7]

Three years after the death of the greatest of the Hohenzollerns the French Revolution began. Among its first accomplishments was the destruction of French feudalism and the creation of an independent propertied peasantry. What the benevolent despots had been vainly attempting to achieve for fifty years was accomplished by liberal parliamentarians in the course of the single night of August 4, 1789. And once the Revolution embarked on a course of conquest and destroyed the old political order, the rulers of Central Europe hastened to mold their states in the image of victorious France. As one state after another abolished personal servitude and feudal prerogative, the peasant of Germany emerged at last out of the bondage which he had endured since the Middle Ages. Schleswig-Holstein adopted a program of rural emancipation in 1804, Nassau and Bavaria in 1808, and Hesse-Darmstadt in 1811, while the oppressed villager of

Hanover and Hesse-Kassel became a free citizen of the Kingdom of Westphalia or the French Empire, enjoying the civic
benefits of the Code Napoléon. Even in Swedish Pomerania
an edict of 1806 gave the serf his freedom, but at a high price,
for the land was declared to be the property of the nobleman, and the peasant often got his first taste of liberty with
a notice of eviction from his holding.[8]

As important as the emancipation of the serf was the regu-
larization of his economic status by the abolition of manorialism. Here again the rulers of the Napoleonic Era were following in the footsteps of the Age of Enlightenment, but
they acted more energetically and more swiftly than had the
benevolent despots. The years from 1806 to 1813 were rich
in legislation defining the nature of peasant dues and transforming them into money liabilities. Bavaria, Nassau, Hesse-
Darmstadt, and the Kingdom of Westphalia were the leaders
in the substitution of a landlord-tenant for a noble-serf relationship. Not only did they order the commutation of servile
obligations into rents, but they also established a legal standard for the extinction of the rents themselves. The peasant
could liquidate many of the fees to which he was subject by
paying the nobleman an amount varying as a rule from
twenty to twenty-five times their annual value. This provision
represented a significant advance beyond what the eighteenth
century had been able to achieve, for it made possible in
theory the development of a free rural population owning
landed property unencumbered with corporate legal restrictions. As yet only certain categories of obligations were subject to redemption, and since contracts by which the peasant
obtained clear title to his holding usually required the consent
of both parties, the landlord could postpone the extinction
of his manorial rights indefinitely. Yet a breach had been
made in the wall of feudal privilege, a breach which was
bound to grow wider with time.[9]

Prussia, enjoying a decade of peace purchased by the Treaty

of Basel, felt the influence of the French Revolution later than the rest of Germany. Blind to the dangers which threatened his kingdom, Frederick William III pursued in leisure the work of rural reform initiated under benevolent despotism, and between 1799 and 1806 he promulgated decrees freeing many of the serfs on the royal domains and commuting their servile obligations into rents. His awakening came on the morrow of the Treaty of Tilsit with the appointment of the historic Stein ministry, which at once proclaimed the abolition of serfdom. On October 9, 1807, came the edict ending hereditary servitude and declaring land a free commodity purchasable by all citizens regardless of class. Besides personal independence the peasant was also to enjoy the economic freedom to dispose of his holding as he saw fit. He could buy, sell, borrow, and mortgage. The balance between noble and serf property which Frederick the Great had created in 1764 was thereby destroyed, and the countryman found himself exposed to the risks of a free rural economy.[10]

While the edict emancipated the rural population, it did not attempt to define the rights of the peasant to the soil. Not until Hardenberg became head of the Prussian ministry did the government finally undertake the task of dividing the land between the former serf and his former lord. The law of September 14, 1811, the first to deal with the complex question of property relationships, was basically a conservative measure. To begin with, it applied only to those farms numbering about 161,000 which were held under favorable categories of tenure. Secondly, it provided for the extinction of manorial claims to such holdings by a novel system of land cession. Unlike his fellow in southwestern Germany, the villager of Prussia did not have to pay in money for a clear title to his farm. Instead he could surrender to the nobleman a portion of his property, one third if he possessed a heritable customary tenure, one half if he held a life tenancy or limited lease. He thus won his independence by enlarging the eco-

nomic resources of the aristocracy, and his liberation consequently contributed to his ultimate decline.[11]

The laws of 1807 and 1811 helped perpetuate and strength-
en the dominant position of the great estates east of the Elbe.
The aristocrat, who was freed from the feudal obligation to
protect the serf, provide him with lodging, feed him in hard
times, and maintain him in possession of his land, became an
agricultural entrepreneur. He improved efficiency, increased
production, reduced costs, and proceeded to devour his weaker
competitors. As for the peasantry, having been deprived of
economic stability and weakened by the loss of property, it
soon discovered that freedom from the restrictions of serfdom also meant freedom to go down in the struggle for
financial survival. A few of the reformers like Baron Stein
himself and Christian Scharnweber foresaw the disruptive
consequences of emancipation and urged the adoption of remedial legislation. But the government, reluctant to arouse
the opposition of the nobility, preferred to strengthen the
alliance between king and Junker by sacrificing the interests
of the village.[12]

The Restoration did not alter in any fundamental respect
the character of the land reforms adopted by the states of
Central Europe during the period of French hegemony. As
a matter of fact, the agrarian legislation promulgated between
1815 and 1848 was only a logical extension of principles first
established during the Age of Enlightenment and the Napoleonic Era. It accentuated tendencies which had already
existed before the Congress of Vienna, sharpening the con-
trast in rural conditions between east and west. In the former
the peasant continued to lose his farm to the great landowner. In the latter the commutation and extinction of peasant dues advanced steadily, although the process was still far
from complete at the time of the Revolution. The dualism
which had developed in the agriculture of Germany under

benevolent despotism reached its culmination under legitimist conservatism.

As soon as the political reorganization of Europe was completed in 1815, the lands of the German Confederation resumed their programs of rural liberation. It is true that in a few cases such as Hanover and Hesse-Kassel the agrarian legislation of the Napoleonic Era was revoked, but before long even these reactionary states felt obliged to introduce measures designed to conciliate the peasantry. Elsewhere, especially in the southwest, manorial dues and services were steadily being transformed into rents which could be liquidated by payments amounting on an average to about twenty times their yearly yield. The details of reform differed from state to state and from one servile obligation to another, for each category of feudal privilege required distinct commuting legislation, and governments could not exercise the same degree of control over the lands of the nobility as over the estates of the crown. Throughout Central Europe, however, the outcome of emancipation was the emergence of agriculture from a condition of corporate manorialism into an age of capitalistic enterprise.

Baden, which in the eighteenth century had become a leader in the movement for peasant liberation, continued to work with zeal for the improvement of agricultural conditions under the Restoration. So rapidly did its government deal with the land problem that by 1848 legal arrangements for the extinction of most obligations were already on the statute books. In Württemberg the most important laws dealing with the abolition of servile dues and labor services were those of October 27, 28, and 29, 1836. The decree of March 17, 1832, initiated the economic emancipation of the peasantry of Saxony. Hanover and Hesse-Kassel, still governed in the spirit of the petty tyrants of the Holy Roman Empire, were frightened into reform by the uprisings of 1830. Of the more important states of western Germany only Bavaria failed to advance the work begun by the Montgelas ministry in 1808, for there the nobility was influential enough to postpone the abolition of manorial land tenure until the middle of the century.[13]

East of the Elbe the peasantry did not fare as well. Even before the fall of Napoleon the government of Prussia had hesitated to undermine the position of the aristocracy by allowing the countryman to obtain title to his land, and after 1815 the obstacles to rural emancipation became greater still. The Junkers, their hold on the army and the bureaucracy strengthened, began to urge the government to revise the edict of 1811 in their favor. The answer to their agitation was the declaration of May 29, 1816, which restricted the right to extinguish manorial dues by land cession to those peasants whose holdings were *spannfähig*, large enough to support a team of draft animals. By and large, only farms of more than eight hectares belonged to this class, and the declaration therefore had the effect of reducing by nearly two thirds the number of those eligible to gain full possession of their properties. It reflected the determination of the state to maintain the landowning aristocracy as its chief beneficiary and hence its chief supporter.[14]

The last major agricultural achievement of the reform era in Prussia was the order of June 7, 1821, defining the economic status of perpetual lessees, peasants enjoying the highest category of tenure. This class, which had been excluded from the provisions of the legislation of 1811 and 1816, was now enabled to obtain unencumbered ownership of the land through the payment of an amount equal to twenty-five times the annual value of the dues to which its holdings were subject. By the terms of the measure it might theoretically have formed the nucleus of a farmer aristocracy in eastern Germany, personally free and economically independent, yet by reason of its small size it never found itself in a position to challenge the supremacy of the Junker. The order affected fewer than 200,000 peasants, while millions continued to perform manorial services and pay manorial fees. And even these were better off than the rustics of the Mecklenburgs who won their freedom in 1820, but lost all property rights to the soil.[15]

Because of the form which rural emancipation assumed in Central Europe the aristocracy was able to survive in the era of industrialism which opened after 1815. Having adjusted to the demands of a new economic age, it retained social prestige and political influence throughout the nineteenth century. In the states of the west the nobleman became increasingly an absentee landowner, deriving the bulk of his wealth from peasant dues. Since his rights as a feudal overlord were converted into annual dividends, his direct control over the soil weakened. Yet the change was by no means unfavorable to him, for it relieved him of financial responsibility and provided him with an assured income. Some proprietors, especially among the mediatized nobility, opposed the commutation of manorial obligations, and a few even proceeded to absorb peasant land in order to enlarge their own estates. The typical aristocrat of the Rhine or the Neckar, however, was willing to sell his prerogatives, provided the terms were advantageous and the price right.

The Junker of Brandenburg or Pomerania, on the other hand, drove a hard bargain with German agriculture. The extinction of servile dues brought him about 400,000 hectares, while the division of commons and the free purchase of peasant farms extended his holdings still farther. Through rents and liquidation payments he also obtained approximately 260,000,000 marks, which could be devoted to the improvement of his land and the modernization of his equipment. Under the Restoration the latifundia of the Prussian aristocracy grew apace, becoming centers of the capitalistic practice of agriculture characteristic of the country east of the Elbe. Seasonal migratory labor displaced the settled rural population on the estates, the fluctuations of the world food market came to govern their cultivation, and the industrial by-products of farming became as important as farming itself. The landowner was not only an entrepreneur engaged in the production of grain, but also more and more a distiller of alcohol, a refiner of sugar, and a manufacturer of brick.[16]

Yet the establishment of a free system of land ownership which allowed the aristocrat to seize the farms of the peasantry exposed him in turn to financial disaster. Nobleman as well as commoner could sink into debt and insolvency whenever the grain market fell. For example, during the farm depression of the Twenties many urban investors, after purchasing mortgages on landed property at low cost, managed to gain possession of extensive holdings through foreclosure. All in all, one third of the Junker estates in Prussia passed into the hands of bourgeois owners in the years of agricultural instability which followed the era of reform, while in adjacent Mecklenburg-Schwerin middle-class proprietors outnumbered noble landlords by the middle of the century. The burden of indebtedness of the Prussian aristocracy doubled between 1805 and 1845, rising from 162,000,000 to 325,000,000 marks. Faced with the threat of bankruptcy, the nobility had recourse to entailment as a weapon against grasping creditors, but even this device proved inadequate for the purpose of economic security. Land continued to change hands so rapidly that by 1885 only 13 per cent of the latifundia of East Prussia had been in the possession of the same family for more than fifty years.[17]

When the great landowner could not resist the destructive effects of a capitalistic organization of the agrarian economy, what was the peasant to do? In the early nineteenth century the social cohesion of the country population began to weaken, as conflicting interests came to divide the wealthier villagers who were able to survive the consequences of reform from those disappearing into the ranks of the rural proletariat. In the north and east it was the small farmer who succumbed first to the pressures exerted by the large estate, for his share in the division of common lands was not enough to compensate him for the loss of meadow and forest rights. Sinking deeper and deeper in debt, unable to cultivate his barren plot profitably, he was eventually forced to sell out and become a laborer on the land of the nobleman. Between 1816 and 1859 the latifundia of Prussia swallowed up some 7,000 large peasant holdings and more than twice as many smaller properties. The growth of a landless agricultural proletariat was most rapid in Pomerania, Silesia, and of course the Mecklenburgs, but it was also observable in Schleswig-Holstein, Hanover, and even as far south as Thuringia and Hesse-Darmstadt.[18]

The lot of the agricultural laborer varied from region to region. In some states he was normally a cotter or crofter, receiving a small plot of land as well as a wage in return for his services. In others he was simply a migratory worker, a hand on a field gang, unsure of future employment and exposed to harsh exploitation. As a rule his earnings maintained him only at the barest subsistence level, and the district president of Danzig admitted to a British visitor that "this price of labour, or amount of 30 dollars . . . a-head annually, yielding no more than what a person wants for bread, salt, clothing, taxes, and minor objects, cannot be diminished without lessening the power of labour and its usefulness."[19] According to the estimate of a board of economists in 1848 the minimum annual expenditure of a peasant family for the necessities of life was about 348 marks, an amount which the average laborer on the land could acquire only if his wife and children were also at work. Since more than 2,000,000 persons in Prussia and the Mecklenburgs earned all or part of their livelihood as farm hands, the unfavorable conditions of agricultural employment affected a high proportion of the rural population east of the Elbe.[20]

In the west rural impoverishment was an even more serious problem, yet the agricultural proletariat of states like Baden, Württemberg, and Hesse-Darmstadt was composed not of landless laborers but of peasants whose holdings were too small to be farmed efficiently. Here a rise in the birth and survival rates beginning in the eighteenth century had led to an overpopulation whose effects were disastrous. The villager, free from fear of the competition of aristocratic latifundia, partitioned his lands among his children again and again, defying the advice of economists who urged a more rational system of agriculture. During the Forties, Friedrich List analyzed the "dwarf economy" practiced along the Neckar and the Main, and spoke of entire villages in which not one plow was in use any more because of the small size of the holdings. Thomas C. Banfield noted the land hunger of the Rhineland: "The pride of the German peasant is to be a small landowner. The sacrifices made to gratify this longing are incredible, as is the tenacity with which he clings to his land in all changes of fortune. The price paid for small lots of land in the valley of the Wüpper [sic] and the adjoining districts would frighten an English farmer."[21] Between 1833 and 1847 the number of villagers in Saxe-Meiningen meeting the property qualification for membership in the state diet declined by more than a third. Everywhere the peasant farm was shrinking and the peasant income declining, while the rural population continued to subdivide, to procreate, and to grumble about hard times.[22]

The complaint of the peasant that the authorities were indifferent to his plight was not without justification, for the rulers of Germany failed to meet the agrarian problem with sufficient determination. The countryman, whose economic situation would have been difficult in any case, had to cope with the additional burden of manorial services, obligations, and disabilities. In no region of Central Europe did the work of emancipation reach its conclusion before the middle of the century. The noble was still judge and sheriff to his peasants, he still nominated teacher and preacher, he still held exclusive hunting and fishing privileges, he still enjoyed special woodland and pasture rights. Countless oppressive servile dues remained in force throughout the nation, and the commutation of these liabilities into rent was a painfully slow process. Moreover, Article XIV of the Act of Confederation protected the property rights of the mediatized aristocracy, excluding wide areas of the west from the competence of reform legislation. The liberation of agriculture, still only in its beginning, was unable to satisfy all the extravagant hopes which it had inspired in the village.[23]

Even those peasants who were able to commute or liquidate their obligations discovered that they had not freed themselves from economic bondage but only altered its form. Instead of surrendering a portion of their grain to the lord or working a number of days on his land, they now paid him a fixed rent which had to be met in times of depression as well as prosperity. Since the capital required for the extinction of dues was beyond the reach of most farmers, the great need of the rural population became easy credit, and without it the emancipation laws were often only so much paper. Some of the states began to cope with this problem by founding rent banks to extend long-term loans to the peasantry. Saxony, for example, took the lead in establishing credit institutions for the countryside with the law of March 17, 1832. The governments of Württemberg, Baden, and Hesse-Darmstadt sought to expedite reform by assuming the liquidation costs of a few of the more onerous servile obligations. Yet these were palliatives, not cures. The farmer who actually attempted to achieve financial independence soon learned that liberation could lead to debts and foreclosures.[24]

Twenty years after the inception of the reform program in Hanover more than half of the manorial fees were still in effect. In Schleswig-Holstein farmers who were permitted to liquidate their obligations in 1819 continued to pay redemption dues as late as 1853. Loans by state banks to the peasantry of Saxony amounted to 33,000,000 marks by 1846, while repayments were less than 500,000 marks. As for Prussia, only about 240,000 peasants in the eastern provinces had actually become free proprietors under the terms of the emancipation laws, 70,000 by land cession and 170,000 by financial settlement. The lack of capital, the inadequacy of reform legislation, the expense of commutation, the rise in indebtedness, the growth of latifundia, the land hunger induced by overpopulation, all in combination constituted an insuperable obstacle to the creation of an independent peasantry in Germany. They engendered among the rural masses a growing dissatisfaction with freedom which reached its culmination in the great agrarian uprising of the spring of 1848.[25]

In the final analysis, the peasant was a victim of far-reaching economic changes which he did not initiate and which he could not control. In the course of barely half a century he lost the security which had been his under manorialism, gaining in return a liberty to which he was not accustomed. The problem of adjustment facing him was aggravated by the lack of resources to defend his new status. After centuries of bondage, he was left to shift for himself in a world of bankers, industrialists, and landlords. Emancipation in the abstract was an act of justice, but in practice it proved to be a dangerous policy. Had the state protected the rural population in freedom as it had done in serfdom, the agrarian problem would not have assumed so serious a character. The rulers of the Restoration, however, dealt with land reform by legislative fiat pure and simple, ignoring its political and social consequences. Thereby they loosened the bonds which had given the rural community its cohesion. The peasantry, deserted by those on whom it called for help, bewildered by its new rights and duties, finally turned to revolution in order to cope with the perplexing questions which the nineteenth century had thrust upon it.

THE IDEOLOGICAL CONFLICT

THE growth of a capitalistic economy working such profound changes in industry and agriculture was also responsible for the political tensions of the years preceding the revolution. The benevolent despotism of the eighteenth century was a mode of government appropriate to a nation of serfs, artisans, and aristocrats, but in the age of the factory and the railway it became a parasitic relic of a bygone age commanding neither loyalty nor respect. Hence the system of legitimate rule established in Europe after the Congress of Vienna, blind to the transformation of society which the French Revolution had introduced, failed to achieve a lasting stability. And the generation which reached maturity after the battle of Waterloo lived through a time of bitter conflict, as the world of the past fought to remain alive.

In Germany the wave of reform which originated in the struggle against French oppression was succeeded after 1819 by an era of reaction. The promise of representative government and economic unity implicit in the Act of Confederation remained a dead letter. After lengthy consideration by one committee after another, Prussian constitutional projects were finally shelved, and in place of a parliament Frederick William III created provincial diets chosen by the estates of the realm to act in a purely advisory capacity. Even in those states of the south and west where written instruments of government were promulgated the competence of the assembly remained carefully restricted, with the right to initiate legislation, to control the armed forces, and to supervise the enforcement of laws reserved for the crown. As for the Diet of the Confederation meeting in Frankfurt, it turned out to be no more than a convenient instrument of conservative rulers for the suppression of the liberal opposition. By its decrees those who in 1813 had been hailed as heroes of the movement for national emancipation became a decade later demagogic agitators to be dismissed from their official posts and hounded into exile or prison.[1]

The statesmen of the reaction assumed that parliamentarianism commanded the support of no more than a small minority of the population of Germany, a minority composed of visionary academicians, sensationalistic journalists, and bourgeois malcontents. The aristocracy certainly was unquestioningly loyal to a monarchy which repaid its devotion with favor and patronage. While here and there in Central Europe there arose an aristocratic liberalism inspired by the teachings of English free traders, the example of French constitutionalists, and a native tradition of resistance to royal absolutism, the highborn reformer was an exception. Far more typical was the Prussian Junker or Württemberg landowner who wore the king's uniform in a guard regiment or in the diplomatic service, dedicating himself to a defense of the crown, because a limitation of royal power must lead to the destruction of his own prerogative. His reward was a privileged position in the social hierarchy from which he could look down on the moneygrubbing banker and the closefisted industrialist.

The masses too remained by and large indifferent to constitutional doctrines. What did concepts of natural right, social contract, popular sovereignty, and legal equality mean to the lower classes engaged in the exhausting struggle for economic survival? Their civic attitude usually found expression in a naïve provincial patriotism and a reverence for the ruling prince, for fundamentally the peasant and the artisan were conservatives, suspicious of newfangled theories and respectful toward tradition. Occasional radicals like Karl Follen or Georg Büchner might dream of leading a hungry mob against kings and princes, but the practical results of their agitation were only a few secret meetings of rebellious workingmen and intellectuals, a fiery pamphlet or two, an infrequent assassination. To a later age grown accustomed to war and revolution they became the prophets of things to come. In their own time, however, their influence was slight, for the proletariat ignored demands for governmental reform until the eve of the Revolution.

Yet the lower classes did long for change, but by change they meant first and foremost an improvement in their economic status. The artisan robbed of his livelihood by industrialism, the peasant forced to sell his farm to the nobleman, the factory worker cheated of his wages by the truck system—all favored reform providing relief from physical want. But they did not put their trust in the leaders of the liberal opposition, those well-to-do outsiders who propounded impious civic ideas and moved in a mysterious world of newspapers and political clubs. Their pleas were sent instead to the prince, the father of his people, who would surely protect them, as he had protected their fathers before them. Only at mid-century did the masses finally participate in open insurrection, although in doing so they responded not to political agitation, but to a desperate economic need.[2]

Theories of constitutionalism found favor only in the eyes of the bourgeoisie. The French Revolution revealed to it the weaknesses of benevolent despotism and gave it a taste of emancipation. Kings had fallen, armies had scattered, and yet society had not degenerated into wild anarchy. Instead, careers had been thrown open to talent and ability had become the measure of worth. The doctrines of liberty, equality, and fraternity had crossed the Rhine with French bayonets, forcing on Central Europe an era of reform whose special favors were reserved for the third estate. Since military occupation and financial extortion accompanied reform, the war against the foreigner which began in 1813 aroused genuine enthusiasm among all classes. But the burgher who fought at Bautzen or Leipzig believed that victory on the battlefield also meant political freedom and social equality, and in defending the fatherland he was upholding his new dignity as a free citizen.

The peace which came with the Congress of Vienna was a bitter disillusionment to him. The middle class, now beginning to move toward economic domination, found itself excluded from every position of political influence. The 100,000 inhabitants of Cologne and Aachen sent only 3 delegates to the diet of the Rhine Province, while the nobility numbering less than 7,000 was represented by 25. Throughout Prussia there were twice as many aristocratic as bourgeois members of provincial assemblies. In the Mecklenburgs the legislature was the scene of repeated but vain attempts by middle-class deputies to reduce the prerogatives of the landowners. In Hanover an estate which passed from the hands of a noble to a commoner lost its representation in the diet. Even in the south, in the heart of German liberalism, the aristocracy retained control over parliament by virtue of the prevailing class system of election.[3]

To the ambitious Cologne manufacturer or Berlin banker the political system of the German Confederation was intolerable. In neighboring France the July Monarchy was enthusiastically endorsing the cult of *enrichissez-vous*; across the English Channel in Great Britain the industrial middle class was making a triumphant entry into the House of Commons after the Reform Act of 1832; but in Central Europe the self-made man who had demonstrated his merit by amassing a fortune in mining or railroading could never achieve political eminence. In dealing with his government he saw himself overtaxed and underprivileged, while do-nothing sons of the nobility found preferment at the court and in the army. In conducting business with other states he paid heavy tolls and coped with the intricacies of a dozen different monetary systems and business codes. Even in the management of his private financial affairs he was constantly harassed by bureaucratic supervision and outmoded regulation.[4]

In a report submitted to the ministry of the interior on February 2, 1844, Governor of the Rhine Province Justus von Schaper disclosed the source of opposition to the policies of the Restoration:

> The disgruntlement and dissatisfaction which are becoming evident in this province do not emanate from the lower classes, but from the so-called educated groups which . . . desire to put their ideas about freedom of the press and popular representation into practice at any cost. To this class belong mostly the lawyers, doctors, and merchants, who hope by the means which they advocate to achieve a greater importance, for no one believes that they have only the welfare of the country in mind, as they maintain. Yet they all belong more or less to the well-to-do class of society, and they are very far from being in sympathy with communistic tendencies. Still, I can well believe that they would be prepared to make use of communism in order to achieve their purposes or at least to create an unrest which they would then exploit in their own entirely private interest.[5]

In its search for a theory of state expressing its civic aspirations, the bourgeoisie came upon liberalism, which had constructed a new philosophy of man and society out of the practical experiences of English parliamentarianism and the ethical teachings of the Age of Enlightenment. The Holy Roman Empire, economically backward and politically divided, had contributed little to its development. Throughout the eighteenth century Germany had endured without complaint the sometimes enlightened, sometimes benighted rule of its hundred princes, and when the French Revolution came, it found itself drawn irresistibly into a great war for European hegemony. Fighting without conviction first on one side, then on the other, it became at last the war booty of the victorious Napoleon. Only through defeat was it exposed to political ideas which had been germinating in the West for more than a hundred years. And from its conqueror it acquired at last a sense of national community and a respect for constitutional rule.

Although liberalism spoke a language addressed to all mankind regardless of origin or class, it differentiated in practice between the well to do who had proved their ability to govern by economic success and the masses whose innate incapacity was reflected in their proverty and ignorance. Maintaining that participation in government was not among those inalienable rights with which all men are endowed, it upheld an aristocratic organization of politics, while changing the qualification for admission to the ruling elite from birth to wealth. Since it sought an equality of opportunity rather than status, it could denounce the monopoly of power held by the nobility, and at the same time express a profound distrust of the wild passions and dark instincts of the lower classes.[6]

In his memorandum of December 31, 1830, for example, the liberal businessman David Hansemann argued that the constitution of an enlightened people ought to be based on majority rule, but majority rule must not invite mob rule: "By majority . . . we are never to understand one determined by counting heads, but rather the true strength of the nation, which, while it is also to have no interest other than that of the numerical majority, yet differs essentially from it, since by its better education, greater insight, and its property it has a larger stake in the maintenance of a stable, vigorous, and good government. It is the task of the latter to find this true majority and to use it to good purpose."[7]

In effect liberalism favored government by a minority composed of men of property and intelligence drawn from the ranks of the old aristocracy of status and the new aristocracy of talent. The citizen who was not entitled to participate in the processes of lawmaking, however, should still enjoy protection against tyrannical oppression, he should still enjoy freedom of speech and of the press, the right of assembly and petition, immunity from religious persecution, and security against judicial arbitrariness. The state was to be made conformable to the dictates of natural law and human ethic, and the will of the prince was to bow before the dignity of the sovereign citizen whose freedom was bond for his loyalty. Liberty would strengthen the nation not by increasing its powers of coercion, but by investing it with a new and vital moral principle.

Out of personal freedom was to develop a united country governed in accordance with the doctrines of parliamentarianism. The German Confederation would become a federal union while its diet would assume the role of a representative assembly speaking for a new nation. The member states should preserve their political identities in the reorganization of Central Europe, maintaining the monarchical form of government and the traditional class system. But they would have to promulgate written constitutions providing for an elective legislature empowered to take part in the formulation of laws and the determination of budgets.[8]

Essentially what the liberals demanded was the recognition of the growing importance of the middle class by its admission to a voice in government. Their ideal was the *juste-milieu* between absolutism and mob rule, between the anachronisms of autocracy and the horrors of revolution. Their quest for the golden mean of statecraft led them to a system of representation which could exercise a salutary restraint on the ruler without becoming subservient to the lower classes. In accordance with the prevailing views of the parliamentary movement in Europe, the leaders of German constitutionalism were unanimously opposed to manhood suffrage. Silvester Jordan, who had suffered years of martyrdom in a Hessian prison for his advocacy of political reform, wanted only property owners admitted to the ballot. The famous *Staats-Lexi-kon* of Karl von Rotteck and Karl Welcker, a bible of early liberal thought, assured its readers that to exclude the masses from voting was no more than just. Eminent public figures like Paul Pfizer and Gustav Rümelin of Württemberg, Hein-rich Laube and Karl Biedermann of Saxony, Ludolf Camp-hausen and Gustav Mevissen of Prussia were all in agreement that popular sovereignty did not mean a franchise for the mob. Only the aristocracy and the middle class, especially the middle class, possessed the practical experience and civic in-telligence to determine the vital interests of the state.[9]

In economics liberalism also defended the interests of the bourgeoisie by demanding the creation of conditions favorable to the growth of industrial capitalism. It urged the expansion of the Zollverein to embrace all of Germany, the removal of restrictions on the growth of the factory system, freedom of movement, freedom of occupation, and freedom of enter-prise. Railways, rivers, telegraphs, roads were to become part of a united system of transportation and communication serv-ing a national market. Such residues of the past as artisan guilds, corporate monopolies, trade privileges, and mercan-tilist regulations should be swept away to make way for a system of liberty under which skill and ambition could find a fit reward. For among the most precious rights of the citizen was the freedom to exercise his talent in the pursuit of finan-cial gain, and only through it could the aptitude and in-genuity of a progressive people contribute to the welfare of the state.[10]

True, in the struggle for economic survival some would have to go down, but poverty and hunger were part of the game; they were the price which society must pay for in-dustrial progress. Germany could not eat its cake and have it too; it could not build factories without inflicting hardships. A misguided sentimentality which ignored the hard truths of nature and society would in the long run ruin the rich without benefiting the poor. Hansemann was only expounding the accepted doctrines of laissez-faire economics when he wrote:

> The dangerous spirit of the lower classes is nourished by an application of philanthropy to statecraft which does honor to humanity, but which in its consequences is most pernicious. We insist that no one suffer distress, and so one institution after another is founded to feed and clothe the poor, to educate their children, to care for the old, to help poor mothers, etc. And almost all the poor to whom aid has been given in this fashion achieve for a shorter or longer period of time or even for their lifetime a much better position than those needy persons who struggle against unfortunate living conditions with their own earnings or those of their families. Here lies the most direct, the most open invitation to wastefulness and laziness, the two vices which will most effectively nourish among the lower classes good-for-nothings dangerous to the public safety. And that nothing may be lacking to arouse in these classes the belief that as a matter of duty they must be taken care of very nicely as soon as they find themselves in some measure destitute, the alms of Christian charity are in many places transformed into annually increasing poor rates.[11]

The liberal opposition with its program of cautious constitutionalism and unrestricted industrialism, however, did not win the support of all opponents of royal autocracy. Under the Restoration there developed in Central Europe a more radical democratic movement, egalitarian in politics and interventionist in economics. Its model was not the narrow parliamentarianism of Guizot, but the virtuous republicanism of Robespierre or better still of Madame Roland. It preached an aristocratic commonwealth defended by the masses and led by the propertied bourgeoisie. Like the middle-of-the-road moderates the democrats favored a closer union of the German states and the creation of an economic system favorable to the growth of industrial capitalism, yet they were more sensitive to social problems and to the need for a broad popular basis to political reform. Hence their insistence on manhood suffrage, their demand for welfare legislation, their advocacy of the republican form of government. Although also middle-class in outlook, they differed from the liberals in theory by their rejection of gradualist compromise and their emphasis on immediate and radical reform.[12]

Still, their bark was worse than their bite. Behind the bold words lurked a deep-seated bourgeois fear of the great unwashed, of the hungry mob to be pitied yet distrusted. Democracy was the brave lion tamer, one hand fondling the awful beast from the slums, the other firmly gripping the whip. Johann Jacoby, the radical physician from Königsberg who during the Revolution dared defy the king of Prussia to his face, maintained at one moment that "we must begin at once to do something to relieve the distress of the working class," and then spoke in almost the same breath of the "anarchist activities of a mob too lazy to work." Julius Fröbel and Franz Zitz were prepared to abandon the republican ideal or at least accept a "republican monarchy." Franz Waldeck, the "Westphalian peasant king," and Wilhelm Zimmermann, democratic professor from Stuttgart, deplored proletarian indifference to social grace and intellectual subtlety. As for economic and social reform in behalf of the masses, the program drafted by the radicals at their meeting in Offenburg on September 12, 1847, did not go beyond a demand for the introduction of a progressive income tax and the pious declaration: "We call for an adjustment in the disparity between labor and capital. It is the responsibility of society to elevate and protect labor."[13]

To their conservative enemies and liberal rivals the democrats were dangerous subverters of society, but in fact nothing was farther from their minds than the surrender of control over the government to the proletariat or the destruction of the economy of private property. While their position was well to the left of the liberals, they were also worlds removed from the handful of socialists who were vainly attempting to win influence among the working classes of the large cities. Even the most extreme among them, even Gustav von Struve and Friedrich Hecker, were closer in spirit to the Jacobins of 1793 than to the Communist League of 1847. They analyzed social problems in purely political terms, the concept of class struggle was repugnant to them, they saw in revolution only a glorified coup d'état, and they stoutly refused to admit workers or peasants to their councils, resisting all suggestions from the socialist camp for a grand coalition of middle-class and proletarian radical organizations.[14]

Thereby they probably acted with greater wisdom than they realized, for throughout his life Karl Marx suffered from an uncontrollable penchant for the domination of united fronts. Yet they also earned the undying enmity of the socialists and that special contempt which the orthodox reserve for the backslider. Friedrich Engels castigated them shortly after the revolution in a vitriolic prose: "These poor, weak-minded men, during the course of their generally very obscure lives, had been so little accustomed to anything like success, that they actually believed their paltry amendments, passed with two or three votes majority, would change the face of Europe."[15] And fifty years later Franz Mehring still could not bring himself to forgive them for refusing to dance to the socialist tune: "Petty bourgeois democracy . . . had freed itself from medieval, parochial fancies only to be taken all the more firmly in tow by the middle class. . . . It did not dare to follow with perseverance any consistent, independent policy, habitually losing even the desire to do so, as soon as it faced the choice between bourgeoisie and proletariat. At such moments it blindly embraced the most advanced political party of the bourgeoisie."[16]

Yet why should the democrats have entered into an alliance

fraught with such great danger and promising so little reward? They were separated from the socialists by an impassable ideological gulf, and there was no visible advantage to be gained from an association with a few wild-eyed doctrinaires haranguing the world from beyond the pale of civic respectability. The lawyers, teachers, petty merchants, and small businessmen congregating in republican clubs had nothing in common with proletarian agitators like Wilhelm Weitling or Stephan Born who had never attended a university or been invited to a salon. Even Karl Grün, Friedrich Engels, and Karl Marx, socially acceptable, were spiritual émigrés more at home in the utopian socialist circles of Paris and London where they had developed their taste for radical theorization than in the stodgy atmosphere of Biedermeier Germany. The democrats instinctively shunned any partnership with the socialists, who were thus left alone to face political ostracism.

Their names have since become enshrined in the hagiography of the left, but in their own day they could find comfort only in the faith of a true believer. The influence which they exerted on the world of their time was insignificant, and the proletariat, the chosen people of dialectical materialism, preferred to follow other prophets. In 1843, after the suppression of the *Rheinische Zeitung* which Marx had edited, the district president of Cologne assured the authorities in Berlin that it had never won popularity among the masses, that its only supporters had been a handful of radical enthusiasts. The *Manifesto of the Communist Party* failed to arouse interest even at police headquarters. The socialists sought to console themselves with the thought that the revolution which they believed to be imminent would soon justify their theory of history, but it came and went, apparently unaware of the teachings of Marx and Engels. Not one of their followers sat in the assemblies of 1848, not one of the uprisings was inspired by their doctrines. Of all the political organizations in opposition to aristocratic monarchism theirs was the weakest.[17]

In response to the criticisms raised against it by rationalist opponents the Restoration proceeded to adapt its philosophy of state to the temper of a generation grown weary of civic chaos. Accepting Bossuet's apotheosis of the throne and Hobbes's identification of civil war with social disintegration, it also enlisted in its cause the institutional historicism and political romanticism of Edmund Burke. The legitimist of the nineteenth century defended established authority not only because it was divinely ordained, but even more because it was the expression of a process of organic growth linking the present with the past. Deeply rooted in the instincts and sentiments of a nation, tradition possessed a vitality which defied dispassionate analysis. The liberal doctrinaire, seized with a mania for constitution making and paper reform, saw in it only an obstacle to the realization of mechanically perfect schemes of government. But to the conservative it was the basis of civilization, a haven against revolution and war which summoned the world to a return to the throne, the altar, and the corporate society.

In his own country Burke suffered the proverbial fate of the prophet. Most Victorians were too busy amassing wealth, extending the suffrage, controlling abuses of the factory system, and bringing Christianity to the heathen to ponder the metaphysical subtlety of legitimist political doctrine. East of the Rhine, however, his writings became gospel for the stanch conservatives who had found their Rome in Vienna and their Maecenas in Metternich. On the banks of the Danube Adam Müller and Friedrich von Gentz composed their treatises against revolution, while the Austrian chancellor fought at the European Areopagus to translate their theories into practice. Too much the eighteenth-century skeptic to embrace without reservation the mysticism of romanticist thought, he nevertheless did not hesitate to use it for his own purposes as an ideological justification of his statecraft.

In northern Germany conservatism tended to be less refined, less subtle, less prone to abstract speculation. It was still able to attract intellectuals like the poets Heinrich von Kleist and Achim von Arnim who battled for king and fatherland in the pages of the *Berliner Abendblätter*. Its chief protagonists, however, were landowning Junkers opposed to liberalism not only because of theoretical disagreements, but also because of fundamental economic and social interests. Field Marshal Hans Yorck von Wartenburg, Duke Karl of Mecklenburg, Count Otto von Voss-Buch, General Karl von Köckeritz—these were the champions of the old Prussian tradition which the reformers were undermining. Their enemy was not to the west in revolutionary France; he was right in their midst, in Berlin, in Potsdam, in Königsberg, destroying before their eyes the heritage which had made their country great. For were not the followers of Stein liberating the peasantry, introducing industrial freedom, concocting constitutional schemes, and trampling on the historic rights of the nobility?[18]

In defending the feudal agrarian society which they had dominated for centuries the aristocrats were fighting for their existence. Ahead of them loomed the specter of a rapacious capitalism with its banks, its paper riches, its cutthroat competition, and its boundless ambition, overwhelming the nobility to become arbiter of the destinies of Prussia. All the distrust of a conservative landowner for the doctrinaire alien reformer found voice in the diatribe against Stein composed by General Ludwig von der Marwitz:

> He . . . began to revolutionize the fatherland. He began the war of the propertyless against property, of industry against agriculture, of the transitory against the stable, of crass materialism against the divinely established order, of imaginary profit against justice, of the present moment against the past and the future, of the individual against the family, of speculators and countinghouses against fields

and trades, of government bureaus against relationships derived from the history of the country, of learning and conceited talent against virtue and honorable character.[19]

The Junker, resisting liberalism with the same courage which he had traditionally displayed on the field of battle, found his reward after 1815 in a renewed political ascendancy. It was he who now had the ear of the king, who sat in the councils of state and jailed his opponents. The system of municipal self-government established in 1808 was restricted in 1831, the plan for a written constitution never advanced beyond the establishment of provincial diets, the dominant economic position of the latifundia survived the emancipation of the peasantry, and the aristocratic monopoly of higher positions in the civil service and the armed forces remained unbroken. Conservatism succeeded in reviving the alliance between crown and nobility formed under benevolent despotism, and while the doctrines of liberalism still constituted a serious threat to royal authority, their effectiveness was reduced through the activities of police censors and the efforts of conservative publicists who found a warm welcome in the Berlin of the Restoration.

Among those devoting their talents to the battle against radical thought were Leopold von Ranke, Karl Ludwig von Haller, Karl Jarcke, and the brothers Ludwig and Leopold von Gerlach. In periodicals like *Berliner Politisches Wochenblatt*, *Historisch-politische Zeitschrift*, and *Evangelische Kirchenzeitung* they advanced their legitimist theories of state, attacking liberalism at its most vulnerable point, its indifference to the social consequences of an unrestrained individualism. They deplored the decline of the guild and the growth of a ruthless competition which industrial freedom had introduced, and they condemned the liberation of the peasantry for its destruction of the traditional system of reciprocal rights and obligations between lord and serf. Since ownership had ceased to imply moral responsibility and had come to represent a purely economic relationship of man to property, the bonds of tradition had weakened, and the community had lost its sense of purpose. Now only the recognition of the religious foundations of society could restore to man that sense of inward discipline of which liberalism had deprived him.[20]

Conservative influence won new strength in 1840, when Frederick William IV assumed the crown of Prussia and the world beheld the rare spectacle of a romantic Hohenzollern. Berlin had long had a reputation as the drab capital of industrious, colorless rulers who collected armies and taxes with a miserly passion, indifferent to the splendors which had made Versailles and Schönbrunn famous. The new king, however, did not conform to the pattern. He was a child of the early nineteenth century, sharing its emotionalism, its introspection, its aesthetic and religious tastes. His interests lay in theology, literature, and art rather than military science or financial administration, and in the piety and mysticism of the Middle Ages he sought a spiritual refuge from the atmosphere of self-confident secularism which was the companion of a triumphant industrialism. He was Hamlet haunted by some stern ancestral ghost.

Frederick William IV discussed his views with a small group of friends gathered about the throne. Count Anton zu Stolberg-Wernigerode, General Ludwig von Thile, Baron Christian von Bunsen, General Joseph von Radowitz, and the Gerlachs were among those who shared the monarch's outlook and enjoyed his confidence. Zealously conservative in politics and uncompromisingly orthodox in religion, they helped him formulate his philosophy of state and plan that return to godly ways which lay close to his heart. In the conversations between the king and his intimates lay the germ of the political and social policies which he attempted to put into execution in the later years of his reign. They strengthened him in the determination to resist demands for constitutional reform and to maintain the absolutist tradition of

Prussia. Yet the justification of autocratic power was to lie in the uses to which it was put, in the defense of the poor and the weak, in the advancement of social justice, in the works of Christian charity. For the ruler who devoted himself to the welfare of his subjects, who protected the masses against a pitiless capitalism, had nothing to fear from a morally bankrupt parliamentarianism.

Collaboration between crown and proletariat against the liberal bourgeoisie was widely discussed in conservative circles during the Forties. In his journal *Janus* Viktor Aimé Huber urged the government to champion the interests of the workers by encouraging the growth of labor associations. The youthful Hermann Wagener, still only a minor government official, began to develop his theories of a monarchy of economic reform, theories which met with the approval of the influential *Rheinischer Beobachter* of Cologne. And Count Stolberg-Wernigerode was advising the king to abandon his ambitious building program and use the funds instead for philanthropic undertakings calculated to win the support of the masses.[21]

It was Radowitz, however, who best understood the nature of the social problem created by industrialism and its relationship to statecraft. A Catholic in the rigidly Protestant court of Berlin, a member of a family which had become German less than a century before, he had a broader vision and a more universal sympathy than the Junkers among whom he lived. To them he was only an upstart foreigner, all the more suspect because of his studies abroad, his interest in music and painting, his experiences as a diplomat in Frankfurt and Karlsruhe. But Frederick William IV found in him an understanding comrade to whom he could impart his innermost thoughts. The brilliantly unstable king and the urbane general, sharing the conviction that an enduring system of government must represent a moral principle, agreed in their view of the ethical problems lying behind political issues. Out of their common philosophy of state arose the belief that an enlightened absolutism of material welfare was the most effective remedy against the spread of seditious sentiment among the lower classes.[22]

In his *Gespräche aus der Gegenwart über Staat und Kirche* published in 1846 Radowitz preached the doctrine that only with the support of the proletariat could conservatism defy the might of the bourgeoisie. The protagonist of the work, Arneburg, outlined a plan of action capable of saving the Hohenzollerns from the fate of the Bourbons:

> I shall not give up the fight. Our princes have not yet exhausted the resources with which they may survive the struggle against triumphant mediocrity. Let them but have the courage to turn to the masses. There, among the lower and most numerous classes of the population, are their natural allies, there are unspent forces, there are natures capable of feeling gratitude and respect, natures responsive to instruction. There, most important of all, are beings more disposed to a return to piety than that public of newspapers, citizen assemblies, and chambers of deputies which has been demoralized by the evil education of the times and which has lost its loyalty and faith.[23]

Frederick William IV was slow to act on good advice. He was a thinker, a visionary, not a doer. Finally, however, he began to take the first hesitant steps toward the establishment of that mutual understanding between upper and lower classes which would make the position of the throne impregnable. Seizing the opportunity presented by a trade exposition in Berlin in 1844, he helped found the Central Society for the Welfare of the Working Classes, a philanthropic organization engaged in charitable activities among the urban masses. The industrial law which he promulgated the following year contained provisions for the establishment of labor associations authorized to extend aid to needy members. In his early plans for the convocation of a united diet composed of members of the provincial assemblies he even proposed to grant special representation to the workingman. And when epidemic and famine descended on Silesia, the government prepared a program of extensive public works to relieve the distress of the unhappy province.[24]

Yet events were moving too fast for the bemused king. While he spun his dreams at Sans Souci, the political atmosphere of the Forties grew increasingly tense. Party struggles reached new heights of acrimony, economic discontent became louder, and the great depression of the middle years of the decade played directly into the hands of the opponents of the Restoration. There were many who realized that the country was heading for a major crisis which must bring about a fundamental change in the structure of its government. In the summer of 1846 the Baden liberal Karl Mathy, for example, noted an intensity, an excitement in public life which seemed to infect everyone about him. Sensing the great happenings which were awaiting his generation, he exclaimed in exultation that "a fresh, animated spirit is sweeping over Germany."[25]

A fresh, animated spirit was indeed sweeping over Germany, and before long it would turn into a storm destroying the established order and preparing the way for a new nation of unity and freedom.

THE HUNGRY FORTIES

THE great depression of the Forties enabled the various groups in opposition to the Restoration, groups disparate in social composition and economic objective, to overcome their differences and form a single political force. For the masses it came as the climax of a long series of disasters extending over thirty years, intensifying the disruptive effects of capitalism in industry and agriculture, accelerating the decline of the master handicraftsman and the independent peasant, and driving the proletariat of Germany from Europe to America in a great wave of emigration. To the middle class it brought new courage and new resourcefulness, providing constitutionalism with a mass following ready to use violence for the overthrow of the old order. Some of the liberals even came to feel that a civilized revolution, a revolution of maximum enthusiasm and minimum bloodshed, might compel the government to share its power with the bourgeoisie without inviting the danger of mob rule. The economic crisis thus prepared the way for the spring uprising of 1848 by endowing the political opposition with popular support and forcing it to adopt more radical tactics.[1]

The crisis itself was one of a series of depressions which had shaken Europe at approximately ten-year intervals since the defeat of Napoleon. The growth of new forms of financial control over manufacture encouraged speculative investment in business enterprises and led to a succession of paper booms and crashes. In 1815 the end of hostilities and the sudden demobilization of armies produced deflation, unemployment, and hunger. Industry recovered rapidly, however, entering a new period of expansion which continued until 1825, when the output of capital goods outstripped demand and a new depression set in. During the next decade production rose once more, reached the saturation point, and then collapsed in 1835. The Revolution of 1848 came in the midst of the most serious of these periodic crises, bursting upon a Europe suffering from famine and disease, frightened by the red specter of socialism.

In Germany the prosperity of the early Forties based on railway construction and factory expansion came to an abrupt end in the later years of the decade. Great Britain had been suddenly shaken by an economic crash which had important repercussions on the Continent, affecting the commerce of ports like Hamburg and Bremen and inflicting hardship on the industries of such inland cities as Karlsruhe, Mannheim, and Offenbach. The decline in foreign demand for German goods became more marked after 1846, when the Austrian annexation of Cracow deprived the eastern provinces of Prussia of one of their most valuable markets. For the tiny republic established by the Congress of Vienna had become an important center of the contraband trade by which wares from Germany penetrated the tariff walls surrounding Poland and the Habsburg crownlands; and its destruction put an end to the advantage which entrepreneurs like the textile manufacturers of Silesia had enjoyed by virtue of superior skill and cheap labor. Between 1844 and 1847 the export of unbleached linen yarn from the Zollverein fell by almost 40 per cent, while other branches of industry suffered losses less serious, but heavy enough to arouse consternation in financial circles. By 1848 Germany was experiencing the most severe economic crisis since the days of the Continental system.[2]

What made the depression even more calamitous was its coincidence with one of the last major famines in Europe. For more than a century crop failures had been becoming less frequent, as scientific farming, agricultural specialization, and improved means of transportation provided the Continent with a relatively stable food supply. But when a blight ruined the potato harvest of 1845, the lower classes from Ireland to Silesia were suddenly deprived of their staple food. In the following year, with the failure of both the grain and potato crops, starvation became a tragic reality in countless cities and villages between the Shannon and the Oder.

The Zollverein, normally an exporter of grain, was forced to import about 165,000,000 liters of rye in 1846, and in 1847 its purchases rose to more than 250,000,000 liters. Hoping to reduce the inflated cost of living, Prussia decided to suspend the import duty on grain and to abandon the mill tax, yet the situation could no longer be controlled by the manipulation of tariffs or the juggling of taxes. All of Europe was now desperately bidding for foodstuffs, and the repeal of the English corn laws in 1846 intensified the already exorbitant demand for wheat and rye. Austria sought protection in an embargo on the export of cereals, but most of its neighbors in Central Europe preferred to wait patiently for better times. And so while the lower classes of East Prussia were sinking into semistarvation, the landlords of the province sold the bulk of their crop abroad, where it brought a better price than the famished masses at home could afford to pay.

The average rise in the cost of food in Germany from 1844 to 1847 was about 50 per cent. The sharpest increases, moreover, occurred in those commodities most important as the daily fare of the lower classes. In Prussia, for example, the price of rye and potatoes more than doubled, while luxury items like pork rose only 25 per cent, and butter which was eaten regularly only by the well to do remained relatively stable. Conditions in the south were no better, and in some western cities like Coblenz they were considerably worse. Everywhere hunger, disease, and unemployment were arousing among the masses a mood of hostility toward the Restoration.

The depression touched bottom in the summer of 1847, and then the downward course of the economy came to a halt. By the following spring Europe was on the road to recovery.

Without the support of government subsidies and public works, without the stimulus of devaluated currencies and restricted competition, the entrepreneur of Germany overcame hard times and began to fashion a new prosperity. By the time of the March days of 1848 the cost of food had dropped far below the record heights of the preceding year and was approaching the normal levels of 1844. Hence the popular uprising inspired by privation came too late to affect the course of the economic crisis, and instead a new industrial boom took the wind out of the sails of the Revolution and helped assure the triumph of the reaction.[3]

For the time being, however, the depression drove the proletariat into a partnership with bourgeois liberalism and thus made possible the overthrow of the old order. It intensified all the ills which had plagued German society since the beginning of the century, exposing the artisan to new dangers and forcing the small rural proprietor closer to bankruptcy. Under its pressure the vague restlessness of the masses turned into revolutionary enthusiasm, discontent developed into sedition. By the late Forties the popular literature dealing with social problems was becoming increasingly acrimonious, even ominous in tone. There were shrewd observers of the political scene who realized that an insurrection of the lower classes was a distinct possibility, for signs of widespread disaffection were there for all to see. The countryman sinking into debt ever since the promulgation of land reform now faced total disaster, as mortgage obligations increased so rapidly that in states like Württemberg they almost doubled in value during the economic crisis. Failure to meet tax and commutation payments became a common occurrence in the overcrowded lands of the west, and foreclosures and public sales of the holdings of insolvent farmers multiplied. Critical conditions in the country drove countless agricultural workers to the city, where they joined the ranks of the unemployed to swell still further the heavy labor surplus. Governments which hoped to win popular approval by the promulgation of new commutation laws discovered that the villager who did not have enough money for clothing and shelter was not interested in schemes of rural reform. They found, therefore, solace in the reflection that since mass privation was the natural outcome of overpopulation, the misery of the lower classes was only the price of their incontinence.[4]

The peasantry, close to the soil and familiar with husbandry, could usually scrape up enough food to keep body and soul together. For the artisan masses of the city, however, there was no relief from hunger. After 1845 thousands of journeymen and apprentices were thrown out of work, as their masters sought to ward off bankruptcy by curtailing expenditures. Even those fortunate enough to find employment worked as much as fourteen hours a day to earn a meager subsistence for their families. Silesian weavers unable to make ends meet were forced to sell their looms and then rent them back during the brief periods when work was available. The Thuringian guildsman, swallowing his self-respect, was ready to offer himself as a mere hand on a road gang. Throughout Germany the proud artisan was sinking into a bottomless sea of unskilled day labor.[5]

The true proletarian of the Forties was the handicraftsman. As for the industrial worker, he too had to endure the long working day, the reduced income, even unemployment, but after a decade of prosperity he was in a better position to face economic misfortune than the long-suffering artisan. Since during the depression mechanical production did not contract as rapidly as the output of the handicraft system, the demand for trained factory labor remained on the whole stable. Wages paid by industrial enterprises were consistently higher than those which the guild shop could offer, and while a linen weaver in Westphalia was earning barely one mark for a week's work, an unskilled hand in a textile mill could get twice as much and more. Hence the spirit of insurrection throve among the artisan masses who soon became the shock troops of revolution, whereas the employees of iron foundries and locomotive works were as a rule only interested by-standers in the great events of 1848.[6]

The economic crisis had a catastrophic effect on urban living conditions. In the Rhineland, which on the whole suffered less than the eastern provinces of Prussia, 25 per cent of the population of Cologne was dependent on public assistance during the worst days of the depression. In the larger cities of Bavaria a third of the inhabitants received some form of charity in 1847. The situation was still more desperate in Baden, where in a town like Pforzheim 70 per cent of the workers were unemployed. In Solingen, famous throughout Europe for its cutlery, one out of every three families was destitute. Farther west the silk weavers of Krefeld suffered such heavy losses that 3,000 looms out of 8,000 were made idle. The lace and toy industries of Saxony were prostrate, typhus raged in the mountain villages, and thousands of idle workers wandered aimlessly through city streets. Even in Berlin, the proud metropolis of the north, there were no more than 20,000 citizens in a population of 400,000 whose earnings or properties were large enough to be taxed.[7]

The number of beggars and vagabonds in Bavaria and the Palatinate nearly doubled. In Prussia about 8 per cent of the population was exempt from direct taxation because of poverty, and only 3 per cent was officially classified as well-to-do. While between 1841 and 1850 the inhabitants of Berlin increased by 30 per cent, expenditures for poor relief grew more than 60 per cent. In a relatively prosperous city like Hamburg meat consumption in 1846-50 was less than two thirds of what it had been twenty-five years before. In the countryside the death rate in many districts rose as much as 200 per cent, and masses of paupers marched in organized processions through the hungry villages hunting for scraps of food or a few coins.[8]

In the wake of famine and epidemic came crime and vice. From Nassau and Hesse-Darmstadt came reports of a growing international traffic in children, a traffic fed by impoverished parents forced to sell their sons and daughters to speculators in human degradation. The unfortunate youngsters, usually transported abroad, begged for alms or engaged in streetwalking to support themselves and enrich their exploiters. And the export of immorality from Central Europe was tragic evidence of its oversupply at home. The Thuringian peasant who could not afford the price of wood stole his fuel in the timberlands of the nobility or the state. Many a Silesian handicraftsman out of work decided to try his hand at pickpocketry or burglary. By 1846 about one tenth of the population of Berlin found its normal source of livelihood in prostitution and crime. If the efficient bureaucracy of the Prussian capital could not cope with the difficulties created by the depression, what were the somnolent authorities of a provincial town to do but shrug their shoulders and pretend not to notice the social evils about them?[9]

There was one avenue of escape from the misery engulfing Germany. After 1845 emigration became an increasingly popular solution for the economic problems which confronted the lower classes. The discontented, the unwanted, the unfortunate could find a new life in remote regions across the sea. The peasant who had lost his holdings along the Main or in the Black Forest might become an independent farmer on the fertile soil of Wisconsin or Missouri. The handicraft trade destroyed by steam and iron in Saxony or Silesia might be pursued with profit in the growing communities of the New World. Overpopulation, unemployment, land hunger, all the problems facing the statesmen of the Restoration on the eve of the Revolution drove Europeans in the hundreds of thousands to lands in the Western Hemisphere. The world of the nineteenth century managed to provide free scope for the energies of the talented and ambitious, because the poor and discontented could always be dumped on the shores of a distant continent.

The figure of the liberal ancestor fleeing tyranny and injustice in Germany to breathe the free air of the United States has become enshrined in millions of hearts in the American Midwest, but the truth is that for every Carl Schurz among the emigrants there were hundreds who wanted nothing more than a secure livelihood. Most Forty-eighters were escaping poverty and famine, not the executioner or the jailer. As a matter of fact, they were not even Forty-eighters at all, but Forty-sixers or Forty-seveners. They were hungry, tired men carried to foreign countries and alien peoples in their search for a refuge from the economic crisis. Moreover, while the landless farmer and unemployed worker were crossing the Atlantic, the bourgeois liberal usually stayed home to preach his doctrines and defend his interests.[10]

The connection between emigration and depression was apparent long before the Revolution. Once the War of Liberation was over, the surplus population of southern Germany began to overflow into Switzerland, Holland, and the United States, although throughout the Twenties the number of those leaving remained less than 5,000 annually. It grew somewhat in the following decade, but total overseas emigration in the Thirties was still only 168,000. The centrifugal forces of the new century had not yet broken down the traditions and loyalties of an earlier age; industrialism and overpopulation had not yet created that uprooted mob which was soon to descend on the New World. A powerful and prosperous state like Prussia continued to attract immigrants from other regions, and between 1823 and 1840 700,000 more persons settled inside its frontiers than left them. Only in some of the poorest districts of Bavaria, Württemberg, and Hesse-Darmstadt was there a significant exodus during these years, and even there the destination of many of the wanderers lay within the German Confederation.[11]

Then came the Hungry Forties, and the trickle of emigration grew into a flood which carried almost 500,000 persons to America. In 1840 the number of those leaving Central Europe was still about 34,000; by 1846, when the full effects of the economic crisis were first felt, it had mounted to 93,-000; and one year later it rose above 100,000. The movement of population then began to slow down. In 1848, the year of the Revolution, it decreased by 20 per cent, and in 1850, although the reaction was in full swing, those migrating numbered only 82,000 persons. But soon the exodus swelled again, and by the end of the decade 1,000,000 had wandered overseas. It is significant, however, that political developments had only a slight effect on emigration, since in 1849, 1850, and 1851, in the period when liberalism was suffering the bitterest persecution, the tide of emigrants actually ebbed. Economic conditions, on the other hand, influenced it very obviously, for it rose during the years of depression in the middle Forties, subsided before the advance of prosperity in 1848, and then grew again after 1851 with the return of hard times.[12]

In the Bavarian provinces there was a close correlation between land hunger and population movement. The aggregate of permanent departures from Württemberg and Baden was greatest in those regions which suffered most heavily from the subdivision of agricultural holdings. In Hesse-Darmstadt variations in the numbers of those leaving the state were directly related to fluctuations in the price of rye. Most emigrants were clearly landless peasants and unemployed handicraftsmen, and since aristocratic circles and conservative philanthropic organizations encouraged the establishment of overseas settlements for the surplus population of Germany, the ruling classes manifestly did not identify the migrants with the liberal opposition. They believed rather that a planned, carefully controlled emigration was a useful means of alleviating mass suffering and popular discontent. And in a sense they were right, for many a hungry proletarian from the Old World became a prosperous, self-satisfied farmer or businessman on the western side of the Atlantic.[13]

Yet not every victim of the depression could leave Europe to seek his fortune overseas. The cost of passage from Bremen or Antwerp to New York even in the wretched quarters of the steerage was high enough to keep at home thousands eager to emigrate. Other thousands felt too deeply attached to their families and homes to abandon them forever. The severest privation could not destroy their roots in German society, and they preferred to endure distress in their native land rather than face the long, difficult adjustment to a new life in a new country. Still, the reluctance of the peasant to leave his village did not make hunger and hardship easier to bear. The unemployed artisan might be afraid to burn his bridges behind him by sailing for America, but he was still the bitter enemy of industrialism. Emigration could not and did not solve the economic problems of Central Europe, and depression, famine, and overpopulation continued to plague the masses and drive them to insurrection.

In the years just before the Revolution there were mass hunger riots in almost every state of Germany. Lacking firm leadership and intelligent purpose, the participants in the disorders could do little more than loot a few food stores, stone the homes of unpopular officials, perhaps engage in futile clashes with the military. The propertied classes, moreover, remained uniformly hostile to these outbursts of lawlessness and collaborated with the authorities in their suppression, for mob violence was a two-edged sword. Turned against royal absolutism it might force the government to make concessions which liberalism had been vainly demanding for years; but it could also lead to anarchy, to a war of all against all in which even private property, the holy of holies of the bourgeois economic ethos, would not be spared. Not until 1848 did parliamentarianism swallow its scruples and agree to lead

the masses against legally constituted authority, and in so doing it transformed the blind uprisings of the depression into
a full-fledged revolution guided by a mature philosophy of
state and capable of effective political action.

Before bourgeois and proletarian concluded their alliance
against the crown, however, the masses waged their struggle
for a better way of life in hopeless isolation. When in 1846
the railway workers of Brandenburg struck in protest against
a reduction in wages, their leaders were at once arrested by a
detachment of cuirassiers dispatched to the scene of disorder.
An attempt by the lace makers of Annaberg in Saxony to
destroy the machines which were threatening them with starvation led only to their imprisonment. The Polish uprisings of
1846 in Cracow and Posen aroused unrest in the rural districts of eastern Prussia. In 1845 there was an encounter between populace and garrison in Leipzig. Soon thereafter riots
broke out in Nürnberg and Regensburg in Bavaria, in Eiter-
feld in Hesse-Kassel, and in Schöningen in Brunswick. In
Stuttgart soldiers stormed barricades and fired at the mob,
and even sleepy Württemberg towns like Ulm and Tübingen
had their moments of violence. The disaffection spread as far
east as Bohemia, where Prague, Eger, and Pilsen witnessed
disturbing displays of mass rebelliousness.[14]

The most significant of these precursors of revolution was
the wave of disorder which broke over Prussia in the spring
of 1847, as food prices reached new heights. In the provinces
clashes between unemployed workers and the police had become a common occurrence, but now the authorities of the
capital itself had to face a hungry mob engaged in pillage and
destruction. On April 21 the market places of Berlin became
a battlefield on which plundering hordes resisted the charges
of the royal cavalry. The next day the rioters received rein-
forcements from the slums of the outlying districts, and the
municipal garrison was finally mobilized. By this time the in-
surgents, no longer content to loot food stores and wine shops,

were erecting barricades, attacking troops, and stoning the palace of the king's unpopular brother Prince William. For four days the "potato revolution" raged in the frightened city before law and order were finally restored, and respectable citizens once again ventured to show themselves on the public squares.[15]

That such lawlessness was possible in the heart of the classic land of obedience to established authority was irrefutable proof of the demoralizing effects of the depression. Many inveterate conservatives now realized that hardship was driving the masses to sedition. Even statesmen most prone to see an international revolutionary conspiracy behind every tumult had to admit that proletarian riots were the effect of hunger rather than ideology. At the United Diet of 1847 the most eloquent plea in behalf of suffering Silesia came not from one of the liberal delegates so insistently demanding constitutional reform, but from a high-born defender of the principle of legitimacy, Prince Felix Lichnowsky. In his speech of May 17 the young aristocrat pointed to the source of popular discontent in his province:

> The unfortunate weavers, . . . when they were no longer able to support themselves by their usual occupation, were forced to work with cotton. Not only in Silesia but also in Westphalia, as I learned only yesterday from Westphalian manufacturers, thousands of workers turned from linen to cotton. There arose consequently such an overproduction that neither employers nor employees could survive. Numerous factories were forced to shut down, others went into bankruptcy. Among these were very many well-intentioned, kind owners who were reluctant to exploit their workers, although their own deficits mounted. Competition declined, and the freedom of the worker disappeared, for the more abundant and varied the articles being produced, the more independent the position of the worker.

Heartless manufacturers oppressed the poor workers, who no longer had the choice of seeking employment with a more humane owner.

This is perhaps the cause of those sad events which have recently taken place in Silesia. I believe it to be hunger, not communistic ideas. He who wants joy in life must have more than his daily bread. He must be able to contemplate tomorrow with a sense of security for himself and his family. As long as there was a sure, an honest livelihood, none of the Silesian weavers paid any attention to communistic agitation. They did not despair of themselves nor of their fate, they did not despair of their king nor of their God. And then at last despair was aroused among them by hunger.[16]

Most parliamentary leaders, however, were too absorbed in the intricacies of party struggle to look beyond the walls of legislative assemblies and committee rooms. They perceived that Germany was approaching a political crisis which must force absolutism to seek an understanding with its foes, but in their opinion the terms of such an understanding would be decided at some quiet conference in a royal palace, not on barricades manned by an ill-smelling mob. Liberalism, still hesitating to use violence to wring concessions out of the Restoration, remained aloof from the popular disorders and uprisings of the Forties, anxious to benefit from the embarrassment of the conservatives, but unwilling to add to it by an endorsement of illegality. The masses were to frighten the aristocracy, while the middle class stood by ready to gather the fruits of the struggle.

The strategy followed by the bourgeois opposition as Central Europe moved closer to civil war accounts for the growing intensity of constitutional agitation and the increased bitterness of the legislative conflict. After 1845 each political school, convinced that important changes in government were in the offing, prepared to derive the greatest possible advantage from the impending crisis. Each attempted to formulate its demands more precisely; each sought to impose a more disciplined organization on its followers. The liberal press, openly defying censorship regulations, launched attacks on established policies and institutions. In the parliamentary assemblies of the smaller states criticisms of the leadership of the German Confederation became more frequent and more insistent. Even in the large states, even in Prussia and Austria, the opponents of absolutism displayed an audacity which would have been unthinkable ten years before. And while the forces of discontent gained new strength with every passing month, the aging statesmen of the Restoration watched in helpless inaction, sensing that their system was approaching its end.

On September 12, 1847, the Baden radicals met in the small town of Offenburg at the foot of the Black Forest to decide on the course of action to be followed in the crucial days ahead. Gustav von Struve and Friedrich Hecker, the firebrands of the democratic movement in the south who dominated the gathering, won its endorsement of their platform. The two would-be sans-culottes were not yet ready to urge the establishment of a republic of virtue, but they did call for a sweeping political and social reform of the nation. They demanded condemnation of the Carlsbad decrees of 1819, of the Frankfurt decrees of 1831 and 1832, and of the Vienna decrees of 1834 as instruments of reaction and oppression. Freedom of speech, freedom of the press, freedom of assembly, and freedom of conscience were to be proclaimed for Germany; the Diet of the Confederation was to become a true parliament representing the people of a united fatherland; standing armies should disappear to make way for a popular militia obedient to the general will; the income tax and enlightened economic legislation were to protect the interests of the masses; and the special privileges and immunities of the feudal aristocracy should be abolished for all time. The radicals were in effect asking the old order to decree its own destruction, threatening it with revolution, if it should refuse to commit political suicide.[17]

The Offenburg program was the declaration of independence of the left wing of parliamentarianism. Ever since 1839 the leaders of the constitutional movement had met each year to discuss current problems and plan future tactics. At these informal gatherings republicans and monarchists sat at the same table, exchanging ideas, reconciling differences, presenting a united front against the common enemy. Now the united front was broken. The extremists withdrew from the grand coalition of opposition parties, taking the first step on the road which was to lead them from treasonable speeches to fantastic Putsches to exile in America. With them went a good deal of the political energy and popular appeal which liberalism had hitherto displayed. The rift in the ranks of the foes of absolutism was to grow wider and deeper, until by the time of the Revolution moderates and radicals looked on each other in undisguised hostility, unable to unite their forces in the work of national reconstruction.

The issues dividing the two camps were defined with greater exactness only a few weeks after the meeting in Offenburg. On October 10, 1847, the notables of the liberal parties of the south and west gathered in the Half-Moon Inn in Heppenheim near Darmstadt. The parliamentary leaders of Bavaria and Hesse-Kassel were not present, because their state legislatures were in session and they were needed at home to guide their followers in the struggle against conservatism. But the fame and importance of those who did attend more than made up for the absentees. Among them were Karl Mathy and Friedrich Bassermann from Baden, David Hansemann and Gustav Mevissen from the Rhineland, Friedrich Römer from Württemberg, Heinrich von Gagern from Hesse-Darmstadt, and August Hergenhahn from Nassau, men who within a year would hold the reins of power in their hands. The fiction that this was a meeting representing the entire political opposition was maintained and even given a semblance of truth by the presence of the graybeard of Baden radicalism, Adam von Itzstein. Yet he was only a pathetic, lonely old man, completely out of place in this convention of moderate reformers representing the bourgeoisie of wealth and education.

The policies approved at Heppenheim reflected the cautious temper of liberalism, just as the program adopted at Offenburg a month earlier breathed the spirit of feverish enthusiasm which had seized the radicals. The moderates hoped to achieve national unification not by the overthrow of the Diet of the Confederation, but by the extension of the competence of the Zollverein over political questions. They too sought the establishment of freedom of speech and assembly and the reform of justice and administration, but their tone was more restrained, more conciliatory. They spoke of a reduction in expenditures for the armed forces rather than the abolition of standing armies. They emphasized the need to improve methods of poor relief and combat mass privation, carefully avoiding references to disparity between capital and labor. Above all, they hastened to assure the world of law and order that their demands were intended to be no more than a subject of peaceful deliberation at the next annual assembly of the leaders of constitutionalism.[18]

Meanwhile in the north the Prussian liberals were going through a dress rehearsal for the revolution which was about to overwhelm Europe. The economic crisis releasing a flood of popular dissatisfaction finally persuaded Frederick William IV to implement the promise of a national legislative assembly implicit in the laws of January 17, 1820, and June 5, 1823. It was characteristic of the monarch that his constitutional plans should succeed in antagonizing his conservative supporters without conciliating his reformist opponents;

for the United Diet established by the decree of February 3, 1847, was neither fish, flesh, nor good red herring. It was neither a representative body in the parliamentary sense nor a gathering of medieval estates of the realm. It was a meeting of members of the provincial diets designed to still the clamor for reform by offering the shadow of popular government without the substance. Its powers were undefined, its future remained uncertain, and its composition conferred on the landed aristocracy a degree of influence out of all proportion to its size. The only effect of such a transparently artificial legislative device was to transfer the scene of party conflict from the provincial capitals to Berlin.[19]

Whatever lingering hopes the liberals might still have entertained were dashed by the address delivered by the king on April 11, 1847, at the opening session of the diet. It was an address worthy of Frederick William IV, brilliant, affecting, and hopelessly unrealistic: "I am moved to declare solemnly that no power on earth will ever succeed in prevailing on me to transform the natural relationship between prince and people, the relationship which by its inward truth has made us so powerful, into a contractual, constitutional one. Never will I permit a written sheet of paper to come between our God in heaven and this land, as if it were a second Providence, to rule us with its paragraphs and supplant the old sacred loyalty."[20] The reply of the Prussian bourgeoisie militant was short and to the point. Romantic conservatism might compose fancy phrases, but the key to the strongbox was in the hands of the middle-class opposition. On June 8, in the course of a discussion of the government request for new appropriations, Hansemann recited the liberal businessman's credo: "When questions of money arise, there is an end to *Gemütlichkeit*."[21]

No compromise between two so diametrically opposed theories of government was possible. For seven weeks the great debate in the royal castle in Berlin continued without budging either side from its position. The king would not recognize the claims of the liberals, he would not grant demands for periodic meetings of the diet, for its right to participate in the formulation of new laws, and for the guarantee of its status in a written constitution. His opponents fought back with the only weapon at their disposal by refusing to approve financial arrangements for the pet project of the ministry, the construction of a railway between Königsberg and Berlin. Even the delegates from East Prussia, the chief beneficiary of the proposed plan, voted overwhelmingly against it, sacrificing economic interest to constitutional principle. The control of finances became the crucial issue in the struggle between royal prerogative and parliamentary claim, and the king, deciding at last to end the hopeless deadlock, adopted a course which two hundred years before had led a Stuart to the scaffold. On June 26 the United Diet came to an end, and Frederick William IV prepared to return to the system of personal rule on which his dynasty had built its greatness.

The outcome of the unsuccessful experiment in representative government was an aggravation of political tension in Prussia. Constitutional issues long submerged beneath the petty interests of everyday life rose to the surface to become the subject of discussion in newspapers and coffeehouses. The liberals had been unable to wrest concessions from the monarchy, but they had gained valuable experience in the technique of party struggle. Important members of the parliamentary movement in the western provinces like Ludolf Camphausen, Baron Georg von Vincke, Hermann von Beckerath, and David Hansemann had met and worked with such leaders of the aristocratic opposition of the east as Alfred von Auerswald, Count Maximilian von Schwerin-Putzar, and the brothers Ernst and August von Saucken. Together they had successfully resisted royal pleas and threats, gaining new confidence in their cause and in themselves. The last opportunity for a peaceful settlement of the rival claims of crown and bourgeoisie vanished in the summer of 1847, and revolution was left as the only means to resolve the vital problems of state.[22]

Only two weeks after the opening of the United Diet a hunger riot broke out in Berlin, and the assembled delegates beheld scenes of mass violence. It was as if some frightful apparition had suddenly entered the chamber, interrupting the orderly proceedings and forcing itself on the attention of the representatives. For a brief, terrible moment the hunger of the street stalked through the halls of the Hohenzollern castle. Then it was all over, and the members could return to their debate over legislative rights, control of finances, and periodicity of parliamentary sessions. Yet a vague anxiety continued to trouble their deliberations. They had been compelled to the realization that all mankind was not divided into conservatives and liberals eloquently disputing with each other across the conference table. There was also the mob, indifferent to theories of government, bent only on plunder and destruction. The gulf separating the well to do from the masses was so wide that no amount of constitutional speculation or social philosophizing could bridge it. The proletariat might make an uprising and unmake it, it might create a new political order and destroy it, it might elevate commoners to the seats of power and cast them down again. The Revolution would soon show that.

PART TWO

REVOLUTION

Es sind drei Fragen vorzüglich gewesen, für welche sich das deutsche Volk am Unzweideutigsten und am Nachdrücklichsten auf materiellem Grund und Boden erhoben hat. . . . Diese Fragen waren die Frage über die Befreiung des Grund und Bodens von seinen Lasten; es war die Frage über die Regulirung des Gewerbewesens, und es war die Frage der commerciellen Einheit und Consolidirung des deutschen Bundesstaates.

BERNHARD EISENSTUCK (1848)

6

THE SPRING UPRISING

THE year 1848 opened amid widespread portents that all was not well with the Europe of the Restoration. In Switzerland the victorious federal army was forcing liberal measures and Protestant prejudices on the conservative and Catholic Sonderbund. Across the Continent in Copenhagen the new king Frederick VII was promising his people a written constitution, while the party of the Eider Danes prepared for the incorporation of Schleswig into Denmark and a conflict with fellow liberals on the other side of the border in Germany. And south of the Alps Ferdinand II of the Two Sicilies first provoked his subjects into one of their periodic uprisings, and then sought to save himself by promulgating a constitution and agreeing to act the parliamentary ruler.

No insurrection, however, was complete without France. It was the course of events in Paris which transformed sporadic violence into a revolutionary movement involving all of Europe. In the last week of February the Orleanist Monarchy fell, and the old order realized at last that it faced a terrible danger. Not only had Louis Philippe been forced to abdicate, but his government had collapsed suddenly, ignominiously. For almost twenty years he had been the bourgeois king, an astute ruler teaching the world how to combine regal dignity with business acumen. And then one day there were riots in the streets of his capital. The next day Guizot, the symbol of the *juste-milieu*, resigned, while the populace howled for his life. One day more, and the monarch himself was slipping out of the Tuileries through the back entrance, making his way in disguise to the coast, being smuggled out of France by the British consul in Le Havre. He and his queen arrived in England as Mr. and Mrs. Smith, without honor, without dignity, and perhaps worst of all, without money.

The news that Louis Philippe had been driven from his throne by an enraged mob thoroughly frightened the rulers of the Continent. If the king who had prided himself on his successful adjustment to the demands of the new age could suffer such a humiliating fate, who dared consider himself safe? The only thing to do was to come to terms with the opposition, before it grew impatient and seized by force what it had been denied by negotiation. In France it had taken only three days to replace a moderate monarchy with a radical republic. A less stable throne might topple in a matter of hours. The weaker the government, the quicker its head to surrender before the enemy. The petty princes of Europe, afraid of their subjects and unsure of their armies, were therefore the first to desert the sinking ship of the old order.

Nowhere were they more numerous than in Germany, nowhere were they more anxious to appease the Revolution. Frightened by reports of peasant insurrections in the provinces and artisan riots in the cities, they hastened to make peace with the liberals whom they had been imprisoning or exiling for thirty years. In Baden, the most progressive of the secondary states, the grand duke appointed Karl Mathy as his prime minister and sent Karl Welcker to Frankfurt to represent him at the Diet of the Confederation. Paul Pfizer and Friedrich Römer entered the reformed government of Württemberg. Heinrich von Gagern became head of the cabinet in Darmstadt, putting an end to the long despotic rule of Baron Karl du Thil. Gottlieb von Thon-Dittmer took office in Bavaria, Ludwig von der Pfordten was named to the ministry in Saxony, and in Hanover Johann Stüve accepted the secretaryship of the interior. As the uprising spread eastward and northward, one ruler after another capitulated to the opposition, and by the middle of March most of them had already dismissed their conservative advisers, issued their pledges of constitutional rule, and embraced with more or less genuine fervor the cause of freedom.

The old order was not dead, however, as long as Metternich was in power. The Austrian chancellor had weathered many a political storm in his long career, and now, while the timid and unscrupulous were trimming their sails, he continued to rally the dispirited conservatives. Yet his days were also numbered. In Hungary the magic eloquence of Louis Kossuth was turned against the "charnel house of the Vienna system," the provincial diet of Lower Austria joined in the growing demand for reform, and the Viennese populace led by university students clamored for the dismissal of the ministry. The coup de grâce was finally delivered by the dynasty which Metternich had served so faithfully. With the proverbial ingratitude of the Habsburgs, Archdukes Johann, Franz Karl, and Ludwig demanded that he sacrifice himself for the imperial house; and on the night of March 13, after almost forty years in office, the aged prince submitted his resignation. But he remained the grand aristocrat to the last, and his exit was calm and dignified, executed with a savoir-faire which the bourgeois monarchy of France had never been able to master.

The fall of Metternich removed the last obstacle to a complete victory of the Revolution in Central Europe. The government of Prussia had become so apprehensive the moment it learned about the proclamation of the republic in France that, according to a Berlin dispatch of February 28, "it is impossible to describe the amazement, the terror, the confusion aroused here by the latest reports from Paris crowding on each other almost hourly."[1] The king, attempting to execute an orderly withdrawal from his position of the previous year, announced on March 14 that he would call the United Diet into session once again to deal with the pressing problems of state. But when the news of the success of the revolution in Vienna reached him, his retreat turned into a rout. By March

18 the cabinet of Ernst von Bodelschwingh-Velmede had submitted its resignation, and the moderately liberal Count Adolf von Arnim-Boitzenburg was entrusted with the task of forming a new ministry. On the same day a royal patent proclaimed that the government favored a constitutional reorganization of the German Confederation, that Prussia must promptly adopt a program of internal reform, and that the diet would meet on April 2 instead of April 17 as originally planned, so that the work of national regeneration might begin at the earliest possible moment.

Yet the Revolution always seemed to be one step ahead of the king. Only a few hours after the publication of his patent the Berlin mob was engaged in a wild struggle with the troops of the garrison. It all began with a misunderstanding, with a few shots fired by an unknown hand, and then in no time barricades appeared on the streets, and the rioters were demanding the withdrawal of the soldiery from the city. "I have seen the barricades of 1830 and those of 1848 [in France]," wrote the French chargé d'affaires in Berlin Adolphe de Circourt, "but no spectacle as terrible as that of this day has been revealed to me."[2] Nor to Frederick William IV. On March 19 he gave in to the insurrection, ordering the military to suspend action against the barricades. The troops retired from the capital, and the king was left in effect a prisoner of his subjects whom only recently he had been treating as rebels and whom now he was proclaiming his friends.

That same day he was forced to pay homage to those killed resisting his authority. On March 20 he issued an amnesty for all political prisoners, and sworn foes of the regime like the Polish revolutionary Ludwik Mierosławski left jail to be hailed as heroes of the struggle for liberty. On March 21 he paraded through the city adorned in the liberal tricolor, addressing the civic guard, swearing allegiance to national unity, extolling political freedom. The heir of Frederick the Great had become a German Louis Philippe, but the bitter cup had not yet been drained. From the provinces came reports of popular disaffection and mass violence, of republican schemes and separatist plots. All of the king's assurances of parliamentary reform, all of his public demonstrations of patriotic enthusiasm had been in vain. District President of Cologne Karl von Raumer informed the government on March 27 that only the admission of the leaders of the constitutional party to the cabinet could prevent the disintegration of Prussia, and two days later Frederick William IV took the hateful step. He dismissed Count Arnim who had been in office less than two weeks and appointed a new ministry composed of the men most bitterly opposed to him the year before at the United Diet, Ludolf Camphausen, David Hansemann, Alfred von Auerswald, and Count Maximilian von Schwerin-Putzar. With this tacit admission that the old order was bankrupt, the country logically passed into the receivership of the liberals.[3]

By a miraculous turn of fortune the lawyers, the journalists, the professors, the merchants, the industrialists, all who under the Restoration had been only despised ideologists suddenly found themselves entrusted with the conduct of government in Central Europe. The court aristocracy and landed nobility lost their monopoly of political influence, as a nation of peasants and artisans turned for guidance to middle-class leaders inspired by a dream of parliamentary government and industrial might. For to the liberals the Revolution was only the first step in a reorganization of society and the creation of a new civic order based on talent and wealth. Behind their blueprints of federal union and individual freedom rose the vision of a land of factories, banks, railroads, and steamships in which political and economic liberty were one.

Yet the bourgeoisie alone had neither the strength nor authority to impose its views on Germany. Only in alliance with other classes could it defeat its aristocratic rivals, only by exploiting the discontent of the proletariat could it win the following needed to maintain itself in power. The liberals gave the Revolution its leadership, but the artisans provided it with defenders and martyrs. Everywhere during the spring uprising the hungry guildsmen fought for a restoration of the corporate system and the victory of man over wealth. Among those who fell in the streets of Berlin on March 18 were two students, thirteen merchants, and seventy-four handicraftsmen. As Rudolf Virchow, the young physician with a social conscience, wrote to his father on May 1: "You are right when you maintain that it was essentially the workers who decided the revolution, although I believe that you in the provinces do not realize fully that this revolution is not simply political but fundamentally social."[4]

The artisan did not wait until the establishment of constitutional government to press his demands for a return to guild regulation of production. Violence which put oppressive officials to flight could also destroy hated machines, and the news of the successful revolution in Paris became for Central Europe the signal for widespread attacks on factories and business establishments. Government reports from Düsseldorf described the extensive devastation of property by impoverished handicraftsmen, as unruly mobs in the Rhineland and Westphalia paraded through the streets, stoned the residences of the rich, and set fire to mills. On March 27 Governor Franz von Eichmann in Coblenz informed Minister of the Interior Alfred von Auerswald that the masses were close to insurrection. And three days later the *Bayerische Landbötin* announced to its readers: "In most cities of the Rhine Province (Prussia) more or less violent scenes have occurred, as for example in Cologne, Düsseldorf, Krefeld, Bonn, Coblenz, and especially in the factory districts of the Berg highlands, where blood has actually flowed in some instances."[5]

In March a nail factory recently established in Schmalkalden was wrecked by Thuringian handicraftsmen who saw their livelihood threatened by mechanization. In April the Vogtland villagers of southern Saxony destroyed mills in Elterlein and Mittweida. The weavers of Chemnitz held a huge demonstration protesting the introduction of weaving machinery and the construction of textile factories. Berlin industrialists were forced to maintain a private police force to protect their property against disgruntled workers, and special detachments of the civic guard were held in readiness to oppose attacks of the populace against workshops and plants. Every large city had its frightening moments, when a clash between the defenders of law and order and a mob bent on violence seemed unavoidable. But in most cases the authorities managed to patch up a peaceful settlement of economic differences, and the artisan contented himself with insulting epithets and broken windows.[6]

Disorder was especially common in the west. The cutlers of the Rhine Province launched a campaign of destruction against iron foundries during which they wrecked the great plant in Burg an der Wupper. The weavers of Viersen forced the leading entrepreneur of the town, the well-known Friedrich Diergardt, to promise rectification of old grievances. But as soon as the victors had dispersed to celebrate their triumph, the frightened industrialist ordered a reduction in output and escaped to Berlin. In near-by Krefeld textile dealers hastened to conclude an agreement with the weavers to forestall an uprising. On March 27 they granted the workers the status of master artisans, recognized their guild as a bargaining agent, and agreed to the peaceful adjustment of trade disputes. The weavers of Elberfeld won a great victory on March 31, when the merchants of the city agreed to a pact regulating production, restricting the use of machinery, and stabilizing prices. In Solingen the riots which began on March 16 forced local middlemen to agree to the abolition of the truck system and the closing of company stores and inns.[7]

Transport workers were as determined as weavers to settle

old scores. Ever since the introduction of the railroad in the Thirties, teamsters and freightmen had been fighting a losing battle against the locomotive. With each passing year more goods and passengers traveled by steam to save time and money, while horses, wagons, and shippers remained idle. It was the familiar story of the ruin of the worker by technology. But in 1848 wagoners who had long petitioned government authorities for restrictions on railway transportation decided at last to take the law into their own hands. On the night of April 5 a mob wrecked a section of the Taunus Railroad near Kastel in Nassau, tearing up ties, threatening company employees, and demolishing a station house. Service on the line had to be suspended until regular troops supported by the civic guard finally succeeded in restoring order. The damage could be repaired without difficulty, but the impression created by the sabotage was lasting. "The incidents are, to put it bluntly, a tragedy for our city," wrote the Mainz correspondent of the liberal *Neueste Nachrichten*. "They contribute directly and indirectly to the business depression and unemployment, they bring humiliation and dishonor to our inhabitants, and they undermine the freedom of the state and of the entire fatherland."[8]

In the meantime unemployed sailors on the Rhine were waging war against the steamship. In the last days of March and early April traffic between Mainz and Cologne came to a halt, as independent shipowners, boatmen, stevedores, towers, and even innkeepers and blacksmiths joined in organized attacks against the vessels of the large companies. The latter, refusing to be easily intimidated, attempted to maintain operations by supplying their crews with protective equipment and ordering them to proceed on their runs in the face of resistance by the boatmen. But when the rioters began to use muskets and even cannon against steamboats, the company directors decided to beat a retreat. An unaccustomed quiet settled over the great stream, and the most important inland waterway of Germany lay paralyzed, presenting one more problem for the newly-appointed liberal governments of the riverain states.

It was solved by a compromise which offered the embattled shippers temporary relief from competition. On April 18 a committee representing the proprietors of sailing vessels met in Cologne and adopted a set of resolutions urging the suppression of all joint-stock express companies, the prohibition of the transport of goods by steamboat, the exclusion of capitalists from freight enterprises, the establishment of a carriers guild, and the elimination of ship fees. It also appealed to the national assembly about to meet in Frankfurt am Main for support against "tradesmen in the service of Mammon." In their reply the steamship companies naturally rejected demands for their dissolution, but they did promise to reduce the number of ports of call, to refrain from building new ships, and to end the use of coal barges for the transport of manufactured wares. These concessions were enough to bring hostilities along the Rhine to an end, and the flow of traffic gradually returned to its normal course.[9]

Boatmen on the Danube also had their day of reckoning, although there the struggle between guildsman and industrialist was complicated by rivalry among the lands of the German Confederation. The Ulm Steamship Company, which had been founded with the aid of the government of Württemberg, claimed the right to engage in the carriage of goods on the river regardless of state boundaries or local monopolies. In defense of its position it cited Articles CIX-CXVI of the Treaty of Vienna, Article XIX of the Act of Confederation, and the federal resolution of August 3, 1820, dealing with freedom of navigation on the interstate rivers of Central Europe. The Austrian shippers guilds, however, would not recognize the abrogation of their ancient rights by high-sounding documents which lawyers in the big city had drafted. The imperial cabinet gave them a measure of support in the decree of March 31, 1830, confirming many of the traditional privileges of municipal associations of boatmen and freighters. Thus each party to the dispute was convinced of the justice of its cause and considered the other an unlawful intruder.

The competition between sail and steam became especially intense in the late Forties, for with the decline in traffic which accompanied the great depression every piece of freight assumed importance. The Revolution finally brought the conflict to a head, as sailors and stevedores took it on themselves to enforce what they believed to be their rights. When vessels from Ulm attempted to take on a cargo in Linz, the mob used violence to force their departure and warned that total destruction awaited them on return. Far from suppressing the disorder, the municipal authorities supported the guildsmen, and the dispute was eventually submitted to the Frankfurt Parliament, which voted on August 11 to refer it to the provisional central government. A decision was thus postponed indefinitely, and the Austrian boatmen were left masters of the field.[10]

Industrial workers too breathed the air of freedom during the spring uprising, yet they fought for limited objectives and with conventional weapons, they fought for advantage, not survival. Unlike the artisan, they did not seek to destroy industrialism, but to win a more secure position within it. In Berlin the printers organized a strike to enforce demands for higher pay, and their easy victory persuaded the publishers of Leipzig and Dresden to grant similar terms to their employees. In Cologne laborers clamored for a more favorable rate of pay, for the proclamation of the right to work, and for the legal recognition of trade associations. And in Breslau, the center of industrial unrest in the east, talk of a general strike was so widespread that employers hastened to make peace with their workers before the mob got out of hand. While the factory worker thus succeeded in winning shorter hours and better wages during the Revolution, he did so through demonstration, not violence.[11]

The crumbling governments of the Restoration, badly shaken by disorders in the town, collapsed completely in the face of an insurrection in the country. The most serious rural uprising in Germany since the days of the Reformation burst forth in the early weeks of March, when the suppressed resentment of generations unloosed a wave of looting and burning. The peasantry rose against manorial dues and obligations, against antiquated hunting privileges and forest rights, against land hunger and population pressure, contributing directly to the establishment of a new system of government whose nature it did not understand and whose aims it did not approve.

The agrarian revolt was particularly violent in the smaller states of the south, where rural discontent was at its worst. As Circourt traveled from France to Berlin to assume his diplomatic duties, he could sense the uneasiness and excitement gripping the countryside: "We spent a few hours in Hanover. This little capital still reposed in peace, but there was unrest in the neighboring Duchy of Brunswick, and frightful disorders were taking place in Thuringia, Swabia, and Franconia, affecting especially governments of the third and fourth magnitude, and threatening the persons and attacking the properties of members of the upper nobility in particular. Strange persistence of the popular instinct! The Jacquerie . . . of 1848 broke out in precisely the same districts and followed the same course of pillage and arson as the peasant revolt of 1525 which was suppressed in a manner so cruelly peremptory by the Swabian League and Emperor Charles V."[12]

Frightened statesmen reading dispatches about rural anarchy must also have felt that history was about to repeat itself. In Baden the peasants of the Odenwald and the Black Forest marched on the castles of the aristocracy, destroying, plundering, and taking special care to burn records of owner-ship and indebtedness. The estates of Prince Karl von Lein-ingen were ravaged by the mob, and his beautiful palace Waldleiningen, modeled after Windsor Castle, was long threatened with serious damage. On March 6 the populace of Neckarbischofsheim forced Count Karl von Helmstadt to sign an agreement renouncing his right to hunt on communal lands. At Amorbach on the Bavarian border the rioters emu-lated their heroes of the great peasant war by submitting twelve articles demanding the end of the special forest privi-leges of the nobility and the cancellation of all outstanding dues and obligations. The fine residences of the Adelsheims and the Rüdts were attacked and looted. In Möggingen, Bod-man, Hausach, Boxberg, Reicholzheim, and Freudenberg villagers conspired, demonstrated, coerced, compelled noble-men to sign renunciations of property rights, and watched with obvious satisfaction as revenue offices went up in smoke. Even to enthusiastic liberals the insurrection on the land was beginning to look like a Frankenstein monster.[13]

From Baden the uprising spread northward into Hesse-Darmstadt, Nassau, and the Rhineland, and eastward into Württemberg, Bavaria, and Saxony. In Starkenburg the mob turned on the castles of Erbach and Fürstenau, forcing the landlords to surrender their manorial prerogatives. Out of Oberhessen came reports of rural riots and threats of violence, as when the inhabitants of Büdingen obliged Prince Ernst von Ysenburg to end his purchases of village farms. Duke Adolf of Nassau promised a gathering of 30,000 in Wies-baden to introduce a program of political reform and issued an amnesty for all prisoners convicted of violating forest and hunting ordinances. But instead of placating his subjects, these measures only encouraged them to seek compensation for past injuries in the destruction of game and the devasta-tion of woodlands. The peasants of the Rhine Province and Westphalia hunted deer, felled trees, and pillaged castles. In vain did popular statesmen like Heinrich von Gagern condemn their conduct and remind them that "only by law and order, which my oath and my conscience constrain me to maintain, can anything good prosper and be permanently achieved."[14] It was too late for moralizing.

Concessions were no more effective than exhortations in restraining the countryside. On March 9 Prince August zu Hohenlohe-Oehringen agreed in principle to the elimination of manorial dues on his ancestral estates. A few weeks later King Wilhelm I of Württemberg surrendered his hunting privileges. Early in April Prince Leiningen issued a declaration renouncing judicial and police powers and voicing the devout assurance that "when, by the union of the classes possessing property, freedom and law shall be firmly established, rights and possessions secured against arbitrary aggression from whatever quarter emanating, then it will become a sacred duty to turn attention to the poor labouring population, and by wise legislation and other appropriate measures to place them in such improved circumstances as will insure their ready co-operation in the preservation of order."[15] Yet the rural uprising continued to grow, driving the ruler of Hohenzollern-Hechingen from his palace, terrorizing the Franconian districts of Bavaria, decimating the game of Thuringia, wrecking the picturesque castles of the Saxon aristocracy.[16]

Across the Elbe the revolution on the land was less severe and less publicized. In later years, moreover, silence, disinterest, and distortion prepared the soil out of which grew the popular image of the hard-working Prussian peasant, loyal to king and obedient to authority. The conservatives carefully cultivated the legend of the patriotic countryside, a legend which received endorsement from the pen of Bismarck, the demigod of his generation. In his memoirs the Iron Chancellor left a vivid account of his experiences in the March days which breathes the spirit of the unregenerate reactionary of 1848. He told how the villagers of Schönhausen, horrified by the news of the conflict in Berlin, prepared to march on the capital to rescue the monarch and save the country from the wild-eyed radicals. Only the indecision of Frederick William IV and the confusion of the court stood in the way of a counterrevolution whose successful outcome was beyond doubt. The defeat of the old order during that terrible spring was the result of a tragedy of errors rather than an expression of dissatisfaction among the mass of the population.[17]

Yet how trustworthy is the word of a bitter old man, who had never made a fetish of accuracy, writing almost fifty years after the event? Whatever the conduct of the peasants on the Bismarck estates, elsewhere in Prussia they did not hesitate to exploit the disorder created by the Revolution to press their economic demands. Not long after the Schönhausen rustics were supposed to have declared themselves ready to die for king and fatherland, the populace of Pomerania and Brandenburg was intimidating the aristocracy, electing democratic deputies, and dreaming of a redistribution of landed property. In Silesia violent outbreaks assumed such serious proportions that the government did not dare enforce the legal claims of the landlords, lest an encounter between troops and the mob lead to a major uprising. Count Stolberg-Wernigerode feared that the smallest incident might set off an insurrection of the hungry farmers. Even Bismarck himself did not always display that calm confidence which he professed half a century later in his apologia. On April 2, 1848, he admitted to his wife that "Silesia is . . . close to dissolution." And as late as July 2 he was writing from Reinfeld: "Only here and there a spark shows that beneath the ashes of seeming tranquillity all the glow of desire for a plot of land is still alive among the day laborers."[18]

Other states of the north also faced the terrors of a peasant uprising. In Schleswig-Holstein the patriotic enthusiasm aroused by the war against Denmark did not blind the masses to opportunities for self-advancement. Agricultural workers were especially adept in extorting concessions from landlords who were too deeply involved in the struggle against the foreign enemy to deal effectively with internal unrest. More than one farm laborer managed to move up the social scale from cottager to crofter and beyond to lessee. In the Mecklenburgs the oppressed peasantry wrecked castle Torgelow, wrung money out of the frightened aristocracy, and manhandled stewards, overseers, and the proprietors themselves. While arbitration commissions sought to arrange a peaceful settlement of agricultural disputes, sporadic outbreaks of violence continued to trouble the grand duchies for more than a year. The rural insurrection spread beyond the frontiers of Germany proper to Austria, Bohemia, and Galicia, destroying vestiges of manorialism in the Habsburg crownlands and inspiring among countrymen throughout Central Europe the hope for economic security.[19]

For the banker and industrialist, however, these were times of doubt and fear. For more than a year business had been in the doldrums, unable to make headway against mounting competition, contracting markets, and declining prices. And now the Revolution came, destroying what little confidence remained. Who was rash enough to consider plans for the future, when mobs were burning factories and a class war loomed ahead? Growing unemployment fed the armies of the insurrection, as lack of credit multiplied business failures. The report of a committee investigating labor conditions offered a sound analysis of the causes of the economic collapse: "If we consider once again the circumstances which have created great distress at the present time, we find that they lie above all in the fact that domestic commerce is lacking in confidence, that property appears to be threatened by constant agitation, and finally that concern about a disruption of foreign trade and of markets abroad has caused the extinction of almost all spirit of enterprise."[20]

The stock exchange reflected the ordeal of the business

world. On February 28, after the news of the fall of Louis Philippe reached Berlin, shares on the Bourse dropped 8 to 10 per cent. By the middle of March government bonds had fallen to 84, and early in April they reached 64. The Bank of Prussia was forced to raise its discount rate from 4 to 5 per cent, after losing 24,000,000 marks in specie in the course of a single month. Between February 18 and April 1 the bottom fell out of railway securities, as the Berlin-Anhalt Railroad stock dropped from 114 to 79, and the Berlin-Potsdam Railroad preferred shares went from 102 to 80. Silesian mortgages which throughout the famine of 1847 had never been below 95 per cent of par slipped to 83. In two months the value of Württemberg bonds on the Frankfurt exchange tumbled from 102 to 71. A Prussian government loan could be floated only at 5 per cent, although the normal rate was 3.5. And in Austria, where public confidence was weakened by the national movements in Bohemia and Hungary and by the war in Italy, capital began to flow out of the country, and investors descended on the treasury to cash their state securities. There was only one way to prevent bankruptcy. On April 2 the government imposed an embargo on the export of specie.[21]

To the businessman of Germany the Austrian decree was the culmination of a series of reverses which had begun six weeks before. As trade decreased, as liquid assets evaporated, as the stock market crashed, the depression turned into panic. Cash became king, for the most stable gilt-edged securities were being offered for sale at a heavy discount. Reputable banking houses, drained of their last reserves by fearful depositors, suspended payment. The great firm of A. Schaaffhausen in Cologne, the mainstay of 170 factories and 40,000 workers, could no longer absorb its losses, and on March 29 it was forced to admit bankruptcy. And then on top of everything else came the news from Vienna that the imperial cabinet had prohibited the shipment of hard money out of the country. Now the Hanseatic importer of tropical wares, the

Leipzig book dealer, the Bavarian industrialist, the Rhenish financier would receive payment in a depreciated paper currency which could not even be applied to the liquidation of old obligations, because the balance of trade had for some time been distinctly favorable to Germany. "Financial problems are pushing politics into the background," commented Mevissen on learning of the failure of the Schaaffhausen bank. "If credit cannot be revived, the existing order is lost beyond salvation."[22]

When the March ministries came to power, their immediate objective became the re-establishment of respect for the law. The statesmen of the Restoration had fallen because they could not cope with the outburst of popular disorder which the Revolution had released. The princes had then turned to the opposition as the only force in political life capable of gaining control over the uprising before it turned into anarchy. Hence the task of the liberals was the suppression of the same insurrectionary energies which had brought them victory. In their eyes plebeian violence had done its work the moment it drove the conservatives from the councils of state, and now its persistence would only undermine the new order as it had destroyed the old. Since economic stability was to be created out of mass chaos, the bourgeois masters of Central Europe had to deal with the problem which every leader of revolution from Danton to Kerensky has faced, the problem of taming the mob without being devoured by it. It is a tribute to their statesmanship that they managed to effect the transition from proletarian lawlessness to constitutional stability with dispatch.

The first of the devices employed to achieve this goal was an appeal to the national sense of decency. Throughout the spring liberalism rained proclamations and manifestoes on the people of Germany. The Saxon ministry issued a plea for the suppression of anarchy and the maintenance of order. The community council of Mannheim urged the citizens of Baden to prove by their discipline that they were worthy of freedom. The municipal government of Berlin assured the lower classes that since their interests were now fully protected, all justification of lawlessness had disappeared once and for all. The electoral committee of Stuttgart adopted a resolution warning that the establishment of a republic would aggravate the problem of unemployment. Bureaucrats, judges, and clergymen joined the crusade for public self-control, while popular leaders like David Hansemann, Heinrich von Gagern, and Alexander von Soiron sermonized against the sins of rebelliousness and false pride. The address which Karl Welcker delivered on March 26 in Heidelberg expressed the temperate mood of the victorious opposition: "Do not mistake license for liberty, nor suppose that because much must be remodelled, all must be overturned. Far be such a thought from us: let us progress, but steadily and thoughtfully."[23]

Concessions accompanied exhortations. Prussian municipalities received authorization to abolish the duty on ground cereals and to introduce in its place a direct assessment from which handicraftsmen and day laborers were exempt. Philanthropic citizens founded employment bureaus, raised relief funds, and urged the nation to buy domestic in preference to imported goods. City fathers sought to create work by ambitious public enterprises, by beautifying parks, building fortifications, and improving roads and canals. To conciliate the peasantry the March ministries in Nassau and Saxe-Meiningen put an end to unpopular game and forest restrictions; in Prussia and Hesse-Darmstadt they proclaimed their intention to deal with the land problem speedily and effectively; and in Württemberg and Baden they promulgated important rural reforms.[24]

The most effective method of restraining revolutionary exuberance, however, was the use of armed force. Soldiers who in March had fought to destroy barricades became in April defenders of freedom. They quelled peasant riots on the Baltic Sea and along the Lake of Constance. They patrolled the streets of Mainz and Posen, ready to subdue proletarian insurrections and disperse artisan mobs. Everywhere they were now received with open arms by the well to do, who had decided that the fury of the masses could be as oppressive as the tyranny of kings. With the encouragement of the authorities, moreover, the urban bourgeoisie organized a civic guard composed of men of property ready to defend law and order. Finding themselves in control of the state apparatus which they had spent a lifetime opposing, the liberals promptly proceeded to use it in the enforcement of public tranquillity.[25]

They acted with the same vigor to restore economic stability. The great need of the business community was credit, and since private means could no longer supply it, state funds were made available to industrial and commercial enterprises. The government of Saxony agreed to open loan offices in Chemnitz and Leipzig, while in Prussia the law of April 15 established banks of issue supported by the resources of the public treasury. The Camphausen cabinet received an impressive vote of confidence on April 10, when the United Diet empowered it to incur obligations of 75,000,000 marks for "the maintenance of credit at home and the support of trade, manufacture, and agriculture." Armed with this parliamentary mandate, it was free to extend aid to merchants and millowners, to rehabilitate banks and finance companies, and to gratify an old wish of the middle class by creating an independent ministry of commerce, industry, and public works.

Its policies led to a miraculous recovery of the economy. The industrialist who had been living in trembling anticipation of the red republic found instead a regime which defended his property and protected his credit. Once he realized that his universe was not about to collapse after all, he returned to work with renewed determination. On April 4, when the Prussian cabinet presented its financial program to the

United Diet, shares on the Berlin stock exchange rose 4 per cent. During the next week the market continued to improve, and on April 10, as the government program was receiving the final approval of the assembly, bonds which had stood at 61 ten days earlier reached 80 amid general rejoicing. The writer Karl Varnhagen von Ense noted jubilantly in his diary: "Government securities have risen. Everyone is full of joy and feels a new courage."[26] Only here and there some captious critic like the young landowner from Schönhausen would suggest that the bourgeoisie apparently identified the interests of industrial capitalism with the welfare of the people. But for most men of importance profits were growing, stocks were climbing, and once again all was right with the world.[27]

By the end of April the tide of revolution was ebbing. The moderates had successfully met the first test of their right to govern, for the popular movement which had swept them into power did not force them closer to a democratic state and a socialistic economy than they wanted to go. Thanks to their efforts differences in wealth, distinctions in social status, even monarchical institutions survived the storm, and the stage was now set for thorough but orderly reform. On the ruins of the mass insurrection of the March days the middle class prepared to erect its edifice of constitutionalism. The palm of victory went not to the street agitator and barricade warrior but to the parliamentary representative and government bureaucrat. From the four corners of Central Europe, from Prussia and Austria and Baden and Saxony and Bavaria and Hanover and thirty other states liberals began to gather in Frankfurt am Main to re-create Germany in their own image.

THE FRANKFURT PARLIAMENT

THE Thermidor of the Revolution came in June. By the time spring turned into summer, the momentum of the European uprising had been spent in quarrels among the victorious liberals. In France the dreams of the February insurrection vanished, as troops of the republic battled workers for four awful days, killing thousands in the streets and exiling thousands more to Algeria. In Prague the hostility of Czech and German reached a tragic climax during the meeting of the Slav Congress. While the revolutionaries wrangled over the terms of Bohemian autonomy, Prince Alfred zu Windischgrätz in command of the imperial garrison played the *tertius gaudens* by proclaiming a state of siege and bombarding the city into submission. As for Italy, the national enthusiasm which greeted the March days was stifled by the rivalry between Naples, Rome, and Turin. Field Marshal Joseph Radetzky emerged from the Quadrilateral at the head of the Austrian armies, retook Vicenza, and speedily subjugated most of Venetia.

In Germany the Revolution came to a halt even earlier. Without fully realizing it, the March ministries deprived themselves of a valuable asset, when they suppressed the spring uprising. True, they could not afford to ignore the danger of a new proletarian rebellion, but by acting against it with such unrelenting thoroughness they destroyed the insurrectionary élan of the masses once and for all. By the time the parliamentarians prepared to gather the spoils of victory, the Revolution was finished, and the middle class stood isolated. Yet the prestige which it had won by directing and then suppressing popular disorder was so great that it was able to remain in power for almost a year. Its spell was broken only when the princes of Central Europe finally realized that liberalism, like the emperor of the fairy tale, was actually naked. In vain did the bourgeois constitutionalists then invoke the magic formulas of freedom and unity which had carried them to victory the previous spring. The spirit of mob violence had been exorcised beyond recall.

All of this, however, lay in the distant future. To liberals exulting in the glorious spring of 1848 every prospect was rosy. Absolutism had capitulated, disorder had been checked, and the waste of the insurrection was about to be made good by the enlightened statesmanship of a new age. The leaders of the constitutionalism of the south gathered in Heidelberg on March 5 to prepare the ground for national reconstruction. But they decided that the time for regional meetings was past, since the task before them was no longer the planning of parliamentary maneuvers but the government of a country, a task with which only an assembly of the best political minds could deal. They therefore resolved to convoke a meeting of the notables of liberalism, and appointed a committee of seven to decide its composition and prepare its agenda. A week later invitations were on their way to all parts of Germany.

The purpose of the preliminary parliament which opened in Frankfurt am Main on March 31 was to determine the means by which constitutional order could be brought out of revolutionary confusion. Not even the larger states were able to cope with this problem unaided, and the Diet of the Confederation was too frightened and too discredited to assume the lead in the achievement of reform. Hence a private gathering of liberal leaders without popular mandate or legal status became by default the source of authority for a nation in a political vacuum. It could decide whether to complete the destruction of the monarchical system which lay helpless before it or to retain the old organization of the state in the service of the new order. The issues which had divided liberal from radical at Offenburg and Heppenheim in 1847 arose again during the deliberations in St. Paul's Church. This time, however, the prize was not the leadership of a disorganized minority party but the future of Germany.

The committee of seven presented the program of the moderates. Prepared by Karl Welcker and endorsed by prominent liberals like Heinrich von Gagern and Friedrich Römer, it urged the establishment of a federal union headed by a liberal monarch and governed through a constitution drafted by a national assembly. The radicals countered with the motion introduced by Gustav von Struve at the first meeting of the preliminary parliament. They sought the realization of their Offenburg program, but their tone was bolder and their intention more explicit than a year before. They still thundered against standing armies, aristocratic privileges, and tyrannical bureaucracies, but now they also openly preached republicanism and demanded for the worker "a share in the profits of labor." Struve made his obeisance to bourgeois sensibilities by including in his address a tribute to "security of property" and "prosperity, education, and freedom for all." Yet behind his professions of respectability lurked the Montagnard with a dash of socialism, the protagonist of egalitarian democracy and controlled economy.

The preliminary parliament, forced to choose between the discreet constitutionalism of the liberals and the utopianism of the radicals, promptly made up its mind. It dealt the extremists the first blow by refusing to grant their program a place on the agenda. It continued to demolish their hopes by voting 368 to 143 against a motion that it remain in permanent session. It rejected the demand of the left for a purge of those members of the Diet of the Confederation who had in the past approved repressive measures. And it added insult to injury in failing to make room for Struve and Hecker on the committee of fifty named to supervise the election of delegates to the national assembly. Frankfurt was clearly no place for republican doctrinaires with visions of Jacobinism.

Even before the deliberations came to an end, about forty members of the preliminary parliament left the meeting to appeal over the heads of the self-appointed representatives of the people to the people themselves. On April 12 they raised the banner of rebellion in Constance, hoping to revive the mass movement which a month before had conquered Europe. The Revolution, however, was over, and the call of the left was answered only by a few thousand peasants and workers, by German émigrés in France and Switzerland, by adventurous students and visionary intellectuals. Such is not the stuff of which successful Putsches are made. By the end of the month the Baden uprising had been crushed, and with its end the last sparks of the March days died out.[1]

Having laid the ghost of insurrection, the preliminary parliament could turn to the election of the national assembly. One delegate was to be chosen for every 50,000 inhabitants, but since the census was thirty years old, approximately 75,000 persons actually resided in the average constituency. While direct elections were recommended, a motion to require them was defeated 317 to 194, so that the states were left free to decide the question. The suffrage was not to be restricted by requirements of property, religion, or class, and yet liberalism could not conquer its deep-rooted distrust of the masses. Although the minutes state that on April 1 the delegates agreed to bestow the right to vote on "every citizen who has reached his majority," this clause appears in a significantly different form in the final compilation of resolutions approved by the assembly. There it reads: "Every independent citizen who has reached his majority is eligible to vote." According to the presiding officer Karl Mittermaier and the members of the secretariat the crucial adjective appeared in the original motion at the time of adoption, but was inadvertently omitted from the published minutes. Be that as it may, the decision to enfranchise only those possessing independence provided state governments with an effective defense against mob rule.[2]

When the preliminary parliament concluded its last session on April 3, the princes of Germany breathed a sigh of relief. The gathering of the liberal leaders had come and gone without declaring war against traditional institutions. It had chosen instead to follow the path of legality by recommending the convocation of an elective convention to determine the future of the nation. It had even presented its defeated enemies with an opportunity to atone for past sins through the enactment of reform laws. Such consideration did not go unappreciated, and at its meeting of April 7 the Diet of the Confederation granted legal sanction to the resolutions adopted by the constitutionalists a week earlier. The old and the new continued to co-operate during the critical days which preceded the meeting of the national assembly, the members of the diet adopting progressive measures, the committee of fifty issuing public declarations against republicanism, anarchy, and revolution. As the breach between moderate and radical grew wider, there developed a tacit alliance between moderate and conservative directed against the common enemy on the left. The Frankfurt Parliament was the offspring of this union.[3]

On May 18, when 330 delegates from all the lands of Germany marched in solemn procession across the *Römerberg* to St. Paul's Church, the world saw the incarnation of a profound national longing for freedom and unity. The enthusiasm of the moment, however, obscured the class predispositions and special interests which accompanied the representatives of the people into the assembly hall. For the men of the Frankfurt Parliament brought to their task ideas and policies inadequate for the government of a society of peasants and artisans torn by the disruptive influences of the Industrial Revolution. They were never more than intelligent, hard-working, middle-class politicians doomed to defeat in a time out of joint, because fate had placed on them a burden beyond their strength.

Failure was inherent in the circumstances which led to the domination of the national assembly by the propertied bourgeoisie. In one state after another liberalism employed a variety of electoral devices to exclude the masses from the polls. In Württemberg and Hanover workers were declared ineligible to vote, because they received wages from their employers and hence could not be considered independent. Saxony and Baden decided that servants and farm hands living with their masters were in a state of subordination and unqualified for the ballot. In Bavaria the law disfranchised all who did not pay a direct tax. In Prussia recipients of public charity lost the right to vote. And in large cities everywhere the sizable floating population of seasonal workers, wandering journeymen, day laborers, and out-and-out vagabonds could not participate in the elections because of strict residence and citizenship requirements.[4]

The will of the people was further purged in electoral colleges, for despite the recommendations of the preliminary parliament the delegates to the national assembly were chosen directly only in Württemberg, Hesse-Kassel, Schleswig-Holstein, and the free municipalities of Frankfurt, Hamburg, and Bremen. Eager to counter the influence of radical agitators, poll officials repeatedly violated the secrecy of the ballot and winked at open attempts to bribe voters. In Cologne, where 25,000 persons had received public assistance during the depression, almost one third of the population was disfranchised, and conditions were not much better in eastern cities like Berlin and Breslau. Frankfurt declared its numerous resident aliens ineligible for the suffrage, while the committee of fifty persistently looked the other way. On April 16 the Hamburg patriciate finally granted the vote to apprentices and factory workers, but then it nullified the effects of its generosity by holding the elections on April 18, 19, and 20, giving the populace no time to prepare for the exercise of the franchise. Even in tiny Hohenzollern-Hechingen the government excluded from the polls all bachelors, Jews, and foreign members of the civil service.[5]

These exertions were in most cases unnecessary, for the apathy of the electorate was the most effective guarantee against the dangers of a broad suffrage. Only in Baden, Saxony, and the Rhineland did party struggles arouse interest among the lower classes, and even there indifference from below as well as restriction from above minimized the political influence of the proletariat. In cities like Freiburg, Karlsruhe, and Pforzheim the moderate candidates of the bourgeoisie were consistently victorious over the democrats who appealed to the masses. Newspaper reports from Chemnitz commented on the lack of popular interest in the elections. In Annaberg only about 500 out of 2,000 eligible voters cast their ballots. The press of the Saxon Vogtland criticized citizens who found time to visit inns and beer cellars but could not appear at the polls. In Leipzig 15,000 men qualified for the vote, but less than 6,000 used their prerogative. Elsewhere political consciousness was rarer still. "The incomprehensible unconcern which many potential voters manifest by absenting themselves at the time of election is deplorable," was the discouraged observation of the *Bayerische Landbötin* in Munich. "In one precinct of approximately 400 eligibles only 106 voted, in another of about 600 only a little more than 200 participated. What are we to expect from the rural districts, when in the capital there are so many completely ignorant, incompetent slackers?"[6]

Scattered results of the elections suggest that participation did not usually exceed 50 per cent, and often it was no more than 30. Adult males, constituting one fourth of the population of Central Europe, numbered about 19,000 in the average constituency. Yet in Frankfurt am Main Friedrich Jucho was chosen delegate after receiving 6,650 votes out of 8,611. In a hotly contested election in the Hersfeld district 10,303 ballots were cast. More typical were the proceedings in nearby

Kassel, where the moderate Philipp Schwarzenberg defeated his republican rival 7,862 to 57. In Württemberg constituencies with more than 10,000 voters were uncommon, and Paul Pfizer was conceded a victory after winning 4,213 ballots. In one Schleswig-Holstein district the successful candidate received 6,000 out of about 8,000 votes. In Hamburg 23,000 persons in a population of 180,000 took part in the elections. In Leipzig only some 40 per cent of the adult male inhabitants went to the polls, and in Plauen and Ölsnitz the proportion of voters was approximately the same. Absence of interest may have been even more important than lack of legal qualification in reducing exercise of the franchise, but in any case the class abstaining or excluded from the suffrage was largely the economically dependent and politically indifferent proletariat.[7]

Chosen in a manner predisposing it in favor of the enlightened bourgeoisie, the Frankfurt Parliament could not reflect the multiplicity of interests of the German people. It was not the inept professorial parliament of the conservative myth, but neither was it an assembly of selfless patriots completely dedicated to shining ideals of liberty and brotherhood. It was the creation of a liberal middle class resolved to make its dominant position secure in a new system of government. Its members did not march into St. Paul's Church from the academician's ivory tower or the martyr's prison cell. They came from the government bureau, from the newspaper room, from the landed estate, from the business office, from the bank, from the shop, and even from the pulpit. There were indeed 49 university professors among them, but the parliamentarians par excellence of 1848 were jurists, who numbered more than 200 in the Frankfurt Parliament. They were joined by 40 school principals and teachers, 35 writers and journalists, 30 merchants and industrialists, 26 clergymen, and 12 physicians. Far from being the parliamentary freak which peers out of the pages of a thousand histories, the national assembly bore a family likeness to other European legislative bodies which throughout the nineteenth century attempted to govern the universe in accordance with the imperatives of the bourgeois ethic. And it suffered from an excess rather than lack of narrow practicality, for in its exclusive concern with the interests of a single class it lost sight of the broad masses on whose backs it had climbed to power.[8]

In the world outside St. Paul's Church the clamor for industrial regulation and rural reform was growing louder, but within all was dignity and decorum. Four handicraftsmen and one lonely peasant sat in awed silence, while their polished colleagues prepared blueprints of a New Jerusalem. As for the ninety dispirited members of the nobility, they seemed to be completely resigned to the triumph of constitutionalism. Even the most determined among them, those meeting in the Café Milani, were basically cautious reformers. The uncompromising foes of the new order like Otto von Bismarck, Hermann Wagener, and Leopold von Gerlach sulked in their tents far from Frankfurt, and the right wing of the national assembly was consequently composed of some forty moderate conservatives like Georg von Vincke, Maximilian von Schwerin-Putzar, and Joseph von Radowitz, men who only the year before had been considered representatives of progressive tendencies in the aristocracy. Now they were playing the unhappy dual role of reactionaries to the liberals within the parliament and turncoats to the counterrevolutionaries without.[9]

The left was in a similar predicament. It was treated with suspicion by the constitutional monarchists of the center, and yet it could not embrace the unabashed egalitarianism of a Wilhelm Weitling or even a Friedrich Hecker. Try as it would, it was unable to overcome its instinctive distaste for rabble-rousers like Friedrich Kapp and Saul Buchsweiler who rubbed elbows with workers in proletarian drinking places. At their national congresses the democrats refused to conclude an alliance with the socialists of the *Neue Rheinische Zeitung*, they rejected proposals that the masses be invited to join their organizations, they even avoided references to republicanism in order to prove their respectability. The thought of anarchy inspired in them the same horror which it aroused among the conservatives. Julius Fröbel, who presided in June at a great radical meeting in Frankfurt, warned the masses against the disintegration of the united front which had been formed during the spring uprising: "Hostility between the working class and the middle class, between the people and the bourgeoisie may not lead to a more thorough reform of our social conditions, but may rather jeopardize the outcome of our entire movement and cheat democracy of its hopes."[10]

What was the left to do? Like faithful Penelope it found itself forced to unravel at night what it had painfully woven by day. Inside St. Paul's Church it sought to prod the moderates to act with greater boldness, while outside it attempted to restrain the hotheads anxious to organize a new uprising. Radical deputies like Ludwig Simon and Lorenz Brentano who formed the party of the Donnersberg invoked the revolutionary trinity of liberty, equality, and fraternity; but when on September 16 the mob invited them to dissolve the Frankfurt Parliament and proclaim themselves an insurrectionary republican convention, they hesitated, trembled, and declined. For months they had looked with disapproval on the cautious policies of the liberal majority, and only yesterday they had been appalled by the conclusion at Malmö of an armistice with Denmark. Now, however, they dared not take the fateful step. At a meeting of the democratic factions with a combined membership of more than a hundred delegates only nineteen voted in favor of rebellion. The others stood aside and watched in helpless inaction, as the uprising which they could have led was crushed. Then they returned to the assembly hall to be greeted by the derisive cries of the moderates. Their weakness was that they were neither conservative enough nor radical enough, and so they remained politically paralyzed, while the Revolution followed its course to a tragic conclusion.[11]

With the right fighting a hopeless rear guard action against constitutionalism and the left dissipating its energies in futile factionalism, the liberals of the center dominated the Frankfurt Parliament. Organized in the parties of the Kasino, Landsberg, Augsburger Hof, and Württemberger Hof, they commanded the allegiance of a majority of the delegates. And while they differed among themselves in questions of particularist loyalty, religious conviction, and financial interest, they were one in their condemnation of conservative efforts to undo the Revolution and of radical attempts to extend its scope. Central Europe was to attain political might and economic greatness through the talent which the bourgeoisie could enlist in its service. "The tendency of our times is to assure for the middle class a preponderant influence over the state," announced Heinrich von Gagern.[12]

Throughout the spring the moderates continued to fear that the Revolution had gone so far that they were in imminent danger of a class war. Had not thousands of workers and peasants taken part in open violation of the rights of ownership? Had not some of them even repeated the blasphemy of Proudhon that property is theft? Before it could begin to prepare its program of parliamentary reform, the new order had to be sure that its deliberations would not be disturbed by a mob demanding a redistribution of wealth and an obliteration of social distinction. The men in St. Paul's Church firmly believed that under modern conditions only a prosperous bourgeoisie could build an enduring state. To confuse political freedom with economic equality was to destroy the incentive to efficiency, for differentiation in status was the condition of all progress. As Joseph Schneider of Vienna told the national assembly: "I am certainly well aware that we will always have an aristocracy of wealth and that we will always have an aristocracy of intellect, human nature unfortunately being what it is. But those, gentlemen, are natural aristocracies to which all may aspire and to which all may ascend. An aristocracy of birth, however, is never natural and neither is it necessary."[13]

The thought of a new mass uprising directed against the bourgeoisie troubled the early sessions of the Frankfurt Parliament. In April the committee of fifty had discussed the appointment of an executive committee to suppress the "anarchy and rebellion" with which the impotent Diet of the Confederation could no longer cope. Events since then had made still more apparent the need for an effective instrument of government to protect liberalism against attacks from the left as well as the right. The first major achievement of the national assembly was therefore the creation of a provisional central government.

For a time the moderates sought the collaboration of the states in this undertaking, but when the negotiations proved too complicated, Heinrich von Gagern made his "bold move." On June 24 he urged the delegates to establish the new executive solely by virtue of the constitutional powers which the people of Germany had vested in them, and four days later the law defining the competence of the provisional central government was adopted. On June 29 the likable but spiritless Archduke Johann of Austria became an imperial regent authorized to enter into diplomatic relations with foreign states, to enforce the decisions of the representatives of the nation, and to defend life and property against lawlessness.[14]

The parliamentarians in Frankfurt could now turn to the task for which they had been summoned, the preparation of a constitution for the united fatherland. Before all else they concerned themselves with the formulation of those personal freedoms which would form the cornerstone of a happier future for the individual and the community. The national assembly began its deliberations of the Fundamental Rights of the German People on July 3 and completed them on December 21. During those six long months it debated the principles of equality before the law, of freedom of speech, of religious toleration, and of judicial independence. It proclaimed the sanctity of private property, it described the rights of citizenship, it eliminated the remnants of servile obligation, and it prescribed the maintenance of representative legislatures and responsible ministries in the governments of the several states. On December 28, a few days after their adoption in St. Paul's Church, the Fundamental Rights were published in the official gazette and thus went into force about twelve weeks before the completion of the other sections of the constitution. To their authors they represented an achievement so benevolent in effect that even a brief postponement of their promulgation seemed undesirable.[15]

To later generations grown accustomed to victories of blood and iron the Fundamental Rights of the German People have appeared blind to political reality. To be sure, the kindly professors meant it all for the best, but their doctrinaire preoccupation with the finer points of constitutional theory allowed the insurrectionary ardor of the masses to cool. Instead of standing their enemies against the wall and shooting them, they lectured and discussed as if they were conducting a seminar in some provincial university. How many students have shaken their heads in sad amusement before the familiar picture of the academician fiddling while Germany burned? Too many, no doubt, for it is a false picture. In deciding to devote valuable months to a definition of the freedom of the citizen the Frankfurt Parliament was not indulging a penchant for abstract theorization. Its purpose was the eminently practical one stated in the preamble to the Fundamental Rights themselves: "They are to serve as a norm for the constitutions of the German states."[16]

The new order emerging out of the chaos of the March days required a statement of ultimate principles to guide the consolidation of its victory in constitutional form, and the national assembly sought to meet this need by expressing the cherished convictions of liberalism through the Fundamental Rights. They arose not from a theoretical concern with parliamentary forms, but out of the practical experience of a bourgeoisie about to realize the hopes of thirty years. Parliamentarians in Berlin, Vienna, Munich, Dresden, Karlsruhe, Hanover, and a dozen other state capitals could now proceed with their projects of reform, safe against radicals and reactionaries alike. The Frankfurt Parliament had forged a guarantee that the triumph of constitutionalism would lead the nation to the golden mean of statecraft between freedom and security.[17]

The stamp of middle-class liberal doctrine also appeared in those sections of the constitution which dealt more directly with the form of the government of Germany. They established a federal union strong enough to defend itself against hostile attacks from abroad and particularist threats at home. At its head was to stand a monarch endowed with the dignity of the imperial title but restricted in his power by an elective diet and a responsible ministry. While he conducted foreign affairs, declared war and concluded peace, exercised command of the armed forces, and enforced the laws of the realm, parliament enjoyed supreme authority in lawmaking. It alone could approve taxes, expenditures, treaties, and laws. It determined the budget and the civil list, it interpellated members of the cabinet and investigated the conduct of the bureaucracy, it impeached ministers and overrode the veto of the emperor. Finally, there was to be a national judiciary competent to try cases involving disputes between the central government and the subordinate members of the federation, conflicts among the states, and violations of private rights through official action.

The constitution breathed the spirit of a *juste-milieu* dear to the bourgeois reformer. There was only one note which sounded strange to an ear accustomed to the language of German parliamentarianism. The law of April 12, 1849, dealing with the election of delegates to the lower chamber of the legislature maintained almost unqualified manhood suffrage. Only the insane, the criminal, the bankrupt, and the pauperized could be barred from the polls. Otherwise not even the familiar requirement of independence was used to withhold the ballot from the worker, the peasant, the domestic, the farm hand, and the day laborer. In theory at least the lower classes were in a position to decide the future of the state, to experiment with its political institutions, and to tamper with its economic practices. What is more, they received these powers from the same men who throughout the Revolution had never tired of warning the world against the dangers of popular tyranny. When the representatives of the nation first met in St. Paul's Church not even the most optimistic of the radicals dared hope that the majority would ever agree to entrust its fortunes to the masses. Yet within a year the impossible had occurred.

It was the result of a bitter party struggle. As late as January the liberals in the constitutional committee and on the floor of the national assembly were still arguing for the disfranchisement of factory workers, journeymen, and servants. Only as the Frankfurt Parliament became increasingly divided in the contest between the Austrophil *grossdeutsch* faction and the *kleindeutsch* champions of Prussia was the left able to make its influence felt. By selling its votes to the highest bidder a hopeless minority became the decisive element in a vital political conflict. At first it enjoyed the support of the Austrians who helped it to revise the constitution in a democratic sense so as to make it unpalatable to Frederick William IV. Then in March it entered into a compact with the *kleindeutsch* delegates by which the Prussians won the imperial crown for their king and the radicals gained the generous electoral law while renouncing their republican sympathies. Both parties to the bargain were violating their innermost convictions, both felt the pangs of a guilty conscience. But if anything was to come of all their labors, principle had to be sacrificed to expediency.[18]

They could find consolation in the establishment of industrial and commercial unity. For right and left, in agreement that the foundation of political greatness was material prosperity, worked in a spirit of friendly collaboration to ensure its achievement. The deliberations dealing with the national economy lack the bitter acrimony and dramatic denouement of the great debate over the federal government. Yet this absence of contentiousness, far from indicating that the Frankfurt Parliament considered the subject unimportant, was rather the outcome of agreement among all parties on the need to overcome the traditional financial parochialism of Central Europe. The chairman of the economic committee Friedrich von Rönne voiced the unanimous sentiment of St. Paul's Church in his speech of June 3:

> The liberated German nation is eager to reap the fruits of its political emancipation. It demands law and order, it demands the revival of industrial activity, it demands above all more remunerative work. It demands the political unity of Germany so that it can break the chains which bind domestic commerce and which even now still separate one German state from another. It demands the political unity of Germany so that it can win for its country the eminent position in foreign commerce and in world trade to which it can rightly lay claim by virtue of its geographic position, its greatness, and the skill of its people, especially of its commercial and industrial classes. The divided states of Germany have until now been in no position to assert this claim against foreign nations, but the united states of Germany will know how to enforce it.[19]

The national assembly went to work with determination to bring about the economic consolidation which the bourgeoisie had been urging since the Congress of Vienna. The federal government was empowered to introduce a common and uniform system of weights, measures, currencies, and tolls. It was to exercise jurisdiction over railways, roads, rivers, canals, posts, and telegraphs. It had the authority to supervise the industry, trade, and transportation of the nation, to appoint consular officials, to negotiate commercial agreements, to determine import duties, and to control the establishment of banks and the emission of paper money. On November 24, 1848, moreover, the Frankfurt Parliament adopted the code governing the use of bills of exchange drafted the year before at a conference of the German governments in Leipzig. It also sought to strengthen the position of German commerce by creating a single national tariff area, at the same time appeasing the free-trade predilections of the Hanseatic cities by a constitutional provision for their exclusion from the customs union. Finally, it removed the dues and charges on domestic interstate river traffic, while the vessels and cargoes of foreign shippers remained subject to discriminatory fees.

In the meantime the provisional central government was getting ready to carry out the integration of the economy of Central Europe. It prepared a lengthy report on the amalgamation of the various German monetary systems and submitted it to the states for study and comment. Christian Wiedenmann of the ministry of justice composed a memorandum outlining a national commercial code and began to draft its text. Johannes Fallati and Philipp Schneider presented comprehensive reports on the formation of a federal consular service. And the ministry of commerce went so far as to draw up two laws dealing with navigation on interstate rivers, one concerned with technical problems of maintenance and improvement, the other providing for the elimination of dues levied by the riverain states.[20]

The optimism of the liberals was contagious. Holland, fearful of reprisals by St. Paul's Church against its vessels, approached the provisional central government in the late summer of 1848 with the offer of a treaty of navigation. Since the stake of the Netherlands in the Rhenish trade was considerable, Frankfurt decided to demand a high price for its friendship. It went without saying that the Dutch would have to agree to the abolition of fees on shipping entering and leaving the delta of the Rhine. They must also provide storage facilities for goods in transit across their territory, they must put an end to the petty annoyances inflicted on German merchants, and they must offer their collaboration in the establishment of freedom of movement on the river from Switzerland to the North Sea. Unfortunately, by the time these terms were transmitted to The Hague, the national assembly was drawing to a close, and soon afterward the victory of the reaction disrupted the *pourparlers* once and for all.[21]

No economic issue aroused greater differences of opinion than the tariff problem. Throughout the Forties the free-trade doctrines of the commercial north had been in bitter conflict with the protectionist demands of the industrial south, and with the outbreak of the Revolution each side saw a new opportunity to win official approval of its views. The *Zollvereinsblatt*, founded by Friedrich List and still faithful to his theories, maintained that "the first thing the German parliament must do for the customs union is to extend it. The unity of all of Germany in import duties and trade policies is the basis for all further economic progress of the state."[22] The chamber of commerce of Flensburg, on the other hand, felt that "our trade interests are hardly to be reconciled with those of the German Zollverein, and we very much fear that our adherence to it would offer little compensation for our former circumstances and connections."[23] A compromise between two so directly opposite views was clearly impossible.

Immediately after the spring uprising the protectionists launched a campaign for an upward revision of tariff rates.

At the second session of the Frankfurt Parliament on May 19 they introduced a motion preparing the way for an increase in import duties. On July 14 they returned to the attack, and on October 9 they made an effort to extend the customs of the Zollverein to the entire nation. They also succeeded in winning a majority on the important economic committee, where Friedrich von Rönne, Bernhard Eisenstuck, Karl von Bruck, Gustav von Mevissen, Karl Mathy, and Moritz Mohl fought for the exclusion of foreign manufactures. They formed the General German Association for the Protection of Native Labor which worked tirelessly to open the eyes of the public to the advantages of economic nationalism. They spared neither time, effort, nor money to bring their views before the Frankfurt Parliament, and their efforts were endorsed by dozens of petitions descending on St. Paul's Church from Stuttgart, Heidelberg, Karlsruhe, Mannheim, Erfurt, Wiesbaden, Krefeld, Solingen, Nürnberg, Munich, and a hundred other cities and towns.[24]

Yet they met their match in Arnold Duckwitz, the Bremen businessman who had become minister of commerce in the provisional central government. To the demands of the protectionists he countered with a statement of economic policy emphasizing freedom of trade which on December 16 received the approval of the national assembly. He was then free to draft a tariff schedule lower than the prevailing one, to prepare legislation establishing a national customs union, and to open negotiations for commercial treaties with the United States, Belgium, France, and Holland. As for his critics, he could always reply to their strictures by pointing to countless requests for lower import duties submitted by coastal cities like Memel, Tilsit, Königsberg, Elbing, Danzig, Kolberg, Stettin, Rostock, Wismar, Lübeck, Bremen, and Hamburg. Now aggressive, now conciliatory, now engaged in controversy, now avoiding open conflict, Duckwitz fought his opponents to a standstill, and when the national assembly concluded its deliberations, neither party could claim victory.[25]

On March 28, 1849, the great debate came to an end, as the Frankfurt Parliament announced to the world the promulgation of a new constitution for Germany. Ten months had elapsed since that May afternoon when the representatives of the people had marched in pomp and ceremony to St. Paul's Church for their first meeting. Since then they had overthrown the rule of the landed aristocracy and put in its place the hegemony of the middle class. They had proclaimed the reign of parliamentary government and economic progress. They had pronounced the old provincialism dead and supplanted it by a new sense of national patriotism. They had held out before their countrymen a vision of unity and freedom arising out of the ruins of the old order. The tree of liberty, watered by the blood of those who died on the barricades, had finally borne its paper fruits amid the eloquent oratory of the national assembly, and the liberals could now contemplate with satisfaction the completed plans for a bourgeois never-never land which they had prepared with such painstaking care. All that remained was to translate them into a reality of flesh and blood.

8

THE WORKER AND THE REVOLUTION

"The world has probably never seen a political assembly composed of a greater number of noble, learned, conscientious, and patriotic men," was Carl Schurz's judgment of the Frankfurt Parliament. "But it lacked the genius for recognizing opportunity and swiftly taking time by the forelock. It forgot that in a wildly excited age history does not wait for the thinker, and so it was doomed to fail in everything."[1] In the ripe wisdom of his long years of achievement the democratic hero of two continents was looking back somewhat patronizingly to that ill-starred first national assembly of his native land. He had been one of the many who in 1848 had turned in eager anticipation to the sages gathered in St. Paul's Church. He could remember how the hopes which had flowed so freely in the springtime of the Revolution began to run dry during the autumn. And he was still pondering the great enigma of a triumphant parliamentarianism completing its constitutional labors and inaugurating the reign of freedom, only to find itself defenseless in the face of a revived conservatism.

Why had all the grand plans of representative government and economic progress turned into mere museum exhibits for the edification of the scholar? For most liberals as for most conservatives the Frankfurt Parliament had frittered away its great opportunity, because it was too busy making speeches and preparing reports to deal with the vital problems of state. The insurrectionary ardor of the masses which had achieved the miracle of the March days cooled, while the members of the national assembly talked and wrote and voted. They accomplished their task with the pedantic thoroughness of the academician, but in the meantime history marched past them to bestow its favor on a helmeted and spurred reaction. The moral of the story found classic expression in Bismarck's speech of September 30, 1862, before the budget committee of the Prussian legislature: "The great questions of the time are decided not by speeches and majority resolutions. That was the great mistake of 1848 and 1849. They are decided by iron and blood."[2]

Yet the thesis that the Revolution was talked to death by petty lawyers and absent-minded professors raises more questions than it purports to answer. The debate in St. Paul's Church was certainly crucial, but as deliberations of parliamentary conventions go, it was not excessive. As far as Germany is concerned, the national assembly of 1848 could not match the accomplishments of the national assembly of 1919 which drafted a constitution in six months, but it acted with greater dispatch than the Italian national assembly of 1946 which was in session eighteen months, or the French national assembly of 1789 which continued to meet for two years. It was not the passage of time which destroyed revolutionary fervor, but the failure to satisfy the needs which had inspired it. The Frankfurt Parliament, far from being the do-nothing gathering of garrulous politicians portrayed by a fraudulent tradition, displayed considerable ingenuity in dealing with the political and economic problems of Central Europe. It asserted its views clearly and boldly, and it acted with decision and promptness. The causes of its defeat are not to be found in vapid mentality or ineffectual artlessness.

They must rather be sought in the policies followed by liberalism which disrupted the united front of bourgeois and proletarian forged during the March days. Once the common foe fell, the common purpose vanished, and the victorious alliance disintegrated into its component elements. During the spring uprising of 1848 the middle class was able to enlist the aid of the worker and the peasant; during the spring uprising of 1849 it could command only its own slender resources. In the course of one year it had squandered its popular following, and by ignoring the wishes of the lower classes it destroyed the one force which might have perpetuated its domination of the state.

Only with the masses of declassed masters and unemployed journeymen behind it could a political party achieve power during the Revolution. The first to discover this truth were the radical socialists of the Rhineland. In vain did Karl Marx, Friedrich Engels, Andreas Gottschalk, Karl Schapper, and Fritz Anneke seek to awaken the spirit of insurrection among factory workers, the bearers of the revolutionary tradition in France and England. In Central Europe their arguments fell on deaf ears. The *Neue Rheinische Zeitung*, struggling to win the attention of the world, was read by at most six thousand subscribers. Attempts to form an alliance between the socialists and the democrats collapsed, when neither side could overcome its distaste for the principles and tactics of the other. And the mill hand himself remained indifferent to shibboleths of class conflict and economic justice. He wanted only a higher wage and a shorter working day, not the good society of dialectical materialism.[3]

The moderate socialists of eastern Germany like Stephan Born and Christian Nees von Esenbeck were more successful, because they wisely avoided the ideological doctrinairism of the Rhenish extremists with its messianic complex. The program which they adopted in Berlin late in August emphasized such objectives of "social democracy" as the organization of trade unions, the establishment of improved working conditions, the promulgation of factory laws, the abolition of internal customs duties, and the repeal of discriminatory suffrage restrictions. In their appeal to the Frankfurt Parliament, moreover, they maintained that they were loyal defenders of law and order whose faith in parliamentarianism could be shaken only by a rejection of their just demands. These professions of respectability proved more persuasive than the maledictions of the western intransigents, for they managed to establish local party organizations in a few cities like Berlin, Breslau, Munich, Leipzig, Hamburg, and Cologne. Their followers, however, never numbered more than twelve thousand, and the claim advanced in their address to St. Paul's Church that they spoke in the name of "several million workers" was pure fantasy.[4]

The truth was that the industrial worker refused to play the role of downtrodden plebeian which socialist theory had chosen for him. He remained faithful to king and fatherland, he felt flattered when the bourgeoisie invited him now and again to join the civic guard, and he resented the insistence of the left that he was a proletarian. For it was humiliating to be identified with an uprooted artisan who had neither work nor hope nor pride. As the aristocrat of the lower classes, the factory employee felt himself far above the destitute handicraftsman, and he held on tenaciously to the sense of social superiority which made his hard life more endurable. Many a discouraged radical like Hermann Kriege was forced to the conclusion that a revolutionary working class was simply not to found in Central Europe.[5]

Yet it was there right before their eyes, only they could not see it. Captives of their own theories and phrases, the socialists expected the masses to march straight from the factory against the citadel of capitalism, and when the mill hand remained at his machine, they decided that their time had not yet come. Had they but looked around them, they would have found a numerous and desperate proletariat ready to accept revolutionary leadership. Countless artisans had fought the armies of the king and defended the cause of freedom, only to discover that the new order ignored their petitions and sent troops against their demonstrations. If socialism had been willing to exploit their grievances as liberalism had done, it too might have won a great victory on the barricades of a new insurrection. But the gospel of Marx had nothing good to say about the guild system, and so the handicraftsman was forced to look for his prophets elsewhere, while the Pharisees of the left continued their search for the ideal working class of revolutionary orthodoxy.

Ignored by the radicals and distrusted by the liberals, the urban masses waged a lone campaign against industrialism. Their first tactic was a direct attack on factories and machines which opened early in March and continued for about eight weeks. It failed, when parliamentarianism used armed force to suppress disorder. Then the artisan turned to the arts of persuasion. During the next twelve months he continued to agitate, educate, and plead. He drafted petitions, he issued proclamations, he founded associations, he convoked congresses. While socialist theorists bewailed the political immaturity of the factory worker who would rather spend his time in a beer cellar than at a political meeting, the guildsman was attending demonstrations, signing manifestoes, and exchanging fraternal greetings with his fellows throughout Germany. The labor movement which arose out of the Revolution was first and last a handicraft movement.

Sometimes the artisan participated in assemblies summoned primarily to defend the interests of his particular occupation. On April 18, 1848, for example, delegates of the Rhenish boatmen gathered in Cologne to direct the struggle against the steamship companies. The plea for economic survival which they sent to the committee of fifty was supported by thousands of sailors, stevedores, towers, and shippers unable to withstand the competition of the great freight concerns. Between June 11 and June 14 a trade convention representing the printers of 141 cities deliberated in Mainz and drafted a petition to St. Paul's Church demanding restriction of machinery, regulation of employment, establishment of equitable wage scales, and the creation of benefit funds for the sick and disabled. From July 20 to July 25 a congress of tailors sat in Frankfurt urging the suppression of industrial freedom, the closure of all shops selling ready-made clothes, and the limitation of admission to the needle trades.[6]

A more common form of artisan organization was the regional association of various occupations threatened by the factory system. In Leipzig, Halle, Augsburg, Tübingen, Tuttlingen, Bonn, Bremen, and Rostock guildsmen subscribed to mass declarations of support for corporate regulation of manufacture and commerce. On June 13 the tradesmen of Hanover assembled in the capital of their state to express opposition to economic freedom and insist on the maintenance of their ancient privileges. Six days later the First Constituent Handicraft Parliament of the Province of Silesia met in Breslau. On July 9 in Wolfenbüttel the masters of Brunswick demanded the restoration of guild control over industrial production. On August 3 delegates from several trade societies in Saxe-Meiningen gathered in Hildburghausen to concert common policies. And on October 27 King Maximilian II of Bavaria granted an audience to a deputation of handicraftsmen from Swabia to assure his subjects that he was deeply disturbed by the hard times which they had to endure.[7]

The step from local assemblies of guildsmen to a national artisan congress was obvious. It was broached in an appeal "to our brothers in trade" issued on April 19 by 391 masters in Bonn, an appeal which aroused warm interest among the workers of Magdeburg, Karlsruhe, Gotha, and Offenbach. It was implied in the petition which the carpenters of Bremen circulated among craft organizations in the north before submitting it to the committee of fifty. It was advocated in the open letter addressed to "all guild comrades of Germany as well as to all citizens and heads of families" which twenty-two Leipzig trade societies published on April 22: "We are therefore sending this open letter to all German guilds, and we call on them to consider the great labor problem their own cause and at the same time to see in it a general national question. In so doing they should adhere to the guild system, since it is a priceless asset without which this problem can never be satisfactorily solved and without which Germany will never again know happy days."[8] If efforts to destroy the corporate organization of industry succeeded, economic anarchy would inevitably result: "Journeymen will dictate laws to masters, and all the practices which are now common in France and which undermine the last remnants of diligence, prosperity, and respect will march in triumph with flying colors and martial music, as it were, across Prussia into Germany."[9]

The decision to convoke a national artisan congress was finally taken by the Assembly of Delegates of the North German Handicraft and Industrial Class meeting in Hamburg from June 2 to June 4. Organized by the guildsmen of Lauenburg with the aid of the masters and journeymen of Hamburg, the assembly was attended by 186 representatives from Prussia, Hanover, Brunswick, Bremen, Hamburg, Schleswig-Holstein, Oldenburg, the Mecklenburgs, and Hesse-Kassel. First it adopted by unanimous vote a resolution condemning economic liberalism. Then it went on to demand "a common code of social legislation for all Germany which will assure to each member of civil society a remunerative position commensurate with his capacity for work." And at its last session it approved a motion to issue a call for a congress of handicraftsmen to convene in Frankfurt in six weeks. Prior to adjournment the delegates elected a committee of seventeen to make the necessary preparations for the gathering and to submit a statement of grievances to St. Paul's Church.[10]

On June 5 and 6 the committee met to prepare the address. Its spirit was high, and the message which it composed was in effect the handicraftsman's declaration of independence. The liberals in the Frankfurt Parliament were told in clear terms what the artisan masses expected of the Revolution:

1. We declare ourselves most firmly opposed to indus-

trial freedom, and we demand that it be abolished insofar as it exists in Germany by a special paragraph of the fundamental law of the nation.

2. We declare ourselves to be competent and qualified to conduct our own affairs and hence also to undertake the solution of the social problem.

3. We are notifying the eminent parliament that on the basis of the general right of assembly we have called a meeting of delegates of the handicraft and industrial class from all parts of the German fatherland to take place in Frankfurt am Main on July 15 of this year in order to prepare the draft of a general handicraft and industrial code and to lay it before the eminent parliament.[11]

While St. Paul's Church was still rejoicing at the establishment of the provisional central government, delegates to the artisan congress began to arrive in Frankfurt. About fifty were present on July 15, when the first session opened in the *Römer*. In the historic hall where once the Holy Roman Emperors celebrated their coronation rites the humble tradesman took his seat to voice opposition to the economic and social forces of a new age which was about to overwhelm him. By the time the assembly concluded its meetings on August 18 the membership had grown to more than a hundred representatives from Prussia, Austria, Bavaria, Württemberg, Baden, Hesse-Darmstadt, Hesse-Kassel, Nassau, Saxony, Hanover, Holstein, Mecklenburg-Schwerin, the Hanseatic cities, Brunswick, and Oldenburg. In its negotiations with the Frankfurt Parliament it could justly claim to speak for the handicraftsmen of the entire nation.[12]

The preface to the industrial code which the artisan congress drafted described the source of the economic ills of modern society: "Can anyone blame . . . the German handicraftsman, who has only a little breath of life left in him, if he gathers his last reserves of strength and pronounces before

Germany and before his representatives in the German parliament a solemn protest against economic freedom, a protest to which millions of unfortunates subscribe?"[13] During the French Revolution, in a moment of political irresponsibility, the National Assembly had decreed the abolition of all controls over industry. The consequence, argued the congress, was the rise of a small group of wealthy merchants and manufacturers fattening with the misery of the lower classes, and the growth of a propertyless and uprooted proletariat always ready to embark on revolution, because only in revolution did it see an opportunity to improve its wretched condition. The same fate awaited Germany, unless it abandoned the policy of encouragement to factories and contempt for guilds.[14]

The solution to the problems confronting the tradesman was outlined in the industrial code itself. It called in essence for a return to the corporate organization of production. The right to engage in a handicraft occupation was to be conferred only on guild masters whose competence had been tested by an artisan association and whose numbers had been restricted in accordance with consumer demand. To be sure, the factory was to remain in existence, but its competition with the small shop would be limited by discriminatory taxation and output regulation. Economic conditions were to be supervised by local guild corporations, which were to appoint members to municipal guild councils, while the latter in turn chose regional guild chambers to advise state legislatures on manufacturing policy. At the apex of the pyramid would stand a national craft assembly regulating the common affairs of all trade organizations and suggesting needed legislation to the national parliament. An autonomous federal industrial government was thus to function side by side with the autonomous federal political government, for to the tradesman the establishment of one was the natural corollary of the existence of the other.

The program of the artisan congress also embraced far-reaching changes in commonly accepted economic and social policies. Demands for protective tariffs on industrial goods and favorable commercial treaties with foreign states were not in and for themselves unusual. But suggestions that the state introduce a progressive income and property tax, that it found government banks to extend easy credit to the handicraftsman, that it provide free education for the children of the poor, and that it substitute deportation for capital punishment had a suspiciously radical sound to liberal ears. As for proposals that the nation guarantee gainful employment to all workers and assume the financial burden of support for the ill and the maimed, every man of means knew that this was socialism pure and simple, and that in France it had led from national workshop to subversion to class warfare.[15]

The tradesman in the *Römer* realized that he was trying to swim against a powerful economic current, but he had no choice. The industrial code was his ultimatum to the new order. With it he would continue to defend the liberal cause, without it he would seek other allies. As the artisan congress concluded its sessions, Martin May, the master butcher from Frankfurt who was presiding officer, defied the industrialist and financier to do their worst: "We may be sure that speculation and usury will oppose us with all their resources, for what is at stake is their domination over industriousness. Yet the German handicraftsman has come of age, and he will no longer endure the yoke of slavery imposed by the money interests."[16]

The industrial code met with the approval of tradesmen throughout Germany. Only in the Palatinate was there serious opposition to its aims. There the French had introduced economic freedom fifty years before, and in the course of two generations a tradition of enterprising individualism had taken root among the winegrowing peasants and the petty shopkeepers and handicraftsmen. They made their peace with the mills of Ludwigshafen and Frankenthal, and many of them even learned to dabble in commercial ventures themselves. The fortunate ones held their own, the losers found employment in the ironworks or emigrated to America. Hence the worker on the left bank of the Rhine, facing conditions essentially different from those which prevailed farther east, felt little kinship with the guildsman of Hanover or Brunswick or Saxony. He did not participate in the great artisan congresses in Hamburg and Frankfurt, his petitions to St. Paul's Church condemned efforts to restore corporate regulations, and at the Palatine handicraft assembly in Neustadt an der Haardt on January 14, 1849, he even expressed his approval of laissez-faire economics. In his attitude toward the factory system he was closer to his French neighbors on the other side of the border than to his compatriots in Central Europe.[17]

For the latter were firmly opposed to free enterprise. Here and there among them could be heard strictures about the industrial code, but they were usually directed against its detail rather than objective. Organizations of journeymen, for example, expressed reservations about some of the proposals of the German Handicraft and Artisan Congress. Since their delegates had been excluded from the deliberations in the *Römer* by the independent tradesmen, they formed their own assembly under the name General German Labor Congress. Meeting from July 20 to September 20, they followed the debates of the master artisans and then presented to the Frankfurt Parliament a program of their own. In it they sought to advance their interests by advocating a minimum wage, a shorter working day, and the right to wander freely from state to state in search of employment. Among their resolutions were also demands for manhood suffrage, planned emigration to relieve overpopulation, and employee representation in the guild system.

Yet despite their differences with the masters over the particulars of corporate regulation journeymen were equally uncompromising foes of industrial freedom. Fundamentally what they sought was an improved economic position within the handicraft trades, and the growth of the factory consequently threatened them no less than their employers. Their address to St. Paul's Church criticized economic liberalism in language recalling the artisan congress. They too pointed to conditions in France, "the nation divided into millionaires and beggars," as an example of the effects of anarchic Manchesterism. They too warned of the impending triumph of usury and speculation over honest toil. Only the promulgation of comprehensive social legislation protecting the worker against the evil powers of wealth could save Germany from the danger of a new revolution. Otherwise the establishment of political freedom would remain a meaningless gesture. Thus in its hostility to the world of business the program of the General German Labor Congress agreed with the industrial code of the German Handicraft and Artisan Congress.[18]

Numerous memorials attested the approval of the artisan of Central Europe for the economic principles espoused in Frankfurt by the two handicraft assemblies. The industrial committee of Esslingen called for the suppression or restriction of mills competing with tradesmen. In Teschen there was a suggestion that the government establish production quotas for every occupation in order to reduce economic insecurity. The guildsmen of Celle reminded St. Paul's Church that commerce was only the tinsel of a nation, labor its marrow. The citizens league of Kassel demanded state regulation of business establishments to control the amount of capital invested, the number of workers employed, and the volume of goods manufactured. The Bamberg trade association expressed the view that factories should sell their wares only abroad. The handicraftsmen of Hanover proposed that no master practice more than one trade. In Limburg and Kiel resolutions urged the promulgation of a national industrial code to alleviate the distress of the lower class. And from

Baden-Baden and Gotha came sweeping condemnations of industrial freedom.[19]

A particularly moving plea for relief from poverty was submitted to the artisan congress by the Brunswick weavers guild:

> Germans! In complete confidence we turn to you with the request that you consider carefully and act justly. It is too well known to require much explanation that through government blunders and lawlessness the capitalists were permitted to enter our trade at will and to manufacture with the aid of their financial resources the products of our trade, frequently by the use of machinery. They did not care that thousands of shops and families were ruined and thus exposed to want and starvation. Proof of this can be seen in Silesia and Saxony, for after the Silesians were deprived of their bread, were they not fed with grapeshot? Was this then the only salvation of the state existing by the grace of God? It is sad that we have always had such governments, for surely they must have recognized so grave an injustice, and yet they did not act accordingly. . . . Fortunately we Germans have finally put an end to laws which are senseless and harmful to the people. As for the fact that the weaver trade has until now been a free occupation, we must put an end to that too, since from it has certainly sprung the greatest cause of our calamity. The evidence proves it.[20]

The industrial code of the artisan congress became the rallying point of the German guild system, and the record of petitions presented to the national assembly refers time and again to statements of support for its provisions. Now it cites "an endorsement by the tradesmen of the city of Schweinfurt of the resolutions adopted by the Handicraft and Artisan Congress in Frankfurt am Main"; now it speaks of "a declaration of assent to the resolutions of the Handicraft and

Artisan Congress in Frankfurt am Main submitted by the skilled workmen and handicraftsmen engaged in the technical trades in Innsbruck"; now it mentions "a request by the handi-craft associations of the Province of Saxony, namely, Witten-berg, Wernigerode and environs, Ilsenburg, Hasserode, Wul-ferstedt, Eilenstedt, Oschersleben, Gerbstedt, Wettin, Barby, Arendsee, Stassfurth, Atzendorf, Borne, Förderstedt, Genthin, Sandau, Oebisfelde, Alsleben, Besedau, Strenz, Nauendorf and Belleben, Magdeburg, and Osterburg, for the promul-gation as law of the draft of a handicraft and industrial code prepared by the artisan congress in Frankfurt am Main."[21]

The voices clamoring for protection against the banker, the merchant, and the industrialist made themselves heard in legislative assemblies. While the handicraftsman demanded a return to the precapitalistic tranquillity of the guild, the bour-geois parliamentarian was extolling the economic virtues of a competitive capitalism. But since liberalism could not afford to ignore completely the wishes of the masses, the artisan movement won a few tactical victories.

The most important of these came in Hanover, where only the year before a new industrial law had facilitated admission to the practice of an occupation. Yet in order to soften the blow against the guildsman the government had agreed to postpone enforcement of the measure until July 1, 1848. Thereby it unwittingly saved him from disaster. For as soon as the spring uprising broke out, artisans began to demand repeal of the legislation, and Minister of the Interior Johann Stüve was too wise and too insecure to risk the wrath of the mob. On June 15 he executed a retreat from economic freedom by introducing important changes in the code for the regulation of industry. Of 291 paragraphs 36 were elim-inated or altered, and the attempt to destroy the powers of trade associations and abolish corporate controls over produc-tion was in effect abandoned.[22]

In Prussia the new order was not as ready to sacrifice its

principles. It agreed to mediate between employer and employee, and the ministry did what it could to encourage the conclusion of industrial agreements. The constituent convention, moreover, appointed a commission to investigate trade conditions and recommend economic legislation. The poverty-stricken weavers of Silesia and Westphalia received a modest disbursement of public funds. On September 5 the government delighted the protectionists by ordering a temporary increase in tariff duties on imported textiles. It even took steps to put an end to the truck system disliked by mill hand and artisan alike. Since during the March days factory owners in the western provinces had learned a valuable lesson, many declared themselves opposed to company stores and wage payment in goods. In October the cabinet presented to the legislature the draft of a law requiring the remuneration of factory labor in cash. Parliamentary approval and royal sanction would in all probability have been forthcoming, but on December 5 the conflict between king and assembly led to the dissolution of the chamber, and the bill was lost in a mass of unfinished business.[23]

Still, despite their occasional efforts to end industrial abuses the liberals refused to meddle in those practices of laissez-faire economics legalized by the decrees of September 7, 1811, and January 17, 1845. When on June 3 a motion to suppress freedom of industry was introduced in the constituent convention in Berlin, it could not find the required number of seconders and never came to a vote. This unambiguous endorsement of Manchesterism moved Baron Erasmus von Patow, the recently appointed minister of commerce, industry, and public works, to congratulate the lawmakers on their rejection of the proposal: "I consider it my duty to offer thanks to the assembly for having withheld support from . . . the motion. I can assure you that I receive numerous requests for the complete abrogation of industrial freedom, and in this decision I shall find the desired ground for opposing such requests with determination."[24]

Throughout Germany the conflict between political expediency and economic conviction troubled the liberals. The Bavarian government established a chamber of industry to represent the interests of the handicraftsman, but it ignored requests for a conservative revision of the law of September 11, 1825. While the ministry of Hesse-Darmstadt was conferring on the tailors guild in the capital a monopoly of the clothing trade, it was also preparing to revoke all exclusive commercial and industrial privileges. The toymen of Saxe-Meiningen could not prevail on their duke to restore corporate controls, although he did agree at last to restrict the activities of papier-mâché manufacturers. And shippers protesting to the Frankfurt Parliament against the competition of steamship lines were told that suffering was the price of progress. The Rhenish states went so far as to reduce a few of the dues levied against sailing vessels, but they would not even hear of proposals to dissolve the great freight companies.[25]

Confronted by artisan demands for the restoration of the guild system, constitutionalism palliated, temporized, hemmed and hawed, but in the end it had to refuse. It acted with a fatal logic which was its undoing. Since it believed in economic freedom no less firmly than in political freedom, what could it say to pleas for the prohibition of machinery and the restraint of competition? Usually it maintained a discreet silence in touchy questions of industrial regulation, but when its patience was exhausted, it could express itself with a brutal candor:

We may feel a very grave concern for the present sad plight of our artisan class, and yet we must condemn the means which the assembly of handicraftsmen in Frankfurt suggests for its improvement. This complete ignorance of the ideas which are fermenting in our time, this disdainful rejection of all interests outside the realm of personal advantage, this contempt for the demands of science, this shameless passion for monopoly not only in the conduct of business but also in the debate regarding its needs, this open declaration of war against technological progress, they are all tragic evidence of an intellectual poverty which would be utterly inexplicable in view of the level of German education, were we not to remember that the first manifestation of a long suppressed freedom degenerates only too easily into abuse. Are we then to recreate the prosperity of our cities by putting together again the ruins of corporate control, by introducing once more the Middle Ages within the demolished walls, by turning basic social and economic laws upside down, by associating the right to work not with skill and the prerogative of man, but with institutions devised in the interest of monopoly and explicitly calculated to achieve monopoly, by forcing the profit motive into a strait jacket, by destroying the foundations of free domestic competition which is the source of industrial progress, by imposing on the factory the dead weight of a taxation system whose purpose is the protection of handicrafts, by imprisoning commerce within absurd restrictions, by forcing journeymen and apprentices into the position of pariahs in relationship to the patriarchal guild master? . . . The national assembly would have to declare itself bankrupt in justice and intelligence, before it could recognize the competence of the artisan congress to settle the unsolved problems of industry.[26]

A conflict between bourgeois and proletarian was unavoidable, because the differences in their social philosophies and economic interests were too profound to be adjusted. Their friendship had suffered the first rude shock when liberalism suppressed the spring uprising of the urban masses. It received a further blow after the artisan discovered during the summer that the new order had no intention of supporting him in the struggle against industrial capitalism. It reached the breaking point in the autumn, as the national assembly prepared to write economic freedom into the constitution.

Paragraphs 133 and 158 of the Fundamental Rights of the German People gave the citizen the authority to establish his domicile wherever he liked, to acquire full residence privileges, to purchase any property, and to pursue every occupation. An industrial code promulgated by the federal government was to determine the conditions under which these rights could be exercised, but in view of the economic outlook of parliamentarianism it was obvious that the new order would not hesitate to overthrow the guild system. Had not Justin von Linde announced from the floor of St. Paul's Church that "there is not the slightest doubt in the assembly that the people of Germany must obtain freedom of movement and freedom of industry?"[27]

The Frankfurt Parliament proved true to its colors. On July 21 the task of preparing an industrial code was assigned to the economic committee, but by February, when its report was completed, the national assembly was already engaged in the bitter party struggle which ended in dissolution, and one more ambitious project was left to molder in the Frankfurt archives. Yet a small corner of the curtain had been lifted, and Germany caught a glimpse of stagehands changing the scenery and moving the properties for the grand constitutional spectacle. It saw the wishes of artisan meetings and guild petitions ignored in a state paper urging the removal of government controls over manufacture, the abolition of the coercive powers of trade corporations, and the freeing of admission to handicraft occupations. For the urban proletariat there could no longer be any doubt about the economic intentions of the middle class. Liberalism was a more zealous champion of the factory and the bank than conservatism in its heyday had dared to be.[28]

With the publication of the economic committee's report on an industrial code the last links in the great coalition of social classes forged in the March days broke. Moderates preached that competition was a necessary stimulus to progress, radicals criticized corporate guilds as survivals of the authoritarian age, and socialists sneered at "small tradesmen, whose entire manufacturing system is a mere relic of the Middle Ages." The artisan masses therefore turned in the one direction still open to them. During the year which followed the spring uprising they completed the circle from conservatism back to conservatism again. They offered their support to the crown on terms of social stability and economic regulation, the same terms which they had presented to liberalism. Once the bargain was concluded, they ended where they had begun, loyal to king and hostile to revolution.[29]

9

THE PEASANT AND THE REVOLUTION

THE Revolution was all things to all men. To the bourgeois liberal it meant the establishment of a new nation of parliamentary government and material prosperity. To the guild master it meant the restoration of corporate control over industrial production. To the peasant it meant above all the abolition of manorialism and the redistribution of landed property. Each fought for his own cause, and therefore their common victory destroyed their common purpose. Once the Restoration fell, the new order began to dissipate its energies in a futile strife of social classes and political factions which made possible the ultimate triumph of the reaction.

By its devotion to economic freedom the middle class alienated the country no less than the city. During the spring uprising the peasantry had collaborated with the proletariat and the bourgeoisie in the struggle against absolutism, and as long as the liberals could count on the support of the village, they had nothing to fear from aristocratic agitation. But something happened between the defeat of conservatism in 1848 and its victory in 1849 to destroy the spirit of insurrection among the rural masses. The same rustic who had forced constitutionalism on the princes of Germany during the March days remained indifferent to its repudiation twelve months later. And his defection from the new order doomed the Revolution.

For the monarchists the change in attitude of the rural population was entirely understandable. It was an article of their faith that while the town breeds subversion, the village is the home of a simple, becoming patriotism. During the Fifties the eminent sociologist Wilhelm Riehl analyzed the character of the peasantry to the satisfaction of every good reactionary:

There is an unconquerable conservative force within the German people, a hard core which withstands all change, and that is our peasantry. It is truly a unique social class, and no other nation can offer a pendant to it. The man of education may be inclined toward conservatism by his understanding, but the peasant is conservative as a matter of habit. In the social conflicts of our time the peasant has played a more important part than most of us realize, for he has formed a natural barrier against the growth of French revolutionary doctrines among the lower classes of society. Only the stolid resistance of the peasants saved the German thrones in March 1848. We are told that the revolution stopped short of the thrones. Yet this is not entirely true, for it was the peasants who stopped short of the thrones. Their stolidity was by no means fortuitous, stemming as it did from the essential character of the German countryman. In our fatherland the peasant exercises a political influence which he enjoys in few other countries of Europe. The peasant is the future of the German nation, and the life of our people is constantly refreshed and rejuvenated by the peasantry.[1]

The Junker no doubt found it reassuring to learn that the rural masses were psychologically incapable of insurrection. But what of the spring uprising? Notwithstanding conservative interpretations of the popular ethos, the peasant had engaged in a revolution. During the March days he had turned against the aristocratic landowner and supported a bourgeois ideology, but in return he expected material benefits denied him by the Restoration. He abandoned his old loyalties to find the answer to the agrarian problem in constitutional government. Only the failure of the new order to meet his economic demands gradually destroyed his faith in parliamentarianism.

The spring uprising was clear evidence of the inadequacy

[157]

of the agricultural policies of the old order. In the lands of
the southwest the benevolent despots of the Age of Enlightenment and the constitutional rulers of the Restoration had
pioneered in the elimination of personal servitudes and the
extinction of manorial dues. Yet it was precisely there that
the agrarian revolt assumed the most alarming form. The
emancipated villager of the Black Forest or the Odenwald
or Franconia was as restive under the contractual obligations
of free tenancy as his grandfather had been under the customary fees of hereditary serfdom. Beset by population pressure, crop failure, and soil exhaustion, he could not afford
the high cost of liquidation or even commutation. What he
wanted was the undisputed ownership of the land obtained
by the abrogation of aristocratic property rights. Through
the Revolution he hoped to throw off once and for all the
weight of economic dependence, the weight of rent remittances, mortgage fees, and interest payments.

On March 14, as the Jacquerie was spreading from state
to state, a member of the Württemberg legislature admitted
the gravity of the revolution on the land:

> There are at this moment only two methods for pacifying
> the populace and for preventing the occurrence of a still
> greater disaster. One would be a friendly agreement be-
> tween nobility and peasantry. But under present conditions
> this is almost impossible, for the peasants do not want to
> pay any more. They want abrogation, not commutation. . . .
> The peasants at this moment, moreover, would submit such
> foolish demands to the proprietors that the latter would
> refuse. What are we then to do? . . . We ought to eliminate
> the tithe, but we can decree its repeal now, and then leave
> the scale of compensation to a future chamber enjoying the
> confidence of the people and working in co-operation with
> the government.[2]

The predicament of the new order, however, came to an

end within a few weeks, for by the end of April the peasant insurrection had been forced into submission. The rural masses which had at first sought to end the complex of manorial dues by force were soon obliged to plead their cause in petitions to ministers and legislators. They discovered that there was a subtle distinction between liberty and anarchy which made it heroic to throw stones at the soldiery of a reactionary prince, but criminal to burn the fields of an extortionary landowner. The citizen of a constitutional state did not march with scythe and flail against the castle to demand redress of grievances. He held meetings and composed addresses to his elected representatives. And in the meantime he continued to meet his legal obligations, for property was the foundation stone of society.

After the spring uprising farmers in countless obscure villages began to gather to draft appeals to St. Paul's Church. From Waldkappel in Hesse-Kassel came a petition for "the abolition without compensation of feudal and manorial burdens, especially land taxes and servile fees as well as hunting privileges." The residents of Eichelberg, Weiler, and Eschenau in Württemberg demanded the elimination of all personal and property obligations, "because in a state built on a democratic basis the will of the people must be recognized as the highest law of the land." The Leipzig lawyer Heinrich Graichen was authorized by the citizens of Oberfrohna, Langenhennersdorf, Bahra, Schwand, and Toberitz to present to the national assembly a request for the eradication of all residues of feudalism. As for the inhabitants of Kallmerode in Prussia, they were clearly thinking of themselves when they proposed "the total exemption from all servile fees, money dues, and crop rents of those poor communities which derive little or no profit from their barren land and soil."[3]

In his memorials to state governments the peasant expressed himself even more voluminously. He informed the Baden legislature that "the commutation of tithes by the present method brings distress rather than benefit to those who pay them, because they are ruined in the process." In Saxony he advocated the division of the latifundia among needy farmers to stem the flow of population from agriculture to industry. In the Mecklenburgs he circulated demands for the revocation of the judicial, administrative, and hunting privileges of the aristocracy. The authorities of Upper Bavaria discovered that rural participation in the Revolution arose out of economic hardship rather than political disaffection. And Frederick William IV was informed by his cabinet that Silesia expected him to decree the abolition of all manorial obligations.[4]

From the County of Ravensberg in Westphalia came a plea for government assistance in the creation of a class of independent peasant proprietors. The two thousand petitioners proposed to achieve their purpose by ingenuously radical means:

1. The establishment of mortgage banks as an aid to farming.
2. The abolition of all feudal dues without compensation.
3. The reformation of the existing system of taxation, the repeal of all direct and indirect taxes, and the substitution for them of a single progressive income tax.
4. The introduction of a system of local government based on truly democratic principles, namely, the principles of self-government of the community and equal political status for all of its members who are of age.
5. The regulation of the status of rural laborers (workers employed by the large landowners).[5]

The peasant wanted first and last emancipation from economic bondage, and the classic revolutionaries would have lived up to the occasion. Robespierre was too sober a statesman to rely on slogans of liberty, equality, and fraternity for the conversion of the village, nor did Lenin preach dialectical materialism to illiterate muzhiks. Their alliance with the countryside was based not on doctrinal agreement but economic interest. They expropriated the aristocracy and divided its possessions among the rural masses, bartering fields and flocks for votes and soldiers. Once the hungry farmer accepted their gift, he became their partner in crime. The French republic of virtue and the Russian soviet state were saved by peasants in uniform who valued a few acres of land more than the teachings of political theory.

The leaders of German liberalism, however, were neither Jacobins nor Bolsheviks. They were only industrious bourgeois politicians, conscientious and sincere enough, but completely incapable of opportunistic audacity. They feared bloodshed and insurrection, because once the mob broke the chains of habitual obedience, there was no telling where it would stop. The Revolution had provided them with an opportunity to translate their theories into practice, yet they were always a little ashamed of the illegitimate origin of their authority. They sought to maintain a spurious respectability through the fiction that the new order was only the legal extension of the old. Hence they left the princes on their thrones, hence they convoked the national assembly by the authority of the Diet of the Confederation, hence they paid constitutional homage to the particularism of the past. But the lot of the parvenu was not easy. To the masses they became snobs too good to hobnob with former friends, to the patriciate they remained climbers eager to rise above their station. At the end they earned the contempt of all.

In approaching the agrarian problem the Frankfurt Parliament resolved to walk the tightrope of dogmatic rectitude. Yet Anton von Schmerling, the suave Austrian aristocrat who became minister of the interior in the provisional central government, warned the new order of the need to appease the countryside: "The self-interest of all German governments demands that the broad masses of the German people receive as soon as possible the material relief which they are entitled to expect as a result of the March revolution. It demands that the agricultural population of Germany be entirely freed from the burdens which have oppressed it for centuries, and that it be brought to realize through direct benefit . . . that the peaceful and legal course adopted by the German national assembly has not been without advantage for it."[6] The democratic physician from Kalbe Wilhelm Löwe was more vivid in his appeal: "If there is any cause at all to fear the proletariat, then it is of the agricultural proletariat that we must especially beware. . . . It has aroused the most frightful passions in the heart of man, and it has bred a barbarism which may carry all the achievements of civilization to the grave. Let us therefore rather carry the Middle Ages to the grave."[7] And his party colleague, the Silesian schoolteacher Adolf Rösler, combined radical predilections with a gymnasial Latinity in his address to St. Paul's Church: "I speak to you in behalf of tranquillity and German unity. Grant legally what will otherwise happen anyway illegally. The peasant war stands without the gate. *Hannibal ante portas.* Think about that, gentlemen."[8]

The liberals were at a loss. Had they fought against royal authority only to prepare the way for anarchic democracy? In endorsing the Revolution they had hoped to establish the inalienable human rights to life and property on a firm legal basis. And now they were being asked to destroy the only moral justification of the March days by promulgating laws more arbitrary than any which absolutism had sanctioned. They had to refuse. Before the peasant could become a loyal citizen of the state, he would have to learn that ownership is inviolable, that social inequality is decreed by nature, and that Providence itself divides mankind into the rich and the poor.[9]

There was another reason why the new order could not agree to jettison the nobility. Not only was it unjustifiable in theory, but it could prove practically very dangerous. If constitutionalism had been sure that the uncompensated elimination of manorial obligations would pacify the countryside, it might have been willing to swallow its scruples. But would the lower classes see the difference between rural and urban property, between the landowner and the industrialist, between the manor house and the factory? Having once gotten a taste of expropriation, would they not rather develop such an appetite for the possessions of others that society would be plunged into the horrors of class war?

Paul Pfizer described the red specter haunting the legislative halls of Central Europe during the spring uprising:

> Every demand to abolish existing feudal dues and revoke rights which have until now been recognized by the state and protected by the courts because of the injustice, severity, and oppressiveness which may to some extent have come to be associated with them, every such demand . . . to break down by a stroke of the pen the distinction between right and wrong must be rejected. For we know that from the destruction of ledgers and registers of landed holdings it is but one step to the destruction of mortgage records and promissory notes, and from the destruction of promissory notes it is again but one step to the division of property or a common ownership of goods.[10]

On one side sounded warnings against the violation of proprietary rights; on the other rose demands for the abolition of manorial obligations. Confronted by this dilemma, the new order decided to trim sail. Wherever possible it postponed hard and fast commitments in agricultural disputes until popular passions subsided. But if neither temporization nor intimidation proved feasible, it offered concessions of sufficient scope to allay peasant excitement without kindling peasant enthusiasm. The rural legislation resulting from the March days was consequently neither original in principle

nor radical in application. It was a palliative by which liberalism mitigated rather than solved the agrarian problem.

The peasant insurrection achieved its greatest success in
Baden, where long before the Revolution progressive rulers
had been actively transforming customary dues into contractual rents on lands directly subject to their jurisdiction.
But the prerogatives of the mediatized nobility were protected
by Article XIV of the Act of Confederation, and proud aristocrats who still cherished memories of past greatness refused
to surrender their historic rights. In 1848 the sight of castles
burning in the spring sun brought them to their senses. By
March 10, when the government introduced a bill liquidating
all servile obligations, they were ready to make peace on
almost any terms. The lower chamber of the legislature gave
the measure its unanimous approval, and even in the upper
house only one member dared cast his vote against it. To be
sure, there were those like Count Waldkirch zu Binau who
wryly suggested that capitalists might emulate the example
of landowners by canceling the debts of the poor. Yet even
they realized that the only alternative to amortization was
expropriation, and the new agricultural law destroying manorialism once and for all was promulgated on April 10.[11]

In Württemberg the peasant was not as fortunate, although
there too he managed to extort important concessions from the
aristocracy. It did not take him long to discover that the pillage of a country house here and there and the devastation
of a few game preserves could work a remarkable change of
heart among bourgeois statesmen, mediatized noblemen, and
even crowned heads. At the end of March the king surrendered the royal hunting privileges, and a few weeks later
he issued an amnesty for violators of forest regulations. At
the same time the legislature was swiftly approving a bill
extinguishing several classes of manorial obligations. The law
of April 14 provided for the elimination of servile fees by
payments varying from twelve to sixteen times their annual

value. The government, moreover, agreed to advance the required capital in long-term credit at 4 per cent interest. Yet some of the most important customary dues like the tithe were still in effect, rural income continued to languish, and farm indebtedness remained dangerously high. In the face of the complex problems of Swabian marginal agriculture, liberalism remained as helpless as conservatism had been.[12]

In Bavaria overpopulation and land hunger were less serious, but rural reform was even more urgent. Whereas the rulers of Württemberg and Baden at least sensed that all was not well with the peasantry, no such doubts troubled the Wittelsbachs. Their agrarian policy had remained unchanged since the days of Montgelas. While King Ludwig I was transforming his provincial capital into the Florence of Germany and titillating his subjects with exotic amours, the faithful countryside paid its four hundred manorial dues and grumbled. Xenophobia and piety seemed to make of the mountain villagers unpromising material for a revolution, but when the spring uprising came, they too forgot their vaunted loyalty.

That was when the government began to pay attention to the wishes of the countryside. On March 27 the lower chamber of the legislature solicited the crown to order "the unavoidable commutation of land and feudal obligations and the repeal of mischievous hunting privileges." The advice was sound but unnecessary, for the ministry was already busily drafting a new agricultural law, and a few weeks later the measure was submitted to the diet. It won parliamentary approval, received the royal signature, and went into effect on June 4. Fees derived from bondage were abolished outright, and while the more lucrative dues on landed property remained, the peasant now satisfied them in money rather than labor or produce. What is more, he could liquidate them by remittances equivalent to eighteen times their annual value, borrowing the required capital from the public treasury at reasonable interest. Yet although the losses suffered by landowners under the terms of abrogation were sometimes as high as 33 per cent, economic conditions were so precarious that many farmers preferred the familiar burdens of manorialism to the unknown risks of free ownership.[13]

The pattern of peasant violence, liberal promise, and rural concession appeared again and again during the Revolution. Disturbed by the spring uprising, the government of Hesse-Darmstadt issued the usual pardon for infringements of forest ordinances, revoked exclusive hunting rights, extended commutation legislation to the possessions of the mediatized nobility, and abolished aristocratic judicial privileges. In Nassau the March days introduced a period of confusion during which the promulgation of agricultural reform was neither advisable nor feasible, for the farmer was defying the tax collector and playing the free proprietor in open violation of the law. Not until the end of the year did the authorities recover from fright long enough to assert themselves. On December 24 they provided for the liquidation of all tithes at sixteen times annual value and for amortization at 5 per cent. As for Hesse-Kassel, the elector made his concessions with that petty calculation which had become a tradition with his house. While the decree of August 26 declared most manorial dues commutable, the cost of extinction was twenty times annual value, the credit extended to the countryside was inadequate, and several of the more important prerogatives of the nobility remained untouched.[14]

In central Germany the peasant insurrection did not assume the same alarming proportions as in the south and west, and agricultural policy was therefore less conciliatory. The rulers usually contented themselves with a minor extension of earlier emancipation laws, as in Saxony and Hanover, or with the elimination of a few hunting and judicial privileges, as in Brunswick and Saxe-Meiningen. It is true that for the peasantry of some of the smaller principalities the revolution brought substantial benefits. The Weimar villager, for in-

stance, managed to free himself from many servile obligations and to consolidate his scattered holdings. Early in 1849
the government of Saxe-Altenburg introduced a program of
rural improvement eliminating manorial obligations. Even
tiny Schwarzburg-Rudolstadt took steps to end aristocratic
prerogatives and servile dues. But the example of these progressive measures was wasted on the larger states, which preferred to solve the agrarian problem by pretending that it
did not exist.[15]

When the country west of the Elbe served the time, what
could be expected of the conservative strongholds of the east?
The nobility of the Mecklenburgs, resisting all attempts to
curb its influence, succeeded in frustrating the hopes of agricultural reform aroused by the spring uprising. All that the
governments of the two Junker commonwealths would undertake was to mediate disputes between landlords and peasants
and to lease state domains to propertyless farm hands. And
in neighboring Schleswig-Holstein it was every man for himself. While foreign armies marched back and forth across the
duchies, the villagers of Dithmarschen and Wagrien proceeded to make demands on the squirearchy. Their audacity
was sometimes rewarded with a garden plot or a bit of mead-
owland, but the new order made no effort to disguise its
opposition to every manifestation of mob violence.[16]

In the meantime the Prussian constituent convention was
humbling the pride of the landowning aristocracy. On August
11 came a decree ending the privileged juridical and fiscal
status of the nobility, while on October 31 its hunting rights
were abrogated. The government also gave a pledge to alleviate the economic burdens of manorialism, and at the end of
April it announced its decision to draft an agricultural reform
bill. But the days turned into weeks and the weeks into
months, while the discussion of a state constitution monopo-
lized the attention of the legislators. Finally on October 9
the parliamentary mountain brought forth a mouse by order-

ing a halt to the negotiation of commutation agreements until a new law dealing with the agrarian problem should appear. There matters stood when the chamber was dissolved early in December.[17]

While the states were mollifying the peasantry with a patchwork of generous promises and temporizing measures, the national assembly was considering the agrarian problem *sub specie aeternitatis*. The task before it was the translation of economic concepts originating in manorial feudalism into those appropriate to industrial capitalism. To destroy all medieval institutional relics root and branch would inflict havoc on established rights, yet to leave them untouched would impede economic development. It therefore attempted by constitutional surgery to remove the dead tissue of the past without injuring the living body of the present. As it turned out, the operation was a textbook success, although neither doctor nor patient survived it.

The Frankfurt Parliament made short work of the class prerogatives of the aristocracy. Liberal resentment of high birth and high life redounded to the advantage of the peasantry, for the Fundamental Rights of the German People annulled servile disabilities, abrogated dues originating in the status of subordination, liquidated financial, judicial, and personal immunities derived from feudalism, and abolished the nobility as an estate and revoked its titles and dignities.[18]

There were those who saw a dangerous precedent in this unceremonious destruction of ancient rights, but most parliamentarians agreed with Heinrich Ahrens that there was a fundamental difference between bourgeois retribution and proletarian lawlessness:

We are dealing here only with civic equality, not with that crude, materialistic, communistic equality which seeks to do away with all natural differences in intellectual and physical endowment and to neutralize their consequences

[168]

in employment and in the acquisition of wealth. Civic equality is founded on right and justice. And justice, far from destroying the differences which arise out of the nature of man and the course of history, sees in them only the various aspects and forms which the organization of human nature assumes and which point toward one goal, the total development of human society in all its provinces and in all its relationships. . . . Hence the proposition that all men are equal before the law does not imply that a consistently uniform system of legislation leveling all differences ought to be introduced. It means rather that to all persons and things established in the same position the same laws must apply.[19]

The emancipation of the citizen from absolutism led logically to the liberation of his property from manorialism. The middle-class ethic, seeing in wealth the gratification of a natural acquisitive instinct rather than the appurtenance of a hereditary social position, had little patience with such practices as primogeniture, entailment, and mortmain. Paragraph 165 of the German constitution extended the right of ownership to include free disposition of landed holdings, while Paragraph 170 decreed the abolition of all estates in tail except those in the possession of a ruling house. The protests of aristocratic families like the Heynitzes, the Preuschens, the Bodelschwinghs, and the Schönburgs, moreover, aroused little sympathy among bourgeois statesmen who could still remember slights suffered under the Restoration.[20]

The argument that the repeal of inheritance restrictions would encourage the subdivision of farms and contribute to the impoverishment of the countryside was demolished by the brilliant Moritz Mohl amid the applause of his liberal colleagues:

Some will perhaps say that the institution of primogeniture is an aid to the maintenance of an industrious peasant class. But an industrious peasant class, gentlemen, ought not and needs not to maintain itself by the crutches of primogeniture. It maintains itself by its diligence and thrift. I have as yet to see anyone who works and saves go down and sink into ruin. Let us not provide for the maintenance of an industrious peasant class by creating a peasant aristocracy alongside a proletariat of day laborers. Let us rather make property obtainable by every man who is industrious, thrifty, and skillful. Freedom and equality, gentlemen, in economic matters as in political questions![21]

Parliamentarianism, however, would go only so far in the emancipation of the rural masses. Its destruction of the remnants of manorialism was not to be construed as an assault on the rights of ownership. These were sacred. To abolish obligations arising out of an unnatural condition of servitude was no more than just, but to lay violent hands on aristocratic deeds of title was an entirely different matter. The boundary between economic prerogative and economic equity could not be transgressed with impunity, for the system of private property was no stronger than its weakest link. Theodor Schneer was only expressing a bourgeois commonplace when he warned St. Paul's Church: "If you do not respect property in one instance, then you will see that those for whose benefit you committed the violation are also not respected. The propertyless, who are more numerous than the propertied, will lose the last vestiges of regard for ownership. They will no longer treat with consideration those goods which others acquired through injustice. Remember that respect for property is the basis of all civilization, and that the banner of justice must be raised side by side with the banner of freedom."[22]

It was not enough that Paragraph 164 of the German constitution declared property inviolable. The national assembly also proceeded to abrogate manorial modes of tenure and to commute customary dues on land. It attempted, in other words, to complete the transition of agriculture from a medieval system of landholding to a modern form of ownership by translating indefinite obligations into contractual rents, by eliminating outmoded qualifications of the rights of property, and by destroying vestigial practices of feudalism and serfdom. The prerogatives of the nobility as hereditary caste were annulled, but its claims as legitimate proprietor were respected. The liberals would not compromise their principles for partisan advantage. Right was right, and perplexed peasants therefore had to learn that while marriage fees were now illegal exactions, harvest tithes still remained valid obligations.[23]

Yet the distinction between dues derived from personal subservience and those originating in property rights was artificial. Both categories of obligations arose at the same time, for the same reason, in the same process. It was not the feudal baron but the nineteenth-century bureaucrat who created these subtle nuances in the economic institutions of the Middle Ages. Attempting to reorganize an antiquated system of agriculture in accordance with the demands of industrial capitalism, he began to manufacture classifications and divisions where none had previously existed. The differentiation of servile duties from rent liabilities was only the legal fiction of parliamentarians resolved to overthrow the domination of the landed aristocracy without endangering the position of the moneyed bourgeoisie.

In the country as in the city liberalism was acting on the postulates of classical economics with respect to the exercise of ownership, the status of dependence, and the employment of labor. It substituted a cash nexus for the corporate bond, and in place of the outworn institution of personal servitude it prepared to establish a system of financial compulsion. Thus it carried on the historic mission of benevolent despots like Margrave Karl Friedrich and enlightened statesmen like Baron Stein, the mission of emancipation, commutation, and rationalization. In so doing, however, it renounced the advantages of a policy of opportunism. As a child of the Revolution it might have expropriated the nobility and formed an alliance with the peasantry capable of withstanding reactionary blandishments. As the party of law and order there was nothing for it to do but continue the work which conservatism had begun and which conservatism could conclude. At the end it was overthrown in the name of the same legality which it had upheld with such scrupulousness.[24]

For the rural masses did not share the compunctions of bourgeois constitutionalists. To them all means improving their economic status were justifiable. What did they care about property rights and contractual obligations? They wanted relief from population pressure and land hunger, not sermons and half measures. In the March days their hopes had seemed so close to realization. And then, instead of abolishing manorial obligations and partitioning aristocratic estates, constituent conventions began to promulgate laws which were fundamentally the same as those which legitimate princes used to issue. Rents in money were as burdensome as fees in kind, crops and prices were no better under parliamentarianism than under absolutism. In all things which really mattered the new order was indistinguishable from the old. Little by little the peasant lost the enthusiasm inspired in him by the spring uprising, and liberalism was left at last to shift for itself in the impending struggle with the forces of reaction.

10

THE FALL OF LIBERALISM

By the end of 1848 the bourgeoisie of Europe was in retreat before the forces of a revived conservatism. It was symptomatic of the altered political situation that everywhere the moderate heroes of the spring uprising were being displaced by the leaders of the far left and the far right. Lamartine was now only a mediocre poet who had once dabbled in affairs of state, Robert Blum died before a firing squad in Brigittenau, and a sad pontiff was meditating on his errors in the exile of Gaeta. The men of the hour were the Kossuths, Mazzinis, and Bakunins whose impassioned visions reflected the feverish state of Continental radicalism *in extremis*. Here and there the curtain fell even before the year was out. From the Hofburg in Vienna a new emperor and a new prime minister began to pursue legitimist policies in the tradition of the Holy Alliance. In France a tired and frightened nation entrusted its fortunes to Louis Napoleon, a sphinx without a riddle. And Frederick William IV renounced his parliamentary faith with the same romantic fervor with which he had embraced it a few months before.

For Germany developments in Prussia determined the outcome of the Revolution. The secondary states, which even under the Restoration had rarely dared defy the wishes of the two leading powers of Central Europe, lost their last illusions of independence after the spring uprising. Commanding neither the armies nor the resources of the Habsburgs or the Hohenzollerns, they were helpless before the triumphant bourgeoisie. Once Austria and Prussia made peace with constitutionalism, there was no course open to them but surrender. The petty princes, waiting until the new order had become sufficiently enervated to make a counterrevolution

[173]

possible, watched in dismay, as parliamentarians overrode their wishes, dismissed their favorites, curtailed their prerogatives, and reduced their incomes.

A measure of comfort awaited them on December 2 in the news of the abdication of Ferdinand I of Austria, for it was obvious that the emperor was being retired on account of the pledges he had made to liberalism. His youthful successor Francis Joseph did not disappoint them, and with his accession the Hofburg adopted a program of undisguised reaction. But the vigorous resistance of the Magyars to Habsburg centralization absorbed all the energies of the new government for almost a year. Not before 1850 was it able to turn its full attention to affairs in the north, and by then its enemy was no longer the liberal nationalism of Frankfurt but the conservative nationalism of Berlin. Hungarian troops fighting along the Danube enabled Prussia to pursue an independent policy in Germany for the first time since the days of Frederick the Great, and during about twelve months Frederick William IV was in a position to determine the fate of Central Europe.

Those who had watched him ride through the streets of his capital after the March days had seen only a frightened, middle-aged figure on horseback, pathetically eager to please the world with his political conversion. The army was demoralized, the aristocracy grumbled and sulked, the bureaucracy could only whine. Never before had a Hohenzollern suffered such mortification at the hands of his subjects. All the historic props of the dynasty had suddenly toppled, and the monarch was left to the mercy of his opponents. In the chaotic atmosphere of the spring uprising all thoughts of stemming the tide seemed not only quixotic but dangerous, and the bewildered king could think of nothing to do but drift with the current.

There was one statesman, however, who saw the situation in clearer perspective. For Radowitz the Revolution was more than an unmitigated disaster. It was also the opportunity for a political reorganization of Germany under Prussian auspices and the introduction of a conservative program of social reform. Liberalism with its narrow outlook and shopkeeping philosophy could not in the long run satisfy the needs of a modern nation. While the spring uprising had created a serious danger for legitimate rulers, it had also removed the obstacles to a reconstruction of their states on a sounder foundation. For the time being they must accept the new order, but only until it had alienated the masses by its inevitable inequities. When the right moment came, the princes were to overthrow the tottering system of constitutionalism and establish in its place a monarchism of civic justice and economic welfare. Out of the fires of insurrection a new royalism of the mind and heart would emerge to defend the thrones of Christendom.

In his correspondence with the king Radowitz advocated a struggle against liberalism with the aid of the lower classes. On March 16, shortly before the Berlin uprising, he wrote: "The socialist movement considered as the struggle of the proletariat for a secure existence and for the organization of labor: This new enormous force has been ridiculed as utopian or been suppressed by means of the police. If left to shift for itself, it will certainly destroy the entire organization of modern states, regardless of what constitution they adopt. But precisely because it stands outside doctrinaire politics, it can provide new and large resources for the monarchical principle and may form a powerful counterweight even within the representative system."[1] The catastrophe which overwhelmed the government a few days later did not shake his conviction, for on March 28 he was still maintaining: "The socialist elements, which unhappily for our times have fallen into the hands of political radicalism, must be divorced from it. The proletariat as such is far from republican, although this is a very popular error. Any form of government which defends its interests boldly and wisely, which advocates the progressive income tax, the system of poor relief, the regulation of conflicts between capital and labor, will have 'the common man' on its side and thus a powerful force. This is admittedly a dangerous course, but what is not dangerous right now?"[2] And in his memorandum of April 20 he continued to urge "a fearless advance with grand measures in favor of the proletariat: the question of the progressive tax, the regulation of the relationship between capital and labor, the system of poor relief."[3]

It required more resolution than Frederick William IV possessed to act on this advice. Throughout the spring he was troubled by memories of the March days, by the smell of gunpowder and the sight of corpses. He was ready to admit that his friend's plan was "profound and true," and he was firmly determined to oppose republicanism with all means at his disposal. He hesitated, however, to endorse an untried program of social reform, and his reply to Radowitz referred to it only in passing: "I want it with the help of God, but I am terribly short of men who can assist me. Nevertheless, the Lord in whom I truly place my trust will aid."[4]

Still, the argument in favor of a conservative policy of material welfare intrigued the king, even if it did not entirely convince him. On April 21 he communicated his views to Leopold von Gerlach, who left a gloomy account of the interview:

Thereupon I went to the tearoom of the queen, but the king called me back and read to me a letter with a memorandum from Radowitz describing what we ought to do now. The king found everything in it admirable, but I was less impressed. The gist of Radowitz's advice was that the king must now follow the path of constitutionalism and champion the working class, the so-called proletarians, against the bourgeoisie. His suggestions even went as far

[176]

as the communistic progressive tax, which he expressly recommended. What is more, and this is a frightful thought,
the king must remain in the background and leave everything to his ministers. In case it should come to a republic,
he urged war. What bad advice![5]

To Gerlach as to most Prussian aristocrats Radowitz was
still the parlor revolutionary, the papist, the alien. They distrusted his radical economics and opportunistic politics. In his
proposals they saw only devious subtleties which confused
right with wrong and played directly into the hands of the
enemy. Theirs was the uncompromising conservatism of
Junkers accustomed to the blind obedience of peasants and
soldiers. They approached statecraft with the same uncompli-
cated assurance with which they managed estates or maneu-
vered troops. It was their conviction that the spring uprising
had been nothing more than an inflated riot engineered by
foreign agitators, by Frenchmen, Poles, and Jews. At first the
weakness of the king had prevented the restoration of law and
order by the army, but now the parliamentary farce had gone
far enough. "We must have a reaction," Bismarck told Reinhold von Thadden-Trieglaff in June.[6]

The news that Minister of Finance David Hansemann was
preparing to end the tax exemptions of the nobility and to
extinguish the manorial obligations of the peasantry became
the immediate occasion for the formation of a conservative
party. Shaking off the lethargy which had seized them after
the March days, the Junkers resolved to found a newspaper
willing to defy the liberal press. Landlords concerned for the
safety of their possessions proved generous with funds, and
in Hermann Wagener they found a publicist of considerable
gifts. The *Neue Preussische Zeitung*, which first appeared in
the early weeks of summer, won immediate attention by the
boldness with which it challenged the shibboleths of the hour.
Its device with the Iron Cross and the motto "Forward with

God for king and fatherland!" proclaimed an unrepentant royalism, and its pages summoned the nation to "true freedom and true progress," to regard for the church, to love of country, and to hatred for the works of revolution. Yet it was as hostile to the bureaucratic absolutism of enlightened monarchy as to the radical egalitarianism of popular democracy. Opposing the paper constitutionalism of doctrinaire speculation with the historic constitutionalism of national tradition, it sought a restoration of the corporate balance between crown and estates which had prevailed in the Middle Ages.[7]

After the successful inauguration of their journalistic enterprise the Junkers opened an ambitious recruitment program. While the Frankfurt Parliament was painstakingly elaborating its blueprints of freedom, the plains beyond the Elbe began to sprout with "Fatherland Associations," "Prussian Associations," and "Associations for King and Fatherland." Black-and-white Hohenzollern cockades appeared in the sea of revolutionary tricolors, and here and there amid the cheers for the new fatherland could be heard the voices of particularism. The shades of the Great Elector and Old Fritz paraded before gatherings of farmers, memories of Yorck and Blücher were refurbished in village inns, loyal countrymen chilled at tales of outrages inflicted on their king by the reds in the capital. Landowners, moreover, knew how to strengthen dynastic devotion by the judicious distribution of favors, and more than one peasant won a mitigation of manorial obligations by signing a declaration of allegiance to his sovereign.

By the middle of the summer the conservatives were ready to challenge liberalism in its stronghold. On August 18 and 19 the Association for the Protection of Property and the Advancement of the Welfare of All Classes met in Berlin to concert measures in opposition to the agricultural policies of the ministry. The designation "Junker Parliament" which the democrats derisively bestowed on the assembly was apt, for among its leading figures were Hans von Kleist-Retzow, Ludwig von Gerlach, Ernst von Bülow-Cummerow, Otto von Bismarck, and Reinhold von Thadden-Trieglaff. These proud noblemen of the eastern marches prepared to fight the new order with its own weapons. They deliberated, debated, resolved, and voted in the best parliamentary fashion, discussing problems of taxation, agreeing on common legislative objectives, and appointing committees to court public opinion and direct the struggle against constitutionalism. Before the eyes of startled bourgeois statesmen arose the phantom of a popular reaction led by the aristocracy and defended by a proletariat disillusioned with their achievements.[8]

The Junkers openly announced their readiness to outbid parliamentarianism for the support of the lower classes. The program by which they strove to return to power spoke of the need for economic reform in the same breath in which it swore loyalty to the throne. It called on the nobility to protect the weak and oppressed, while to the lower classes it preached the virtues of faithfulness and obedience. "If this honorable assembly shares my views," Bülow-Cummerow told the Association for the Protection of Property, "we will refrain from all political dispute and thus avoid conflicts leading to disunion. Material interests have a significance outweighing all others, and by pursuing them we will always be on firm ground. Let us exert all our energies to advance these interests. If we are successful, we can count on the approval of the broad masses of the population and of all propertied groups. . . . Let us work toward our goal harmoniously, actively, wisely, and boldly."[9]

In industry conservative strategy was to champion the handicraftsman against the millowner. The nobleman and the artisan discovered that they had common foes in financiers, manufacturers, and merchants. Both were threatened by the growth of industrial capitalism, both sought security in a privileged status for their corporate rights. From its first days the *Neue Preussische Zeitung* condemned "anarchic industrial freedom" and emphasized the need to revive craft trades. In the pietistic circles in which the Gerlachs moved there was talk about the defense of man against the machine. Influential aristocrats like Count Otto von Schlippenbach appealed to all men of good will to help feed the hungry and shelter the homeless. And Hermann Wagener was only one of many reactionary intellectuals endorsing with enthusiasm a handicraft movement which parliamentarianism feared and condemned.[10]

In agriculture the conservatives acted with greater circumspection. While Radowitz suggested with characteristic venturesomeness that the state hasten the elimination of manorial obligations by paying one third of the extinction cost, most Junkers found such a remedy more pernicious than the disease. They were not prepared to purchase political success by the sacrifice of their economic interests, and their appeals to the countryside envisioned a rectification of abuses in the forms of landownership rather than an alteration in the forms themselves. Basically they did not promise to do more than the liberals, but to do it more promptly and more effectively. They agreed only to the surrender of judicial and police privileges, the commutation of servile dues, and the establishment of rural credit institutions.[11]

The moment was favorable to a reaction. The vitality of the new order had been slowly sapped by the conflict between those who feared that it was going too far and those maintaining that it was not going far enough. On one side were the respectable, the timid, the wealthy, those who had always considered the revolution a dangerous experiment. For them the course of events was confirming the direst prophecies of the sages of the *juste-milieu*. On the night of June 15 they watched in alarm as the populace looted the Berlin arsenal, seizing arms which might be used before long in a new insurrection against established authority. They read frightening newspaper accounts of the death of Prince Felix Lichnowsky and General Hans von Auerswald, lynched on September 18 by a Frankfurt mob aroused through radical oratory. And at the end of October they heard a democratic congress endorse demands for the public ownership of the transportation system, the introduction of a progressive income tax, and the establishment of national workshops. Faced with the danger of social anarchy, these reluctant rebels began to entertain second thoughts about popular sovereignty.

Dissatisfaction was also rife on the other side, among the artisans and mill hands who had fought to make possible the victory of the Revolution. They were discovering that the new order was slow to fulfill extravagant promises made in the heat of battle. Wages remained low, hours were still long, and guilds proved as powerless as before, while industrialists continued to expand factories and build machines. To be sure the hungry could always earn a pittance in the public works, but this was a far cry from the vision of financial security which had been held out to the lower classes on the barricades. While the civic guard excluded the handicraftsman from its ranks, the police spied on his clubs and the constituent convention ignored his petitions. Bitter and disillusioned, the masses were ready to withdraw from the alliance with the middle class which had brought them so little advantage.[12]

The incompatibility of bourgeois and proletarian was dramatically demonstrated on October 16 in the clash between the civic guard and the Berlin mob. A few days earlier a group of canal diggers in Köpenick had destroyed a recently installed mechanical pump, and the authorities retaliated with the summary dismissal of about a hundred of them. The outcome was a labor demonstration complete with revolutionary slogan, red flag, and armed escort. Taunts led to threats, threats to stones, stones to bullets, bullets to barricades. Before the day was over ten workers had been killed by the guardians of public safety. Liberalism had shown that it could defend itself against friends even more successfully than against enemies, and on the morrow the city council adopted by unanimous vote a resolution of thanks to the police for their devotion to duty. At the same time a request submitted by the populace to the constituent convention for the punishment of the instigators of the disastrous encounter was shunted to the ministry of justice, where it was promptly lost in the labyrinth of the bureaucratic machinery.[13]

The conflict on the field of Köpenick reflected in microcosm the tragedy of the Revolution. It brought a sense of foreboding to parliamentarians, but in the conservative camp all was jubilation. The *Neue Preussische Zeitung* editorialized with malicious satisfaction:

The Berlin civic guard seems now to have reached the conclusion that there are situations and occasions when it is permissible to fire not only on the people, but even on "the sovereign people itself." As long as the brutal soldiery maintained "law and order," its first duty was to allow itself to be stoned to death peacefully. But as soon as such an attack is directed against the civic guard, it becomes high treason against the sovereignty of the people and must be suppressed in blood. And yet the attacks and insults to which the soldiers had been exposed were just as great, and the soldiers themselves are children of "the same sovereign people." While now the opponents were only seduced children of the nation, at that time they had been seducers and men in whom not a single drop of Prussian blood flowed.[14]

Discord between the propertied and the propertyless brought new resolution to the vacillating king of Prussia. After the spring uprising he succeeded in persuading himself that he believed all the things he was saying to win popular support, and for a few weeks he managed to play the constitutional monarch with convincing realism. But it was not long before he tired of the liberal masquerade. By June he was once again a romantic legitimist, confessing to Bismarck his displeasure with the constituent convention, and bluntly telling Camphausen that "after this ministry I shall move not to the left, but to the right." Throughout the summer he continued to mutter about the dangerous policies of parliamentarianism and the unshakable loyalty of the countryside, although he could not bring himself to face the risk of a new insurrection. What finally persuaded him was the spontaneous acclaim which met him on all sides as he traveled to Cologne for the cathedral festival on August 14. Here was unmistakable proof of the fidelity of his people, and in a letter to his sister Alexandra Feodorovna, empress of Russia, he overflowed with gratification:

> Despite its exhausting demands the journey to Cologne was a refreshing draught for me. Never until my dying day will I forget the love and devotion which greeted me in our ancient lands, in Brandenburg, Magdeburg, in Minden, Ravensberg, the County of Mark, and the faithful Cleve country. All of that is genuine and unembellished, and it could be read in eyes filled with tears even more clearly than in deafening shouts of joy. Also in the Berg valleys, in Elberfeld and Barmen, and in the Münster region I was never received as warmly and joyfully as now. The reception in Cologne was sincere and true in the wild enthusiasm of the moment, and for the good people of Cologne the moment was great and moving and exalted.[15]

Convinced at last that the nation was on his side, the king decided to dispense with parliamentary rule and take the reins in his own hands. The liberal statesmen of the March days had been replaced early in the summer by ministers reflecting the political leanings of the cautious bourgeoisie and progressive bureaucracy. While not as actively reformist as the Camphausen government had been, the Auerswald cabinet sought to maintain harmonious relations with the constituent convention, and thereby it incurred the displeasure of the court. When it showed itself unable to resist legislative claims to control over the army, the holy of holies of royal prerogative, Frederick William IV accepted its resignation and began to look for advisers made of sterner stuff. By the middle of September he was discussing the organization of a conservative ministry with Hermann von Beckerath, but the man who had once led the Rhenish opposition to kingly arbitrariness refused to become the cat's-paw of the reaction. That was when the call went out to General Ernst von Pfuel, who had endeared himself to nationalist circles by the dispatch with which he had suppressed the Polish insurrection in Posen. Having successfully coped with a dangerous revolutionary like Ludwik Mierosławski, the brave soldier would surely be able to handle the Unruhs, Waldecks, and Jacobys of the assembly in Berlin.

The general, however, turned out to be a paper tiger. He was awed by the strange world of parliamentary decorum, the world without obsequious orderlies and aides. His tone before the constituent convention was conciliatory, even respectful. He assured its members that he looked forward to the completion of the constitution, that he proposed to give them a faithful account of his activities, and that he would suppress reactionary agitation in the armed forces. In a chosen instrument of conservatism such sentiments were intolerable, and within four weeks after the appointment of Pfuel the king was looking for his successor. He approached Gustav von Bonin, then Franz von Eichmann, and finally Radowitz himself, but they all managed to beg off for one reason or another.

In the meantime the reactionaries could see the political situation going from bad to worse. Soon after opening plenary discussion of the constitution on October 12, the assembly resolved to strike the time-honored formula "by the grace of

God" from the title of the sovereign. On the 16th came the tragic clash between the civic guard and the canal workers. Ten days later a democratic congress in Berlin began its deliberations with republican speeches and radical demands. And on the evening of the 31st a wild mob besieged the constituent convention to demand aid for the crumbling revolutionary government of Austria. The time was ripe for a reaction, perhaps overripe. The king overcame his fears at last, and on November 2 Prussia learned that it had found its savior in the person of Count Friedrich Wilhelm von Brandenburg.

Born of the morganatic marriage between Frederick William II and the beautiful Countess Sophie von Dönhoff, the man of the hour was more of a Hohenzollern than his royal nephew. As commanding general in Silesia he had maintained harsh discipline in radical Breslau, and as political head he was equally unyielding toward radical Berlin. There was a military peremptoriness about the corrective decrees which swiftly descended on the bewildered capital. The session of the constituent convention was transferred to the provincial isolation of the town of Brandenburg and prorogued until November 27. The civic guard was disbanded, martial law was proclaimed, and the parliamentary hall was occupied by soldiers. While the prime minister hoped that the country would acquiesce in the reassertion of the kingly prerogative, he was ready, as befitted a good officer, to use muskets to enforce obedience. General Friedrich von Wrangel in command of the troops in the marches had been waiting impatiently since the first weeks of autumn for the summons to avenge the disgrace of the spring uprising. The good tidings came at last, and on November 10 he led his 13,000 men into the city.[16]

The first test of the counterrevolution proved a success. During the March days the Berlin mob had fought against the troops with unrelenting determination. Eight months later the same troops re-entered the capital without firing a shot. The *Neue Preussische Zeitung* crowed triumphantly in its headlines about the "total victory without bayonets of General Wrangel." The brother of the king, the future William I, noted that "the troops have found a friendly reception." The *Neue Münchner Zeitung* found that "the city is completely peaceful." The *Bayerische Landbötin* concurred. Even Wilhelm Löwe, the democratic leader in the Frankfurt Parliament, conceded that "this city maintains the most exemplary order, while the troops march in." Liberalism could no longer conjure up the spirit of insurrection at will. It waved the magic wand and repeated the secret incantation, but no barricades arose in its defense. It stood alone in a rising tide of reaction.[17]

The parliamentarians tried to assure each other that the people were still with them, and the *Neue Rheinische Zeitung* even affected an air of insouciance: "It is no wonder that in a city of 420,000 inhabitants with about 30,000 burghers, where many are born reactionaries for pecuniary considerations, so to speak, there are a few thousand men of wealth who are glad 'to get back to the good old days,' as the Berliner puts it."[18] But the new order was whistling in the dark. The truth was that all classes of society welcomed the return of monarchical authority. The bourgeoisie saw in troops the guardians of law and order against the dark forces of anarchy. Workers, remembering recent battles with the civic guard, cheered "Papa" Wrangel as their champion against middle-class exploitation. And the ladies found a uniform as irresistible as ever. In vain did liberalism call on the country to oppose the reaction with the weapons of passive resistance. Its appeal remained unanswered.[19]

The conservative coup culminated on December 5 in the dissolution of the constituent convention and the promulgation of a constitution by royal decree. The court, reluctant to risk a frontal assault on the new order, preferred to divide its enemies by granting the shadow of their demands without the substance. The state charter paid its respects to liberalism in a bill of rights, an elected legislature, and an independent judiciary. Yet it was also careful to confer on the sovereign exclusive control of the armed forces, an absolute veto over legal enactments, and the authority to issue emergency decrees between sessions of parliament. This was a constitutional document without teeth, a document establishing royal domination under the guise of popular rule. For the militant radicals it did not give enough and for the out-and-out reactionaries it gave too much, but to thousands tired of party strife it offered an acceptable compromise between freedom and security.[20]

The conservatives, however, would not content themselves with the suppression of parliamentarianism. Their ambition was to win a public vote of confidence in the elections to the legislature. They could have manufactured a paper victory easily enough by manipulating suffrage requirements, and there were many frightened bourgeois statesmen like David Hansemann who urged the government to disfranchise the masses. As a matter of fact, the law of December 6 did restrict the right to vote for members of the lower chamber to "independent citizens," so that the *Neue Rheinische Zeitung* confidently assured its readers that "they want to exclude all servants, journeymen, etc. from eligibility for the ballot." But the cabinet surprised friend and foe alike by deciding on December 19 that no one should be barred from the polls for reasons of dependence, while Minister of the Interior Otto von Manteuffel added to the general wonderment by instructing local officials to protect the electorate against improper influence. The forthcoming vote was to be a free popular referendum on the policy of reaction.[21]

Since Frederick William IV agreed with his advisers that the support of the countryside was vital to his cause, he made a resolute effort to conciliate the peasantry. A royal patent of December 5 spoke of "the improvement in the condition of the rural population, which is especially close to our heart," and promised the prompt enactment of measures dealing with the commutation of manorial dues, the annulment of feudal privileges, and the elimination of tax exemptions. Article XXXVIII of the constitution prohibited the establishment of new entailments, while Article XL put an end to the police powers of the nobility. On December 20 the government issued a decree providing for the extinction of servile obligations in Silesia, and on January 2 the right of private jurisdiction was abolished without compensation. It was common knowledge, moreover, that the ministry was working day and night to draft a law settling the agrarian problem once and for all.[22]

Conservatism knew also how to play on urban grievances. The *Neue Preussische Zeitung*, seeing in the artisan a potential ally, summoned guilds to an attack on political and industrial freedom. The gruff Wrangel displayed surprising geniality toward a visiting labor delegation and even offered to contribute 150 marks to the welfare fund of the machinists' association. In an address to the voters of Nessin near Kolberg the king himself assured the country of his concern for "the poor and the propertyless, whose lot I am most anxious to improve." To demonstrate that his words were more than pious generalities, Minister of Commerce August von der Heydt convoked in Berlin on January 17 a commission composed of 24 handicraftsmen and 20 manufacturers and merchants to consider a revision of economic legislation. The bureaucracy of the capital listened in respectful sympathy to the wishes of the artisan representatives, the government submitted to them the draft of a new industrial law, and their sovereign received them in a warm and gracious audience. There could be no mistaking which way the wind was blowing. The reaction was bidding for the friendship of the urban proletariat by offering the prospect of a revival of corporate trade regulation.[23]

The elections of January 22 vindicated the conservative strategy. Their outcome was a limited but distinct victory for the royalist cause, a victory all the more remarkable in view of the catastrophe which had befallen legitimism the preceding year. The government could count on about 184 members of the lower chamber, while its opponents numbered only 160. Unregenerate Berlin returned all nine democratic candidates, but the towns and villages of the provinces supported the court. Dyed-in-the-wool reactionaries like Leopold von Gerlach still growled about the rebels who had managed to worm their way into the assembly. The radicals, on the other hand, were profoundly depressed by what they had to recognize as a popular rebuke to their fire-eating tactics. Yet to most discerning observers like Gustav Mevissen or even Otto von Bismarck it was clear that public opinion was turning toward counterrevolution in its quest for stability.[24]

The results at the polls dispelled the last doubts of the government regarding the wisdom of its economic policy. The commission considering the correction of industrial abuses did not conclude its deliberations until January 30, eight days after the elections, but a promise to follow its recommendations could still influence the electoral colleges, which were to meet February 5. "You see how conciliatory toward you we have been," Minister Heydt told one of the Westphalian representatives at the trade conference. "Now be grateful and do not send us too many democrats."[25] He assured the members that their wishes would soon be met in favorable legislation, and he proved as good as his word. On February 9 the cabinet promulgated two emergency measures which halted the trend to industrial freedom inaugurated forty years before by Hardenberg.

In some seventy crafts admission became contingent on guild approval through trade examinations and apprenticeship requirements. The simultaneous practice of several occupations and the store sale of artisan wares were restricted, while the truck system of wage payment was prohibited outright. Benevolent labor associations, originally established under the law of January 17, 1845, were strengthened by the provision that shop owners and manufacturers could be compelled to contribute to their funds. If local conditions proved favorable, moreover, industrial councils representing employers and employees were to be established to investigate economic conditions and advise the government of needed reforms. Finally, wherever feasible municipal authorities could organize trade courts authorized to deal with disputes between masters and journeymen, industrialists and mill hands, and merchants and helpers.[26]

The peasantry also found a champion in conservatism. The address with which Frederick William IV opened the session of the legislature on February 26 announced his intention to submit to it "laws for the commutation of manorial obligations, for the uncompensated abolition of some of these obligations, and for the establishment of loan banks." Even as he spoke, Minister of the Interior Manteuffel was putting the final touches to the measures. Many of the Junkers protested against the sacrifices they were being forced to make, while the king hesitated and the queen prayed. Manteuffel, however, remained adamant, and his views finally prevailed. On April 10 the proposals of the cabinet won royal assent, and two weeks later they were presented to parliament. Their enactment was postponed for almost a year, for the lower house was dissolved on April 27 after its endorsement of the Frankfurt Parliament. But the government had clearly shown a willingness to pay as much for rural favor as liberalism had offered.[27]

The Prussian experiment in political reaction and economic reform was observed with great interest by conservative circles throughout Central Europe. At first they still feared a new uprising in favor of parliamentary government, but developments in eastern Germany soon taught them how to defeat constitutionalism at its own game. If they conciliated the populace with welfare legislation, the new order would find itself deserted by the lower classes. The legitimists soon mastered the art of the *quid pro quo*, while the bourgeois statesmen of the revolution prepared for the retreat from national prominence to retirement or exile.

During the spring and summer of 1849 the reaction prosecuted with vigor the program of agricultural improvement initiated the previous year under liberal auspices. In Württemberg the tithe was commuted on June 17, feudal jurisdiction was annulled on July 4, and hunting privileges were ended on August 17. In Nassau the law of April 14 provided for the extinction of all remaining manorial obligations by payments equivalent to eighteen times their annual value. In Hesse-Darmstadt the decree of May 2 abolished the status of servility and the dues derived from it. The Thuringian principalities were busily engaged in the elimination of labor services, the liquidation of tenure fees, and the extension of farm credit. Everywhere radical clubs were being dissolved and conservative ministries were taking office, but the peasant saw in the counterrevolution only the executor of a policy of rural reform. Since neither the bourgeoisie nor the aristocracy was prepared to satisfy his most cherished ambition, the achievement of free proprietorship through the expropriation of the landlords, he settled for a compensated emancipation, and thereafter his interest in the struggle between constitutionalism and absolutism waned. The last act of the Revolution was played out on a crowded stage, but before an empty house.[28]

In industry conservatism could afford to do more than merely outliberalize the liberals. It bid boldly for the support of the urban proletariat by reintroducing corporate regulation of production. Through the association of an economic with a political reaction it hoped to create a mass following for the policy of counterrevolution. Hence the royalist victory in Prussia was followed by the promulgation of the two emergency measures of February 9 revitalizing the atrophied guild system. On April 3 Nassau, a stronghold of industrial freedom for thirty years, imposed residence and examination requirements on the artisans of the duchy. In June the toy-men of Sonneberg celebrated a great victory when the government of Saxe-Meiningen established corporate control over their trade. And in Saxe-Gotha the four provisional statutes of September 24 accorded a high degree of occupational self-government to the handicraftsmen of the capital city and of the towns of Ohrdruf, Waltershausen, and Ichtershausen.[29]

By the time the members of the Frankfurt Parliament finished their work, the political situation was radically different from what it had been when they first entered St. Paul's Church amid the hurrahs of the crowd. Then absolutism was humble and particularism weak as a result of the March days. Austria and Prussia, torn by revolution, teetered on the brink of dissolution. The national assembly was all that stood between society and chaos. At that moment liberalism could have imposed on the old order whatever parliamentary settlement it liked. But a year had now elapsed, and conservatism had found new hope and new courage. Since dynastic loyalty was once again a rival to national patriotism, it was no longer possible to dictate terms to kings and princes. The execution of a program of constitutional reform was feasible only with the co-operation of at least one of the two leading states of Central Europe, and Francis Joseph had already announced his preference for a unified Habsburg state over a unified Germany. It was therefore as much by necessity as choice that on March 28 the Frankfurt Parliament voted unenthusiastically to offer the imperial dignity to Frederick William IV.

In its summons to the Hohenzollern Hamlet liberalism was leaning on a broken reed. As early as December he had spoken sneeringly of "the crown from the gutter," coining a phrase immortalized in a thousand textbooks, and in April he confided to Hermann von Beckerath in a classic understatement that he was no Frederick the Great. The delegation which came to invite him to accept the German crown was met with a refusal, although it was characteristic that even the royal "no" was hedged in with qualifications and conditions. The declination of Prussia to embrace parliamentarianism forced a cruel dilemma on the national assembly. It could admit defeat, or it had to attempt to complete its mission by reviving the spirit of insurrection which had once moved mountains. For the moderates there was no choice. They packed their bags, said their farewells, and went home. The radicals who were left masters of St. Paul's Church decided to give effect to the federal constitution by popular force. The Revolution therefore ended as it had begun with a spring uprising.[30]

There was, however, a world of difference between the March days of 1848 and the May days of 1849. The masses which had once battled in streets and fields for the victory of the new order watched impassively as it went down in defeat twelve months later. The only support that constitutionalism could still find was the militant petty bourgeoisie of Dresden, Breslau, Elberfeld, Düsseldorf, Karlsruhe, and Kaiserslautern. In place of the peasants and workers who would no longer fight for freedom the parliamentary cause was forced to seek its champions among professional revolutionaries like Mikhail Bakunin, visionary artists like Richard Wagner, idealistic students like Carl Schurz, and radical politicians like Lorenz Brentano. It found in them followers who could strike poses and deliver speeches, but who were no match for the disciplined troops of the reaction. Only in the southwest, where the regular army decided to throw in its lot with the Revolution, did the insurrectionary government manage to hold out for more than a few days. And there too the proletariat turned a deaf ear to pleas for assistance. In the Palatinate no more than about 8,000 men in a population of 600,000 responded to democratic appeals, while in Baden with 1,300,000 inhabitants only some 40,000 rallied to the defense of republicanism.

Yet even in this hour of supreme danger the middle class remained true to itself. It met disaster with unsullied ideology and consistent principle. It would not compromise with the counterrevolution, but neither did it coquet with the masses. Friedrich Engels who advised the dissolution of the civic guard, the arming of the workers, and the adoption of the red flag found himself ostracized by the high command of the insurrection. Well-to-do citizens were asked to support the uprising by voluntary contribution, for confiscation was logically incompatible with the doctrines of parliamentarianism. And the proletariat of Elberfeld was warned against transforming the struggle for constitutional liberty into a war of class interest: "Citizens, the city is in the hands of the people. Now the people must show its appreciation of true freedom. Therefore no single individual ought to decide questions of person and property, and still less ought the people to attack person or property. Let the motto of a free people be: 'The person is inviolable, property is sacred!' "[31]

On July 23 Rastatt, the last stronghold of democracy, fell, and with its surrender the revolution was at an end. Gone were the hopes which had inspired liberalism in its years of innocence under the Restoration. A new age was opening which would see in the enthusiasms of the March days nothing more than the growing pains of a national adolescence. Something youthful and ingenuous vanished from the political life of Central Europe after 1848, and in its place came the disillusioned egotism of an acquisitive society worshipping its cakes and ale. The heroes of this society, mirroring the unscrupulous energy of their time, found their destiny not in the realm of ideals but on the battlefield of deeds. One of them who had seen the rise and fall of German parliamentarianism composed its epitaph with that brutal directness which was to bring him fame as the Iron Chancellor. "They inflicted on us a revolution," wrote Bismarck on July 4, 1850, "with which not even 10,000 inhabitants of the kingdom besides the Poles were in fundamental agreement, and then they won sympathy for it only by promising the moon to the peasants and the workers."[32]

PART THREE

REACTION

Es giebt nur ein Mittel der Herrschaft, der Herrschaft über freie Menschen und Christen, und das
ist der Dienst, der Dienst für die Hebung der bis
dahin gesellschaftlich und staatlich unterworfenen
Klassen, und alles "Königthum wird fortan ent-
weder ein leerer Schatten oder eine Despotie werden oder untergehen in Republik, wenn es nicht den
hohen sittlichen Muth hat, ein Königthum der
socialen Reform zu werden."

HERMANN WAGENER (1855)

11

THE CONSERVATIVE FIFTIES

TIME has been unkind to the reaction. After dwelling with painstaking detail on every obscure putschist of the Revolution, the scholar usually dismisses the Fifties with a few remarks about obscurantist tyranny and hurries on to grapple with the Bismarckian enigma. The liberal will neither forget nor forgive aristocratic oppression of parliamentarianism. Even the confirmed monarchist prefers to find his heroes in other reigns. For were not the years of legitimist counter-revolution years of national humiliation? Was not the Habsburg star in the ascendant, while Frederick William IV and his camarilla toyed with hopeless schemes and visions? The conservatism which descended on Germany after the fall of the new order has found no champion, because it would not march in step with history. Overshadowed by the aspirations of the Forties and the achievements of the Sixties, it has been consigned to abuse and oblivion.

The charges against the reaction are not without foundation. Those who measure government by the yardstick of diplomatic success can point to the defeat of the movement for national unification and the restoration of the German Confederation in all its inadequacy. For weakness of purpose in Berlin made possible the revival of Austrian influence among the secondary states sighing for their freedom. When the Frankfurt Parliament collapsed after the historic refusal of "the crown from the gutter," it was still not too late to establish a German federal union under Prussian auspices. Public opinion was ready to support a bold program of internal reorganization, the Habsburg armies under the notorious Julius von Haynau were engaged in a bitter campaign against Hungarian independence, and the minor princes were powerless to resist demands for a restriction of their prerogatives. If Frederick William IV had succeeded in making himself master of Germany in the spring of 1849, the Hofburg in Vienna would have faced an irrevocable fait accompli. But such a policy of opportunism required cool nerve and strong determination, and the king possessed neither. His only resources were good intentions and a vivid imagination.

He opened his diplomatic campaign boldly enough. On May 15, 1849, a proclamation announced his intention to pursue the work of unification by summoning a national assembly ready to collaborate with the princes in the preparation of a federal constitution. Before the month was over Saxony and Hanover had given their reluctant consent to the Prussian plan, and four weeks later 148 former members of the Frankfurt Parliament met in Gotha to express their approval of the projects emanating from Berlin. Radowitz, who had been entrusted with the mission of organizing the new federation, worked with unflagging zeal to coax and bully the secondary states into submission. By the end of the summer only Bavaria, Württemberg, Holstein, and a handful of the minor governments had not succumbed to his threats, and their feeble resistance was kept alive only by promises of future support which the Austrian prime minister Prince Felix zu Schwarzenberg was whispering in their ears. But how much longer would they hold out? Frederick William IV could see his dearest ambitions fulfilled; he could see a united fatherland, a conservative parliament, a grateful people, and all without bloodshed and without expense. It was almost too good to be true.

Then in the early days of autumn the fortunes of Prussia turned. The king had accepted the pledges of support of the secondary states at face value, confident that the details of unification could be settled at leisure in future conferences. The cunning of the weak deceived him so completely that the mass desertion of his allies which followed the revival of Habsburg influence came as an unexpected calamity. In

August the Austrian government concluded peace with Sardinia, and then with the aid of Russian troops it completed the subjugation of Hungary. By October, with Magyar generals swinging from the gallows of Arad, Vienna could once again play a major role in the affairs of Germany.

It immediately began to offer stout resistance to the designs of Frederick William IV, and on September 30 Prussia apprehensively agreed to share with Austria the authority formerly vested in Archduke Johann as imperial regent. This first sign of weakness in Berlin encouraged the princes to betray their promises to Radowitz. When the assembly chosen to consider a constitution for the national union met in Erfurt on March 20, 1850, important members like Hanover and Saxony had already withdrawn from the undertaking. Two months later in Frankfurt they reconstituted the Diet of the Confederation under the presidency of Austria, and the two leading powers of Central Europe found themselves involved in an open struggle for political supremacy.

The issue was decided by Nicholas I of Russia. Frederick William IV was not the man to meet adversity with resolution, and the legitimist counselors on whom he now leaned for support had long entertained serious misgivings about the new departure in Prussian policy. Only Radowitz continued to plead the national cause in Berlin, while the king weakened from day to day, until the danger of war against heavy odds broke down his last scruples of pride. When in October 1850 both Austria and Prussia prepared to intervene in Hesse-Kassel to put an end to the constitutional conflict in the electorate, hostilities seemed unavoidable. But the czar turned the military scale in favor of Vienna. Count Brandenburg and Prince Schwarzenberg traveled to Warsaw to present their views to the autocrat whose decision would determine the future of the national movement. Without hesitation Nicholas endorsed the proposals of the Hofburg, leaving his royal brother-in-law no choice but to abandon as gracefully as possible his project for a reorganization of Germany. Radowitz resigned from the cabinet amid the jubilation of his Junker opponents, and Manteuffel who was promoted to the premiership took the road to Canossa. On November 29 in Olmütz he signed a punctation by which his government renounced the plan for a new union and agreed to a revival of the German Confederation. Habsburg diplomacy had won a splendid victory which the face-saving stipulation that federal reform would be considered in the near future could not disguise.[1]

Only in its commercial policy was the Prussian government able to withstand the importunities of Vienna. It countered the suggestion of the ill-starred Baron Karl von Bruck that the Austrian crownlands be admitted to the Zollverein by opening negotiations with the free-trade states of the north. In 1851 Hanover was persuaded to enter into a tariff association with Prussia in return for an advantageous system of revenue distribution and a significant reduction in import duties. Having thus strengthened its position on the seacoast, the Berlin cabinet could bring pressure to bear on the southern courts through the threat to terminate the customs union treaties in 1853. Economic necessity overcame Habsburg sympathies below the Main, and the Zollverein was extended for another twelve years under terms dictated by Manteuffel. The sole concessions which the Hofburg gained were a trade agreement and a promise that its request for admission to the customs union would be reconsidered in 1859.[2]

To Prussia, however, the successful defense of its position in the Zollverein was small compensation for a humiliating political defeat. Not since Jena had the Hohenzollern name commanded so little respect. Frederick William IV, after living in a state of intense emotional strain ever since the outbreak of the Revolution, relapsed at last into a morbid introspection from which he never recovered. While he immersed himself more and more deeply in the problems of religion and aesthetics which were always closest to his heart, the kingdom floated aimlessly in the backwaters of European political life. In France the ineffectualness of the Second Republic was replaced by the sham vigor of the Second Empire. The Crimean War came and went, checking Russian ambitions in the Balkans. Count Camillo di Cavour in Italy began to spin a fine web of intrigue out of which he fashioned a new nation. And still Germany drifted.

Manteuffel made an attempt to mask the discomfiture of his government with a show of bravado. "The strong man may retreat a step," he rationalized before the legislature on December 3, 1850, "but he keeps his gaze fixed firmly on the goal and decides in what other way he can achieve it."[3] Yet not even the tried conservatives in the chamber found comfort in his assurances. A franker estimate of the diplomatic situation was given by Prince William, who was destined to see the disgrace of Olmütz avenged on the battlefield of Sadowa: "Confidence in the strength and good will of Prussia, or rather in its savoir-faire, has been shaken for a long time to come."[4] As for the man who would one day lead the national movement to victory, he had not yet seen the light. When the news that Radowitz had fallen reached Bismarck, the bluff squire opened a bottle of champagne and danced around the table for joy. It would take another fifteen years of struggle and reflection to make an iron chancellor out of the wild Junker.[5]

Too weak to play a major role in the councils of the Continent, the reaction was at least able to wreak its displeasure on liberals at home. For the enemies of legitimism the Fifties were a time of humiliation and suffering. Some of them like Wilhelm von Trützschler and Maximilian Dortu were tried before military tribunals and executed. Others such as Gottfried Kinkel and Ludwig von Rango paid for their misdeeds with long prison sentences. In the regular courts political defendants usually fared better, and both Waldeck and Jacoby were acquitted of charges of lese majesty and high treason.

Judicial acquittal, however, was no protection against bureaucratic harassment. Franz Ziegler was expelled from the town
of Brandenburg where he had once been mayor, Hans Viktor
von Unruh lost his position in the civil service, and the sep-
tuagenarian Nees von Esenbeck was grotesquely charged
with concubinage and deprived of his pension. The only ones
to escape official wrath were those like Schurz and Born who
managed to find safety abroad.

Not only was the opposition driven into prison or exile,
but all expressions of its aspirations, all reminders of its suc-
cesses had to be destroyed as well. One of the first achievements of the resurrected German Confederation was the resolution of August 23, 1851, nullifying the Fundamental Rights
of the German People. The red-black-gold tricolor with its
liberal associations was taken down from the Thurn und Taxis
Palace in Frankfurt where the Diet of the Confederation sat. The national fleet created during the revolution to
protect commerce against Danish depredation was sold four
years later at public auction like so much contraband. And
lest any of the states flag in their zeal to destroy political
error, a federal commission was ready to prod them with
threats of military intervention.[6]

In the Habsburg monarchy the conservative policy initiated
by Schwarzenberg was pursued with determination by his
successors Baron Alexander von Bach and Count Karl von
Buol-Schauenstein. The constitution granted in 1849 was revoked, the historic rights of the kingdoms and provinces
were suppressed, and rule by administrative decree became
the order of the day. Centralization and Germanization went
hand in hand, as the dream of the enlightened despots of the
eighteenth century was realized a hundred years too late to
save the state from the disintegrating effects of nationalism.
In his benevolent despotism Francis Joseph was the heir of
Joseph II and Leopold II, but in the clericalism of his political outlook the world could recognize the son of the Arch-

duchess Sophie and of the pious Wittelsbachs. The concordat of 1855, breaking with the Josephinism which had become a tradition with the Austrian government, conferred on the church extensive self-rule and invested it with supervision over educational practice, marriage law, and public morality. Yet the hope that the statecraft of the young emperor would thus find a moral purpose remained unfulfilled, for the reactionary system of the Hofburg was never more than a lifeless contrivance of the official mind incapable of satisfying men in search of an ideal.[7]

Prussian conservatism, while less suave, at least possessed the virtue of inner conviction. In Vienna the civil servant paid lip service to the teachings of absolutism, but in his heart he knew that the mainspring of bureaucratic conduct was professional pride. The experience of generations had taught him to obey altruistic autocracy, liberal reformism, or ecclesiastical restoration with the same impassive complaisance. In the eastern marches of Germany, however, the Austrian form of government was considered sheer Bonapartism. The Junker had never become a servile courtier. There was still something feudal about his attitude toward the crown, for behind the outward appearance of a devoted subject lurked the bold frondeur. His faith in the monarchy arose out of a sense of pride, and his opposition to liberalism was more than a preference for royal over bourgeois rule. It was a defense of the military and economic alliance between ruler and nobleman which the Hohenzollerns had maintained in their lands for a hundred years.

Frederick William IV was therefore not free to emulate the example of Francis Joseph by imposing a Caesarean absolutism on his state. Despite the urgings of the Hofburg he would not abrogate the constitution, although his government did countenance measures calculated to strengthen monarchical prerogative and noble influence. After the spring of 1849 the lower chamber of the legislature was chosen by an electoral system favoring the propertied classes, and in 1853 the upper chamber was transformed into a house of peers. Provisions for the dissolution of entailed estates were repealed in 1852, while a year later the right of local self-government in rural districts was restricted. Through the activities of Minister of the Interior Ferdinand von Westphalen a bureaucratic arbitrariness began to creep into the administration of a country which had always prided itself on a strict observance of the law. The authorities molested newspapers with threats of censorship, political meetings were subjected to police surveillance, even members of the royal family could not escape the vigilance of the secret service. And since piety was considered the most effective antidote against subversion, religious instruction received a new emphasis in the schools at the expense of mundane studies.[8]

The secondary governments willy-nilly followed the example of Vienna and Berlin. Those few which tended toward political moderation were afraid to show themselves tolerant of unorthodoxy, and the others were only too happy to be free of commitments to which they had agreed under duress. In 1850 the Mecklenburgs, abandoning the constitution published the previous year, restored the state compact of 1755. The Saxon cabinet repudiated the reforms adopted during the revolution and returned to the conservative fundamental law of 1831. Georg V of Hanover, a blind king dazzled by the ancient glories of the Guelphs, strengthened his political position in 1855 by reviving aristocratic predomination in the upper chamber of the legislature. And princely duplicity could always be found in Hesse-Kassel, where Elector Friedrich Wilhelm asked the Diet of the Confederation to send him military assistance to help break a solemn constitutional pledge.[9]

Not only the achievements of parliamentarianism but its hopes as well vanished in the aftermath of the revolutionary fiasco. During the Fifties the call for national reform met with proletarian indifference and aristocratic hostility, and even among the faithful bourgeoisie it had to overcome a growing demoralization. In this dark hour the liberals could turn only to the future, appealing to the judgment of history against the verdict of their own time. And history heard their call. For posterity sees the reaction as its critics saw it, blind, despotic, and cruel.

Yet to its contemporary generation it meant above all a period of economic recovery after a terrible depression. It brought with it an increase in production, a relaxation of population pressure, an improvement in the standard of living. Most important, it developed a new understanding of the problems besetting a society in transition from feudal agrarianism to industrial capitalism. The legitimism which emerged out of the ordeal of the Revolution won the masses with a program of welfare legislation. It completed the emancipation of the peasantry, it protected the worker against the mill-owner, and it encouraged the growth of commerce and transportation. Not until the promulgation of the social insurance laws in the Eighties did the ruling classes of Germany again display such a concern for the laboring man. In its struggle against bourgeois liberalism the landed aristocracy raised the banner of tory reform around which nobleman and commoner alike could rally.

It is true that the success of this benevolent reaction arose partly out of developments beyond the scope of government action. The remarkable growth of manufacture after the revolution was by and large a result of private initiative, for middle-class energies which had suffered defeat in politics turned to economics. Pig iron production in the Zollverein grew from 24,000,000 marks in 1848 to 66,000,000 in 1857, coal output rose from 25,000,000 marks to 82,000,000, and the value of mining climbed from 45,000,000 marks to 135,000,000. All in all, capital and consumer goods turned out by industry more than doubled in the course of the decade, while foreign trade increased almost 150 per cent. In finance the discovery of the gold fields of California promoted a speculative boom, as optimistic investors rushed to make their profits on the inflated market. When the bubble finally burst in 1857, the weak went down in bankruptcy, but by then great business establishments like the Disconto-Gesellschaft, the Darmstädter Bank, and the Berliner Handelsgesellschaft had already won recognition as credit institutions of the first rank.[10]

For the masses industrial and commercial prosperity brought a measure of relief from the hardships of the Forties. Not only did expansion of production raise the demand for man power, but the labor supply achieved a new stability which strengthened the bargaining position of the lower classes. Demographic growth, which was particularly rapid during the decades following the Congress of Vienna, began to taper by the middle of the century. Between 1816 and 1837 the normal yearly increase in population was 1.42 per cent, but from then until 1858 it was only .85 per cent. In 1816-34 the Prussian annual birth rate was 412 for every 10,000 inhabitants, in 1835-43 it was 402, in 1844-52 it was 396, and by 1853-61 it had declined to 380. In Bavaria the average number of residents to the square kilometer was 54.1 in 1830, 57.3 in 1840, 59.2 in 1849, and 60.4 in 1858, while in Saxony it was 93.5, 113.9, 126.4, and 132.9. At a time when manufacturing capacity was expanding at an unprecedented rate, the rise in the number of workers available for hire slackened.[11]

Emigration contributed to the establishment of an equilibrium between labor supply and demand. The great exodus of the Forties had been a spasmodic response to a depression which was bringing hunger and unemployment to the masses. Growing by leaps and bounds in the middle years of the decade, it suddenly subsided after the failure of the revolution and the return of prosperity. The reaction had little direct effect on the transatlantic movement of population, and only after economic conditions worsened once again did the flow of landless peasants and uprooted artisans reach its greatest extent. The number of those wandering overseas was 82,000 in 1850; 162,000 in 1852; 252,000 in 1854; 99,000 in 1856; and 56,000 in 1858. Of the 1,000,000 Germans who found new homes abroad between 1851 and 1860, more than 90 per cent came from the exhausted lands west of the Elbe. By their departure they helped improve the standard of living of those who remained.[12]

The fluctuation of wages was a faithful measure of the industrial boom and the tight labor supply. Between 1846 and 1850 the pay of miners rose 4 per cent, of printers 9 per cent, of construction laborers 10 per cent. A mill hand in an Augsburg textile factory getting 278 marks in 1845 received 372 in 1850. The daily earnings of a Württemberg blacksmith were 1.20 marks in 1840-49 and 1.40 in 1850-59. After touching bottom in 1847, the real income of workers in industry, transportation, and agriculture rose so rapidly that in 1850 it attained the highest level in about twenty years. While the improved economic position of the proletariat was to some extent a result of increased productivity made possible by the mechanization and rationalization of manufacture, its main source was the business expansion stimulated by the return of political stability after 1848.[13]

Some of the gains made by labor in the early Fifties, however, were wiped out by the increase in the cost of living which accompanied economic recovery. The heavy influx of American and Australian gold, the sudden distention of the international credit structure, the blind optimism of the stock exchange, all combined to set off an inflationary wave which did not ebb before the great crash at the end of the decade. Until 1851 wages mounted steadily, while the price of food remained more or less stable at a point well below the famine level of 1846 and 1847. But then quotations on the overconfident market began to climb so rapidly that few workers could hold their own in the race between income and outgo. A liter of wheat which in 1849 cost 11 pfennigs rose in 1855 to 22 pfennigs. Between 1850 and 1855 the price of rye increased 150 per cent, of potatoes and barley 125 per cent, of oats and peas 100 per cent. The cost of beef, pork, and butter did not expand as greatly, but even in times of prosperity meat and dairy products were a rare luxury for a proletarian family. By 1857 the speculative fever was spent, but not before it had nullified much of the economic advance achieved by the lower classes immediately after the revolution.[14]

As a matter of fact, throughout the decade widespread impoverishment remained a serious problem for the states of Central Europe. The mayor of Breslau, where almost 32,000 inhabitants out of 104,000 depended on charity, described pauperism as "a malignant, cancerous growth threatening to infect the healthy core of the country." Economic conditions in Silesia were particularly bad, for unemployment in the depressed textile industry was increasing, wages were declining as much as a third, and by 1854 Zollverein exports of linen were only half of what they had been ten years before. But reports from other regions showed that mass privation was a national evil. Berlin was having its difficulties with the support of the sick and the needy. Out of Düsseldorf came the complaint that the burden of municipal taxation for poor relief was growing insupportable. In Prussia in 1855 288,000 persons, 4 per cent of the population, lived entirely by alms. In Bavaria there were 15 beggars and vagabonds for every 1,000 inhabitants, while in the Palatinate with its dwarf farms and petty trades the proportion of paupers was almost twice as great.[15]

Yet despite extensive poverty, rising prices, and an uneven distribution of the benefits of industrialization the German standard of living was significantly higher in the Fifties than in the Forties. Employment was steadier, income larger, hope brighter. The sufferings of the lower classes were real enough, but they were not as intense as ten years before. Besides, where in Europe were conditions better? In the east the Russian peasant still endured serfdom, bound body and soul to the whim of the aristocracy. Across the Rhine in France the empire turned out to be as bourgeois as the republic had been, while Napoleon III was too busy winning military glory in the Crimea to remember a treatise on the extinction of pauperism which he had once composed in the prison of Ham. As for the Great Britain of Queen Victoria, a million vagrants roamed its cities and villages, and Benjamin Disraeli was writing about the two nations, the rich and the poor, separated from each other by an impassable gulf of resentment.

In Germany at least the economic and social problems created by the growth of industrial capitalism won more attention among the upper classes than anywhere else on the Continent. Publicists and academicians like Lorenz von Stein and Johann Karl Rodbertus were propounding their theories of a monarchy of mass welfare. Hermann Wagener appealed to the chivalrous instincts of the nobility in behalf of the weak and the poor. Viktor Aimé Huber looked to the state for aid in the establishment of worker associations. The views of Paul de Lagarde were not fully developed until the empire, but it was in the Fifties that he was first drawn to the labor question. Even Leopold von Ranke, forced out of the ivory tower by the Revolution, prepared memoranda for Frederick William IV which have an unexpectedly practical ring:

For he who serves the state with his life has also a claim on it for his support. The soundest policy would be to satisfy this claim, since as a matter of fact it is dangerous to train year after year the entire youthful population in the use of arms, and then alienate a large and physically perhaps the most vigorous part, leaving it exposed to the agitation of the enemies of all order. Either we must exempt the propertyless from the duty to serve in the army, or we must place them under an obligation to the state even after their period of service by the prospect of gainful employment. Since the first course is out of the question because it would reduce our military strength, nothing remains but the second alternative. The idea arises that under certain conditions the state ought to organize labor and perhaps recognize the right to work, yet it must also respect private enterprise. We may well agree that the state in times of peace should provide employment under military supervision for those workers especially who are physically fit for service in war. As formerly the character of the army was transformed from that of an unruly crowd to a disciplined association, so now the activity of manual workers must be regulated. We could create labor cohorts for the many necessary public works, the control of rivers, the reclamation of lands, etc., etc. Political rights, on the other hand, could be granted the propertyless only to a very small extent, just as the Roman republic formed out of the entire mass of proletarians only one century entitled to vote in a total of 193.[16]

The political leaders of Prussia were strongly influenced by the gospel of a conservatism of public service. To be sure, there were those in Berlin who preferred obedience to intellectual originality. Ferdinand von Westphalen of the ministry of the interior, Karl von Raumer superintending ecclesiastical affairs and public instruction, Karl von Hinckeldey at the head of the police, in such men the efficient bureaucrat had completely repressed the constructive statesman. But elsewhere greater wisdom prevailed. During his ten years in the cabinet Manteuffel showed himself sympathetic to the ideal of social justice, and his agrarian and industrial policies were planned to improve the lot of the masses. Absorption in foreign affairs did not blind Radowitz to the importance of domestic developments. Although after 1850 he was no longer a direct participant in politics, he continued to remind the rulers of Europe of their obligations to their subjects: "If the state does not turn to the solution of the social problem when the established authorities are still in full possession of power, then this problem will be forced on it at a time when government stands weak and helpless before anarchy."[17] From his diplomatic post in Frankfurt Bismarck urged the adoption of a program of economic reform as an instrument of state-craft. And the king himself remained faithful to the teach-ings of Christian charity which he had embraced before the Revolution, reiterating his conviction that in dealing with the masses the crown "cannot trample on these people."[18]

The Junkers also developed a growing awareness of the moral responsibilities of a governing aristocracy. Never before had they attempted to define their political mission in such universal terms, never again were they to identify themselves so closely with the economic interests of the broad masses. In Friedrich Julius Stahl they found an eloquent expounder of the legitimist philosophy of state summoning the nobility to a defense of the spiritual tradition of the nation. Their party program of 1856 attacked the enemy head on: "Liberalism has dissolved the ties whose purpose was to bind the com-ponent elements of society to each other, to offer them mutual support, to place them in a vivifying and fructifying relation-ship to one another. It has given rise to a wasteful, destruc-tive struggle of all against all."[19] Advocating a corporate eco-nomic ethic, they argued that the worker and peasant needed the protection of a benevolent throne even more than the nobleman, for without assistance from above they were pow-erless to resist the social decay with which industrialism was infecting the world. Plebeian and patrician should therefore join forces in a common hostility to the liberal bourgeoisie.[20]

In its last decade of political hegemony feudal agrarianism came closest to the realization of its political and economic ideals. It restored the throne and the altar to their honored place in society, it strengthened guild regulation of industrial life, it defended the worker against the machine, it consummated the legal liberation of the countryside without destroying the paternalistic character of the village life, and it concluded a firm alliance between aristocracy and proletariat. The growth of the factory system was too vigorous to be checked by theories and decrees, but in their quixotic attempt to turn back the clock the conservatives won the loyalty of those who were becoming the victims of technological progress.

Is it any wonder that the policies of the reaction enjoyed the approval of the masses? The man in the street, too busy earning a meager livelihood to participate in the struggle of political parties, remained indifferent to questions of civil rights and constitutional procedures. On election day he frequently stayed away from the polls, but his sympathies were on the side of legitimism. In Prussia the parties of the right remained in the majority until the establishment of the regency of Prince William in 1858, and even afterward liberalism drew its strength from the bourgeoisie rather than the proletariat. As late as the elections of October 20, 1863, the third class of voters composed of the poorer elements of society proved more favorable to the government than the first two classes representing the well to do. It is true that throughout the Fifties the bureaucracy attempted to influence the electorate by threats, exhortations, and promises, but the efforts of an overzealous officialdom did no more than strengthen the royalist predisposition of the nation.[21]

The camarilla about Frederick William IV, which always maintained that the most loyal supporters of the crown were among the masses, criticized the three-class system of election for conferring an excessive parliamentary influence on wealth. Stahl condemned it as "illegal and pernicious," asserting that some day it would bring disaster to the nation. Leopold von Gerlach urged the adoption of a new electoral law dividing the voters by social classes and occupational groups instead of income categories. The *Neue Preussische Zeitung* feared that the liberals would turn the tables on legitimism by amassing sufficient financial resources to win a majority in the legislature. Ernst von Bülow-Cummerow conceded that under constitutional government men of property ought to enjoy special privileges, but in his appraisal of the suffrage regulations he spoke of "arbitrariness and bureaucratic enactments." Westphalen worked hard to limit the political role of money by introducing corporate voting. And many years later Bismarck stated in the legislature of the North German Confederation that "a sillier, wretcheder electoral law has never been devised in any state."[22]

As a matter of fact, the firmest defenders of the three-class system were not bitter reactionaries but disillusioned liberals. In a letter to Prince William which he wrote at the end of 1848 Hansemann described manhood suffrage as "the most dangerous experiment in the world," and a few months later he told Radowitz that a state which tolerated a mass franchise could not survive. Gustav von Mevissen, in sympathy with the attempt to establish the preponderance of wealth in public affairs, favored the transformation of the upper chamber of the legislature into a house of peers. Ludolf Camphausen cautioned the king that an unrestricted suffrage was incompatible with monarchy, ascribing his own endorsement of it during the spring uprising to the pressure of the moment. When in May 1849 the Prussian government began to look for an electoral device sure to produce a submissive parliament, the Rhenish leaders advanced the proposal that ballots be weighted in accordance with a property classification of the voters. Their plan was adopted, although in the cabinet the warmest support for it came not from Brandenburg and Manteuffel, representatives of the military aristocracy and the conservative bureaucracy, but from political moderates like August von der Heydt and Adalbert von Ladenberg.[23]

The true legitimist recognized in a propertied suffrage the cloven hoof of the doctrine of *enrichissez-vous* which the July Monarchy in France had preached, but for many liberals the repeal of the equal franchise was a source of comfort. All around them they saw the triumphs of a "red reaction," a reaction compounded of aristocratic demagoguery and proletarian blindness. Where were men of education and wealth to find escape from this scene of social confusion and ideological betrayal? Some like Lothar Bucher and Alexander Pagenstecher broke with the beliefs of 1848 to seek new leaders and new policies for the deliverance of the fatherland. Hermann von Beckerath and Werner von Siemens were among the many turning from the disappointments of the national cause to brilliantly successful careers in finance and industry. But those who remained close to the political scene never tired of warnings against the perfidy of the lower classes. "The rule of the masses has begun in Europe," wrote Mevissen in 1850, "although they have not been trained to rule. They have freed themselves from the burdens, partly imaginary, partly real, which once oppressed them, and violent revolutions rapidly following one another have placed the reins of power in their hands. These masses, however, must still acquire the education needed for government, they must still acquire the measure of self-control necessary for the achievement of social purposes."[24]

In the radical camp prospects were even bleaker. The liberals could at least vent their spleen against the fickle mob and await the day when the three-class system would bring them parliamentary victory. For the democrats there was no such consolation. Wedded to manhood suffrage and majority rule, they could only cling to the fiction that the proletariat was still on their side. At first they refused to be discouraged by the failure of the insurrection of 1849, and when the government in Berlin introduced its new electoral law, their response was a boycott of the polls. Early in the reaction they were able to point to the high degree of abstention from voting as proof of popular approval. But in 1855 they made the mistake of abandoning the tactic of passive resistance and calling on their followers for support in the elections. The outcome was a disaster, the lowest participation in the franchise of the decade and a chamber overwhelmingly conservative in composition. Even the most rabid republicans were now forced to recognize that they were an isolated and futile minority.[25]

Only in the headquarters of the Communist League in London was there still an unshaken faith in the ultimate triumph of a popular revolution. From the other side of the English Channel the political situation on the Continent seemed to offer the rich promise of a future struggle of the oppressed against their oppressors. The feudal reaction in alliance with the middle class had won a temporary success over the masses, but the logic of economic development made new conflicts inevitable. Next time, however, the socialists would be better prepared to seize the opportunities which the predestined hour presented. Marx addressed the non-existent insurgent legions of Germany in an inflammatory manifesto, warning them against the political blandishments of the democrats. And Engels summed up the lessons of 1848 with the panache of a defiant rebel: "The workers and peasants who today suffer under the rule of the saber as severely as the petty bourgeois have not gone through the experience of the recent uprising without effect. Moreover, having to avenge their killed and murdered brothers, they will see to it that in the next insurrection they, and not the petty bourgeois, take the helm."[26]

It was all in vain. The lower classes were not ready for the gospel of dialectical materialism. They still yearned for the innocence of a precapitalistic economy in which every man earned his bread and knew his place. They sought to escape from the factory age, not to dominate it. The ideal of traditionalist legitimism was more intelligible to the independent artisan and small farmer than the vision of a classless society which Marxism offered to them. While both socialist and conservative opposed to bourgeoisie, they did so for diametrically opposed reasons. One looked to a cataclysmic future, the other to a pastoral past. The proletariat accepted the leadership of the nobility in the struggle against industrialism, because it too saw its salvation in the return to a corporate, static social order. Together they fought against the machine, against the countinghouse, against the bourse, until economic progress pushed them out of its way. After a decade of reaction the world of guilds and hamlets succumbed, and with its fall a way of life came to an end.

THE ECONOMICS OF REACTION

A FEW months after meeting Schwarzenberg at Olmütz, Manteuffel confessed to Prince William his sympathy with the social predilections of his Austrian opponent: "I am pretty much in agreement with him on one point, namely, a thorough contempt for the present generation, especially for the so-called educated class. One characteristic of this class is a combination of arrogance and cowardice, both sprung from godlessness. The sound elements of the nation, and we still have those, thank God, are to be found in the rural folk, but they make little noise and are therefore rarely noticed."[1] For Sans Souci as for Schönbrunn the great enemy of royal authority was the bourgeoisie infected with seditious ideas and inflated ambitions. It was from this source that revolution drew nourishment, for great wealth, especially moneyed wealth, was a constant temptation to subversion. To find true civic virtue, therefore, the state must look to the peasant hut, the artisan shop, and the Junker manor house.

Rewarding its proletarian friends and chastising its middle-class enemies, the reaction introduced a program of economic reform in Central Europe whose most enduring achievement was the completion of rural emancipation. The conservatives who returned to power in the Fifties saw in agriculture not only the foundation of national greatness, but also a counter-weight to liberal industrialism. Since without the support of the rural masses the crown could not resist the encroachments of constitutionalism, expediency forced on landowning noblemen a policy of agrarian improvement. Sometimes they justified it by arguments of *noblesse oblige* derived from the feudal tradition, sometimes they emphasized the close connection between agricultural and military efficiency, sometimes they frankly acknowledged that their interest in the peasantry was primarily political. Yet whatever their motives, they destroyed manorialism once and for all.[2]

The rural reforms adopted by the reaction were necessarily shaped by the economic developments of the preceding fifty years. The Gerlachs inveighing against the social consequences of the liberation of the village sang the praises of an aristocratic patriarchalism rooted in the Christian sense of communal responsibility, but they could not undo the great changes which enlightened princes and liberal ministers had initiated at the turn of the century. The time for a feudal revival had long since passed. It was even too late for the proposal advanced by Hans von Kleist-Retzow that the government halt the rise of a landless proletariat by creating a vigorous class of small peasant proprietors. The spread of latifundia in the east and the growth of population in the west had made the position of the villager so precarious that no degree of state solicitude could restore the security he had once enjoyed. All that was practicable was to cut the few ties still binding agriculture to the past and allow the farmer to strike out for himself.

Most conservatives, recognizing the handwriting on the wall, strove to facilitate the transition from the old to the new system of landholding. In Prussia the work of emancipation which had languished since the days of Hardenberg was resumed after the revolution. As soon as Frederick William IV had executed the coup of December 5, 1848, the best talents among the legitimists turned to the work of agricultural reform. Stolberg-Wernigerode and Kleist-Retzow proceeded to draft the outline of a measure commuting servile dues, while Bülow-Cummerow composed minutes and memoranda based on his forty years of experience as landowner and gentleman-farmer. But Leopold von Gerlach, criticizing the government for its neglect of aristocratic interests, appealed to divine wisdom to rectify the errors of a blind officialism. And the king himself was as usual too bewildered by the flood of conflicting proposals to act with determination. He waited in indecision until he could delay no longer, and then he followed the voice which was clearest and firmest.

It was Manteuffel's. The minister of the interior had turned his attention to rural affairs immediately after entering the cabinet. His was the mind of the Prussian bureaucrat, incapable of lofty vision, but conscientious, painstaking, resolute. He approached questions of statecraft with a hard common sense and an inbred distrust of ideological formulas, qualities invaluable to a regime suffering from verbosity and nerves. Since he was too matter-of-fact to share the romantic extravagances of the king and the camarilla, he could never overcome the hostility of the clique of reactionary doctrinaires at the court. Yet by endowment and training he was admirably equipped for the execution of a program of agrarian improvement. By the early spring of 1849 he had completed the preparation of two decrees establishing criteria for peasant proprietorship and extending credit to the independent farmer. What is more, he had persuaded Frederick William IV to approve his projects, and on April 23 they were submitted to the legislature. Four days later, however, the government dissolved the lower chamber, and the slow process of legal enactment had to begin all over again. Parliamentary discussion began at last in November, continued through December and January, came to an end in February, and on March 2, 1850, the measures received the royal signature.[3]

The first provided for the liquidation of the servile obligations of virtually all landholders, whatever the category of their tenure or the size of their property. Peasants excluded from the benefits of earlier emancipation legislation because their leasehold was unfavorable or their farm small were now enabled to become free proprietors by converting manorial dues into money rents and extinguishing them through payments equivalent to eighteen times their annual value. The second law made available the financial resources needed for the purchase of rural independence by establishing loan banks to advance long-term, low interest credit to villagers. Thus the state assumed direct responsibility for the liberation of the countryside, strengthening the movement of agriculture toward a free and individualized form of organization.

The magnitude of its achievement can be gauged by a comparison of the number of those affected by the emancipation laws of the era of liberal reform with those profiting from the agrarian legislation of the reaction. Between 1811 and 1848 about 70,000 peasants in the eastern provinces of Prussia freed themselves of dues by land cession, and another 170,000 through the remittance of money. The two measures of March 2, 1850, on the other hand, made possible in the course of only fifteen years the extinction of the obligations of close to 640,000 farmers, almost all of them paying in cash and thus avoiding the loss of property. The figures speak for themselves. For the rural masses between the Elbe and the Vistula liberation from manorialism came not in the early years of the nineteenth century but in its middle period. And conservatives like Manteuffel and Brandenburg were their benefactors more than liberals like Stein and Hardenberg. For only after the Revolution had taught the powers that be the importance of the agrarian problem, did they act with boldness to meet its complexities.[4]

In central Germany the achievements of rural reform were less far-reaching. The liberation of the countryside had begun with eighteenth-century benevolent despots, it had made rapid progress under French domination, even the Restoration had given it cautious support, and the Revolution had brought it to its final stage. Odds and ends were all that was left for the conservatives in the Fifties. In Saxony they promulgated the law of May 15, 1851, providing for the completion of the commutation of servile obligations. Hanover, Saxe-Altenburg, and Schwarzburg-Rudolstadt permitted the alodification of lands held in feudal tenure, encouraged the division of commons, and facilitated the consolidation of scattered holdings. In Saxe-Weimar the decrees of March 9 and March 14, 1850, abolished manorial jurisdiction and revoked the privileged legal status of special classes of persons and goods. Indeed, along the entire left bank of the Elbe the reaction was a period of agricultural experimentation, modernization, and progress.[5]

In the south and west the destruction of manorialism had been practically concluded during the Revolution. Only the electoral Hessian government still faced unfinished business, but on November 13, 1849, it finally revoked the judicial privileges inherent in the ownership of an estate, and on June 20, 1850, came a law governing the commutation of the remaining servile obligations. The peasant of Hesse-Kassel became as independent as the peasant of Bavaria or Württemberg or Baden. He too was now tried for his misdemeanors in public courts and atoned for them in public jails, paid money rents instead of labor services, bought, sold, divided, and subdivided his property, sowed whatever he wanted and reaped whenever he pleased, and with the coming of hard times borrowed and defaulted and emigrated. He too was now a free man.[6]

Rural reform, however, could not overcome the dualism of aristocratic latifundium and impoverished small farm. The Elbe remained a dividing line between two systems of agriculture, each with its own economic practice, class structure, and political outlook. To the east stretched the great estates of the Prussian plain, owned by proud Junkers and tilled by propertyless laborers. In the west were the overworked holdings of a teeming peasantry more fertile than the soil. On one side the self-seeking of the nobility had established a lopsided form of landownership; on the other side fifty years of peace and medical progress had created a dangerous overpopulation. Here the source of agricultural difficulties was social, there it was demographic. But throughout Central

Europe land hunger remained, and the flow of dispossessed farmers from the fields grew. Freedom merely translated the conditions of peasant subservience from medieval into modern terms.

Agricultural adjustment to the world of finance was easiest in the states of the west, where the upper classes looked on land as a source of revenue rather than the appurtenance of a privileged social status. The aristocrat of Franconia or Swabia, normally finding a career in the diplomatic service or in some ornamental cavalry regiment or at the court, was willing to lease out his estates and become an absentee landlord in the English manner. There were few personal ties between him and the peasants, and as for the tradition of conservative patriarchalism, it meant little in the polite society which congregated in Ems and Homburg. The old rural order fell of its own weight, leaving the countryman to shift for himself as an independent landholder.

In Prussia, however, the transition from a manorial to a free organization of farming was more difficult. So powerful were the political influences opposed to agrarian emancipation that the best-intentioned reforming statesman could not have overcome them. The villager had to pay for his freedom in amortization remittances which around the middle of the century amounted to more than 200,000,000 marks, and in the transfer between 1816 and 1859 of some 21,000 holdings from peasant to noble hands. On the right bank of the Elbe the latifundium remained king. Even before the reaction 62 per cent of the land in Pomerania had belonged to properties of 150 hectares or more, in Posen 55 per cent, in Silesia 50 per cent, in Brandenburg 46 per cent. By the Fifties a lasting improvement in the position of the farm vis-à-vis the estate was no longer possible. The course of rural development had strengthened the strong and weakened the weak, leaving the masses of the countryside in the grip of a domineering aristocracy. The outward forms of personal servitude could be destroyed by legislative fiat, but its social and financial concomitants remained the incubus of agriculture in the east long after feudalism was dead.[7]

The state was partly responsible for the continuing subordination of the peasant. It could not establish the economic and it would not establish the political conditions essential to his independence. The nobleman might in any event have retained a preponderant role in the countryside because of his financial resources, but the government underwrote his domination by giving him a privileged civic status. The law of June 5, 1852, legalized once again the maintenance of entailed estates, the law of May 7, 1853, turned the upper house of the legislature into a chamber of peers, the law of May 24, 1853, revoked the right of self-government in rural communities, and the law of April 14, 1856, restored the manorial police authority of the magnates. Before the reaction came to an end the Junkers managed to regain most of the prerogatives which had been theirs before the Revolution. Their hostility to Manteuffel's agrarian reform program was thus mollified, while the countryman himself did not usually mourn the loss of freedoms which he had never comprehended. In a favorable environment, however, they might have gradually developed into an instrument of his liberation from aristocratic oppression. As it was, the nobility perpetuated its hegemony in the social order of Central Europe.[8]

Yet the nemesis of the great landowners appeared before long in the guise of the moneylender. The wealth which they squeezed out of the peasantry kept making its way into other pockets, for the capitalistic form of agriculture exposed the Junker to the vicissitudes of the business world. He tried to stay in step with the times by adopting improved methods of tillage, by making more efficient use of migratory labor, by adjusting output to international demand, and by experimenting with the manufacture of alcohol and sugar. But it was a losing battle. Foreign competition, glutted markets, mortgage obligations, and rural bankruptcies continued to increase amid the Macedonian cries of the aristocrats. From 1835 to 1864 there was a 200 per cent turnover in the ownership of some 12,000 large estates in the eastern provinces, with 14,400 sales, 1,300 foreclosures, and only 7,900 hereditary transmissions. While some noblemen sought safety in the establishment of entails, the inalienability of their holdings could not of itself produce profits or pay debts. Little by little the landlord began to look for a solution to his difficulties in state support, in financial speculation, or in fortune-hunting marriage. By the end of the century he had degenerated into a landed adventurer subsisting on a marginal economy and trading his proud name for government favors and bourgeois alliances.[9]

But what of the villager? For him there were no commissions in the army, no influential friends, no wealthy brides. His liberation had been postponed until it could no longer protect him against Junker greed. In the fifty years which followed the emancipation edict of October 9, 1807, the latifundia of Prussia absorbed 1,000,000 hectares of peasant property, and in some provinces like Pomerania and Silesia 13 per cent of the land under cultivation left the possession of the small farmer. Although estates of more than 100 hectares constituted less than 2 per cent of all holdings in the east, the area under their control rose to 42 per cent. Conditions were worse still in Mecklenburg-Schwerin where the Junker held 60 per cent of the land, or in Mecklenburg-Strelitz where he owned 61 per cent. Even west of the Elbe the rustic's shrinking plot of tired earth could not support the weight of indebtedness created by liberation. In Hanover the cost of freedom was 210,000,000 marks, in Baden 72,-000,000, in Brunswick 30,000,000, in Saxe-Altenburg 7,500,-000, in Waldeck 3,000,000. Those who tried to pay it sank into a financial dependence as oppressive as personal servitude. The others gave up the struggle and sought their fortunes elsewhere, leaving behind them deserted villages like Wernings or Pferdsbach or Wippenbach as a silent testimonial to the destructive force of agricultural progress.[10]

There was no answer to the agrarian problem; there was only escape from it. The state freed the peasant from the burdens of the past, but it could not protect him against the dangers of the future. His safety lay in flight. The masses of the overcrowded countryside began to desert their fields in a mighty internal migration which within the lifetime of one generation completed the urbanization of Germany. They descended on the blast furnaces of the Ruhr, the textile mills of Saxony, the coal mines of Silesia. They doubled and tripled and quadrupled the size of cities like Düsseldorf, Leipzig, and Breslau. They became the "industrial reserve army" which Marx analyzed in the chapter of *Capital* dealing with the general law of capitalist accumulation. In other words, the farmer managed to keep body and soul together by ceasing to be a farmer. Seeking a way out of a doomed agriculture, he entered the service of the industrialism which he could not overcome. Some villagers stayed on the land, struggled, and hungered, but most found a new life in the ranks of the factory proletariat. For neither under liberalism nor under conservatism, neither in the east nor in the west could the small independent cultivator successfully withstand the combined might of money and privilege.

To conservatives rural reform posed a moral dilemma. They were judge and litigant in the same lawsuit, the interests of the landowner and the principles of the statesman were at grips in the same soul. Regarding industrial affairs, however, their counsel was undivided. "It is the sober result of observation," expounded Leopold von Gerlach, "that revolution has power only where almost every organic body has disintegrated, i.e., among arrogant, hungry literati and among atomized factory workers. Whenever revolution encounters an organic body, even if it be decayed and weak, an organic body like an estate of the realm or a craft association, it is forced to retreat."[11]

The reaction was as hostile to laissez-faire individualism in economics as to parliamentary liberalism in politics, for one was no less dangerous to legitimate authority than the other. As far as Bismarck was concerned, the essence of industrial freedom was the principle that "he who can starve best will starve his competitor into bankruptcy, he who produces the shoddiest wares will destroy his rival." Kleist-Retzow summoned the state "to work against the multiplication and brutalization of a demoralized proletariat." Ludwig von Gerlach reminded the upper classes that "only in connection with the duties which rest on it is property sacred, while purely as a means of enjoyment it is not sacred but unclean." And Hermann Wagener maintained that in the interest of the general welfare the government should see to it that "the diligent artisan, tradesman, and manufacturer receive guarantees for the security of their existence and livelihood, that these are at least not jeopardized by unrestricted and thoughtless competition, that proof of competence is required, that the free exercise of a craft is restrained as far as possible by corporate organizations, and that differences in the control of capital are balanced as far as possible by the assurance of credit."[12]

The conflicting economic principles of constitutionalism and legitimism clashed in the parliamentary discussion of the emergency decrees of February 9, 1849, restoring guild control in Prussia. The most eloquent defenders of industrial freedom were such well-known champions of liberal government as the banker Hermann von Beckerath, the entrepreneur Ludolf Camphausen, and the manufacturer Friedrich Harkort. Its opponents were landowning aristocrats like the squire of Schönhausen who had already won a name as an ultra of the ultras. On October 18, 1849, Bismarck launched a scathing attack on financial self-seeking masquerading as doctrinal subtlety:

If we do not fear to restrict the freedom of the individual in other respects, if we do not hesitate to give assistance through lawmaking to those calling for protective duties, why do we hesitate to protect the existence of the artisan class by legal compulsion? The shareholder in railroads demands a guarantee of his dividends, the industrialist, the mineowner, the shipper, the viniculturist, etc., they all demand to be protected in their occupations by tariff laws at the expense of their customers. Why do you not want to grant this favor as well to the more numerous and more moderate class, the artisan class? Factories enrich the individual, but they also breed a mass of proletarians, a mass of undernourished workers who are a menace to the state because of the insecurity of their livelihood. Handicraftsmen, on the other hand, constitute the backbone of the burgher class, of an element whose survival is essential to a healthy national life and whose maintenance seems to me to be fully as important as was the creation of a free peasantry at the beginning of this century for the sake of which the authorities did not boggle at serious infringements of law and property. It is true that industrial freedom may offer the public many advantages. It produces inexpensive goods. But to this inexpensiveness the misery and sorrow of the artisan are poisonously bound, and I believe that the inexpensive garments from the clothing shop may after all lie uneasily on our backs, when those who make them must despair of earning their daily bread honestly.[13]

By approving the emergency decrees the legislature endorsed the government policy of support for the guild system; and within a few years after their promulgation some 4,600 craft corporations had been founded or reconstituted by the artisans of Prussia. On April 3, 1854, a new law designed to strengthen the financial organization of labor welfare funds placed them more directly under state supervision and extended earlier provisions for compulsory participation. For the Westphalian textile workers there were state loans, trade schools, and new equipment. In Silesia economic rehabilitation was initiated with vocational training and industrial modernization. Then came special inducements to encourage the establishment of shops for the production of woolen, carpet, and plush wares. Finally the authorities helped introduce the manufacture of clocks and watches, little by little creating employment for idle spinners and weavers.[14]

To the advocates of industrial freedom the social teachings of the conservatives were sheer folly. Liberal politicians reviled legitimism for its blindness to the demands of progress, Manchestrian economists poked fun at its antiquated theories of production, and the learned publicists of the *Nationalzeitung*, the *Kölnische Zeitung*, and the *Ostseezeitung* predicted its defeat in the struggle against the spirit of the new age. Yet the reaction was not without apologists. Hermann Wagener, for example, defended its program before the Prussian legislature with a shrewd realism:

Recent times have taught us what the handicraftsmen want, and I believe that we now find ourselves in a position to warn the gentlemen on the left not to wait until disturbances arise before dealing with the demands of the handicraftsmen. For then they will once again act in haste and become involved in complications which it will be difficult to disentangle. I believe that the events of the years 1848 and 1849 have taught us that the artisan class desires not political but social improvements. If we want to wean the artisans from the political theory of subversion, then we can do so only by improving their social condition in accordance with the proper theory. Only because their needs had never been adequately met did they fall into the clutches of the party of the left and the men of subversion, for these promised to satisfy their wishes in the desired manner.[15]

Farther west handicraftsmen were also enjoying unaccustomed consideration. Even before the Revolution was over Hanover enacted the law of June 15, 1848, restoring corporate control over production. Ten months later, on April 3, 1849, Nassau broke with economic freedom by introducing residence and competence requirements for the practice of a craft. In Saxe-Gotha the four provisional statutes of September 24, 1849, establishing occupational courts and occupational assemblies were confirmed by the law of September 18, 1851. And in Frankfurt am Main artisans began to press on the senators of the municipal republic the draft of a manufacturing code endorsed by 700 masters providing for the restriction of factories and the formation of a chamber of trade. Disturbed by schemes limiting business initiative, the burgher patriciate blocked the adoption of the industrial charter, but in 1850 the city fathers agreed to establish a vocational council representing the interests of the independent shopkeepers.[16]

The Bavarian artisan also won important concessions. After the promulgation of the industrial law of September 11, 1825, he had found himself completely at the mercy of state officials invested with the life-and-death power to grant economic concessions. Just as his battle against the machine seemed lost, the revolution came bringing with it new hope. First liberalism bid for the favor of the urban masses with the statute of August 3, 1848, creating a chamber of trade to advise the government regarding the wishes of the small producer. Then five years later the conservatives countered with the decree of December 17, 1853, regulating the employment of apprentices, the sale of handicraft wares, and the ownership of artisan shops. To hard-pressed tradesmen the new policy was a godsend.[17]

There were still other means for the propitiation of guilds. For more than fifty years handicraft associations had been fighting tooth and nail in defense of the municipal right to exclude migrants from other communities. By controlling the influx of population they hoped to safeguard their markets, stabilize their earnings, and reduce competition. But freedom of industry led to freedom of movement, and while in most states relaxation of domicile requirements came slowly, the laws of November 26, 1834, in Saxony and December 31, 1842, in Prussia created a high degree of popular mobility. By the time of the Revolution the principle of laissez passer had gained the upper hand, and the Fundamental Rights of the German People proclaimed in Paragraph 133 that "every German has the right to make his abode and domicile in any community of the nation, to acquire real property of any kind and dispose of it, to practice any occupation, to acquire the civil rights of a resident."

Conservatism was less disposed to innovate. As reactionaries replaced liberals in the bureaucracy, official opinion became favorable to artisan demands for labor stability. In a few states such as Prussia it was no longer feasible to impose checks on the right of movement, although there too legitimist newspapers like the *Neue Preussische Zeitung* and legitimist politicians like Count Heinrich von Itzenplitz continued to rail against freedom of migration. Elsewhere, however, there seemed to be time enough to slow the drift of population from country to city. Troubled by the growth of urban pauperism, lawmakers rejected proposals for the abatement of residence restrictions, and here and there they actually reinforced older prohibitions. In Hanover, for example, the code of May 1, 1851, declared the acquisition of a legal domicile dependent on proof of moral character and financial independence, while in Württemberg the statute of May 5, 1852, continued to require of new residents not only economic solvency but honorable reputation as well.[18]

The reaction even made an effort to cope with the rapid growth of population by prohibiting the marriage of persons without means to support a family. In the years following the Congress of Vienna the rulers of Central Europe had begun to impose conjugal restrictions. These were most severe in the Mecklenburgs and in Bavaria, but the Thuringian principalities, the Hessian states, Baden, Hanover, and Nassau also sought to impede improvident marriages. Only Prussia, Saxony, Schleswig-Holstein, and the Palatinate refused to sanction any abridgment of the right of matrimony. In the Fifties conservatism strengthened the policy of marital restriction. Maintaining that it was the indigent and thriftless who were particularly prolific, the reactionary press advocated supervision of places of amusement and the revival of manorial discipline. And governments impressed with such arguments proceeded to extend marriage regulations, as in Württemberg by the law of May 5, 1852, and in Hesse-Darmstadt by the law of May 19, 1852. Yet such measures often raised moral issues as serious as the economic difficulties which they were supposed to solve. The state might decree celibacy, but it could not enforce abstinence. Illegitimacy was highest in precisely those regions where conjugal prohibitions were strictest. While in 1845-50 the percentage of children born out of wedlock was 14.8 in Saxony, 7.5 in Prussia, 7.4 in France, and 6.7 in England, in Bavaria it was 20.5. As for the Mecklenburgs with their exploited peasants and underprivileged townsmen, there the proportionate number of illicit unions was the greatest in Central Europe.[19]

Profiting from the experiences of its neighbors, Prussia rejected the demands of those reactionaries who insisted on the abrogation of the freedom of movement and the limitation of the right of marriage. The Manteuffel ministry was too hardheaded, too matter-of-fact to surrender to the eloquence of romantic legitimism. It sought rather to steer a middle course between artisan demands and business complaints. It would not ban the construction of factories, but by the decrees of February 9, 1849, it did introduce a measure of industrial self-government. It would not seek to reduce the birth rate by marriage prohibitions which invited concubinage and prostitution, but the edict of May 7, 1853, did facilitate emigration through state supervision over companies transporting passengers to the New World. It would not obstruct the movement of population, but it did promulgate the law of May 21, 1855, providing that in the first year of his residence in a new municipality a recipient of public charity remained the charge of his former community.[20]

Liberal arguments in defense of freedom of bargain between employer and employee found little favor among aristocrats who had long upheld traditional against contractual rights. On October 25, 1848, the king had submitted to the constituent convention the draft of a decree outlawing the truck system of wage payment. The constitutional crisis which broke soon afterward made enactment of the bill impossible, but its purpose was fulfilled by Paragraphs 50-55 of the law on industrial councils of February 9, 1849. During the Fifties the government began to enforce with greater vigor the ordinance of February 7, 1837, requiring a suspension of work on religious holidays. It encouraged the negotiation of agreements between employers and employees establishing uniform wage scales. It aided in the settlement of trade disputes through the creation of occupational courts and the appointment of inspectors to ensure compliance with factory regulations. And it sought to revive depressed industries by assisting harassed entrepreneurs with counsel, equipment, and money.[21]

The most important of the measures adopted for the benefit of the worker, however, was the law restricting the employment of minors. The first step toward a limitation of child labor had been the cabinet order of April 6, 1839, barring persons under nine years of age from work in factories, but this pioneer effort was too narrow in scope to end the exploitation of the young. Ten years after its promulgation industry still employed 8,000 workers between nine and twelve, and 24,000 between twelve and fourteen. Soon after the Revolution, therefore, Minister of Commerce Heydt decided to undertake a thoroughgoing revision of the legislation. He consulted with officials in the provinces, with chambers of commerce, trade corporations, manufacturers, journalists, and physicians. Most of them were in agreement that additional safeguards for the welfare of the youth of the nation were needed, and the ministry went to work. Early in 1853 it presented to the legislature the draft of a statute imposing stricter control over the working conditions of juveniles.[22]

The parliamentary discussion of the bill provided an interesting illustration of the conflicting social theories of liberals and conservatives. Opposition to the measure was strongest among the protagonists of constitutionalism in politics and individualism in economics. For such men as Karl Degenkolb, Erasmus von Patow, and Karl von Vincke an attempt to limit the freedom to work was an unjustifiable infringement of the rights of the citizen. In their criticism of the government draft they invoked visions of poor widows dependent on the earnings of their children, they prophesied the ruin of the domestic manufacturer unable to compete with cheap foreign labor, they warned that protection of minors would logically justify demands for state employment of the idle and state support of the disabled. All the dogmas of the dismal science of laissez faire were marshaled in behalf of the sanctity of contract.

From Ignaz von Olfers on the right side of the house came the reply of conservatism: "We have been told of the loss of funds. Gentlemen, there are also destructive funds, and these under discussion would be destructive funds, funds battening on the marrow of the state. We are not obliged to treat the children of the poor as if they were machines. It is our duty as men, as citizens, and as Christians to admit them to the social order, so that they may also enjoy their share of its fruits. For if we allow them to pine away in their childhood, then a grave guilt will hang over us, the educated classes."[23]

The government was victorious, and on May 16, 1853, the

measure became law. The labor of children under twelve was prohibited outright, while those between twelve and fourteen were to work no more than six hours a day. At a time when the minimum age of employment in England and France was eight, in Bavaria nine, and in Baden eleven, Prussia took the lead in the protection of the young against industrial oppression. They were to be exempt from nightwork, they were to receive daily rest periods, and they were to attend public or factory schools. The task of enforcement was entrusted to government inspectors and the regular courts, with violators subject to disqualification from the employment of underage workers and a fine of fifteen marks for each infringement. As to the effectiveness of the legislation, soon after its promulgation reports from Aachen showed that regulations requiring general school attendance could finally be enforced, while in a Westphalian manufacturing region like Arnsberg the number of juvenile laborers began to decline steadily. The hope expressed by Heydt that the state would "guard the growing generation of these workers against the crippling of body and soul" was becoming a reality.[24]

Regulation of child labor, abolition of the truck system, restoration of artisan self-government, elimination of personal servitudes, commutation of manorial obligations, these were the benefits which the reaction brought to the lower classes. The Fifties became a decade of new hope for the farmer and the worker, for the impoverished masses of the countryside and the uprooted proletariat of the city. They became the Indian summer of a social order which had been in decline since the advent of the factory system. A monarchism of public welfare developed in Germany which won the allegiance of the nation with its program of political legitimism and economic stability. Its goal was the fulfillment of the task which Manteuffel described as properly and uniquely its own: "The old feudal society was organized primarily for warlike purposes, for the old feudal states had originated in conquest, whereas today the pursuits of peace predominate and the interests of civil life are in the forefront, i.e., agriculture, industry, commerce, and the arts and sciences. It thus follows as a logical consequence that the princes must concern themselves in the most important fields of activity of civil society and wherever possible place themselves at their center."[25]

13

THE NEW ERA

LATE in the Fifties the reaction began to show signs of political exhaustion. In Austria the tortuous policy followed by the government during the Crimean War alienated Russia without winning the support of France. While the Slavs of the empire would not forget that for a few short months in 1848 they had been free, the Magyars continued to maintain a stubborn resistance against the centralizing policy of the Hofburg. Worst of all, the expenditures incurred through the mobilization of the army and the expansion of the bureaucracy strained the treasury to the breaking point, precipitating an acute financial crisis which weakened the fabric of Habsburg absolutism. For the time being the authorities were still able to hide civic discontent and economic enfeeblement behind a show of aggressive confidence, but with the first serious reverse the mask of bravura was bound to fall.

In Prussia the last years of the reign of Frederick William IV revealed only weakness in foreign policy and stagnation in domestic affairs. At the international conference in Paris in 1856 Manteuffel sat as an unwanted and almost uninvited guest, and a year later he was forced to seek the mediation of the Great Powers in the dispute with Switzerland over Hohenzollern rights in Neuchâtel. The loyal conservatives in the legislature continued to support the cabinet, more convinced than ever that the proof of political wisdom was a refusal to compromise with changing conditions. Yet the social monarchism of the reaction had lost its sense of mission, and there was a profound malaise behind royalist avowals which could still be heard in parliament and in the press. Unable to accept the new, unwilling to abandon the old, legitimism clung to power with a stubbornness born of secret panic.

The lesser governments of Germany found this state of affairs a source of secret satisfaction. What did it matter to them that the interests of the German Confederation were ignored in the councils of Europe, as long as difficulties in Berlin and Vienna enhanced their own importance by enabling them to fish in troubled waters? In 1850 they supported Schwarzenberg against Radowitz's plan for a new national union. In 1855 they supported Manteuffel against Buol's proposal for a mobilization of the federal army. In 1856 they agreed with Otto von Bismarck that a further restriction of representative institutions in Germany was inadvisable. In 1857 they agreed with Johann von Rechberg that a reinforced Austrian garrison should help defend the fortress of Rastatt. It was the heyday of bureaucratic intriguers expert in playing both ends against the middle, the heyday of second-rate statesmen from second-rate states like Ludwig von der Pfordten of Bavaria, Friedrich von Beust of Saxony, Wilhelm von Meysenburg of Baden, and Reinhard von Dalwigk of Hesse-Darmstadt.

The tragic illness of Frederick William IV was the first augury of a new age. For the unhappy king of Prussia the time had always been out of joint. Liberal agitation, revolutionary upheaval, aristocratic reaction, constitutions, parliaments, reforms, restorations—it was all too much for the morbidly contemplative man whom history had forced into a life of action. The cares of state disturbed him, frightened him, depressed him, and finally destroyed him. After suffering a stroke which left him mentally incapacitated in the fall of 1857, he spent the remaining years of his life in a twilight world of melancholy brooding. Prince William assumed the functions of the crown, although at first the ministry hesitated to formalize a transfer of power to the heir apparent who had more than once expressed his antipathy for the extremism of the camarilla. The further postponement of a regency became impossible, however, after a year had passed without an improvement in the condition of the ruler. On October 7, 1858, the queen herself presented to him the document assigning the royal prerogative to his brother. After reading it without a word, he signed; his head sank, and bursting into tears he stumbled out of the room.

The establishment of the regency meant the end of the reaction. No sooner had Prince William become master of the state in his own right, than he carried out a drastic purge of those most closely associated with the previous regime. An inbred suspicion of the abstract and the theoretical turned him against the overzealous royalism fostered by his predecessor. Westphalen, Raumer, the Gerlachs, Stahl, Kleist-Retzow, even the faithful Manteuffel fell from favor, and to take their place the regent summoned middle-of-the-road advisers. As head of the cabinet he appointed Prince Karl Anton of Hohenzollern-Sigmaringen, a grand seigneur with liberal leanings, but his most influential counselor was that same Rudolf von Auerswald who had held the premiership in the summer of 1848. The cabinet also included Count Maximilian von Schwerin-Putzar, leader of the opposition in the United Diet, Baron Erasmus von Patow, minister of commerce during the revolution, and Moritz von Bethmann-Hollweg, well-known for his attacks on the reaction in the *Preussisches Wochenblatt*. Before the year was out parliamentary elections had given an enthusiastic endorsement to the change in policy, for with 23 per cent of the eligible voters participating in the ballot, the party of the extreme right won only 59 seats, while the moderates led by Baron Georg von Vincke returned 210 members.

In Austria the days of the reaction were also numbered. Remembering that during the Revolution parliamentarianism had led to the disintegration of the empire, Francis Joseph in the first years of his reign remained convinced that the greatness of the dynasty depended only on military might. He therefore refused to hear of legislative reform, until the disastrous war with France into which the Hofburg blundered in the spring of 1859 destroyed the twin myths of the invincibility of the army and the infallibility of the bureaucracy. The foundations of Habsburg authoritarianism collapsed at the conference table in Villafranca, and on the morrow of the peace Vienna resolved to accept a constitutionalism deficient and stunted, but a constitutionalism all the same.

Among the minor states political energies dormant for more than a decade began to stir and waken. Early in 1859 Ludwig von der Pfordten retired as the leading minister of King Maximilian II of Bavaria. A year later Grand Duke Friedrich I of Baden dismissed Wilhelm von Meysenburg. In Heidelberg Ludwig Häusser thundered against the perfidious Habsburgs, and in Hanover Onno Klopp warned against the treacherous Hohenzollerns. The *Grenzboten* spoke from Leipzig with the voice of the centralist north, while the *Historisch-politische Blätter* in Munich pleaded the cause of the federalist south. In September 1859 the proponents of a Prussian imperial union formed the National Association, and in October 1862 the Austrophil Reform Association began its agitation for the reorganization of Germany. A period of constitutional conflict and civil war was opening, a period which would culminate in a fundamental alteration of the European balance of power.[1]

For the artisan the recovery of the liberal bourgeoisie from its defeat of 1849 was the beginning of the end. Even before the establishment of the regency in Berlin the economic position of the small shopowner had become hazardous, and throughout the Fifties he had continued to suffer from a chronic overcrowdedness. In numbers handicraftsmen still managed to keep pace with the general growth of population, but their opportunities for advancement were vanishing. Between 1852 and 1858 master artisans in Prussia decreased from 553,107 to 545,034, while journeymen and apprentices increased from 447,502 to 507,198. In Württemberg those engaged in the leading trades grew from 110,141 in 1852 to 126,710 in 1861, but the masters among them declined from 73,634 to 71,151. Independent tradesmen in Bavaria who numbered 151,006 in 1847 totaled only 157,435 in 1861, although their employees were rising from 149,554 to 172,-122. And then there were special cases like the textile industry of Sommerfeld where during the twenty years after 1845 master clothiers diminished by 60 per cent, or the Silesian woolen manufacture in which small producers fell from 2,056 to 1,200 between 1849 and 1861.

Where the artisan shop lost the factory gained. About 15,000 handicraftsmen left Baden in the Fifties to find richer economic opportunities abroad, yet the employees of manufacturing establishments in the grand duchy increased from 17,000 to 50,000. Between 1847 and 1861 masters, journeymen, and apprentices in Bavaria grew only 2.6 per cent, while industrial labor rose 9 per cent. Looms in use in Westphalian homes for the output of woolen cloth fell from 26,900 in 1837 to 18,369 in 1861, but the number of spindles in the average Prussian cotton mill climbed from 828 in 1837 to 1,126 in 1846, 2,627 in 1858, and 5,783 in 1861. At least 80 per cent of all business enterprises in the Zollverein were still owned by independent tradesmen, and those whom they provided with a livelihood constituted almost 60 per cent of all workers engaged in nonagricultural pursuits. But there could be no question that the guild system was heading for disaster.[2]

Convinced that a vigorous artisan class was essential for the defense of their political interests, the conservatives did their best to protect the handicraftsman. They attempted to delimit a sphere of economic activity within which he might find security against the power of money, hoping that the joint-stock company and the corporate association could live side by side without overstepping the imaginary line which divides big business from the small shop. The years of reaction demonstrated how unrealistic such expectations were. The restoration of restrictive control over production was at best a palliative, and once guild organizations realized that it could not revive declining markets or improve living conditions, the exaggerated hopes aroused by the legislation of the early Fifties gave way before a sense of despair.

The Prussian tradesman, for example, found only disappointment in the industrial laws of February 9, 1849. On paper he possessed far-reaching rights of economic regulation, but in practice he was hardly more successful than before in holding his own against the millowner. The welfare funds designed to shield him from impoverishment could not overcome the hostility of the well-to-do merchants and manufacturers whose influence in municipal affairs was predominant. In the entire kingdom only 230 social insurance associations were founded, and of these a mere 60 required contributions from employers as well as employees. The government sought to aid them through the decree of April 3, 1854, reinforcing stipulations for compulsory membership, but even with this assistance they rarely prospered. The industrial councils which were to represent the interests of the skilled craftsman were likewise unable to withstand the opposition of the powerful chambers of commerce. In the first flush of guild optimism following the defeat of the revolution 96 trade assemblies were founded, but by 1854 their number had fallen to 22, and in 1864 the last of them went under. As for the arbitration courts established to mediate in labor disputes, there were never more than 11 of them, and even these few expired quietly in the middle Fifties.[3]

As it became evident that the decline of the guild system was continuing, trade corporations once again began to compose memorials to the government. In the spring of 1851 the industrial council of Berlin was complaining of the shortage of credit for the small shopkeeper and urging the authorities to repair this deficiency out of the resources of the public treasury. Two years later the handicraftsmen of Cologne submitted an address concerning "the sad plight of the artisan class," a plea for survival from the land which for half a century had been the heart of industrial freedom. At each session of the legislature there were new complaints and new warnings. The same dilemma which had faced liberals during the Revolution returned to trouble conservatives during the counterrevolution. Again those in power had to choose between the political advantages of mass support and the economic advantages of factory production. And again they decided to follow a middle course.[4]

To be sure, the reaction saw the problem of the handicraftsman more clearly than had the parliamentarianism of 1848, yet nothing less than an outright suppression of business initiative would have satisfied his wishes. Guild organizations condemned speculation on the stock exchange, they advocated the abolition of department stores, they criticized the increasing division of labor, they deplored the growing burden of taxation, and they advised further restriction of the right to practice a trade. What government could agree to demands so violently opposed to the normal growth of its national economy? As a committee report presented to the Prussian legislature suggested: "The establishment of such a system of compulsion would in any case also require the restoration of abolished rights of sale, monopoly, and coercion, while the importation into cities of domestic and foreign handicraft wares would have to be forbidden."[5]

Even among conservatives only a few were prepared to go that far, and once the new era opened, the bureaucratic attitude toward the artisan began to cool noticeably. As for the liberals, the program of January 13, 1861, adopted by the parliamentary group in Prussia popularly known as Young Lithuania was typical in its condemnation of efforts to limit industrial freedom: "We shall recommend the liberation of trade from the bonds which still exist in our customs duties and consumption taxes to the detriment of the broad masses, and we shall also support a revision of the manufacturing laws, so that regulations which are oppressive and which remind us of the antiquated guild system are repealed, and after the abolition of police concessions free scope is given to all industrial energies."[6]

In a final effort to ward off ruin independent tradesmen prepared to moderate their demands. They would now be willing to settle for minor concessions, they might even consider only a guarantee of the gains they had won in the preceding ten years. To defend the rights of guild corporations, moreover, they organized state and national associations of artisans. Thus when the protagonists of laissez faire proposed the repeal of the industrial laws of February 9, 1849, the aroused shopowners promptly convoked the Prussian State Convention of Handicraftsmen. Meeting in Berlin from August 27 to August 31, 1860, they reaffirmed their opposition to economic freedom as the source of social decay. Two years later, on September 15, 1862, there was founded in Weimar the German Union of Handicraftsmen "to wage a life-and-death struggle against this plague and fraud of liberal industrial conditions." At subsequent meetings in Frankfurt am Main and in Cologne it voiced its disapproval of factories, banks, machines, department stores, and stock exchanges, and in 1864 it submitted to the states of the German Confederation a memorandum urging the adoption of a national code of industrial regulation.[7]

Artisans also attempted to strengthen their alliance with legitimism. Frightened by the growing bourgeois influence in government, noblemen and guildsmen opened an exchange of expressions of fraternal regard. The *Neue Preussische Zeitung* heaped praise on Minister of Commerce Heydt for his defense of the industrial legislation of 1849. Handicraft corporations held out the prospect of a coalition at the polls between landowners and shopkeepers. And monarchist leaders warned tradesmen that only in loyalty to tradition could they find protection against the tyranny of wealth. The conservative Prussian Popular Union, for example, made a bid for the support of the workingman with its program of September 20, 1861:

> Protection and esteem for honest labor, for every property, right, and estate. No favor and exclusive domination for capital. No surrender of handicraft and landed property to the false teachings and usurious artifices of the times. Freedom through the participation of the subject in legislation and through the autonomy and self-government of corporations and communities. Freedom through the maintenance of the protective order. No turn to bureaucratic absolutism and social servitude as the result of an unrestrained and licentious anarchy, and no imitation of the political and social institutions which have led France to Caesarism. Development of our constitution in the spirit of German freedom, in love and devotion to king and fatherland.[8]

As early as the Fifties, however, there had been portents of a growing reluctance among authorities to continue shoring up the tottering system of trade regulation. The government of Württemberg stubbornly refused to yield to artisan demands for new industrial restrictions and even sought to mitigate the severity of existing ones. In Frankfurt am Main reform of the municipal constitution prepared the way for a relaxation of controls over competition. Saxe-Coburg made known its intention to end restraints on commerce and manufacture. But the first major break with the corporate organization of production came in Austria. Ever since 1855 the imperial cabinet had been considering the removal of obstacles to the modernization of industry, although it hesitated to strengthen a middle class suspected of liberal sympathies. The defeat suffered in the war with France settled these doubts, and after Villafranca the Hofburg resolved to win bourgeois support by following a new course in economics as well as politics. The decree of December 20, 1859, gave the nation freedom of enterprise, while the diploma of October 20, 1860, proclaimed constitutional government.[9]

Within a year economic liberalism was on the march westward. In Nassau the law of June 9, 1860, and in Saxony the law of October 15, 1861, abandoned restrictive economic practices. Württemberg, unimpressed by the arguments of guild organizations, removed controls over production by the ordinance of February 12, 1862. In Baden Grand Duke Friedrich I proclaimed his adherence to laissez faire in the statute of September 20, 1862. And then the Thuringian principalities, the Hanseatic cities, and even the minor agricultural states of the north like Oldenburg, Brunswick, Waldeck, and Anhalt joined in the rush to make peace with the factory system.[10]

Those few governments which tried to stave off the downfall of the handicraftsman by retaining industrial regulation soon learned that such efforts were not only costly but futile. Hesse-Darmstadt at first resisted liberal economic demands, but finally by the decree of January 5, 1864, it too facilitated the exchange of goods within the Zollverein, and with the law of February 16, 1866, it introduced complete freedom of enterprise. Bavaria, which had hoped to appease business interests with the ordinance of April 21, 1862, relaxing limitations on the employment of labor, discovered that manufacturers refused to be bought off with half measures, and in the statute of January 30, 1868, the government of the youthful Ludwig II deferred to their wishes. In Prussia the two edicts of June 22 and July 1, 1861, easing the practice of a trade without abandoning the principle of state superintendence failed to satisfy a growing agitation for the total destruction of restrictive regulation. All in all, between the opening of the new era in 1858 and the conclusion of the war with Denmark in 1864 sixteen German lands came to terms with capitalism, by 1866 the number had risen to more than twenty, in 1869 it was thirty.[11]

Only in such unindustrialized states on the seacoast as Mecklenburg-Schwerin, Schleswig-Holstein, and Hanover did the handicraftsman still retain a precarious foothold, and even there the collapse of the guild system came before the decade was out. Yet the coup de grâce was administered not by some bourgeois parliamentarian nurtured on Adam Smith, but by the fire-eating Junker who was making a political career out of his opposition to liberalism. Otto von Bismarck had come a long way since that October of 1849 when he rose in the Prussian legislature to defend man against machine. In those days, arguing that the preservation of an independent class of tradesmen was essential to a healthy national life, he had condemned unrestrained competition, rejected the financial advantages of big business, and endorsed artisan demands for industrial regulation. The logic of the struggle against the constitutional theories of the industrial middle class had perforce made him a supporter of the corporate principle in economic organization.[12]

Then came the years in Frankfurt when Bismarck represented Prussia at the Diet of the Confederation, years marking a turning point in the life of the petty squire who had grown up in the provincialism of the eastern latifundia. He beheld for the first time the complexity of national statecraft and the vitality of bourgeois society, an experience which transformed the callow zealot into a diplomat. By the time of his departure in 1859 for the embassy in St. Petersburg he had renounced the simple political faith which had guided him through the trials of the Revolution. The man who had once celebrated the downfall of Radowitz with champagne was now himself a bitter enemy of Austrian ambitions. And in his acknowledgment that agrarian conservatism could not overcome the forces of nationalism he displayed that remarkable capacity for recognizing a winning idea which he described many years later with a deceptive simplicity: "I have never in my life been a doctrinaire."[13]

Since for Bismarck economic policy was a supplement to political action, his conversion to nationalism led to an acceptance of industrialism. In the early days of his public career he had been too much the Junker to see in popular discontent anything but cupidity or presumption. In April 1848 he complained that "we live in a time of material interests." In September 1849 he announced that "I am of the opinion that the 'dominant principles' of last year were social rather than national in nature." In July 1850 he was still convinced that the opposition had engineered the spring uprising "by promising the moon to the peasants and the workers." But the diplomatic duties which he assumed the following spring soon persuaded him that only in alliance with middle-class strength could his statecraft achieve success. By June 22, 1851, he was writing to Leopold von Gerlach:

> I would consider it most useful, if we were to concern ourselves in good time with questions of German material welfare. The side which seizes the initiative in this matter, whether it be the Diet of the Confederation, the Zollverein, or Prussia alone, will enjoy a great advantage with respect to the sympathies of the participants, since those things *quae numero et pondere dicuntur* are more important to the majority of Germans than to you and me. Although I do not place great value on a uniformity in measures, weights, bills of exchange, and other such knickknacks, and although I consider it difficult to put into practice, yet we should demonstrate our good will and play it up for the sake of the trades, but in the name of Prussia rather than the Diet of the Confederation. It would be most interesting for me to hear whether the negotiations between the Zollverein and Hanover are still continuing and progress-

ing. For the consolidation of the sound elements of northern Germany with ties of material interest, even if it should be purchased with the loss of the southern members of the Zollverein, would not be without conservative influence on the direction of our domestic policy and would enable us to regard with greater equanimity the development of the policy of the Diet of the Confederation.[14]

With this growing appreciation of the energies latent in capitalism, his artless confidence in the salutary moral influence of the artisan shop began to weaken. Were handicraftsmen who morbidly feared all innovation the suitable economic instrument for a program of blood and iron? Could the new Germany be built on a static organization of production to which trade associations still clung? Clearly the corporate guilds would have to surrender their controls over industry for the same reason that the secondary states would have to lose their rights of sovereignty. There was no place for them in an age of Realpolitik. Writing to Hermann Wagener from Frankfurt on April 27, 1853, Bismarck candidly confessed his change of heart:

I have until now expected a great deal from the abolition of industrial freedom, but local conditions prove that this alone will not serve the purpose. Here the guild system has up to the present remained intact, and we are spared none of the disadvantages which it brings, that is, excessive prices for manufactured articles, indifference to customers and therefore careless workmanship, long delays on orders, late beginning, early stopping, and protracted lunch hours when work is done at home, little choice in ready-made wares, backwardness in technical training, and many other deficiencies. . . . Here corporate associations, far from constituting a basis for Christian education and conduct, serve rather as the arena for petty political and personal squabbles and as a device for the successful exploitation of the public and the exclusion of competition.[15]

In the new era Bismarck's apprenticeship came to an end. Exiled at first to the genteel obscurity of ambassadorships in St. Petersburg and Paris, he was finally summoned to the helm in the midst of a constitutional crisis arising out of the conflict between king and legislature over military policy. The role of hard-bitten reactionary had been familiar to him since the days of the revolution, but now the Junker of Schönhausen was playing for bigger stakes than the restoration of the royal prerogative. His objective was the establishment of a political system under which the landed nobility could retain a favored position within the framework of parliamentary government. Since under modern conditions no out-and-out authoritarian regime was viable, the liberals would first be chastised for their overweening ambition, but then conciliated with timely concessions. For only by taking the lead in the movement for national unification could the monarchy win sufficient popular support to withstand the pressure of radical reformism. From his academic chair in Basel, Jacob Burckhardt analyzed the great transformation taking place in Central Europe with a shrewdness unexpected in a mild professor of Renaissance culture: "Bismarck has only taken in hand what would have happened in time anyway, but without him and against him. Seeing that the rising tide of democratic and social forces would somehow lead to a state of unrestrained violence, whether through the democrats themselves or through the governments, he said: '*Ipse faciam*' and waged the three wars of 1864, 1866, and 1870."[16]

Yet not even in the hour of his greatest triumph when at Sadowa the Hohenzollerns became masters of Germany did Bismarck overlook the vital role which the bourgeoisie had played in the rise of Prussia. Long afterward he told a group of admirers: "Discontent among the lower classes may produce a serious illness for which we have remedies, but discontent among the educated minority leads to a chronic disease whose diagnosis is difficult and cure protracted."[17] As soon as Austria had been compelled at Nikolsburg to agree to the dissolution of the German Confederation, he held out the olive branch to the middle class. To be sure, he insisted on a bill of indemnity legalizing the unparliamentary procedures followed in the past, but he was prepared to offer rich gifts in return. Could liberals oppose the creation of a national union which they had been demanding for fifty years, could they criticize the promulgation of a national constitution based on the work of the Frankfurt Parliament, could they quarrel with the adoption of a policy of economic modernization? A few of them were strong enough to resist the blandishments of the Iron Chancellor, but most bowed down before the golden calf of success.

Among the earliest achievements of this new alliance between crown and bourgeoisie on which Bismarck built his state was the final victory of industrial freedom. Soon after the formation of the North German Confederation the ministry submitted to the legislature the draft of a national code of manufacture, and when parliamentary discussion of the measure began to drag, the provisional decree of July 8, 1868, was issued. Its six short paragraphs made a shambles of the rights of trade associations. It enabled the employer to hire as many workers as he wanted, the handicraftsman to practice his calling in defiance of guild regulations, the buyer to purchase his wares in any market and from any dealer. And while the definitive industrial law of June 21, 1869, dealt with the conditions of manufacture in much greater detail, it was equally opposed to the interests of corporate organizations. With its adoption the long struggle between artisan and millowner was over.[18]

The constitution of the North German Confederation, moreover, authorized the government to legislate in civil and criminal law, industry and finance, commerce and transportation, weights and measures, and posts and telegraphs. A bold opportunist like Bismarck knew how to make use of such powers to construct a sound economic foundation for his great political achievement. On November 1, 1867, he promulgated a measure establishing freedom of movement to help adjust the distribution of population to the demand for factory labor. Consular representation of national interests abroad was strengthened by the decree of November 8, 1867. The law of June 5, 1869, introduced uniform business regulations and practices throughout Germany. The Zollverein won a great triumph with the adhesion of the Mecklenburgs and Lübeck in 1868, restrictions on the formation of joint-stock companies fell in 1870, export duties disappeared in 1873, and the creation of the German Imperial Bank fortified the financial structure of the state.[19]

The business community had long hoped that common political institutions would lead to a common system of weights, measures, and coinage. The first two of these objectives were easily achieved by the decree of August 17, 1868, but the adoption of a uniform monetary standard proved to be a more complicated undertaking. At the time of the formation of the empire there were seven legal tender areas and thirty-three banks of issue in Germany, each possessing a high degree of autonomy, each determined to retain its freedom of action. The government had to act cautiously to transform this congeries of mediums of exchange into a national money system. First the law of December 4, 1871, established a central mint office empowered to issue an imperial currency, and then the law of July 9, 1873, provided for the withdrawal from circulation of coinages emitted by state authorities. The arguments of economic experts like Ludwig Bamberger and Rudolph von Delbrück, moreover, persuaded Bismarck to adopt the gold standard, although traditionally silver was the fiscal base everywhere except

Bremen. He thus avoided the problems of bimetallism which soon beset other countries, and within a few years the mark could take its place beside the pound as a mainstay of financial stability in the West.[20]

Unification led to an equally thoroughgoing reform of communication and transportation. In the early Sixties more than twenty independent postal organizations vied with each other in the German Confederation, some like the Prussian and Hanoverian under government control, others like the Hessian and Thuringian administered by the Thurn und Taxis family corporation. These rival systems were amalgamated by the decree of December 18, 1867, and before long the indefatigable Postmaster General Heinrich von Stephan was directing one of the most advanced mail services in Europe. The fees which had for centuries impeded the movement of water traffic began to diminish earlier still, as one after another the rivers of Central Europe rid themselves of burdensome restrictions. The Ems became free in 1851, the Danube in 1856, the Moselle in 1862, the Rhine in 1868, and the Elbe in 1870. Road tolls had been generally abolished in the south even before the Revolution, while in the Hohenzollern lands they disappeared at last by 1875. As for railroads, Bismarck was content to leave them in the hands of private investors or state authorities, but the law of June 27, 1873, created an imperial bureau to supervise the activities of common carriers.[21]

On October 23, 1828, in a conversation with Johann Peter Eckermann, Goethe had expressed a pious wish which millions of his generation shared:

I have no fear that Germany will not become one, for our good roads and our future railroads will play their part. Above all, however, may it be one in mutual love, may it always be one against the foreign foe. May it be one, so that the German thaler and the German groschen have

the same value everywhere in the nation, so that my travel-
ing bag can pass unopened through all the thirty-six states.
May it be one, so that the municipal passport of a citizen of
Weimar is not treated by the frontier official of some great
neighboring state as invalid, as the passport of an alien.
May there no longer be any distinction of native and foreign
among the German states. Furthermore, may Germany be
one in weights and measures, in trade and business, and in
a hundred similar things all of which I could not and would
not enumerate.[22]

Forty-two years later on January 18, 1871, Bismarck
stood in the Hall of Mirrors at Versailles to witness the
proclamation of the German Empire. Goethe and Bismarck,
Weimar and Potsdam, the antipodes of the spirit of Central
Europe were meeting in the creation of a new state capable
of satisfying an intense national longing for political unity
and economic progress. Germany had entered an age in which
military victory, diplomatic success, and industrial might became the idols of a country drunk with good fortune.

Yet the magnitude of its accomplishment obscured the
image of another Germany, a Germany of lackland peasants,
struggling artisans, impoverished shopkeepers, and hungry
journeymen. The fall of a precapitalistic social order went
almost unnoticed in a world bent on getting rich at all costs.
Neither the captains of industry nor the lords of agriculture
rose to defend the handicraftsman in his last hour, for there
was no room for him in the vast market place of capitalism
where men were busy buying, selling, haggling, speculating,
manufacturing, hoarding. One after another the familiar
landmarks of his way of life crumbled and disappeared, first
the corporate prerogatives, then the restrictive regulations,
then the guild associations, then the independent shops.
Finally he himself lost his unique economic identity and sank
into the gray sea of factory labor which was spreading over
the face of Europe. A new era had begun.

CONCLUSION

Die deutsche Revolution von 1848 zeigt nun gewiss
nicht nur allenthalben den oft über das Wirkliche
hinwegfliegenden und ideologisch werdenden Ideal-
ismus, sondern auch—kausal noch mächtiger—das
Wirkliche selber, die massiven und elementaren In-
teressen der Menschen und sozialen Gruppen.

FRIEDRICH MEINECKE (1948)

14

THE ROAD TO UNIFICATION

IN THE FIRST ACT OF *Faust* the protagonist of the greatest
of German dramas, pondering the translation of an enigmatic
passage in the New Testament, meditates on the source of
human destiny:

> 'T is written: "In the Beginning was the *Word*."
> Here am I balked: who, now, can help afford?
> The *Word*?—impossible so high to rate it;
> And otherwise must I translate it,
> If by the Spirit I am truly taught.
> Then thus: "In the Beginning was the *Thought*."
> This first line let me weigh completely,
> Lest my impatient pen proceed too fleetly.
> Is it the *Thought* which works, creates, indeed?
> "In the Beginning was the *Power*," I read.
> Yet, as I write, a warning is suggested,
> That I the sense may not have fairly tested.
> The Spirit aids me: now I see the light!
> "In the Beginning was the *Act*," I write.[1]

The historian will appreciate the perplexity of Goethe's
bemused hero. As he contemplates Germany in the nineteenth
century, he too must choose between the word and the act,
between thoughts and deeds. It becomes his task to appraise
the influence of mind and matter on the course of political
development, finding purpose and direction in the infinite
complexity of an age long dead. And while the search for
the meaning of the past may lead him into error, it is also
the justification of his calling. Through it he may discover an
aspect of truth, without it he becomes an antiquarian.

When posterity looks into history, a familiar image looks
back. It sees what it wants to see, it sees its own problems, its

own interests, its own attitudes. For the liberal the years from Metternich to Bismarck are a period of struggle for constitutional freedom, for the patriot they are an awakening of the national consciousness, for the socialist a step in the development of the class struggle, for the Germanophobe an illustration of the perversity of the Teutonic mind. Each seeks the ideological forces which determine the direction of social development, each finds in them only the reflection of his time. They all exclaim with Wilhelm Mommsen: "In writing or speaking about 1848 we do not stand before a grave, but before political happenings and struggles which still have vitality for our age."[2]

Yet the emphasis on the modern significance of the past exacts a price. It leads to an exclusive concern with those political and economic problems relevant to the life of a later generation, and to the neglect of issues important only to their own time. Here lies the fallacy of the quest for present value in 1848, for in writing about it we do stand before a grave. The starting point of a study of the German Confederation must be the vanished society in which the men of the German Confederation worked, hoped, and fought. Each age has the right to be understood in its own terms. The gospel of unity and freedom, so familiar in a century of world wars, was originally intended for another era and another milieu. As a matter of fact, it was only one of many calls to action competing for the allegiance of a bewildered and frightened nation. To maintain that liberal nationalism was the dominant force among the various political, economic, social, and intellectual influences at work in Central Europe after the Congress of Vienna is a gross oversimplification.

The truth is that there was no German Revolution of 1848. There were rather several simultaneous German revolutions, each with its own ideology and objective, all combining their efforts to achieve the overthrow of an oppressive system of government. One of these, the uprising of the middle class, came to dominate the political scene so completely that to this day it remains the only revolution in the textbook and in the classroom. Its accomplishments, the Frankfurt Parliament, the Fundamental Rights of the German People, and the constitution of March 28, 1849, have found a secure place in history. Yet its fleeting success was made possible only by peasant revolts and artisan riots. As far as the masses were concerned, the insurrection was the outcome of tensions generated by the transition from agricultural manorialism to industrial capitalism. They were prepared to accept the leadership of liberal parliamentarians, but their allegiance to constitutionalism depended on the satisfaction of their material needs.

Uneasy alliances of diverse interests stood behind St. Paul's Church, and the claim that it spoke in the name of a united people was valid only as long as it confined itself to a censure of the past. Once it attempted to build a new order on the ruins of the old, it found itself face to face with the inconsistencies inherent in the coalition of which it was nominally in command. All the irreconcilably opposed claims of handicraftsmen, shopkeepers, manufacturers, bankers, peasants, landowners, day laborers, and factory workers began to pound on the doors of liberalism. The joint purpose of the insurrection vanished with the defeat of its joint foe, and the victors were left to attempt a division of the spoils acceptable to all the allies in the Revolution.

It was an impossible task. Subjected to the conflicting demands of interests and classes which descended on it as soon as it achieved power, German parliamentarianism responded with a program reflecting its middle-class background. The rights of property took precedence over the needs of men, the arguments of the industrialist prevailed over the appeals of the artisan, liberty destroyed security. Given their philosophy of state and society, the constitutionalists had to act with the fatal logic which led ineluctably to their undoing. They clung to their faith in freedom in defiance of the dictates of expediency, while before their eyes a coalition was formed between political conservatism and economic traditionalism. This realignment of popular forces made possible the temporary restoration of the old order, and when the time for an adjustment of national life to changing social conditions came around once again, it was under the auspices of a policy of blood and iron that Central Europe finally embraced the machine age.

BIBLIOGRAPHY

BIBLIOGRAPHY

I. GUIDES TO HISTORICAL MATERIALS

No complete bibliographical account of the scholarly literature dealing with the period of the German Confederation has ever been undertaken. Dahlmann-Waitz, *Quellenkunde der deutschen Geschichte*, 9th ed. (2 vols., Leipzig, 1931-32) names more than two thousand publications, but its treatment of documentary materials is inadequate. The same criticism may be directed against Veit Valentin, *Geschichte der deutschen Revolution von 1848-49* (2 vols., Berlin, 1930-31), which contains a list of some fifteen hundred books and a comprehensive critical essay. Paul Wentzcke, *Kritische Bibliographie der Flugschriften zur deutschen Verfassungsfrage, 1848-1851* (Halle a. S., 1911) is a guide to the pamphlets and tracts of 1848 concerning constitutional problems. The best description of writings appearing since the fall of the Weimar Republic is presented in Jacques Droz, *Les révolutions allemandes de 1848* (Paris, 1957). There is not much else, for the bibliographies in Rudolf Stadelmann, *Soziale und politische Geschichte der Revolution von 1848* (Munich, 1948) and Jacques Droz, "Travaux récents sur la révolution de 1848 en Allemagne," *Revue d'histoire moderne et contemporaine*, 1 (1954) are hardly more than sketches, while the survey in the *Historische Zeitschrift*, CLXX (1950), 660-665 is confined to works written in celebration of the centennial of the March days. The great co-operative histories like Lord Acton's *The Cambridge Modern History*, ed. A. W. Ward, G. W. Prothero, and Stanley Leathes (14 vols., Cambridge and New York, 1902-12); *Histoire générale du IVe siècle à nos jours*, ed. Ernest Lavisse and Alfred Rambaud (12 vols., Paris, 1893-1901); and *Peuples et civilisations*, ed. Louis Halphen and Philippe Sagnac (20 vols., Paris, 1926-45) contain only short lists of obvious titles. Of the attempts to analyze the historiography of the Revolution the most ambitious is the unpublished doctoral dissertation submitted to Columbia University in 1955 by Kurt Schwerin, *The Revolution of 1848 and the German Historians*. More modest in scope are two review articles by Axel von Harnack, "Die Paulskirche im Wandel der Geschichtsauffassung," *Zeitschrift für Politik*, XII (1922) and "Die deutsche Revolution von 1848-49 als Aufgabe für den Geschichtsschreiber," *Sammlung*, III (1948), and a study of the changing fashions in scholarship by J. A. Hawgood, "The Frankfurt Parliament of 1848-49," *History*, XVII (1932). Theodore S. Hamerow, "History and the German Revolution of 1848," *American Historical Review*, LX (1954) criticizes the narrowly political and ideological approaches to 1848.

II. PARLIAMENTARY MINUTES, LAW COLLECTIONS, STATE DOCUMENTS, INTERNATIONAL TREATIES

The most important sources for the history of the Revolution are the verbatim reports of the deliberations in St. Paul's Church edited by Franz Wigard under the title *Stenographischer Bericht über die Verhandlungen der deutschen constituirenden Nationalversammlung zu Frankfurt am Main* (9 vols., Frankfurt am Main, 1848-49) and the official minutes, committee reports, and formal motions appearing in *Verhandlungen der deutschen verfassunggebenden Reichs-Versammlung zu Frankfurt am Main*, ed. K. D. Hassler (6 vols., Frankfurt am Main, 1848-49). The proceedings of the preliminary parliament and of the committee of fifty may be found in *Verhandlungen des deutschen Parlaments* (2 vols., Frankfurt am Main, 1848), while the debates of the constitutional committee of the Frankfurt Parliament were published partly in *Die Verhandlungen des Verfassungs-Ausschusses der deutschen Nationalversammlung*, ed. Johann Gustav Droysen (Leipzig, 1849) and partly in *Aktenstücke und Aufzeichnungen zur Geschichte der Frankfurter Nationalversammlung aus dem Nachlass von Johann Gustav Droysen*, ed. Rudolf Hübner (Stuttgart, Berlin, and Leipzig, 1924). For political developments in Prussia the essential parliamentary records are *Der erste vereinigte Landtag in Berlin 1847*, ed. Eduard Bleich (4 vols., Berlin, 1847); *Verhandlungen des am 2. April 1848 zu Berlin eröffneten zweiten vereinigten Landtages* (Berlin, 1848); and *Verhandlungen der Versammlung zur Vereinbarung der preus-*

sischen Staats-Verfassung (6 vols., Berlin, 1848). During the reaction the deliberations of the legislature in Berlin appeared in *Stenographische Berichte über die Verhandlungen der Kammern.* A wealth of material is also contained in the legislative minutes of the secondary states. For Bavaria there are *Verhandlungen der Kammer der Reichsräthe* and *Verhandlungen der Kammer der Abgeordneten*; for Württemberg *Verhandlungen der württembergischen Kammer der Abgeordneten* and *Verhandlungen der württembergischen Kammer der Standesherren*; and for Baden *Verhandlungen der Stände-Versammlung des Grossherzogthums Baden.*

The law gazettes published by the members of the German Confederation illustrate the policies which the governments of Central Europe were pursuing. The most important of these is *Gesetz-Sammlung für die königlichen preussischen Staaten,* but other significant publications are *Gesetz-Blatt für das Königreich Bayern; Königlich württembergisches Staats- und Regierungs-Blatt; Gesetz- und Verordnungsblatt für das Königreich Sachsen; Sammlung der Gesetze, Verordnungen und Ausschreiben für das Königreich Hannover*; and *Grossherzoglich badisches Staats- und Regierungsblatt.* Then come such journals of the secondary states as *Grossherzoglich hessisches Regierungsblatt; Sammlung von Gesetzen, Verordnungen, Ausschreiben und anderen allgemeinen Verfügungen für Kurhessen; Verordnungsblatt des Herzogthums Nassau; Gesetz- und Verordnungs-Sammlung für die herzoglich braunschweigischen Lande*; and *Chronologische Sammlung der Gesetze, Verordnungen und Verfügungen für die Herzogthümer Schleswig-Holstein.* Finally there are the statute books of minor principalities like *Regierungs-Blatt für das Grossherzogthum Sachsen-Weimar-Eisenach; Sammlung der landesherrlichen Verordnungen im Herzogthume Sachsen-Meiningen; Gesetzsammlung für das Herzogthum Gotha; Gesetzsammlung für das Fürstenthum Schwarzburg-Rudolstadt; Gesetz- und Statuten-Sammlung der freien Stadt Frankfurt; Sammlung der Verordnungen der freien Hanse-Stadt Hamburg*; and *Sammlung der Verordnungen und Proclame des Senats der freien Hansestadt Bremen.* With the achievement of national unification the federal government began to publish *Bundes-Gesetzblatt des Norddeutschen Bundes,* which soon became *Reichs-Gesetzblatt.*

A few years after the Revolution Paul Roth and Heinrich Merck issued a valuable collection of official documents entitled *Quellensammlung zum deutschen öffentlichen Recht seit 1848* (2 vols., Erlangen, 1850-52). The texts of several important state papers may also be found in the two works edited by Wilhelm Altmann, *Ausgewählte Urkunden zur brandenburgisch-preussischen Verfassungs- und Verwaltungsgeschichte* (2 vols., Berlin 1897) and *Ausgewählte Urkunden zur deutschen Verfassungsgeschichte seit 1806* (2 vols., Berlin, 1898). The constitutional laws of Central Europe appear in *Die deutschen Verfassungsgesetze der Gegenwart*, ed. Heinrich Albert Zachariä (Göttingen, 1855), while the best edition of the German constitution of 1848 is by Ludwig Bergsträsser, *Die Verfassung des Deutschen Reiches vom Jahre 1849 mit Vorentwürfen, Gegenvorschlägen und Modifikationen bis zum Erfurter Parlament* (Bonn, 1913). A useful source for the programs, statutes, and memberships of the parties formed during the revolution is Gottfried Eisenmann, *Die Parteyen der teutschen Reichsversammlung: Ihre Programme, Statuten und Mitglieder-Verzeichnisse* (Erlangen, 1848), but there is also *Die deutschen Parteiprogramme*, ed. Felix Salomon (2 vols., Leipzig and Berlin, 1907). The delicate negotiations leading to the formation of the Zollverein are traced in *Vorgeschichte und Begründung des deutschen Zollvereins, 1815-1834*, ed. W. v. Eisenhart Rothe and A. Ritthaler (3 vols., Berlin, 1934). A discerning account of economic conditions in Germany in the Thirties may be found in John Bowring, "Report on the Prussian Commercial Union," *Parliamentary Papers* (1840), XXI. [Johannes] Fallati, "Entwürfe zu einem Flussschifffahrts-Gesetze und zu einem Reichsgesetze über die Aufhebung der Flusszölle und die Ausgleichung für dieselbe nebst Motiven: Aus den Acten des Reichshandelsministeriums der provisorischen Centralgewalt," *Zeitschrift für die gesammte Staatswissenschaft*, VI (1850) exemplifies the reforms in transportation which the provisional central government was contemplating.

The most complete assemblage of European treaties concluded between Waterloo and Sedan is the series edited under the name of G. F. de Martens, *Nouveau recueil de traités d'alliance, de paix, de trêve, de neutralité, de commerce, de limites, d'échange etc.*

et de plusieurs autres actes servant à la connaissance des relations étrangères des puissances et états de l'Europe (16 vols., Göttingen, 1817-42) and *Nouveau recueil général de traités, conventions et autres transactions remarquables, servant à la connaissance des relations étrangères des puissances et états dans leurs rapports mutuels* (20 vols., Göttingen, 1843-75). Sufficient for most purposes, however, is the briefer work of Edward Hertslet, *The Map of Europe by Treaty* (4 vols., London, 1875-91). The texts of Prussian trade agreements negotiated about the time of the formation of the Zollverein appear in *Die Handels- und Schifffahrtsverträge des Zollvereines,* ed. C. A. von Kamptz (Brunswick, 1845). There are also two valuable collections of conventions regulating the international rivers of Central Europe, *Rheinurkunden: Sammlung zwischenstaatlicher Vereinbarungen, landesrechtlicher Ausführungsverordnungen und sonstiger wichtiger Urkunden über die Rheinschiffahrt seit 1803* (2 vols., The Hague, Munich, and Leipzig, 1918) and *Die Elbzölle: Aktenstücke und Nachweise, 1814-1859* (Leipzig, 1860).

III. NEWSPAPERS, LETTERS, MEMOIRS, WRITINGS

One of the best German newspapers was the *Allgemeine Zeitung* of Augsburg, presenting a picture of national and international political developments in the colors of a moderate parliamentarianism. Far to its left stood the *Neue Rheinische Zeitung: Organ der Demokratie,* edited in Cologne by the young firebrand Karl Marx. At the other extreme was the ultraconservative *Neue Preussische Zeitung,* which voiced the sentiments of the reactionary aristocracy of the eastern marches. Good examples of the provincial press were such Munich papers as *Neue Münchner Zeitung, Neueste Nachrichten aus dem Gebiete der Politik,* and *Bayerische Landbötin,* all three liberal in outlook and Bavarian in flavor. More parochial still were the reformist *Hessische Volkszeitung* and the democratic *Freie Hessische Zeitung* of Giessen. *Kladderadatsch: Organ für und von Bummler,* a weekly journal of political satire appearing in Berlin, expressed its radical leanings in story and cartoon. The most influential periodical of the protectionists was *Das Zollvereinsblatt* of Augsburg, while many prominent liberals voiced their convictions in *Staats-Lexikon oder Encyclopädie der Staatswissenschaften*, ed. Carl von Rotteck and Carl Welcker (15 vols., Altona, 1834-43). *Die Gegenwart: Eine encyclopädische Darstellung der neuesten Zeitgeschichte für alle Stände*, ed. August Kurtzel (12 vols., Leipzig, 1848-56) contains articles on public affairs by well-known scholars like Lorenz von Stein, Ludwig Häusser, Karl Vogt, David Friedrich Strauss, and Wilhelm Heinrich Riehl. Brief accounts of world events and the texts of important speeches and documents may also be found in the *Annual Register* of London.

Among the important publications of letters and memoranda by leading political figures are three collections of the writings of Frederick William IV, *Revolutionsbriefe 1848: Ungedrucktes aus dem Nachlass König Friedrich Wilhelms IV. von Preussen*, ed. Karl Haenchen (Leipzig, 1930); *König Friedrich Wilhelms IV. Briefwechsel mit Ludolf Camphausen*, ed. Erich Brandenburg (Berlin, 1906); and *Aus dem Briefwechsel Friedrich Wilhelms IV. mit Bunsen*, ed. Leopold von Ranke (Leipzig, 1873). The last of these, however, should be supplemented with *Christian Carl Josias Freiherr von Bunsen: Aus seinen Briefen und nach eigener Erinnerung geschildert von seiner Witwe*, ed. Friedrich Nippold (3 vols., Leipzig, 1868-71). A selection from the correspondence of the king's heir was published as *Kaiser Wilhelms I. Weimarer Briefe*, ed. Johannes Schultze (2 vols., Stuttgart, Berlin, and Leipzig, 1924), while the papers of the king's chief adviser appear in *Josef von Radowitz: Nachgelassene Briefe und Aufzeichnungen zur Geschichte der Jahre 1848-1853*, ed. Walter Möring (Stuttgart and Berlin, 1922). Prominent parliamentarians describe their hopes and activities in Friedrich von Raumer, *Briefe aus Frankfurt und Paris, 1848-49* (2 vols., Leipzig, 1849); *Johann Gustav Droysen: Briefwechsel*, ed. Rudolf Hübner (2 vols., Stuttgart, Berlin, and Leipzig, 1929); *Ausgewählter Briefwechsel Rudolf Hayms*, ed. Hans Rosenberg (Stuttgart, Berlin, and Leipzig, 1930); and *Max Duncker: Politischer Briefwechsel aus seinem Nachlass*, ed. Johannes Schultze (Stuttgart and Berlin, 1923). The growing restiveness of public opinion under the Restoration is expressed in such collections as *Rheinische Briefe und Akten zur Geschichte der politischen*

Bewegung, 1830-1850, ed. Joseph Hansen (2 vols. Essen and Bonn, 1919-42); *1848: Der Vorkampf deutscher Einheit und Freiheit*, ed. Tim Klein (Ebenhausen-Munich and Leipzig, 1914); *Einheit und Freiheit: Die deutsche Geschichte von 1815 bis 1849 in zeitgenössischen Dokumenten*, ed. Karl Obermann (Berlin, 1950); and J. G. Legge, *Rhyme and Revolution in Germany: A Study in German History, Life, Literature and Character, 1813-1850* (London, 1919).

As soon as the Revolution was over its protagonists hastened to their desks to compose their apologias. Among works written from the point of view of the Prussophil wing of constitutionalism were Rudolf Haym, *Die deutsche Nationalversammlung* (3 vols., Frankfurt am Main and Berlin, 1848-50); Heinrich Laube, *Das erste deutsche Parlament* (3 vols., Leipzig, 1849); Max Duncker, *Zur Geschichte der deutschen Reichsversammlung in Frankfurt* (Berlin, 1849); and Karl Biedermann, *Erinnerungen aus der Paulskirche* (Leipzig, 1849). Karl Jürgens, a Brunswick clergyman, championed the Habsburg cause in *Zur Geschichte des deutschen Verfassungswerkes, 1848-49* (3 vols., Brunswick and Hanover, 1850-57), while the cry of militant democracy could be heard in Wilhelm Zimmermann, *Die deutsche Revolution* (Karlsruhe, 1848) and Bruno Bauer, *Der Untergang des Frankfurter Parlaments: Geschichte der deutschen constituirenden Nationalversammlung* (Berlin, 1849).

Memoirs began to appear in the latter years of the nineteenth century, as the generation of the spring uprising reached old age. For the conservatives there were works like Hermann Wagener, *Erlebtes: Meine Memoiren aus der Zeit von 1848 bis 1866 und von 1873 bis jetzt* (2 vols., Berlin, 1883-84) and *Die kleine aber mächtige Partei* (Berlin, 1885); *Denkwürdigkeiten aus dem Leben Leopold von Gerlachs, Generals der Infanterie und General-Adjutanten König Friedrich Wilhelms IV.* (2 vols., Berlin, 1891-92); and *Ernst Ludwig von Gerlach: Aufzeichnungen aus seinem Leben und Wirken, 1795-1877* (2 vols., Schwerin, 1903). Liberals found comfort in Karl Biedermann, *Dreissig Jahre deutscher Geschichte* (2 vols., Breslau, 1881); Georg Beseler, *Erlebtes und Erstrebtes, 1809-1859* (Berlin, 1884); and Reinhard Carl Theodor Eigenbrodt, *Meine Erin-*

nerungen aus den Jahren 1848, 1849 und 1850, ed. Ludwig Bergsträsser (Darmstadt, 1914). Even the radicals, mellowed by time and experience, presented their side of the story in Julius Fröbel, *Ein Lebenslauf: Aufzeichnungen, Erinnerungen und Bekenntnisse* (2 vols., Stuttgart, 1890-91); *Erinnerungen aus dem Leben von Hans Viktor von Unruh,* ed. Heinrich von Poschinger (Stuttgart, Leipzig, Berlin, and Vienna, 1895); Stephan Born, *Erinnerungen eines Achtundvierzigers* (Leipzig, 1898); and Carl Schurz, *Lebenserinnerungen* (3 vols., Berlin, 1906-12). Economic developments are described by A. Duckwitz, *Denkwürdigkeiten aus meinem öffentlichen Leben von 1841-1866: Ein Beitrag zur bremischen und deutschen Geschichte* (Bremen, 1877) and Rudolph von Delbrück, *Lebenserinnerungen, 1817-1867* (2 vols., Leipzig, 1905), while *Aus dem Nachlass Varnhagen's von Ense: Tagebücher* (14 vols., Leipzig, Zurich, and Hamburg, 1861-70) is a chatty commentary on the passing social scene. The most perceptive of foreign observers was Adolphe de Circourt, *Souvenirs d'une mission à Berlin en 1848,* ed. Georges Bourgin (2 vols., Paris, 1908-1909), but two discerning Americans also expressed their views in [Andrew Jackson Donelson], "The American Minister in Berlin on the Revolution of March, 1848," *American Historical Review,* XXIII (1918) and in Theodore S. Fay, "The Revolution of 1848 in Berlin: Personal Recollection," *Galaxy,* XVI (1873) and *The Three Germanys* (2 vols., New York, 1889).

Collections of the political writings of the Forties appeared as early as the reaction. Radowitz, for example, lived long enough to see his *Gesammelte Schriften* (5 vols., Berlin, 1852-53), and a modest selection of official statements by his royal master was issued in Berlin in 1851 as *Reden, Proklamationen, Botschaften, Erlasse und Ordres Sr. Majestät des Königs Friedrich Wilhelm IV. Vom Schlusse des vereinigten ständischen Ausschusses, am 6. März 1848, bis zur Enthüllungs-Feier des Denkmals Friedrich des Grossen, am 31. Mai 1851.* Twenty years later Johann Jacoby defended his convictions in his *Gesammelte Schriften und Reden* (2 vols., Hamburg, 1872). The memoranda which Leopold von Ranke composed for the king of Prussia during the Revolution may be found in volume XLIX-L of his *Sämmtliche Werke* (54 vols., Leipzig, 1867-90). After the fall of Bismarck the bourgeois statesmen came into their own with Joseph Hansen, *Gustav von Mevissen: Ein rheinisches Lebensbild, 1815-1899* (2 vols., Berlin, 1906); *L. Camphausen*, ed. Mathieu Schwann (3 vols., Essen, 1915); Erich Brandenburg, *Untersuchungen und Aktenstücke zur Geschichte der Reichsgründung* (Leipzig, 1916); and Johann Gustav Droysen, *Politische Schriften*, ed. Felix Gilbert (Munich and Berlin, 1933). But there were also scholars to do justice to prominent conservatives in such works as *Friedrich August Ludwig von der Marwitz: Ein märkischer Edelmann im Zeitalter der Befreiungskriege*, ed. Friedrich Meusel (2 vols., Berlin, 1908-13); *Unter Friedrich Wilhelm IV.: Denkwürdigkeiten des Ministers Otto Freiherrn v. Manteuffel*, ed. Heinrich v. Poschinger (3 vols., Berlin, 1901); *Preussens auswärtige Politik, 1850 bis 1858: Unveröffentlichte Dokumente aus dem Nachlasse des Ministerpräsidenten Otto Frhrn. v. Manteuffel*, ed. Heinrich v. Poschinger (3 vols., Berlin, 1902); and Otto von Bismarck, *Die gesammelten Werke* (15 vols., Berlin, 1924-35). The theories of Friedrich List are expounded in his *Schriften, Reden, Briefe* (10 vols., Berlin, 1927-35).

IV. RECORDS OF THE ARTISAN MOVEMENT

The most important of the minutes of artisan assemblies are *Verhandlungen der ersten Abgeordneten-Versammlung des norddeutschen Handwerker- und Gewerbestandes zu Hamburg, den 2.-6. Juni 1848* (Hamburg, 1848) and *Verhandlungen des ersten deutschen Handwerker- und Gewerbe-Congresses gehalten zu Frankfurt a. M. vom 14. Juli bis 18. August 1848*, ed. G. Schirges (Darmstadt, 1848). The industrial code adopted by the German Handicraft and Artisan Congress was published as *Entwurf einer allgemeinen Handwerker- und Gewerbe-Ordnung für Deutschland berathen und beschlossen von dem deutschen Handwerker- und Gewerbe-Congress zu Frankfurt am Main in den Monaten Juli und August 1848* (Frankfurt am Main, 1848). The deliberations of the General German Labor Congress were not made public, but for the resolutions which it adopted see W. E. Biermann, *Karl Georg Winkelblech (Karl Marlo): Sein*

Leben und sein Werk (2 vols., Leipzig, 1909), II, 441-456. The demands of guild organizations sometimes appeared in print, like the moving *Offener Brief an alle Innungsgenossen Deutschlands so wie zugleich an alle Bürger und Hausväter. Von zweiundzwanzig Innungen zu Leipzig* (Leipzig, 1848), but most of them circulated in manuscript form. There is a collection of more than two hundred of these memorials among the *Akten des Frankfurter Handwerker-Kongresses* in the Frankfurt am Main *Stadtarchiv*.

V. GENERAL WORKS

Until 1890 the figure of the Iron Chancellor loomed so large on the German scene that only here and there appeared a solitary account of the Revolution like Karl Marx's *Revolution and Counter-Revolution*, ed. Eleanor Marx Aveling (Chicago, 1914); A. Bernstein's *Revolutions- und Reaktions-Geschichte Preussens und Deutschlands von den Märztagen bis zur neuesten Zeit* (3 vols., Berlin, 1882); or C. Edmund Maurice's *The Revolutionary Movement of 1848-9 in Italy, Austria-Hungary, and Germany* (New York and London, 1887). A Europe dazzled by the achievements of Bismarck preferred to read the nationalist histories of Heinrich von Treitschke, *Deutsche Geschichte im neunzehnten Jahrhundert* (5 vols., Leipzig, 1879-94) and Heinrich von Sybel, *Die Begründung des Deutschen Reiches durch Wilhelm I.* (7 vols., Munich and Leipzig, 1889-94). During the reign of William II, however, a new interest in the spring uprising arose with the publication of Karl Binding, *Der Versuch der Reichsgründung durch die Paulskirche* (Leipzig, 1892), which was followed in the next twenty-five years by an outpour of major works bearing on the Forties. Among them were Wilhelm Blos, *Die deutsche Revolution* (Stuttgart, 1893); Hans Blum, *Die deutsche Revolution, 1848-49* (Leipzig, 1898); Franz Mehring, *Geschichte der deutschen Sozialdemokratie* (2 vols., Stuttgart, 1897-98) and his writings later assembled in *Zur preussischen Geschichte* (2 vols., Berlin, 1930); Paul Matter, *La Prusse et la révolution de 1848* (Paris, 1903); Erich Marcks, *Männer und Zeiten: Aufsätze und Reden zur neueren Geschichte* (2 vols., Leipzig, 1911); Erich Brandenburg, *Die deutsche*

Revolution 1848 (Leipzig, 1912) and *Die Reichsgründung* (2 vols., Leipzig, 1916); and Adolphus William Ward, *Germany, 1815-1890* (3 vols., Cambridge, 1916-18).

In the liberal atmosphere of the Weimar Republic books about 1848 proliferated and flourished. Some of them like Veit Valentin, *Die erste deutsche Nationalversammlung* (Munich and Berlin, 1919); Wilhelm Appens, *Die Nationalversammlung zu Frankfurt a. M., 1848-49* (Jena, 1920); Ricarda Huch, *Alte und neue Götter: Die Revolution des neunzehnten Jahrhunderts* (Berlin, 1930); and Kurt Kersten, *1848: Die deutsche Revolution* (Berlin, 1933) are works of popularization rather than scholarship; but also during these years Franz Schnabel was writing his brilliant political, social, and cultural synthesis *Deutsche Geschichte im neunzehnten Jahrhundert* (4 vols., Freiburg im Breisgau, 1929-37), and Veit Valentin published the greatest of the histories of the Revolution *Geschichte der deutschen Revolution von 1848-49* (2 vols., Berlin, 1930-31). After the collapse of the republican regime came the pedestrian Paul Wentzcke, *1848: Die unvollendete deutsche Revolution* (Munich, 1938) and the bigoted Klaus Besser, *Das tolle Jahr: Die Geheimleitung einer Revolution* (Munich, 1940). Yet at the same time important contributions to an understanding of nationalism in Central Europe appeared in Erich Marcks's swan song *Der Aufstieg des Reiches: Deutsche Geschichte von 1807-1871/78* (2 vols., Stuttgart, 1936), and in Heinrich von Srbik's massive study *Deutsche Einheit: Idee und Wirklichkeit* (4 vols., Munich, 1935-42). The defeat of the Third Reich brought a revival of interest in the March days, with the failures of German liberalism emphasized by L. B. Namier, *1848: The Revolution of the Intellectuals* (London, 1946); A.J.P. Taylor, *The Course of German History* (New York, 1946); Arnold Whitridge, *Men in Crisis: The Revolutions of 1848* (New York, 1949); and the authors of *The Opening of an Era, 1848: An Historical Symposium*, ed. François Fejtö (London, 1948). Its achievements were stressed by Theodor Heuss, *1848: Werk und Erbe* (Stuttgart, 1948); Rudolf Stadelmann, *Soziale und politische Geschichte der Revolution von 1848* (Munich, 1948); Wilhelm Mommsen, *Grösse und Versagen des deutschen Bürgertums: Ein Beitrag zur*

Geschichte der Jahre 1848-49 (Stuttgart, 1949); and the contributors to *Deutschland, 1848-1948: Beiträge zur historisch-politischen Würdigung der Volkserhebung von 1848-49,* ed. Wilhelm Keil (Stuttgart, 1948). Luigi Salvatorelli, *La rivoluzione europea, 1848-1849* (Milan, 1949) presented an excellent brief account of the Revolution as a European movement, while Priscilla Robertson, *Revolutions of 1848: A Social History* (Princeton, 1952) attempted to capture the feel of "the springtime of peoples."

The definitive economic history of Central Europe in the nineteenth century remains to be written, but Werner Sombart, *Die deutsche Volkswirtschaft im neunzehnten Jahrhundert* (Berlin, 1903) and A. Sartorious von Waltershausen, *Deutsche Wirtschaftsgeschichte, 1815-1914* (Jena, 1920) are sound and judicious. Among useful pioneer works are Alfred Zimmermann, *Geschichte der preussisch-deutschen Handelspolitik* (Oldenburg and Leipzig, 1892); Emil Wolff, *Grundriss der preussisch-deutschen socialpolitischen und Volkswirtschafts-Geschichte vom Ende des dreissigjährigen Krieges bis zur Gegenwart, 1640-1898* (Berlin, 1899); Werner Sombart, *Der moderne Kapitalismus* (2 vols., Leipzig, 1902); Ludwig Pohle, *Die Entwicklung des deutschen Wirtschaftslebens im 19. Jahrhundert* (Leipzig, 1904); and W. Wygodzinski, *Wandlungen der deutschen Volkswirtschaft im neunzehnten Jahrhundert* (Cologne, 1912). Among later publications J. H. Clapham, *The Economic Development of France and Germany, 1815-1914* (Cambridge, 1936) and Gustav Stolper, *German Economy, 1870-1940* (New York, 1940) deserve special mention. Most studies of labor problems in the early Industrial Revolution have come out of the socialist camp, some from moderates like Georg Adler, *Die Geschichte der ersten sozialpolitischen Arbeiterbewegung in Deutschland mit besonderer Rücksicht auf die einwirkenden Theorieen: Ein Beitrag zur Entwickelungsgeschichte der sozialen Frage* (Breslau, 1885); H. Schlüter, "Beiträge zur sozialen Geschichte des Jahres 1848," *Neue Zeit,* III (1885); Eduard Bernstein, *Die Geschichte der Berliner Arbeiter-Bewegung: Ein Kapitel zur Geschichte der deutschen Sozialdemokratie* (3 vols., Berlin, 1907-10); and Max Quarck, *Die erste deutsche Arbeiterbewegung: Geschichte der Arbeiterverbrüderung, 1848-*

49 (Leipzig, 1924), others from such defiant militants as Jürgen Kuczynski, *Labour Conditions in Western Europe, 1820 to 1935* (London, 1937), *A Short History of Labour Conditions under Industrial Capitalism: Germany, 1800 to the Present Day* (London, 1945), and *Die Bewegung der deutschen Wirtschaft von 1800 bis 1946* (Berlin and Leipzig, 1947), and Karl Obermann, *Die deutschen Arbeiter in der ersten bürgerlichen Revolution* (Berlin, 1950). Friedrich Meinecke's classic examination of German political ideals from Frederick the Great to Bismarck appeared in *Weltbürgertum und Nationalstaat: Studien zur Genesis des deutschen Nationalstaates* (Munich and Berlin, 1908) and more briefly in "Zur Geschichte des älteren deutschen Parteiwesens," *Historische Zeitschrift*, CXVIII (1917), but his views were challenged by Erich Brandenburg, "Zum älteren deutschen Parteiwesen," *Historische Zeitschrift*, CXIX (1919). For the growth of governmental institutions Conrad Bornhak, *Geschichte des preussischen Verwaltungsrechts* (3 vols., Berlin, 1884-86) should be supplemented with Heinrich Heffter, *Die deutsche Selbstverwaltung im 19. Jahrhundert: Geschichte der Ideen und Institutionen* (Stuttgart, 1950). *Allgemeine deutsche Biographie* (56 vols., Leipzig, 1875-1912) is essential for biographical data, while *Handwörterbuch der Staatswissenschaften*, 4th ed. (9 vols., Jena, 1923-29); *Staatslexikon*, 5th ed. (5 vols., Freiburg im Breisgau, 1926-32); and *Wörterbuch der Volkswirtschaft*, 4th ed. (3 vols., Jena, 1931-33) are serviceable encyclopedias of politics and economics.

VI. SPECIAL WORKS

The monographic literature on the German Confederation is vast but amorphous. Of the works dealing with the origins of German liberalism Guido De Ruggiero, *The History of European Liberalism*, trans. R. G. Collingwood (London, 1927), the second volume of Franz Schnabel, *Deutsche Geschichte im neunzehnten Jahrhundert* (4 vols., Freiburg im Breisgau, 1929-37), and Jacques Droz, *Le libéralisme rhénan, 1815-48* (Paris, 1949) are particularly good, but for a convenient summary of the social theories of the Rhenish constitutionalists there is Johanna Köster,

Der rheinische Frühliberalismus und die soziale Frage (Berlin, 1938). The development of a conservative theory of society is the theme of Sigmund Neumann, *Die Stufen des preussischen Konservatismus* (Berlin, 1930); Hildegard Goetting, *Die sozialpolitische Idee in den konservativen Kreisen der vormärzlichen Zeit* (Berlin, 1920); Karl Valerius Herberger, *Die Stellung der preussischen Konservativen zur sozialen Frage, 1848-62* (Meissen, 1914); Walter Früh, *Radowitz als Sozialpolitiker: Seine Gesellschafts- und Wirtschaftsauffassung unter besonderer Berücksichtigung der sozialen Frage* (Berlin, 1937); Georg Lüttke, *Die politischen Anschauungen des Generals und des Präsidenten von Gerlach* (Borsdorf-Leipzig, 1907); Jacques Droz, "Préoccupations sociales et préoccupations religieuses aux origines du parti conservateur prussien," *Revue d'histoire moderne et contemporaine*, II (1955); and Ferdinand Tönnies, "Deutscher Adel im neunzehnten Jahrhundert," *Neue Rundschau*, XXIII (1912). The political developments leading to the Frankfurt Parliament are discussed in Karl Biedermann, *Geschichte des ersten preussischen Reichstags* (Leipzig, 1847); Hans Mähl, *Die Überleitung Preussens in das konstitutionelle System durch den zweiten vereinigten Landtag* (Munich and Berlin, 1909); Joseph Hansen, "König Friedrich Wilhelm IV. und das liberale Märzministerium der Rheinländer Camphausen und Hansemann im Jahre 1848," *Westdeutsche Zeitschrift für Geschichte und Kunst*, XXXII (1913); Ludwig Bergsträsser, "Die parteipolitische Lage beim Zusammentritt des Vorparlaments," *Zeitschrift für Politik*, VI (1913); Ulrich Freyer, *Das Vorparlament zu Frankfurt a. M. im Jahre 1848* (Greifswald, 1913); Nanette G. Katzenstein, *Das Vorparlament* (Munich, 1922); and S. Kan, "Predparlament i pervoie badenskoie vosstanie 1848 goda" [the preliminary parliament and the first Baden uprising of 1848], *Voprosy istorii* (1948), no. 5.

Descriptions of the composition and outlook of the national assembly appear in *Biographische Umrisse der Mitglieder der deutschen konstituirenden Nationalversammlung zu Frankfurt a. M.* (Frankfurt a. M., 1848-49); [Robert Heller], *Brustbilder aus der Paulskirche* (Leipzig, 1849); L. Rosenbaum, *Beruf und Herkunft der Abgeordneten zu den deutschen und preussischen*

Parlamenten, 1847 bis 1919 (Frankfurt am Main, 1923); Karl Demeter, "Die soziale Schichtung des deutschen Parlamentes seit 1848: Ein Spiegelbild der Strukturwandlung des Volkes," *Vierteljahrschrift für Sozial- und Wirtschaftsgeschichte*, XXXIX (1952); Ludwig Bergsträsser, "Parteien von 1848," *Preussische Jahrbücher*, CLXXVII (1919); Otto Ernst Sutter, *Die Linke der Paulskirche* (Frankfurt am Main, 1924); and Andrea Frahm, "Paulskirche und Volkssouveränität," *Historische Zeitschrift*, CXXX (1924). Herbert Arthur Strauss, *Staat, Bürger, Mensch: Die Debatten der deutschen Nationalversammlung 1848-49 über die Grundrechte* (Aarau, 1947) analyzes the Fundamental Rights of the German People, while Walter Schneider, *Wirtschafts- und Sozialpolitik im Frankfurter Parlament, 1848-49* (Frankfurt am Main, 1923); Paul Albrecht, *Die volkswirtschaftlichen und sozialen Fragen in der Frankfurter National-Versammlung* (Halle, 1914); and Ludwig Oelsner, "Die wirtschafts- und sozialpolitischen Verhandlungen des Frankfurter Parlaments," *Preussische Jahrbücher*, LXXXVII (1897) examine the economic problems confronting St. Paul's Church. For suffrage legislation there are Georg Meyer, *Das parlamentarische Wahlrecht* (Berlin, 1901); Georg von Below, *Das parlamentarische Wahlrecht in Deutschland* (Berlin, 1909); Gerhard Schilfert, *Sieg und Niederlage des demokratischen Wahlrechts in der deutschen Revolution 1848-49* (Berlin, 1952); Ferdinand Frensdorff, "Die Aufnahme des allgemeinen Wahlrechts in das öffentliche Recht Deutschlands," *Festgabe der Göttinger Juristen-Fakultät für Rodolf von Jhering zum fünfzigjährigen Doktor-Jubiläum am vi. August MDCCCXCII* (Leipzig, 1892); Johanna Philippson, *Ueber den Ursprung und die Einführung des allgemeinen gleichen Wahlrechts in Deutschland mit besonderer Berücksichtigung der Wahlen zum Frankfurter Parlament im Grossherzogtum Baden* (Berlin and Leipzig, 1913); Konrad Repgen, *Märzbewegung und Maiwahlen des Revolutionsjahres 1848 im Rheinland* (Bonn, 1955); "Die hessischen Wahlen zur deutschen Nationalversammlung in Frankfurt a. M. vom 18. April 1848," *Hessenland*, XII (1898); Wilhelm Otto Vollrath, *Der parlamentarische Kampf um das preussische Dreiklassenwahlrecht* (Borna-Leipzig, 1931); and A. Wolfstieg, "Wer ist der 'Vater' des Dreiklassenwahlrechts in Preussen?", *Preussische Jahrbücher*, CLXIV (1916). The triumph of the reaction is portrayed in Wilhelm Blos, *Der Untergang des Frankfurter Parlaments* (Frankfurt am Main, 1924); Karl Enax, *Otto von Manteuffel und die Reaktion in Preussen* (Dresden, 1907); Hans Walter, *Die innere Politik des Ministers von Manteuffel und der Ursprung der Reaktion in Preussen* (Berlin, 1910); and Ludolf Parisius, *Deutschlands politische Parteien und das Ministerium Bismarck: Ein Beitrag zur vaterländischen Geschichte* (Berlin, 1878).

Besides accounts of national developments there are numerous regional studies. Berlin is described in Dora Meyer, *Das öffentliche Leben in Berlin im Jahr vor der Märzrevolution* (Berlin, 1912); Karl Haenchen, "Zur revolutionären Unterwühlung Berlins vor den Märztagen des Jahres 1848," *Forschungen zur brandenburgischen und preussischen Geschichte*, LV [n. d.]; and Ernst Kaeber, *Berlin 1848* (Berlin, 1948). Oscar J. Hammen, "Economic and Social Factors in the Prussian Rhineland in 1848," *American Historical Review*, LIV (1949); Wilhelm Hüttermann, *Parteipolitisches Leben in Westfalen vom Beginn der Märzbewegung im Jahre 1848 bis zum Einsetzen der Reaktion im Jahre 1849* (Münster, 1910); Reinhard Kaeller, *Die konservative Partei in Minden-Ravensberg: Ihre Grundlagen, Entstehung und Entwicklung bis zum Jahre 1866* (Heidelberg, 1912); and Kazimierz and Franciszek Popiołek, "1848 in Silesia," *Slavonic and East European Review*, XXVI (1948) deal with political and economic conditions in the provinces of Prussia. For other states of the north there are Carl J. H. Blume, *Hamburg und die deutschen wirtschaftlichen Einheitsbestrebungen, 1814-1847* (Hamburg, 1934); Hans Pahl, *Hamburg und das Problem einer deutschen Wirtschaftseinheit im Frankfurter Parlament, 1848-49* (Hamburg, 1930); Adolf Werner, *Die politischen Bewegungen in Mecklenburg und der ausserordentliche Landtag im Frühjahr 1848* (Berlin and Leipzig, 1907); and Ruth Wöltge, *Die Reaktion im Königreich Hannover, 1850-1857: Die Rückbildung des Verfassungsgesetzes und die Reformversuche an den Provinziallandschaften* (Tübingen, 1932). Central and southern Germany are discussed by Curt Geyer, *Politische Parteien und öffentliche Meinung in Sachsen von der Märzrevolution bis zum Ausbruch des Maiaufstands, 1848-1849* (Leipzig, 1914); Mathilde Klemm, *Sachsen und das deutsche Problem 1848 (von den Wirkungen der Pariser Februarrevolution an bis zur Einsetzung einer provisorischen Zentralgewalt durch das Frankfurter Parlament)* (Meissen, 1914); Rudolf Krauss, *Das sächsische Vogtland in der Bewegung von 1848-1850* (Würzburg, 1935); Ernst Schocke, *Die deutsche Einheits- und Freiheitsbewegung in Sachsen-Meiningen, 1848-1850: Ein Beitrag zur Geschichte der ersten deutschen Revolution* (Hildburghausen, 1927); Veit Valentin, *Frankfurt am Main und die Revolution von 1848-49* (Stuttgart and Berlin, 1908); J. B. Bekk, *Die Bewegung in Baden von Ende des Februar 1848 bis zur Mitte des Mai 1849* (Mannheim, 1850); and M. Doeberl, *Bayern und die deutsche Frage in der Epoche des Frankfurter Parlaments* (Munich and Berlin, 1922).

Of the biographical works Hermann Wagener, *Die Politik Friedrich Wilhelm IV.* (Berlin, 1883); Herman v. Petersdorff, *König Friedrich Wilhelm der Vierte* (Stuttgart, 1900); and Ernst Lewalter, *Friedrich Wilhelm IV.: Das Schicksal eines Geistes* (Berlin, 1938) are too laudatory to be perceptive. Erich Marcks, *Kaiser Wilhelm I.* (Leipzig, 1897); Paul Hassel, *Joseph Maria v. Radowitz* (Berlin, 1905); and Friedrich Meinecke, *Radowitz und die deutsche Revolution* (Berlin, 1913) are creditable lives of the brother and the confidant of the king of Prussia. The best book about young Bismarck is Erich Marcks, *Bismarck: Eine Biographie, 1815-1851* (Stuttgart, 1951). Hermann v. Petersdorff, *Kleist-Retzow: Ein Lebensbild* (Stuttgart and Berlin, 1907); Alexander Bergengrün, *Staatsminister August Freiherr von der Heydt* (Leipzig, 1908); and Otto zu Stolberg-Wernigerode, *Anton Graf zu Stolberg-Wernigerode: Ein Freund und Ratgeber König Friedrich Wilhelms IV.* (Munich and Berlin, 1926) describe important counselors of Frederick William IV; and *Deutscher Aufstieg: Bilder aus der Vergangenheit und Gegenwart der rechtsstehenden Parteien* ed. Hans von Arnim and Georg von Below (Berlin, 1925) contains sketches of eminent monarchist statesmen. The banner of constitutionalism is raised by Anton Springer, *Friedrich Christoph Dahlmann* (2 vols., Leipzig, 1870-72); Gustav Freytag, *Karl Mathy: Geschichte seines Lebens* (Leipzig, 1870); Alexander Bergengrün, *David Hanse-*

mann (Berlin, 1901); Anna Caspary, *Ludolf Camphausens Leben* (Stuttgart and Berlin, 1902); and Joseph Hansen, *Gustav von Mevissen: Ein rheinisches Lebensbild, 1815-1899* (2 vols., Berlin, 1906). The two prophets of socialism find appreciation and homage in Franz Mehring, *Karl Marx: Geschichte seines Lebens* (Leipzig, 1918) and Gustav Mayer, *Friedrich Engels: Eine Biographie* (Berlin, 1920), while W. E. Biermann, *Karl Georg Winkelblech (Karl Marlo): Sein Leben und sein Werk* (2 vols., Leipzig, 1909) portrays a quixotic champion of the artisan cause.

Georg von Viebahn, *Statistik des zollvereinten und nördlichen Deutschlands* (3 vols., Berlin, 1858-68) is a storehouse of statistical information about the German economy, but there are also valuable official publications like *Tabellen und amtliche Nachrichten über den preussischen Staat für das Jahr 1849* (6 vols., Berlin, 1851-55); *Tabellen und amtliche Nachrichten über den preussischen Staat für das Jahr 1855* (Berlin, 1858); *Tabellen und amtliche Nachrichten über den preussischen Staat für das Jahr 1858* (Berlin, 1860); *Zeitschrift des königlich preussischen statistischen Bureaus; Mittheilungen des statistischen Bureau's in Berlin; Statistisches Handbuch für den preussischen Staat*; and *Preussische Statistik*. Convenient reference works are C.F.W. Dieterici, *Der Volkswohlstand im preussischen Staate* (Berlin, Posen, and Bromberg, 1846) and *Handbuch der Statistik des preussischen Staats* (Berlin, 1861); Wilhelm Kellner, *Taschenbuch der politischen Statistik Deutschlands oder Aufstellung der staatlichen Einrichtungen Gesammt-Deutschlands sowohl als der einzelnen Staaten* (Frankfurt am Main, 1864); and Johannes Müller, *Grundriss der deutschen Statistik* (4 vols., Jena, 1925-28). The finest general account of the early development of the factory system in Central Europe is Pierre Benaerts, *Les origines de la grande industrie allemande* (Paris, 1933). More specialized are such studies of industrialization as T. C. Banfield, *Industry of the Rhine* (2 vols., London, 1846-48); Alphons Thun, *Die Industrie am Niederrhein und ihre Arbeiter* (2 vols., Leipzig, 1879); *Die Rheinprovinz, 1815-1915*, ed. Joseph Hansen (2 vols., Bonn, 1917); Alfred Zimmermann, *Blüthe und Verfall des Leinengewerbes in Schlesien: Gewerbe- und Handelspolitik dreier Jahrhunderte* (Breslau, 1885); and Hans Rosenberg, *Die Weltwirt-*

schaftskrisis von 1857-59 (Stuttgart, 1934). The beginnings of factory legislation are traced in Günther K. Anton, *Geschichte der preussischen Fabrikgesetzgebung bis zu ihrer Aufnahme durch die Reichsgewerbeordnung* (Leipzig, 1891); Lujo Brentano, "Zur Reform der deutschen Fabrikgesetzgebung," *Jahrbücher für Nationalökonomie und Statistik*, XIX (1872); and Alphons Thun, "Beiträge zur Geschichte der Gesetzgebung und Verwaltung zu Gunsten der Fabrikarbeiter in Preussen," *Zeitschrift des königlich preussischen statistischen Bureaus*, XVII (1877), while Wilhelm Friedensburg, *Stephan Born und die Organisationsbestrebungen der Berliner Arbeiterschaft bis zum Berliner Arbeiterkongress, 1840-September 1848* (Leipzig, 1923) and S. B. Kan, "Rabocheie dvizhiniie v Berline v perviie nedeli martovskoi revoliutsii 1848 goda" [the workers movement in Berlin in the first weeks of the March revolution of 1848], *Isvestiia Akademii Nauk SSSR: Seriia istorii i filosofii* (1948), no. 1, eulogize the labor movement organized during the Revolution.

Economic theories and problems growing out of the Industrial Revolution are examined in Eugen von Philippovich, *Die Entwicklung der wirtschaftspolitischen Ideen im 19. Jahrhundert* (Tübingen, 1910); P. Mombert, *Soziale und wirtschaftspolitische Anschauungen in Deutschland vom Beginn des neunzehnten Jahrhunderts bis zur Gegenwart* (Leipzig, 1919) and "Aus der Literatur über die soziale Frage und über die Arbeiterbewegung in Deutschland in der ersten Hälfte des 19. Jahrhunderts," *Archiv für die Geschichte des Sozialismus und der Arbeiterbewegung*, IX (1921); *Die Entwicklung der deutschen Volkswirtschaftslehre im neunzehnten Jahrhundert: Gustav Schmoller zur siebenzigsten Wiederkehr seines Geburtstages*, ed. S. P. Altmann et al. (2 vols., Leipzig, 1908); and Ludolf Grambow, *Die deutsche Freihandelspartei zur Zeit ihrer Blüte* (Jena, 1903). For the Zollverein there are the works of Arnold H. Price, *The Evolution of the Zollverein: A Study of the Ideas and Institutions Leading to German Economic Unification between 1815 and 1833* (Ann Arbor, 1949) and W. O. Henderson, *The Zollverein* (Cambridge, 1939) and "The Zollverein," *History*, XIX (1934), which have largely supplanted the older study by Hermann von Festenberg-Packisch, *Geschichte des Zollvereins* (Leipzig, 1869). Works dealing briefly with German emigration are W. Dieterici, *Ueber Auswanderungen und Einwanderungen* (Berlin, Posen, and Bromberg, 1847); Alexis Markow, *Das Wachstum der Bevölkerung und die Entwickelung der Aus- und Einwanderungen, Ab- und Zuzüge in Preussen und Preussens einzelnen Provinzen, Bezirken und Kreisgruppen von 1824 bis 1885* (Tübingen, 1889); and Marcus L. Hansen, "The Revolutions of 1848 and German Emigration," *Journal of Economic and Business History*, II (1930). Karl Braun, "Das Zwangs-Zölibat für Mittellose in Deutschland," *Vierteljahrschrift für Volkswirthschaft und Kulturgeschichte*, v (1867), no. 4, describes the policy of marriage restriction, while Christian Eckert, *Rheinschiffahrt im XIX. Jahrhundert* (Leipzig, 1900) and Eberhard Gothein, *Geschichtliche Entwicklung der Rheinschiffahrt im XIX. Jahrhundert* (Leipzig, 1903) depict the development of Rhenish shipping.

The best history of German handicraft trades in the nineteenth century is still Gustav Schmoller, *Zur Geschichte der deutschen Kleingewerbe im 19. Jahrhundert* (Halle, 1870). While it by no means supersedes Victor Böhmert, *Freiheit der Arbeit: Beiträge zur Reform der Gewerbegesetze* (Bremen, 1858) and "Deutschlands wirthschaftliche Neugestaltung," *Preussische Jahrbücher*, XVIII (1866) and H. A. Mascher, *Das deutsche Gewerbewesen von der frühesten Zeit bis auf die Gegenwart* (Potsdam, 1866), neither has it been replaced by Kurt von Rohrscheidt, *Vom Zunftzwange zur Gewerbefreiheit* (Berlin, 1898) or G. Kölzsch, *Die Entwicklung der Gewerbefreiheit in Deutschland* (Greifswald, 1920). The advance of industrial freedom in Prussia is described by Hugo Roehl, *Beiträge zur preussischen Handwerkerpolitik vom allgemeinen Landrecht bis zur allgemeinen Gewerbeordnung von 1845* (Leipzig, 1900); Otto Thissen, *Beiträge zur Geschichte des Handwerks in Preussen* (Tübingen, 1901); Hugo C. M. Wendel, *The Evolution of Industrial Freedom in Prussia, 1845-1849* (New York, 1921); and Paul Geissen, *Die preussische Handwerkerpolitik unter Otto von Manteuffel* (Wuppertal-Elberfeld, 1936). Paul Möslein, *Die Gewerbegesetzgebung der thüringer Herzogtümer im 19. Jahrhundert bis zur Einführung der Gewerbefreiheit* (Weimar, 1909) and Wilhelm Engel, *Wirt-*

schaftliche und soziale Kämpfe in Thüringen (insonderheit im Herzogtum Meiningen) vor dem Jahre 1848 (Jena, 1927) examine the plight of the artisan in the Thuringian duchies, while Josef Kaizl, *Der Kampf um Gewerbereform und Gewerbefreiheit in Bayern von 1799-1868* (Leipzig, 1879); Georg Ziegler, *Das bayrische Gewerbegesetz von 1868* (Erlangen, 1908); Anton Höfle, *Die Gewerbeordnung der Pfalz seit der französischen Revolution bis 1868* (München, 1908); Rudolf Bovensiepen, *Die kurhessische Gewerbepolitik und die wirtschaftliche Lage des zünftigen Handwerks in Kurhessen von 1816-1867* (Marburg, 1909); and Wilhelm Ullmann, *Die hessische Gewerbepolitik von der Zeit des Rheinbundes bis zur Einführung der Gewerbefreiheit im Jahre 1866* (Darmstadt, 1903) deal with the decline of the guild system in the south and west.

The most thorough histories of agricultural development are Samuel Sugenheim, *Geschichte der Aufhebung der Leibeigenschaft und Hörigkeit in Europa bis um die Mitte des neunzehnten Jahrhunderts* (St. Petersburg, 1861) and Theodor von der Goltz, *Vorlesungen über Agrarwesen und Agrarpolitik* (Jena, 1899) and *Geschichte der deutschen Landwirtschaft* (2 vols., Stuttgart and Berlin, 1902-03). "Mr. Jacob's Report on the Trade in Corn and on the Agriculture of the North of Europe," *Parliamentary Papers* (1826), XXI; "Die Ablösungsgesetze und andere Gesetze zu Erfüllung der Forderungen des Liberalismus," *Deutsche Vierteljahrs Schrift*, XVII (1854), no. 3, and Werner Conze, "Die Wirkungen der liberalen Agrarreformen auf die Volksordnung in Mitteleuropa im 19. Jahrhundert," *Vierteljahrschrift für Sozial- und Wirtschaftsgeschichte*, XXXVIII [n. d.] are less comprehensive but also less ponderous. The two articles by Carl Johannes Fuchs, "Bauer" and "Bauernbefreiung," *Wörterbuch der Volkswirtschaft*, 4th ed., provide a thoughtful brief description of a complex historical process. For rural conditions between the Elbe and the Vistula see Georg Friedrich Knapp, *Die Bauern-Befreiung und der Ursprung der Landarbeiter in den älteren Theilen Preussens* (2 vols., Leipzig, 1887), *Die Landarbeiter in Knechtschaft und Freiheit* (Leipzig, 1891), and *Grundherrschaft und Rittergut* (Leipzig, 1897); Max Sering, *Die innere Kolonisation im östlichen Deutschland* (Leipzig, 1893); Erich

Jordan, *Die Entstehung der konservativen Partei und die preussischen Agrarverhältnisse von 1848* (Munich and Leipzig, 1914); Karl Reis, *Die Ursachen und ersten Äusserungen der schlesischen Agrarbewegung des Jahres 1848* (Breslau, 1910); Karl Böhme, *Gutsherrlich-bäuerliche Verhältnisse in Ostpreussen während der Reformzeit von 1770 bis 1830* (Leipzig, 1902); and J. Conrad, "Die Latifundien im preussischen Osten," *Jahrbücher für Nationalökonomie und Statistik*, L (1888) and "Agrarstatistische Untersuchungen: Der Grossgrundbesitz in Ostpreussen," *ibid.*, LVII (1891). Hugo Preuss, *Die Junkerfrage* (Berlin, 1897); J. Conrad, "Die Fideikommisse in den östlichen Provinzen Preussens," *Festgabe für Georg Hanssen zum 31. Mai 1889* (Tübingen, 1889); Lujo Brentano "Familienfideikommisse und ihre Wirkungen," *Volkswirtschaftliche Zeitfragen*, XXXIII (1911); and Max Weber, *Gesammelte Aufsätze zur Soziologie und Sozialpolitik* (Tübingen, 1924) deal with the economic position of the landed nobility. The emancipation of the peasantry of the Rhine and the Danube is discussed in Otto Stolz, "Die Bauernbefreiung in Süddeutschland im Zusammenhang der Geschichte," *Vierteljahrschrift für Sozial- und Wirtschaftsgeschichte*, XXXIII (1940), but more detailed accounts may be found in Sebastian Hausmann, *Die Grund-Entlastung in Bayern* (Strasbourg, 1892); Otto Reinhard, *Die Grundentlastung in Württemberg* (Tübingen, 1910); Theodor Knapp, *Neue Beiträge zur Rechts- und Wirtschaftsgeschichte des württembergischen Bauernstandes* (2 vols., Tübingen, 1919); Friedrich Lautenschlager, *Die Agrarunruhen in den badischen Standes- und Grundherrschaften im Jahre 1848* (Heidelberg, 1915); Eugen Katz, *Landarbeiter und Landwirtschaft in Oberhessen* (Stuttgart and Berlin, 1904); and Adolf Nebel, *Die ländlichen Arbeiterverhältnisse in Kurhessen* (Fulda, 1909). The borderlands between the eastern latifundia and the western dwarf farms are depicted by Georg Hanssen, *Die Aufhebung der Leibeigenschaft und die Umgestaltung der gutsherrlichbäuerlichen Verhältnisse überhaupt in den Herzogthümern Schleswig und Holstein* (St. Petersburg, 1861); Werner Wittich, *Die Grundherrschaft in Nordwestdeutschland* (Leipzig, 1896); Karl Georg Immanuel Teuthorn, *Das sächsische Gesetz über Ablösungen und Gemeinheitsteilungen vom 17. März 1832 in seiner*

Entstehung und in seinen Folgen (Leipzig, 1904); Bruno Moll, *Die Landarbeiterfrage im Königreich Sachsen* (Leipzig, 1908); and Otto H. Brandt, *Der Bauer und die bäuerlichen Lasten im Herzogtum Sachsen-Altenburg vom 17. bis zum 19. Jahrhundert* (Gotha, 1906).

Notes

CHAPTER 1

THE ORIGINS OF INDUSTRIALISM

1. *Goethes Briefe* (50 vols., Weimar, 1887-1912), XXXIX, 216.

2. Pierre Benaerts, *Les origines de la grande industrie allemande* (Paris, 1933), pp. 97-126; Werner Sombart, *Die deutsche Volkswirtschaft im neunzehnten Jahrhundert und im Anfang des 20. Jahrhunderts,* 7th ed. (Berlin, 1927), p. 304; Gustav Schmoller, *Zur Geschichte der deutschen Kleingewerbe im 19. Jahrhundert* (Halle, 1870), p. 575; Walter Schneider, *Wirtschafts- und Sozialpolitik im Frankfurter Parlament, 1848-49* (Frankfurt am Main, 1923), p. 12; Ludwig Pohle, *Die Entwicklung des deutschen Wirtschaftslebens im letzten Jahrhundert,* 2nd ed. (Leipzig, 1908), p. 20; Paul Albrecht, *Die volkswirtschaftlichen und sozialen Fragen in der Frankfurter National-Versammlung* (Halle, 1914), p. 3; Witt Bowden, Michael Karpovich, and Abbott Payson Usher, *An Economic History of Europe since 1750* (New York, 1937), pp. 468, 472; Carl Brinkmann, "The Place of Germany in the Economic History of the Nineteenth Century," *Economic History Review,* IV (1933), 135; Jürgen Kuczynski, *Die Bewegung der deutschen Wirtschaft von 1800 bis 1946,* 2nd ed. (Meisenheim am Glan, 1948), p. 198; A. Sartorius von Waltershausen, *Deutsche Wirtschaftsgeschichte, 1815-1914* (Jena, 1920), pp. 167-168.

3. G. Schmoller, *Geschichte der Kleingewerbe,* pp. 162-163, 478; Bruno Moll, *Die Landarbeiterfrage im Königreich Sachsen* (Leipzig, 1908), pp. 17-18.

4. Mathilde Klemm, *Sachsen und das deutsche Problem 1848 (von den Wirkungen der Pariser Februarrevolution an bis zur Einsetzung einer provisorischen Zentralgewalt durch das Frankfurter Parlament)* (Meissen, 1914), pp. 4-5; T. C. Banfield, *Industry of the Rhine* (2 vols., London, 1846-48), II, 20-21, 53-54, 122, 128, 221, 230-231; W. Schneider, *Wirtschafts- und Sozialpolitik,* p. 12; A. Sartorius von Waltershausen, *Wirtschaftsgeschichte,* pp. 167-168; Karl Georg Immanuel Teuthorn, *Das sächsische Gesetz über Ablösungen und Gemeinheitsteilungen vom 17. März 1832 in seiner Entstehung und in seinen Folgen* (Leipzig, 1904), p. 62; B. Moll, *Die Landarbeiterfrage,* pp. 17-18; Jürgen Kuczynski, *A Short History of Labour Conditions under Industrial Capitalism: Germany, 1800 to the Present Day* (London, 1945), p. 19; Heinrich von Treitschke, *Deutsche Geschichte im neunzehnten Jahrhundert* (5 vols., Leipzig, 1879-94), IV, 570; G. Schmoller, *Geschichte der Kleingewerbe,* p. 149; Ernst Kaeber, *Berlin 1848* (Berlin, 1948), p. 9; Dora Meyer, *Das öffentliche Leben in Berlin im Jahr vor der Märzrevolution* (Berlin, 1912), p. 17; Max Quarck, *Die erste deutsche Arbeiterbewegung: Geschichte der Arbeiterverbrüderung, 1848-49* (Leipzig, 1924), pp. 14-15.

5. L. Pohle, *Entwicklung des Wirtschaftslebens,* p. 15; W. Sombart, *Die deutsche Volkswirtschaft,* p. 84; W. Wygodzinski, *Wandlungen der deutschen Volkswirtschaft im neunzehnten Jahrhundert* (Cologne, 1912), p. 119; J. Kuczynski, *Short History,* p. 17; J. Kuczynski, *Bewegung der Wirtschaft,* p. 173; Ernest Denis, *La fondation de l'empire allemand, 1852-1871* (Paris, 1906), p. 99.

6. W. Sombart, *Die deutsche Volkswirtschaft*, p. 173; A. Sartorius von Waltershausen, *Wirtschaftsgeschichte*, pp. 179-180; W. Kähler, "Handel, Bankwesen, Versicherungswesen," *Die Rheinprovinz, 1815-1915*, ed. Joseph Hansen (2 vols., Bonn, 1917), I, 526; Max Muss, "Banken in der Volkswirtschaft," *Handwörterbuch der Staatswissenschaften*, 4th ed.

7. W. O. Henderson, *The Zollverein* (Cambridge, 1939), pp. 139-140; A. Sartorius von Waltershausen, *Wirtschaftsgeschichte*, pp. 29, 176-177; P. Benaerts, *Les origines*, p. 283; J. H. Clapham, *The Economic Development of France and Germany, 1815-1914* (Cambridge, 1936), p. 125; Gustav Stolper, *German Economy, 1870-1940* (New York, 1940), pp. 27, 32; W. Schneider, *Wirtschafts- und Sozialpolitik*, p. 139; L. Pohle, *Entwicklung des Wirtschaftslebens*, pp. 16-17; John Bowring, "Report on the Prussian Commercial Union," *Great Britain: Parliamentary Papers* (1840), XXI, 95.

8. J. G. Legge, *Rhyme and Revolution in Germany: A Study in German History, Life, Literature and Character, 1813-1850* (London, 1919), p. 123. Cf. Karl Beck, *Gedichte*, rev. ed. (Berlin, 1845), p. 20; P. Benaerts, *Les origines*, pp. 308, 319, n. 74, 631; L. Pohle, *Entwicklung des Wirtschaftslebens*, pp. 11, 113; A. Sartorius von Waltershausen, *Wirtschaftsgeschichte*, pp. 96-98; W. Sombart, *Die deutsche Volkswirtschaft*, pp. 239-247; W. O. Henderson, *Zollverein*, pp. 20, 146-147; J. H. Clapham, *Economic Development*, pp. 151-153, 339; Werner Sombart, *Der moderne Kapitalismus: Historisch-systematische Darstellung des gesamteuropäischen Wirtschaftslebens von seinen Anfängen bis zur Gegenwart*, 2nd ed. (3 vols., Munich and Leipzig, 1938), III, 675.

9. Prussia, *Gesetz-Sammlung für die königlichen preussischen Staaten* (1838), pp. 505-516; A. Sartorius von Waltershausen, *Wirtschaftsgeschichte*, p. 95; H. v. Treitschke, *Deutsche Geschichte*, IV, 593; Walther Lotz, *Verkehrsentwicklung in Deutschland, 1800-1900* (Leipzig, 1900), p. 26.

10. W. Lotz, *Verkehrsentwicklung*, pp. 28-30; A. Sartorius von Waltershausen, *Wirtschaftsgeschichte*, pp. 101-104; G. Stolper, *German Economy*, pp. 71-72; J. H. Clapham, *Economic Development*, p. 153; C. Brinkmann, "The Place of Germany," p. 139; L. Pohle, *Entwicklung des Wirtschaftslebens*, pp. 119-120; W. Schneider, *Wirtschafts- und Sozialpolitik*, p. 130.

11. Christian Eckert, *Rheinschiffahrt im XIX. Jahrhundert* (Leipzig, 1900), pp. 238-239, 260-266, 333, 338-339; A. Sartorius von Waltershausen, *Wirtschaftsgeschichte*, p. 107; T. C. Banfield, *Industry*, II, 49; A. Wirminghaus, "Das Verkehrswesen," *Rheinprovinz*, ed. J. Hansen, I, 580; Franz Schnabel, *Deutsche Geschichte im neunzehnten Jahrhundert* (4 vols., Freiburg im Breisgau, 1929-37), III, 425-426; C.F.W. Dieterici, *Der Volkswohlstand im preussischen Staate* (Berlin, Posen, and Bromberg, 1846), p. 258; W. O. Henderson, *Zollverein*, p. 148; L. Pohle, *Entwicklung des Wirtschaftslebens*, p. 10; W. Sombart, *Die deutsche Volkswirtschaft*, pp. 254-255.

12. *Rheinische Briefe und Akten zur Geschichte der politischen Bewegung, 1830-1850*, ed. Joseph Hansen (2 vols., Essen and Bonn, 1919-42), I, 354.

13. A. Wirminghaus, "Verkehrswesen," p. 571; W. Sombart, *Die deutsche Volkswirtschaft*, p. 253; T. C. Banfield, *Industry*, II, 30-35, 197-200; W. Schneider, *Wirtschafts- und Sozialpolitik*, pp. 114-115; *Rheinurkunden: Sammlung zwischenstaatlicher Vereinbarungen, landesrechtlicher*

Ausführungsverordnungen und sonstiger wichtiger Urkunden über die Rheinschiffahrt seit 1803 (2 vols., The Hague, Munich, and Leipzig, 1918), I, 212-283; *The Map of Europe by Treaty*, ed. Edward Hertslet (4 vols., London, 1875-91), I, 75-93.

14. *Vorgeschichte und Begründung des deutschen Zollvereins, 1815-1834*, ed. W. v. Eisenhart Rothe and A. Ritthaler (3 vols., Berlin, 1934), I, 321.

15. *Ibid.*, II, 62, III, 164-165, 525-541. Cf. Arnold H. Price, *The Evolution of the Zollverein: A Study of the Ideas and Institutions Leading to German Economic Unification between 1815 and 1833* (Ann Arbor, 1949), p. 252.

16. P. Albrecht, *Die volkswirtschaftlichen Fragen*, pp. 18, 30; W. Schneider, *Wirtschafts- und Sozialpolitik*, p. 105; W. O. Henderson, "The Zollverein," *History*, XIX (1934), 12; H. v. Treitschke, *Deutsche Geschichte*, V, 451; Karl Rathgen, "Die Ansichten über Freihandel und Schutzzoll in der deutschen Staatspraxis des 19. Jahrhunderts," *Die Entwicklung der deutschen Volkswirtschaftslehre im neunzehnten Jahrhundert: Gustav Schmoller zur siebenzigsten Wiederkehr seines Geburtstages*, ed. S. P. Altmann et al. (2 vols., Leipzig, 1908), II, no. 20, p. 27; A. Sartorius von Waltershausen, *Wirtschaftsgeschichte*, pp. 78-79; W. O. Henderson, *Zollverein*, p. 182; P. Benaerts, *Les origines*, p. 224; Hermann von Festenberg-Packisch, *Geschichte des Zollvereins* (Leipzig, 1869), p. 287.

17. Friedrich List, *Schriften, Reden, Briefe* (10 vols., Berlin, 1927-35), VI, 156.

18. K. Rathgen, "Freihandel und Schutzzoll," pp. 27, 30, n. 1; M. Schwann, "Grundlagen und Organisation des Wirtschaftslebens." *Rheinprovinz*, ed. J. Hansen, I, 219; P. Benaerts, *Les origines*, p. 235; *Vorgeschichte des Zollvereins*, ed. W. v. Eisenhart Rothe and A. Ritthaler, II, 293, n. 1; Rudolph von Delbrück, *Lebenserinnerungen, 1817-1867* (2 vols., Leipzig, 1905), I, 146-147.

19. Hans Pahl *Hamburg und das Problem einer deutschen Wirtschaftseinheit im Frankfurter Parlament, 1848-49* (Hamburg, 1930), pp. 10-11; P. Albrecht, *Die volkswirtschaftlichen Fragen*, p. 18; Georg Jahn, "Freihandelslehre und Freihandelsbewegung," *Handwörterbuch der Staatswissenschaften*, 4th ed.

20. P. Benaerts, *Les origines*, pp. 237, 246; K. Rathgen, "Freihandel und Schutzzoll," p. 27; T. C. Banfield, *Industry*, II, 13-15, 141; W. O. Henderson, "Zollverein," p. 12; P. Albrecht, *Die volkswirtschaftlichen Fragen*, p. 18; H. v. Festenberg-Packisch, *Geschichte*, p. 283; W. Schneider, *Wirtschafts- und Sozialpolitik*, pp. 89-90.

21. Georg von Viebahn, *Statistik des zollvereinten und nördlichen Deutschlands* (3 vols., Berlin, 1858-68), I, 230-236; *Die Handels- und Schifffahrtsverträge des Zollvereines*, ed. C. A. von Kamptz (Brunswick, 1845), pp. 27-40, 120-133, 198-255; H. v. Treitschke, *Deutsche Geschichte*, V, 457; J. Bowring, "Report," pp. 269-271; "Convention of Commerce and Navigation between Her Majesty and the King of Prussia, and the Other Members of the German Union of Customs," *Great Britain: Parliamentary Papers* (1841), XXXI.

22. A. Sartorius von Waltershausen, *Wirtschaftsgeschichte*, p. 110; A. Duckwitz, *Denkwürdigkeiten aus meinem öffentlichen Leben von 1841-1866: Ein Beitrag zur bremischen und deutschen Geschichte* (Bremen,

1877), pp. 36-60, 272; W. Schneider, *Wirtschafts- und Sozialpolitik*, pp. 90-91; W. O. Henderson, *Zollverein*, pp. 159, 161; Carl J. H. Blume, *Hamburg und die deutschen wirtschaftlichen Einheitsbestrebungen, 1814-1847* (Hamburg, 1934), p. 95; *Europe by Treaty*, ed. E. Hertslet, II, 1041-1044.

23. J. G. Legge, *Rhyme and Revolution*, p. 189. Cf. *Hoffmann's von Fallersleben Gesammelte Werke*, ed. Heinrich Gerstenberg (8 vols., Berlin, 1890-93), IV, 28.

24. *Düsseldorfer Zeitung*, September 3, 1843.

25. *Tabellen und amtliche Nachrichten über den preussischen Staat für das Jahr 1849* (6 vols., Berlin, 1851-55), V, 823-824, VI, 1583-1584; *Stenographischer Bericht über die Verhandlungen der deutschen constituirenden Nationalversammlung zu Frankfurt am Main*, ed. Franz Wigard (9 vols., Frankfurt am Main, 1848-49), VII, 5101; *Zeitschrift des königlich preussischen statistischen Bureaus*, I (1861), 50-51; Erich Jordan, *Die Entstehung der konservativen Partei und die preussischen Agrarverhältnisse von 1848* (Munich and Leipzig, 1914), p. 58; P. Benaerts, *Les origines*, pp. 118, 133, 575; G. Schmoller, *Geschichte der Kleingewerbe*, p. 106; G. v. Viebahn, *Statistik Deutschlands*, I, 341, 349, II, 147; Anton Höfle, *Die Gewerbeordnung der Pfalz seit der französischen Revolution bis 1868* (Munich, 1908), pp. 22, 39; Johannes Müller, *Grundriss der deutschen Statistik* (4 vols., Jena, 1925-28), III, 202; A. Sartorius von Waltershausen, *Wirtschaftsgeschichte*, pp. 144-145; Wilhelm Ullmann, *Die hessische Gewerbepolitik von der Zeit des Rheinbundes bis zur Einführung der Gewerbefreiheit im Jahre 1866* (Darmstadt, 1903), pp. 62, 84; J. Kuczynski, *Short History*, p. 25; J. Kuczynski, *Bewegung der Wirtschaft*, p. 196.

26. P. Benaerts, *Les origines*, p. 581; Jürgen Kuczynski, *Labour Conditions in Western Europe, 1820 to 1935* (London, 1937), p. 92; J. Kuczynski, *Short History*, pp. 28-29, 33, 60-62; J. Kuczynski, *Bewegung der Wirtschaft*, p. 197; T. C. Banfield, *Industry*, II, 235.

27. J. Kuczynski, *Short History*, pp. 26, 47-54; Alphons Thun, *Die Industrie am Niederrhein und ihre Arbeiter* (2 vols., Leipzig, 1879), II, 72-76; Alphons Thun, "Beiträge zur Geschichte der Gesetzgebung und Verwaltung zu Gunsten der Fabrikarbeiter in Preussen," *Zeitschrift des königlich preussischen statistischen Bureaus*, XVII (1877), 61, 69; Günther K. Anton, *Geschichte der preussischen Fabrikgesetzgebung bis zu ihrer Aufnahme durch die Reichsgewerbeordnung* (Leipzig, 1891), pp. 92, 149-151; Oscar J. Hammen, "Economic and Social Factors in the Prussian Rhineland in 1848," *American Historical Review*, LIV (1949), 827; P. Mombert, *Soziale und wirtschaftliche Anschauungen in Deutschland vom Beginn des neunzehnten Jahrhunderts bis zur Gegenwart* (Leipzig, 1919), p. 30.

28. Prussia, *Gesetz-Sammlung* (1839), pp. 156-158; Bavaria, *Regierungs-Blatt für das Königreich Bayern* (1840), pp. 97-103; Baden, *Grossherzoglich badisches Staats- und Regierungsblatt* (1840), pp. 41-44; M. Quarck, *Die erste Arbeiterbewegung*, p. 16; P. Mombert, *Soziale Anschauungen*, p. 30; J. Kuczynski, *Short History*, pp. 53-54; G. K. Anton, *Geschichte der Fabrikgesetzgebung*, pp. 32-33; A. Thun, "Beiträge," pp. 69, 82; L. Pohle, *Entwicklung des Wirtschaftslebens*, p. 108; O. J. Hammen, "Economic and Social Factors," p. 827; P. Benaerts, *Les origines*,

p. 586; Lujo Brentano, "Zur Reform der deutschen Fabrikgesetzgebung," *Jahrbücher für Nationalökonomie und Statistik*, XIX (1872), 177; G. Albrecht, "Arbeiterschutz," *Wörterbuch der Volkswirtschaft*, 4th ed.

29. J. Benaerts, *Les origines*, pp. 131, 133; François Fejtö, "Europe on the Eve of the Revolution," *The Opening of an Era, 1848: An Historical Symposium*, ed. François Fejtö (London, 1948), p. 14; Werner Conze, "Die Wirkungen der liberalen Agrarreformen auf die Volksordnung in Mitteleuropa im 19. Jahrhundert," *Vierteljahrschrift für Sozial- und Wirtschaftsgeschichte*, XXXVIII [n. d.], 23; G. v. Viebahn, *Statistik Deutschlands*, I, 144, 148, 341, 349, 361, II, 166-171, 251-257; Adolf Werner, *Die politischen Bewegungen in Mecklenburg und der ausserordentliche Landtag im Frühjahr 1848* (Berlin and Leipzig, 1907), pp. 12-13; Alexis Markow, *Das Wachstum der Bevölkerung und die Entwickelung der Aus- und Einwanderungen, Ab- und Zuzüge in Preussen und Preussens einzelnen Provinzen, Bezirken und Kreisgruppen von 1824 bis 1885* (Tübingen, 1889), pp. 28-29, 38.

30. P. Benaerts, *Les origines*, pp. 143-146, 153, 157; B. Moll, *Die Landarbeiterfrage*, p. 23; L. Pohle, *Entwicklung des Wirtschaftslebens*, p. 20; G. v. Viebahn, *Statistik Deutschlands*, II, 147; W. Sombart, *Die deutsche Volkswirtschaft*, pp. 394-395; G. Schmoller, *Geschichte der Kleingewerbe*, p. 190; *Zeitschrift des königlich preussischen statistischen Bureaus*, I (1861), 24-25.

CHAPTER 2

THE DECLINE OF THE HANDICRAFT SYSTEM

1. A. Höfle, *Gewerbeordnung der Pfalz*, pp. 10, 15; G. Schmoller, *Geschichte der Kleingewerbe*, p. 50; W. Schneider, *Wirtschafts- und Sozialpolitik*, p. 11; Heinrich Waentig, "Die gewerbepolitischen Anschauungen in Wissenschaft und Gesetzgebung des 19. Jahrhunderts," *Entwicklung der Volswirtschaftslehre*, ed. S. P. Altmann et al., II, no. 25, p. 7; W. E. Biermann, *Karl Georg Winkelblech (Karl Marlo): Sein Leben und sein Werk* (2 vols., Leipzig, 1909), II, 21; Victor Böhmert, *Freiheit der Arbeit: Beiträge zur Reform der Gewerbegesetze* (Bremen, 1858), p. 259; Ludolf Grambow, *Die deutsche Freihandelspartei zur Zeit ihrer Blüte* (Jena, 1903), p. 19; J. H. Clapham, *Economic Development*, p. 322.

2. Josef Kaizl, *Der Kampf um Gewerbereform und Gewerbefreiheit in Bayern von 1799-1868* (Leipzig, 1879), pp. 30, 48; Georg Ziegler, *Das bayrische Gewerbegesetz von 1868* (Erlangen, 1908), pp. 7-12; G. Schmoller, *Geschichte der Kleingewerbe*, p. 121; Paul Möslein, *Die Gewerbegesetzgebung der thüringer Herzogtümer im 19. Jahrhundert bis zur Einführung der Gewerbefreiheit* (Weimar, 1909), pp. 6-21, 25-44; Wilhelm Engel, *Wirtschaftliche und soziale Kämpfe in Thüringen (insonderheit im Herzogtum Meiningen) vor dem Jahre 1848* (Jena, 1927), p. 117; W. Schneider, *Wirtschafts- und Sozialpolitik*, p. 11.

3. G. H. Pertz, *Das Leben des Ministers Freiherrn vom Stein* (6 vols., Berlin, 1849-55), VI, 184-186; Carl William Hasek, *The Introduction of Adam Smith's Doctrines into Germany* (New York, 1925), p. 105; H. v. Treitschke, *Deutsche Geschichte*, III, 377.

4. H. Waentig, "Die gewerbepolitischen Anschauungen," pp. 8-9; H. v. Treitschke, *Deutsche Geschichte*, III, 377; C. W. Hasek, *Introduction of Adam Smith's Doctrines*, pp. 144-148; Eugen von Philippovich, *Die Entwicklung der wirtschaftspolitischen Ideen im 19. Jahrhundert* (Tübingen, 1910), pp. 6-7.

5. Prussia, *Gesetz-Sammlung* (1810), pp. 79-87, (1811), pp. 263-280; H. Waentig, "Die gewerbepolitischen Anschauungen," pp. 10-11; Paul Geissen, *Die preussische Handwerkerpolitik unter Otto von Manteuffel* (Wuppertal-Elberfeld, 1936), pp. 17-19; Kurt von Rohrscheidt, *Vom Zunftzwange zur Gewerbefreiheit* (Berlin, 1898), p. 375; C. W. Hasek, *Introduction of Adam Smith's Doctrines*, pp. 147-148; Hugo C. M. Wendel, *The Evolution of Industrial Freedom in Prussia, 1845-1849* (New York, 1921), pp. 11-14.

6. W. E. Biermann, *Winkelblech*, II, 21; V. Böhmert, *Freiheit der Arbeit*, p. 259; H. Waentig, "Die gewerbepolitischen Anschauungen," pp. 12, 14; J. Kaizl, *Kampf um Gewerbereform*, p. 30; J. H. Clapham, *Economic Development*, p. 323; H. Pahl, *Hamburg*, pp. 184-185; M. Quarck, *Die erste Arbeiterbewegung*, p. 98; W. Schneider, *Wirtschafts- und Sozialpolitik*, p. 11.

7. Nassau, *Sammlung der landesherrlichen Edicte und Verordnungen des Herzogthums Nassau* (4 vols., Wiesbaden, 1817-[46?]), III, 117-121; G. v. Viebahn, *Statistik Deutschlands*, III, 545; M. Quarck, *Die erste Arbeiterbewegung*, p. 5; P. Benaerts, *Les origines*, p. 544.

8. Bavaria, *Gesetz-Blatt für das Königreich Bayern* (1825), pp. 127-142; A. Höfle, *Gewerbeordnung der Pfalz*, p. 17; J. Kaizl, *Kampf um Gewerbereform*, pp. 79-80; G. Ziegler, *Gewerbegesetz von 1868*, pp. 14-21; P. Benaerts, *Les origines*, p. 542; H. Waentig, "Die gewerbepolitischen Anschauungen," p. 14.

9. Hesse-Darmstadt, *Grossherzoglich hessisches Regierungsblatt* (1827), pp. 185-200; V. Böhmert, *Freiheit der Arbeit*, pp. 193-196; W. Ullmann, *Die hessische Gewerbepolitik*, pp. 17, 20-21, 28-29, 39-40, 50.

10. Württemberg, *Königlich württembergisches Staats- und Regierungs-Blatt* (1828), pp. 237-286, (1836), pp. 385-434; P. Benaerts, *Les origines*, p. 543; G. Schmoller, *Geschichte der Kleingewerbe*, p. 109; J. Kaizl, *Kampf um Gewerbereform*, p. 30; J. H. Clapham, *Economic Development*, p. 84; H. Waentig, "Die gewerbepolitischen Anschauungen," p. 14.

11. Saxony, *Gesetz- und Verordnungsblatt für das Königreich Sachsen* (1840), pp. 246-253; P. Benaerts, *Les origines*, pp. 543-544.

12. Prussia, *Gesetz-Sammlung* (1845), pp. 41-78; H. Waentig, "Die gewerbepolitischen Anschauungen," pp. 11, 16-17; H.C.M. Wendel, *Industrial Freedom*, pp. 17-41; P. Geissen, *Handwerkerpolitik*, pp. 22-25; J. Kaizl, *Kampf um Gewerbereform*, p. 29.

13. Hanover, *Sammlung der Gesetze, Verordnungen und Ausschreiben für das Königreich Hannover* (1847), pp. 215-257; *Verhandlungen der deutschen verfassunggebenden Reichs-Versammlung zu Frankfurt am Main*, ed. K. D. Hassler (6 vols., Frankfurt am Main, 1848-49), II, 271;

V. Böhmert, *Freiheit der Arbeit*, pp. 262-263; H. Waentig, "Die gewerbepolitischen Anschauungen," p. 22.

14. Bavaria, *Verhandlungen der zweyten Kammer der Ständeversammlung des Königreichs Bayern* (18 vols., Munich, 1827-28), Beylage 36, p. 3. Cf. *ibid.*, I, 145, 424-425, II, 23-24, 56, 87, 420, III, 127, 263, IV, 65, 168, 253-254, V, 77, VI, 317, 414, VIII, 15, 148; *Alphabetisches Repertorium über die Verhandlungen der Stände des Königreichs Bayern im Jahre 1827-28*, ed. Georg von Delling (Munich, 1830), pp. 155-156.

15. Bavaria, *Verhandlungen der zweyten Kammer* (1827-28), I, 321-322, II, 24, 167, III, 166, 263, 587, VII, 280, 384, 577-578, X, 387-388; *Alphabetisches Repertorium*, ed. G. v. Delling, pp. 153-157; B. Ziegler, *Gewerbegesetz von 1868*, pp. 21-23; A. Höfle, *Gewerbeordnung der Pfalz*, pp. 15, 17-18.

16. P. Geissen, *Handwerkerpolitik*, p. 20; K. v. Rohrscheidt, *Vom Zunftzwange*, pp. 458, 461-463; H. Waentig, "Die gewerbepolitischen Anschauungen," pp. 15-18; H.C.M. Wendel, *Industrial Freedom*, pp. 56-58; G. Schmoller, *Geschichte der Kleingewerbe*, p. 80.

17. M. Schwann, "Grundlagen des Wirtschaftslebens," pp. 204, 218, 225; H. Waentig, "Die gewerbepolitischen Anschauungen," p. 18; G. Schmoller, *Geschichte der Kleingewerbe*, p. 80.

18. W. Engel, *Wirtschaftliche Kämpfe*, pp. 13, 112; P. Möslein, *Gewerbegesetzgebung*, p. 25; Veit Valentin, *Frankfurt am Main und die Revolution von 1848-49* (Stuttgart and Berlin, 1908), pp. 112-114; E. v. Philippovich, *Entwicklung der Ideen*, p. 39.

19. *Vorgeschichte des Zollvereins*, ed. W. v. Eisenhart Rothe and A. Ritthaler, III, 206. Cf. *ibid.*, III, 195-198, 201-202; P. Benaerts, *Les origines*, p. 69.

20. Veit Valentin, *Das Hambacher Nationalfest* (Berlin, 1932), pp. 15-17, 31, 36, 48, 50-52, 61-62, 75-76; A. Price, *Evolution of the Zollverein*, pp. 177-179.

21. Alfred Zimmermann, *Blüthe und Verfall des Leinengewerbes in Schlesien: Gewerbe- und Handelspolitik dreier Jahrhunderte*, 2nd ed. (Oldenburg and Leipzig, [1892]), pp. 301-362, 468; Veit Valentin, *Geschichte der deutschen Revolution von 1848-49* (2 vols., Berlin, 1930-31), I, 52-54; H. v. Treitschke, *Deutsche Geschichte*, V, 468-469, 519-520; R. v. Delbrück, *Lebenserinnerungen*, I, 226; Georg Adler, *Die Geschichte der ersten sozialpolitischen Arbeiterbewegung in Deutschland mit besonderer Rücksicht auf die einwirkenden Theorieen: Ein Beitrag zur Entwickelungsgeschichte der sozialen Frage* (Breslau, 1885), p. 108; J. Kuczynski, *Bewegung der Wirtschaft*, pp. 58-59.

22. G. Schmoller, *Geschichte der Kleingewerbe*, pp. 65, 69, 104, 111-112, 122-123, 143-147, 331, 368-383, 634, 638, 643; M. Quarck, *Die erste Arbeiterbewegung*, p. 2; L. Pohle, *Entwicklung des Wirtschaftslebens*, p. 58; C.F.W. Dieterici, *Volkswohlstand*, pp. 253-254; Prussia, *Stenographische Berichte über die Verhandlungen der durch das allerhöchste Patent vom 5. Dezember 1848 einberufenen Kammern: Erste Kammer* (5 vols., Berlin, 1849-50), V, 2298.

23. E. Kaeber, *Berlin 1848*, p. 9; H. v. Treitschke, *Deutsche Geschichte*, III, 377; Karl Valerius Herberger, *Die Stellung der preussischen Konservativen zur sozialen Frage, 1848-62* (Meissen, 1914), p. 2; G. Schmoller,

Geschichte der Kleingewerbe, pp. 121, 429; J. Kuczynski, *Short History*, pp. 24, 34, 36-37, 39, 44-45, 55-57; Eugen Katz, *Landarbeiter und Land-wirtschaft in Oberhessen* (Stuttgart and Berlin, 1904), p. 18; Wilhelm Friedensburg, *Stephan Born und die Organisationsbestrebungen der Ber-liner Arbeiterschaft bis zum Berliner Arbeiter-Kongress, 1840-September 1848* (Leipzig, 1923), pp. 4-6; P. Benaerts, *Les origines*, p. 587; P. Al-brecht, *Die volkswirtschaftlichen Fragen*, p. 4; P. Mombert, "Aus der Literatur über die soziale Frage und über die Arbeiterbewegung in Deutsch-land in der ersten Hälfte des 19. Jahrhunderts," *Archiv für die Geschichte des Sozialismus und der Arbeiterbewegung*, IX (1921), 169-236; P. Mom-bert, *Soziale Anschauungen*, pp. 30-31; W. Sombart, *Die deutsche Volks-wirtschaft*, p. 430; Eugen Barthelmess, "Sozialpolitisches im Revolutions-jahr," *Deutschland, 1848-1948: Beiträge zur historisch-politischen Würdi-gung der Volkserhebung von 1848-49*, ed. Wilhelm Keil (Stuttgart, 1948), pp. 117-121; H. Schlüter, "Beiträge zur sozialen Geschichte des Jahres 1848," *Neue Zeit*, III (1885), 28-29; D. Meyer, *Das Leben in Berlin*, p. 106; V. Valentin, *Frankfurt und die Revolution*, p. 115.

24. *Mittheilungen des statistischen Bureau's in Berlin*, IV (1851), 307-308; *Tabellen und Nachrichten für 1849*, V, 823-824; G. Schmoller, *Geschichte der Kleingewerbe*, pp. 65, 71, 104; W. Sombart, *Die deutsche Volkswirtschaft*, p. 461; W. Ullmann, *Die hessische Gewerbepolitik*, p. 62.

CHAPTER 3

THE AGRARIAN PROBLEM

1. *Tabellen und Nachrichten für 1849*, V, 823-825; G. v. Viebahn, *Statistik Deutschlands*, II, 147, 274, 276, 611, 613-614; *Verhandlungen der Nationalversammlung*, ed. F. Wigard, IV, 2389, 2415; *Mittheilungen des statistischen Bureau's in Berlin*, IV (1851), 307-308; W. Sombart, *Die deutsche Volkswirtschaft*, pp. 394-395, 423; Otto Thissen, *Beiträge zur Geschichte des Handwerks in Preussen* (Tübingen, 1901), pp. 22-23; A. Sartorius von Waltershausen, *Wirtschaftsgeschichte*, p. 7; L. Pohle, *Entwicklung des Wirtschaftslebens*, p. 19; A. Werner, *Die politischen Bewegungen*, p. 103; P. Benaerts, *Les origines*, p. 133; Friedrich Meinecke, "The Year 1848 in German History: Reflections on a Centenary," *Review of Politics*, X (1948), 483; T. C. Banfield, *Industry*, I, 72; W. O. Hender-son, *Zollverein*, p. 11; J. Kuczynski, *Short History*, pp. 14, 25; B. Moll, *Die Landarbeiterfrage*, pp. 22, 41; K.G.I. Teuthorn, *Das sächsische Gesetz*, p. 62.

2. Theodor von der Goltz, *Geschichte der deutschen Landwirtschaft* (2 vols., Stuttgart and Berlin, 1902-03), II, 208-209; Max Weber, *Wirt-schaftsgeschichte* (Munich and Leipzig, 1924), p. 81; W. Engel, *Wirt-schaftliche Kämpfe*, p. 20; G. v. Below, "Fronden," *Handwörterbuch der Staatswissenschaften*, 4th ed.; Friedrich Lautenschlager, *Die Agrarunruhen in den badischen Standes- und Grundherrschaften im Jahre 1848* (Heidel-berg, 1915), p. 26, n. 1; Otto Stolz, "Die Bauernbefreiung in Süddeutsch-land im Zusammenhang der Geschichte," *Vierteljahrschrift für Sozial- und*

Wirtschaftsgeschichte, XXXIII (1940), 54-55; W. Conze, "Wirkungen der Agrarreformen," p. 11; W. Schneider, *Wirtschafts- und Sozialpolitik*, p. 10.

3. W. Schneider, *Wirtschafts- und Sozialpolitik*, pp. 57, 64; Carl Johannes Fuchs, "Bauernbefreiung," *Wörterbuch der Volkswirtschaft*, 4th ed.; Theodor von der Goltz, *Vorlesungen über Agrarwesen und Agrarpolitik* (Jena, 1899), p. 38; A. Werner, *Die politischen Bewegungen*, p. 13; E. v. Philippovich, *Entwicklung der Ideen*, p. 95; L. Pohle, *Entwicklung des Wirtschaftslebens*, p. 36; Heinrich Heffter, *Die deutsche Selbstverwaltung im 19. Jahrhundert: Geschichte der Ideen und Institutionen* (Stuttgart, 1950), p. 201; Georg v. Below, "Grundbesitz: Geschichte des Grundbesitzes," *Handwörterbuch der Staatswissenschaften*, 4th ed.; Heinrich Sieveking, *Wirtschaftsgeschichte* (Berlin, 1935), p. 137.

4. Georg Friedrich Knapp, *Grundherrschaft und Rittergut* (Leipzig, 1897), p. 10; G. v. Viebahn, *Statistik Deutschlands*, II, 572; Georg Hanssen, *Die Aufhebung der Leibeigenschaft und die Umgestaltung der gutsherrlich-bäuerlichen Verhältnisse überhaupt in den Herzogthümern Schleswig und Holstein* (St. Petersburg, 1861), pp. 1-3; F. Gutmann, "Bauernbefreiung," *Handwörterbuch der Staatswissenschaften*, 4th ed.; Werner Wittich, *Die Grundherrschaft in Nordwestdeutschland* (Leipzig, 1896), pp. 1-18; H. Sieveking, *Wirtschaftsgeschichte*, p. 138.

5. M. Weber, *Wirtschaftsgeschichte*, p. 99; Theodor Knapp, *Neue Beiträge zur Rechts- und Wirtschaftsgeschichte des württembergischen Bauernstandes* (2 vols., Tübingen, 1919), I, 155; W. Schneider, *Wirtschafts- und Sozialpolitik*, pp. 15, 56-57; L. Pohle, *Entwicklung des Wirtschaftslebens*, p. 9; Karl Lamprecht, *Deutsche Geschichte* (12 vols., Berlin, 1891-1909), IX, 235-236, 241.

6. W. Schneider, *Wirtschafts- und Sozialpolitik*, p. 58; G. Hanssen, *Aufhebung der Leibeigenschaft*, pp. 34-37, 42, 159; H. Sieveking, *Wirtschaftsgeschichte*, p. 138.

7. M. Weber, *Wirtschaftsgeschichte*, pp. 91-92; H. Heffter, *Selbstverwaltung*, p. 201; Georg Friedrich Knapp, *Die Bauern-Befreiung und der Ursprung der Landarbeiter in den älteren Theilen Preussens* (2 vols., Leipzig, 1887), I, 49-66, II, 33-37, 51-53; W. Schneider, *Wirtschafts- und Sozialpolitik*, p. 57; T. v. d. Goltz, *Vorlesungen*, p. 38.

8. Samuel Sugenheim, *Geschichte der Aufhebung der Leibeigenschaft und Hörigkeit in Europa bis um die Mitte des neunzehnten Jahrunderts* (St. Petersburg, 1861), pp. 409-444; G. Hanssen, *Aufhebung der Leibeigenschaft*, pp. 53-56, 58; T. v. d. Goltz, *Geschichte*, II, 160; W. Schneider, *Wirtschafts- und Sozialpolitik*, p. 15; K. Lamprecht, *Deutsche Geschichte*, IX, 243; G. v. Viebahn, *Statistik Deutschlands*, II, 586-594; E. Katz, *Landarbeiter*, p. 20; H. Sieveking, *Wirtschaftsgeschichte*, p. 137; G. F. Knapp, *Bauern-Befreiung*, II, 464.

9. G. v. Viebahn, *Statistik Deutschlands*, II, 586, 594; K. Lamprecht, *Deutsche Geschichte*, IX, 243; E. Katz, *Landarbeiter*, p. 20.

10. Prussia, *Gesetz-Sammlung* (1806-10), pp. 170-173; G. F. Knapp, *Bauern-Befreiung*, I, 96-114, 126-136, II, 173-178; E. v. Philippovich, *Entwicklung der Ideen*, p. 95.

11. Prussia, *Gesetz-Sammlung* (1810-11), pp. 281-299; G. F. Knapp, *Bauern-Befreiung*, I, 161-171, 259-260, II, 226-264; Emil Wolff, *Grundriss der preussisch-deutschen sozialpolitischen und Volkswirtschafts-Ge-*

schichte vom Ende des dreissigjährigen Krieges bis zur Gegenwart, 1640-1898 (Berlin, 1899), pp. 88-90; Lysbeth Walker Muncy, *The Junker in the Prussian Administration under William II, 1888-1914* (Providence, 1944), p. 25; W. Bowden, M. Karpovich, and A. P. Usher, *Economic History*, p. 274.

12. Georg Friedrich Knapp, *Die Landarbeiter in Knechtschaft und Freiheit* (Leipzig, 1891), pp. 77, 85, 90-91; E. v. Philippovich, *Entwicklung der Ideen*, p. 95; E. Wolff, *Volkswirtschafts-Geschichte*, pp. 89-90; L. W. Muncy, *The Junker*, p. 25.

13. Württemberg, *Regierungs-Blatt* (1836), pp. 545-580; Saxony, *Verordnungsblatt* (1832), pp. 163-266; Wilhelm Kellner, *Taschenbuch der politischen Statistik Deutschlands oder Aufstellung der staatlichen Einrichtungen Gesammt-Deutschlands sowohl als der einzelnen deutschen Staaten* (Frankfurt am Main, 1864), pp. 33-34; "Die Ablösungsgesetze und andere Gesetze zu Erfüllung der Forderungen des Liberalismus," *Deutsche Vierteljahrs Schrift*, XVII (1854), no. 3, pp. 207-208, 210-215; M. Weber, *Wirtschaftsgeschichte*, pp. 99-100; A. Sartorius von Waltershausen, *Wirtschaftsgeschichte*, pp. 12-13; T.v.d. Goltz, *Geschichte*, II, 160; W. Schneider, *Wirtschafts- und Sozialpolitik*, pp. 14-16, 58-59; F. Lautenschlager, *Agrarunruhen*, pp. 11, 13-14, 18-19; K. Lamprecht, *Deutsche Geschichte*, IX, 237-238, 243; G. v. Viebahn, *Statistik Deutschlands*, II, 586-595; T. Knapp, *Neue Beiträge*, I, 161-163, 170-172; Otto Reinhard, *Die Grundentlastung in Württemberg* (Tübingen, 1910), p. 12; B. Moll, *Die Landarbeiterfrage*, pp. 8, 27-28; K.G.I. Teuthorn, *Das sächsische Gesetz*, p. 50; H. Sieveking, *Wirtschaftsgeschichte*, p. 137; *Verhandlungen der Nationalversammlung*, ed. F. Wigard, IV, 2398-2399; W. Wittich, *Grundherrschaft*, pp. 434-445; G. F. Knapp, *Grundherrschaft*, p. 98; A. Höfle, *Gewerbeordnung der Pfalz*, p. 16; T.v.d. Goltz, *Vorlesungen*, p. 101; Ernst Schocke, *Die deutsche Einheits- und Freiheitsbewegung in Sachsen-Meiningen, 1848-1850: Ein Beitrag zur Geschichte der ersten deutschen Revolution* (Hildburghausen, 1927), pp. 8-9; S. Sugenheim, *Aufhebung der Leibeigenschaft*, p. 463; W. Engel, *Wirtschaftliche Kämpfe*, pp. 96, 100; Otto H. Brandt, *Der Bauer und die bäuerlichen Lasten im Herzogtum Sachsen-Altenburg vom 17. bis zum 19. Jahrhundert* (Gotha, 1906), pp. 132-139; E. Katz, *Landarbeiter*, pp. 23-27.

14. Prussia, *Gesetz-Sammlung* (1816), pp. 154-180; Lujo Brentano, *Gesammelte Aufsätze* (Stuttgart, 1889), p. 257; L. W. Muncy, *The Junker*, p. 28; G. F. Knapp, *Bauern-Befreiung*, I, 260-261, 265; G. F. Knapp, *Landarbeiter*, pp. 79-80; J. Kuczynski, *Bewegung der Wirtschaft*, p. 41; G. v. Viebahn, *Statistik Deutschlands*, II, 555; E. Wolff, *Volkswirtschafts-Geschichte*, pp. 88-89.

15. Prussia, *Gesetz-Sammlung* (1821), pp. 77-83; G. F. Knapp, *Bauern-Befreiung*, I, 201-205, 267, 269-270; W. Bowden, M. Karpovich, and A. P. Usher, *Economic History*, p. 274; J. H. Clapham, *Economic Development*, p. 195; A. Sartorius von Waltershausen, *Wirtschaftsgeschichte*, p. 137; J. Kuczynski, *Bewegung der Wirtschaft*, p. 41; T.v.d. Goltz, *Geschichte*, II, 160; H. Heffter, *Selbstverwaltung*, p. 201; A. Werner, *Die politischen Bewegungen*, p. 13.

16. L. W. Muncy, *The Junker*, pp. 25-26; W. Sombart, *Die deutsche Volkswirtschaft*, p. 78; W. Sombart, *Kapitalismus*, III, 335-336; *Tabellen*

und Nachrichten für 1849, IV, 550-551; J. Kuczynski, *Short History*, p. 21; J. Kuczynski, *Bewegung der Wirtschaft*, p. 41; E. Jordan, *Enstehung der konservativen Partei*, p. 28; T.v.d. Goltz, *Geschichte*, II, 181; Ferdinand Tönnies, "Deutscher Adel im neunzehnten Jahrhundert," *Neue Rundschau*, XXIII (1912), 1049; Sigmund Neumann, *Die Stufen des preussischen Konservatismus* (Berlin, 1930), p. 40; Max Sering, *Deutsche Agrarpolitik auf geschichtlicher und landeskundlicher Grundlage* (Leipzig, 1934), p. 29; G. F. Knapp, *Landarbeiter*, p. 85; E. v. Philippovich, *Entwicklung der Ideen*, p. 96.

17. A. Sartorius von Waltershausen, *Wirtschaftsgeschichte*, p. 121; T.v.d. Goltz, *Geschichte*, II, 177, 186-187; W. Sombart, *Die deutsche Volkswirtschaft*, pp. 78, 520; A. Werner, *Die politischen Bewegungen*, p. 23, n. 24; J. Conrad, "Die Latifundien im preussischen Osten," *Jahrbücher für Nationalökonomie und Statistik*, L (1888), 139; S. Neumann, *Stufen des Konservatismus*, p. 37; F. Schnabel, *Deutsche Geschichte*, II, 295; G. v. Viebahn, *Statistik Deutschlands*, II, 1007, 1010, 1019; W. Sombart, *Kapitalismus*, III, 335; "Mr. Jacob's Report on the Trade in Corn and on the Agriculture of the North of Europe," *Great Britain: Parliamentary Papers* (1826), XXI, 72-73; J. Conrad, "Agrarstatistische Untersuchungen: Der Grossgrundbesitz in Ostpreussen," *Jahrbücher für Nationalökonomie und Statistik*, LVII (1891), 831, 844; J. Conrad, "Die Fideikommisse in den östlichen Provinzen Preussens," *Festgabe für Georg Hanssen zum 31. Mai 1889* (Tübingen, 1889), pp. 293-296; L. W. Muncy, *The Junker*, p. 85; E. v. Philippovich, *Entwicklung der Ideen*, p. 100.

18. W. Conze, "Wirkungen der Agrarreformen," pp. 14-15, 20-23; L. Brentano, *Aufsätze*, pp. 257-258; T.v.d. Goltz, *Geschichte*, II, 181, 201; F. Schnabel, *Deutsche Geschichte*, II, 294; W. Sombart, *Kapitalismus*, III, 335-336; W. Sombart, *Die deutsche Volkswirtschaft*, p. 52; K.G.I. Teuthorn, *Das sächsische Gesetz*, pp. 57-59; *Zeitschrift des königlich preussischen statistischen Bureaus*, V (1865), 5, 7-9, XIII (1873), 25; Max Sering, *Die innere Kolonisation im östlichen Deutschland* (Leipzig, 1893), pp. 296-297; A. Sartorius von Waltershausen, *Wirtschaftsgeschichte*, p. 124; G. F. Knapp, *Bauern-Befreiung*, I, 257; G. F. Knapp, *Grundherrschaft*, p. 10; G. Hanssen, *Aufhebung der Leibeigenschaft*, pp. 17-22; E. Katz, *Landarbeiter*, pp. 38, 43; W. Engel, *Wirtschaftliche Kämpfe*, p. 41; Christoph Crössmann, *Die Unruhen in Oberhessen im Herbste 1830* (Darmstadt, 1929), pp. 42-43.

19. "Mr. Jacob's Report," p. 79. The value of the Prussian dollar or thaler was three marks.

20. G. v. Viebahn, *Statistik Deutschlands*, II, 608-610; T.v.d. Goltz, *Geschichte*, II, 271-272; *Tabellen und amtliche Nachrichten über den preussischen Staat für das Jahr 1855* (Berlin, 1858), pp. 198-199; E. Jordan, *Entstehung der konservativen Partei*, p. 66; W. Kellner, *Taschenbuch*, pp. 24-25; G. F. Knapp, *Grundherrschaft*, pp. 8, 10, 36-40; G. F. Knapp, *Bauern-Befreiung*, I, 12-14; J. Conrad, "Latifundien," p. 131.

21. T. C. Banfield, *Industry*, I, 53.

22. F. List, *Schriften*, V, 443; W. Conze, "Wirkungen der Agrarreformen," pp. 2, 11-12; T.v.d. Goltz, *Geschichte*, II, 184; G. v. Viebahn, *Statistik Deutschlands*, II, 566, 573-574; W. Sombart, *Kapitalismus*, III, 379; W. Engel, *Wirtschaftliche Kämpfe*, pp. 20, 213.

23. Ulrich Zeller, "Der Ablauf der Ereignisse," *Deutschland, 1848-1948*, ed. W. Keil, p. 28; T. Knapp, *Neue Beiträge*, I, 164-165, 167, 173-176; F. Lautenschlager, *Agrarunruhen*, pp. 9-10, 13-14, 18-19, 22, 24-25, 69; G. v. Viebahn, *Statistik Deutschlands*, II, 586-587; W. Kellner, *Taschenbuch*, p. 34; E. Katz, *Landarbeiter*, pp. 21-27, 40-41; S. Sugenheim, *Aufhebung der Leibeigenschaft*, pp. 473-474; Adolf Nebel, *Die ländlichen Arbeiterverhältnisse in Kurhessen* (Fulda, 1909), pp. 7-8; G. Hanssen, *Aufhebung der Leibeigenschaft*, pp. 2-3.

24. Saxony, *Verordnungsblatt* (1832), pp. 267-272; E. Jordan, *Entstehung der konservativen Partei*, p. 50; L. Brentano, *Aufsätze*, p. 257; "Ablösungsgesetze," pp. 215-216; K.G.I. Teuthorn, *Das sächsische Gesetz*, pp. 50-52; Fr. Schulte, "Rentenbanken," *Handwörterbuch der Staatswissenschaften*, 4th ed.; W. Schneider, *Wirtschafts- und Sozialpolitik*, p. 15; K. Lamprecht, *Deutsche Geschichte*, IX, 238; G. v. Viebahn, *Statistik Deutschlands*, II, 587-588, 594; F. Lautenschlager, *Agrarunruhen*, pp. 18-19; T. Knapp, *Neue Beiträge*, I, 172; E. Katz, *Landarbeiter*, pp. 24-27; E. Schocke, *Sachsen-Meiningen*, p. 8; W. Engel, *Wirtschaftliche Kämpfe*, pp. 96-97, 101-103.

25. W. Wittich, *Grundherrschaft*, p. 446; G. Hanssen, *Aufhebung der Leibeigenschaft*, pp. 134-135; W. Kellner, *Taschenbuch*, p. 34; G. F. Knapp, *Bauern-Befreiung*, I, 258, 267; E. Wolff, *Volkswirtschafts-Geschichte*, pp. 89-90; J. Kuczynski, *Bewegung der Wirtschaft*, p. 41; S. Sugenheim, *Aufhebung der Leibeigenschaft*, pp. 473-474; Karl Reis, *Die Ursachen und ersten Äusserungen der schlesischen Agrarbewegung des Jahres 1848* (Breslau, 1910), p. 14; Karl Böhme, *Gutsherrlich-bäuerliche Verhältnisse in Ostpreussen während der Reformzeit von 1770 bis 1830* (Leipzig, 1902), pp. 72-73; E. Jordan, *Entstehung der konservativen Partei*, pp. 46-47; *Verhandlungen der Nationalversammlung*, ed. F. Wigard, IV, 2418; F. Lautenschlager, *Agrarunruhen*, pp. 26-27; E. Katz, *Landarbeiter*, p. 32.

CHAPTER 4

THE IDEOLOGICAL CONFLICT

1. H. v. Treitschke, *Deutsche Geschichte*, II, 278, 287, 589, 606-607, III, 364; Heinrich von Sybel, *Die Begründung des Deutschen Reiches durch Wilhelm I.* (7 vols., Munich and Leipzig, 1889-94), I, 58-59, 67-68; F. Schnabel, *Deutsche Geschichte*, II, 282-291; E. Kaeber, *Berlin 1848*, p. 14; L. W. Muncy, *The Junker*, p. 24; W. Kellner, *Taschenbuch*, pp. 66-67; Herbert Arthur Strauss, *Staat, Bürger, Mensch: Die Debatten der deutschen Nationalversammlung 1848-49 über die Grundrechte* (Aarau, 1947), pp. 14-16.

2. Erich Brandenburg, "Zum älteren deutschen Parteiwesen," *Historische Zeitschrift*, CXIX (1919), 68, 73; Erich Brandenburg, *Die Reichsgründung* (2 vols., Leipzig, 1916), I, 294-295; F. Schnabel, *Deutsche Geschichte*, II, 94-95; Rudolf Stadelmann, "Das Jahr 1848 und die deutsche Geschichte,"

NOTES FOR CHAPTER 4

Deutsche Rundschau, LXXI (1948), 104; Hans Krause, *Die demokratische Partei von 1848 und die soziale Frage* (Frankfurt am Main, 1923), pp. 39-40; A. H. Price, *Evolution of the Zollverein,* pp. 175-176; O. J. Hammen, "Economic and Social Factors," p. 826; G. Adler, *Geschichte der Arbeiterbewegung,* pp. 135-136.

3. *Rheinische Briefe,* ed. J. Hansen, I, 30; Wilhelm Zimmermann, *Die Entstehung der provinziellen Selbstverwaltung in Preussen, 1848-1875* (Berlin, 1932), p. 10; Hugo Preuss, *Die Junkerfrage* (Berlin, 1897), p. 41; Franz Mehring, *Zur preussischen Geschichte* (2 vols., Berlin, 1930), II, 241; F. Fejtö, "Europe on the Eve," p. 8, n. 1; E. Jordan, *Entstehung der konservativen Partei,* p. 38; A. Werner, *Die politischen Bewegungen,* p. 30; Ruth Wöltge, *Die Reaktion im Königreich Hannover, 1850-1857: Die Rückbildung des Verfassungsgesetzes und die Reformversuche an den Provinziallandschaften* (Tübingen, 1932), pp. 5-6; H. A. Strauss, *Staat, Bürger, Mensch,* pp. 14-16.

4. *Rheinische Briefe,* ed. J. Hansen, I, 138, 372, 517, 590-591; R. v. Delbrück, *Lebenserinnerungen,* I, 144-145, 183; *Die deutschen Parteiprogramme,* ed. Felix Salomon, 4th and 5th eds. (3 vols., Leipzig and Berlin, 1931-32), I, 26-28; K. Rathgen, "Freihandel und Schutzzoll," p. 25; Alfred Zimmermann, *Geschichte der preussisch-deutschen Handelspolitik* (Oldenburg and Leipzig, 1892), p. 40; A. H. Price, *Evolution of the Zollverein,* pp. 37-38.

5. *Rheinische Briefe,* ed. J. Hansen, I, 622.

6. The best analysis of the development of early German liberalism is by F. Schnabel, *Deutsche Geschichte,* II, 90-214, but sound treatments are also presented in H. Heffter, *Selbstverwaltung,* pp. 137-245, and Guido De Ruggiero, *The History of European Liberalism,* trans. R. G. Collingwood (London, 1927), pp. 211-274. Valuable illustrations of liberal theories and attitudes may be found in the following: Rotteck, "Demokratisches Princip, demokratisches Element und Interesse, demokratische Gesinnung," *Staats-Lexikon oder Encyclopädie der Staatswissenschaften,* ed. Carl von Rotteck and Carl Welcker (15 vols., Altona, 1834-43), IV, 254-255; Pfizer, "Liberal, Liberalismus," *ibid.,* IX, 715; *Rheinische Briefe,* ed. J. Hansen, I, 12-14, 21, 138, 517; *Vorgeschichte des Zollvereins,* ed. W. v. Eisenhart Rothe and A. Ritthaler, I, 326; Erich Marcks, *Männer und Zeiten: Aufsätze und Reden zur neueren Geschichte* (2 vols., Leipzig, 1911), I, 205-206; Alexander Bergengrün, *David Hansemann* (Berlin, 1901), pp. 113, 271; Joseph Hansen, *Gustav von Mevissen: Ein rheinisches Lebensbild, 1815-1899* (2 vols., Berlin, 1906), II, 132; Friedrich Meinecke, "Zur Geschichte des älteren deutschen Parteiwesens," *Historische Zeitschrift,* CXVIII (1917), 57; Andrea Frahm, "Paulskirche und Volkssouveränität," *Historische Zeitschrift,* CXXX (1924), 214, 233-234; Thilo Schnurre, *Die württembergischen Abgeordneten in der konstituierenden deutschen Nationalversammlung zu Frankfurt am Main* (Marburg, 1912), p. 43; Johanna Köster, *Der rheinische Frühliberalismus und die soziale Frage* (Berlin, 1938), pp. 106-107; Jacques Droz, *Le libéralisme rhénan, 1815-1848* (Paris, 1940), pp. 425-426; Wilhelm Mommsen, *Grösse und Versagen des deutschen Bürgertums: Ein Beitrag zur Geschichte der Jahre 1848-1849* (Stuttgart, 1949), p. 171; Georg Erler, *Die verwaltungspolitischen Ideen der 1848er*

NOTES FOR CHAPTER 4

*Bewegung: Ihre Grundlagen u. Auswirkungen unter besonderer Berück-
sichtigung der preussischen Gesetze von 1850* (Münster, 1928), p. 18.

7. *Rheinische Briefe,* ed. J. Hansen, I, 17.

8. *Parteiprogramme,* ed. F. Salomon, 3rd ed. (3 vols., Leipzig and
Berlin, 1920-24), I, 2-5; J. Hansen, "Das politische Leben," *Rheinprovinz,*
ed. J. Hansen, I, 697; *Rheinische Briefe,* ed. J. Hansen, I, 517; W. E. Biermann, *Winkelblech,* I, 261; A. Frahm, "Paulskirche," p. 214; J. Köster,
Frühliberalismus, p. 106.

9. Silvester Jordan, *Versuche über allgemeines Staatsrecht* (Marburg,
1828), pp. 469-470; Rotteck, "Census, insbesondere Wahlcensus," *Staats-
Lexikon,* ed. C. v. Rotteck and C. Welcker, III, 378, 381-382, 385; Rotteck,
"Demokratisches Princip," p. 259; Pfizer, "Liberal, Liberalismus," p. 715;
Erinnerungen aus dem Leben von Hans Viktor von Unruh, ed. Heinrich
von Poschinger (Stuttgart, Leipzig, Berlin, and Vienna, 1895), p. 98;
Johanna Philippson, *Ueber den Ursprung und die Einführung des allgemeinen gleichen Wahlrechts in Deutschland mit besonderer Berücksichtigung
der Wahlen zum Frankfurter Parlament im Grossherzogtum Baden* (Berlin
and Leipzig, 1913), pp. 8-9, 11, 13-14, 19-20, 26, 28; A. Bergengrün,
Hansemann, pp. 113, 271; J. Köster, *Frühliberalismus,* p. 107; A. Frahm,
"Paulskirche," pp. 233-234; T. Schnurre, *Die württembergischen Abgeordneten,* p. 43; J. Hansen, "Das politische Leben," p. 718.

10. *Rheinische Briefe,* ed. J. Hansen, I, 590-591; *Parteiprogramme,* ed.
F. Salomon, 3rd ed., I, 2-5; W. E. Biermann, *Winkelblech,* I, 235;
A. H. Price, *Evolution of the Zollverein,* pp. 37-38.

11. *Rheinische Briefe,* ed. J. Hansen, I, 13.

12. *Parteiprogramme,* ed. F. Salomon, 3rd ed., I, 5-7; Luigi Salvatorelli, *La rivoluzione europea, 1848-1849* (Milan, 1949), p. 87; G. F.
Knapp, *Bauern-Befreiung,* I, 218; J. Philippson, *Ursprung des Wahlrechts,*
pp. 22-23, 76.

13. *Parteiprogramme,* ed. F. Salomon, 3rd ed., I, 6. Cf. Johann Jacoby,
Gesammelte Schriften und Reden, 2nd ed. (2 vols., Hamburg, 1877), II,
11, 13, 17, 22-23, 26; W. Mommsen, *Grösse und Versagen,* pp. 130, 160;
Franz Mehring, *Geschichte der deutschen Sozialdemokratie* (2 vols., Stuttgart, 1897-98), I, 346-347; Wilhelm Zimmermann, *Die deutsche Revolution* (Karlsruhe, 1848), pp. 565-568; Otto Ernst Sutter, *Die Linke der
Paulskirche* (Frankfurt am Main, 1924), p. 43; J. Philippson, *Ursprung
des Wahlrechts,* pp. 22-23; G. Adler, *Geschichte der Arbeiterbewegung,*
p. 317; A.J.P. Taylor, *The Course of German History* (New York, 1946),
p. 69.

14. W. Mommsen, *Grösse und Versagen,* p. 160; G. Adler, *Geschichte
der Arbeiterbewegung,* pp. 133-134, 317; V. Valentin, *Geschichte der
Revolution,* II, 176; F. Mehring, *Geschichte der Sozialdemokratie,* I, 304;
H. Krause, *Die demokratische Partei,* p. 112, n. 1.

15. Karl Marx, *Revolution and Counter-Revolution,* ed. Eleanor Marx
Aveling (Chicago, 1914), p. 148. Engels was the actual author of this
collection of newspaper articles appearing under Marx's name. See Gustav
Mayer, *Friedrich Engels: Eine Biographie,* 2nd ed. (2 vols., The Hague,
1934), II, 30.

16. F. Mehring, *Geschichte der Sozialdemokratie,* I, 346-347.

17. *Rheinische Briefe,* ed. J. Hansen, I, 422; Arnold Whitridge, *Men in*

[304]

Crisis: The Revolutions of 1848 (New York, 1949), p. 208; W. Mommsen, *Grösse und Versagen*, p. 160; G. Mayer, *Friedrich Engels*, I, 245-290.

18. *Friedrich August Ludwig von der Marwitz: Ein märkischer Edelmann im Zeitalter der Befreiungskriege*, ed. Friedrich Meusel (2 vols., Berlin, 1908-13), I, xxxii, 676, II/II, 89, 320, 462; Walther Kayser, "Ludwig von der Marwitz," *Deutscher Aufstieg: Bilder aus der Vergangenheit und Gegenwart der rechtsstehenden Parteien*, ed. Hans von Arnim and Georg von Below (Berlin, 1925), pp. 34, 37; K. v. Rohrscheidt, *Vom Zunftzwange*, pp. 544-545; F. Schnabel, *Deutsche Geschichte*, I, 472; H. Sacher, "Konservative Parteien," *Staatslexikon*, 5th ed.

19. *Marwitz*, ed. F. Meusel, I, 492.

20. Hildegard Goetting, *Die Sozialpolitische Idee in den konservativen Kreisen der vormärzlichen Zeit* (Berlin, 1920), pp. 19-23, 25-26; Georg Lüttke, *Die politischen Anschauungen des Generals und des Präsidenten von Gerlach* (Borsdorf-Leipzig, 1907), pp. 34-35, 37-38; Hans Delbrück, *Erinnerungen, Aufsätze und Reden* (Berlin, 1902), p. 215; F. Tönnies, "Deutscher Adel," p. 1044.

21. H. v. Treitschke, *Deutsche Geschichte*, v, 3-60; Herman v. Petersdorff, *König Friedrich Wilhelm der Vierte* (Stuttgart, 1900), pp. 9, 60; Hermann Wagener, *Die Politik Friedrich Wilhelm IV.* (Berlin, 1883), p. 25; K. V. Herberger, *Stellung der Konservativen*, p. 48; Hildegard Goetting, "Viktor Aimé Huber," *Deutscher Aufstieg*, ed. H. v. Arnim and G. v. Below, pp. 80-81; Herman v. Petersdorff, "Hermann Wagener," *ibid.*, p. 170; G. Adler, *Geschichte der Arbeiterbewegung*, pp. 133-134; O. J. Hammen, "Economic and Social Factors," p. 883; Otto zu Stolberg-Wernigerode, *Anton Graf zu Stolberg-Wernigerode: Ein Freund und Ratgeber König Friedrich Wilhelms IV.* (Munich and Berlin, 1926), pp. 50-52.

22. Walter Früh, *Radowitz als Sozialpolitiker: Seine Gesellschafts- und Wirtschaftsauffassung unter besonderer Berücksichtigung der sozialen Frage* (Berlin, 1937), pp. 34, 62-63, 65-66, 69, 74, 84, 117, 120-121; Friedrich Meinecke, *Radowitz und die deutsche Revolution* (Berlin, 1913), pp. 77-78, 531; Hildegard Goetting, "Joseph Maria von Radowitz," *Deutscher Aufstieg*, ed. H. v. Arnim and G. v. Below, pp. 107-108; H. Goetting, *Die sozialpolitische Idee*, pp. 31-32.

23. [Joseph Maria von Radowitz], *Gespräche aus der Gegenwart über Staat und Kirche*, 2nd ed. (Stuttgart, 1846), p. 280. Cf. *ibid.*, pp. 281-282.

24. *Parteiprogramme*, ed. F. Salomon, 1st ed. (2 vols., Leipzig and Berlin, 1907), I, 1-16; *Rheinische Briefe*, ed. J. Hansen, I, 689-694; Karl Biedermann, *1840-1870: Dreissig Jahre deutscher Geschichte*, 2nd ed. (2 vols., Breslau, [1883]), I, 158-159; H.C.M. Wendel, *Industrial Freedom*, pp. 53-56; J. Köster, *Frühliberalismus*, pp. 71-75; J. Hansen, *Mevissen*, I, 343-346; E. Kaeber, *Berlin 1848*, pp. 10-11; H. Goetting, *Die sozialpolitische Idee*, pp. 34-49; H. Waentig, "Die gewerbepolitischen Anschauungen," p. 17; P. Geissen, *Handwerkerpolitik*, pp. 25, 55; H. v. Petersdorff, *Friedrich Wilhelm der Vierte*, p. 60; O. J. Hammen, "Economic and Social Factors," p. 833; O. z. Stolberg-Wernigerode, *Stolberg-Wernigerode*, p. 52.

25. Gustav Freytag, *Karl Mathy: Geschichte seines Lebens*, 2nd ed. (Leipzig, 1872), p. 243.

CHAPTER 5

THE HUNGRY FORTIES

1. B. Bauer, *Der Untergang des Frankfurter Parlaments: Geschichte der deutschen constituirenden Nationalversammlung* (Berlin, 1849), p. 279; Hans Rosenberg, *Die Weltwirtschaftskrisis von 1857-59* (Stuttgart, 1934), p. 34; P. Benaerts, *Les origines*, pp. 171-172; Marcus L. Hansen, "The Revolutions of 1848 and German Emigration," *Journal of Economic and Business History*, II (1930), 649-650; E. Barthelmess, "Sozialpolitisches," p. 121; F. Fejtö, "Europe on the Eve," pp. 45-46, 48; O. J. Hammen, "Economic and Social Factors," pp. 825, 840.

2. M. Weber, *Wirtschaftsgeschichte*, p. 250; P. Benaerts, *Les origines*, p. 133; A. Sartorius von Waltershausen, *Wirtschaftsgeschichte*, p. 139; H. Rosenberg, *Weltwirtschaftskrisis*, p. 34; A. Thun, *Industrie am Niederrhein*, II, 86; O. J. Hammen, "Economic and Social Factors," p. 831; R. v. Delbrück, *Lebenserinnerungen*, I, 176; A. Zimmermann, *Blüthe und Verfall*, p. 468; W. Schneider, *Wirtschafts- und Sozialpolitik*, p. 45.

3. H. v. Treitschke, *Deutsche Geschichte*, V, 521-522; H. Rosenberg, *Weltwirtschaftskrisis*, p. 34; A. Sartorius von Waltershausen, *Wirtschaftsgeschichte*, p. 136; O. J. Hammen, "Economic and Social Factors," pp. 828-830; P. Benaerts, *Les origines*, p. 598; E. Jordan, *Entstehung der konservativen Partei*, p. 110; H.C.M. Wendel, *Industrial Freedom*, pp. 42, 50, 66; *Zeitschrift des königlich preussischen statistischen Bureaus*, XI (1871), 243; F. Kühnert, "Schlachtvieh- und Fleischpreise in Preussen in den Jahren 1911 und 1912," *ibid.*, LII (1912), 379-380; J. Kuczynski, *Short History*, pp. 32, 63; J. Kuczynski, *Labour Conditions*, p. 94; E. Schocke, *Sachsen-Meiningen*, p. 8; J. Kaizl, *Kampf um Gewerbereform*, p. 142; H. Neisser, "Ausfuhrzölle, Ausfuhrverbote, Ausfuhrregelung," *Handwörterbuch der Staatswissenschaften*, 4th ed.

4. R. Stadelmann, "Das Jahr 1848," p. 104; E. Barthelmess, "Sozialpolitisches," p. 117; G. Adler, *Geschichte der Arbeiterbewegung*, p. 136; V. Valentin, *Frankfurt und die Revolution*, p. 115; H. Krause, *Die demokratische Partei*, pp. 39-40; P. Mombert, *Soziale Anschauungen*, pp. 30-31; H. Schlüter, "Beiträge zur Geschichte," pp. 28-29; J. Kuczynski, *Short History*, pp. 24, 36, 39-40, 44-45, 55-57; W. Sombart, *Kapitalismus*, III, 335, 378-379; M. L. Hansen, "Revolutions of 1848," pp. 649-650; E. Schocke, *Sachsen-Meiningen*, pp. 8-9; W. Engel, *Wirtschaftliche Kämpfe*, pp. 101-103; E. Katz, *Landarbeiter*, p. 36; F. Lautenschlager, *Agrarunruhen*, pp. 34-35; B. Moll, *Die Landarbeiterfrage*, p. 79.

5. W. Friedensburg, *Stephan Born*, pp. 4-6; G. Schmoller, *Geschichte der Kleingewerbe*, p. 82; J. Kuczynski, *Short History*, pp. 32, 36, 40, 44-45; J. Kuczynski, *Labour Conditions*, p. 95; P. Benaerts, *Les origines*, p. 587; W. Engel, *Wirtschaftliche Kämpfe*, pp. 126-127; A. Sartorius von Waltershausen, *Wirtschaftsgeschichte*, p. 86; T. C. Banfield, *Industry*, II, 140, 250; K. V. Herberger, *Stellung der Konservativen*, pp. 3-4; V. Valentin, *Frankfurt und die Revolution*, pp. 113-114; W. Schneider, *Wirtschafts- und Sozialpolitik*, pp. 79-80; P. Albrecht, *Die volkswirtschaftlichen Fragen*, p. 46; L. Salvatorelli, *La rivoluzione europea*, p. 14; R. Stadelmann, "Das

Jahr 1848," pp. 103-104; Karl Adam, "Stände und Berufe in Preussen gegenüber der nationalen Erhebung des Jahres 1848," *Preussische Jahrbücher*, LXXXIX (1897), 296.

6. P. Albrecht, *Die volkswirtschaftlichen Fragen*, p. 4; G. Adler, *Geschichte der Arbeiterbewegung*, p. 136; W. Friedensburg, *Stephan Born*, pp. 5-6; P. Benaerts, *Les origines*, p. 587; J. Kuczynski, *Short History*, pp. 40, 44; A. Sartorius von Waltershausen, *Wirtschaftsgeschichte*, p. 86; W. Schneider, *Wirtschafts- und Sozialpolitik*, pp. 79-80; L. Salvatorelli, *La rivoluzione europea*, p. 14; R. Stadelmann, "Das Jahr 1848," p. 104.

7. O. J. Hammen, "Economic and Social Factors," p. 830; J. Kuczynski, *Short History*, p. 48; A. Thun, *Industrie am Niederrhein*, I, 113, II, 86; T. C. Banfield, *Industry*, II,131, 137-138; Curt Geyer, *Politische Parteien und öffentliche Meinung in Sachsen von der Märzrevolution bis zum Ausbruch des Maiaufstands, 1848-1849* (Leipzig, 1914), p. 60; J. H. Clapham, *Economic Development*, pp. 289-290; W. Friedensburg, *Stephan Born*, p. 4; M. Quarck, *Die erste Arbeiterbewegung*, pp. 12-13; V. Valentin, *Geschichte der Revolution*, I, 87; K. Adam, "Stände und Berufe," pp. 287-288; Karl Haenchen, "Zur revolutionären Unterwühlung Berlins vor den Märztagen des Jahres 1848," *Forschungen zur brandenburgischen und preussischen Geschichte*, LV [n.d.], 87; H. v. Treitschke, *Deutsche Geschichte*, V, 518.

8. A. Höfle, *Gewerbeordnung der Pfalz*, p. 23; V. Valentin, *Geschichte der Revolution*, I, 86-87; D. Meyer, *Das Leben in Berlin*, pp. 34, 37; *Zeitschrift des königlich preussischen statistischen Bureaus*, XLIV (1904), 93; Prussia, *Der erste vereinigte Landtag in Berlin 1847*, ed. Eduard Bleich (4 vols., Berlin, 1847), I, 49-50; G. Schmoller, *Geschichte der Kleingewerbe*, p. 429; H. v. Treitschke, *Deutsche Geschichte*, V, 523; J. Kuczynski, *Bewegung der Wirtschaft*, p. 59; Kazimierz and Franciszek Popiołek, "1848 in Silesia," *Slavonic and East European Review*, XXVI (1948), 376; W. Schneider, *Wirtschafts- und Sozialpolitik*, p. 80.

9. *Verhandlungen der Nationalversammlung*, ed. F. Wigard, V, 3513, VI, 4403-4408; E. Schocke, *Sachsen-Meiningen*, p. 8; W. Sombart, *Kapitalismus*, III, 378; V. Valentin, *Geschichte der Revolution*, I, 86, n. 125.

10. G. v. Viebahn, *Statistik Deutschlands*, II, 246; M. L. Hansen, "Revolutions of 1848," pp. 632-633; O. J. Hammen, "Economic and Social Factors," p. 832; Arthur J. May, "The United States and the Mid-Century Revolutions," *Opening of an Era*, ed. F. Fejtö, pp. 221-222.

11. C. Brinkmann, "The Place of Germany," p. 134; J. Kuczynski, *Short History*, p. 48; G. Stolper, *German Economy*, p. 39; W. Dieterici, *Ueber Auswanderungen und Einwanderungen* (Berlin, Posen, and Bromberg, 1847), p. 34; G. v. Viebahn, *Statistik Deutschlands*, II, 240; P. Benaerts, *Les origines*, pp. 139-140; J. Kaizl, *Kampf um Gewerbereform*, p. 168; A. Höfle, *Gewerbeordnung der Pfalz*, p. 20; T.v.d. Goltz, *Geschichte*, II, 184; E. Katz, *Landarbeiter*, pp. 33, 37.

12. G. Stolper, *German Economy*, p. 39; J. Kuczynski, *Short History*, p. 49; H. v. Treitschke, *Deutsche Geschichte*, V, 491; M. Quarck, *Die erste Arbeiterbewegung*, p. 21; P. Albrecht, *Die volkswirtschaftlichen Fragen*, p. 61; *Zeitschrift des königlich preussischen statistischen Bureaus*, XIII (1873), 2-3; G. v. Viebahn, *Statistik Deutschlands*, II, 241, 247; W. Dieterici, *Auswanderungen*, pp. 6, 38, 40-41; *Mittheilungen des*

statistischen Bureau's in Berlin, IV (1851), 152-153; P. Benaerts, *Les origines*, pp. 139-140; A. Markow, *Wachstum der Bevölkerung*, pp. 162, 199.

13. M. L. Hansen, "Revolutions of 1848," pp. 632-634, 657-658; E. Katz, *Landarbeiter*, pp. 31, 33, 35, 37; *Verhandlungen der Nationalversammlung*, ed. F. Wigard, VI, 4407-4408, VIII, 5712, 5715; G. v. Viebahn, *Statistik Deutschlands*, II, 246; A. Nebel, *Arbeiterverhältnisse*, p. 15; A. Höfle, *Gewerbeordnung der Pfalz*, p. 20; T.v.d. Goltz, *Geschichte*, II, 184; A. Whitridge, *Men in Crisis*, pp. 298-300; W. Schneider, *Wirtschafts- und Sozialpolitik*, pp. 82-83; O. J. Hammen, "Economic and Social Factors," p. 832.

14. G. Adler, *Geschichte der Arbeiterbewegung*, pp. 135-137; L. Salvatorelli, *La rivoluzione europea*, p. 73; V. Valentin, *Geschichte der Revolution*, I, 57-58, 60-61, 222-224; K. and F. Popiołek, "1848 in Silesia," pp. 376-377; J. Kuczynski, *Bewegung der Wirtschaft*, pp. 59-62; O. J. Hammen, "Economic and Social Factors," p. 839; John A. Hawgood, "1848 in Central Europe: An Essay in Historical Synchronisation," *Slavonic and East European Review*, XXVI (1948), 320; Alfred Meusel, "Deutsche Revolution von 1848," *Neue Welt*, III (1948), no. 6, p. 7; H.C.M. Wendel, *Industrial Freedom*, pp. 47-48.

15. D. Meyer, *Das Leben in Berlin*, pp. 86-98; V. Valentin, *Geschichte der Revolution*, I, 83-84; Karl Biedermann, *Geschichte des ersten preussischen Reichstags* (Leipzig, 1847), pp. 130-133; J. Kuczynski, *Bewegung der Wirtschaft*, p. 59; G. Adler, *Geschichte der Arbeiterbewegung*, p. 136; E. Kaeber, *Berlin 1848*, p. 12; H.C.M. Wendel, *Industrial Freedom*, p. 66.

16. Prussia, *Der vereinigte Landtag 1847*, ed. E. Bleich, II, 705.

17. *Parteiprogramme*, ed. F. Salomon, 3rd ed., I, 5-7; V. Valentin, *Geschichte der Revolution*, I, 161; E. Brandenburg, *Reichsgründung*, I, 169-170; Erich Marcks, *Der Aufstieg des Reiches: Deutsche Geschichte von 1807-1871/78* (2 vols., Stuttgart, 1936), I, 246-247; L. Salvatorelli, *La rivoluzione europea*, pp. 71-72.

18. *Parteiprogramme*, ed. F. Salomon, 3rd ed., I, 2-5; V. Valentin, *Geschichte der Revolution*, I, 161-164; H. v. Treitschke, *Deutsche Geschichte*, V, 687-688; E. Brandenburg, *Reichsgründung*, I, 170-171; E. Marcks, *Aufstieg des Reiches*, I, 246-247; Ludwig Bergsträsser, "Die parteipolitische Lage beim Zusammentritt des Vorparlaments," *Zeitschrift für Politik*, VI (1913), 597; A. Frahm, "Paulskirche," pp. 214-215; J. Philippson, *Ursprung des Wahlrechts*, p. 28.

19. Prussia, *Gesetz-Sammlung* (1820), pp. 9-16, (1823), pp. 129-130, (1847), pp. 33-39; Prussia, *Der vereinigte Landtag 1847*, ed. E. Bleich, I, 10; E. Kaeber, *Berlin 1848*, pp. 14-29; F. Fejtö, "Europe on the Eve," p. 8, n. 1; H. Preuss, *Junkerfrage*, p. 41; Conrad Bornhak, *Geschichte des preussischen Verwaltungsrechts* (3 vols., Berlin, 1884-86), III, 223.

20. Prussia, *Der vereinigte Landtag 1847*, ed. E. Bleich, I, 22.

21. *Ibid.*, III, 1507.

22. V. Valentin, *Geschichte der Revolution*, I, 61-83; A. Bergengrün, *Hansemann*, pp. 344-402; H. v. Treitschke, *Deutsche Geschichte*, V, 605-648; *Reden und Redner des ersten preussischen vereinigten Landtages*, ed. R. Haym (Berlin, 1847), pp. 55-73, 162-167, 172-183, 196-205, 259-285, 303-329, 359-393; J. Kuczynski, *Bewegung der Wirtschaft*,

pp. 60-61; F. Mehring, *Zur preussischen Geschichte*, II, 356-357; W. Lotz, *Verkehrsentwicklung*, pp. 28-29; E. Kaeber, *Berlin 1848*, pp. 31-32; Ludwig Bergsträsser, "Parteien von 1848," *Preussische Jahrbücher*, CLXXVII (1919), 196. For Metternich's shrewd observations on the political significance of the United Diet see *Mémoires, documents et écrits divers laissés par le prince de Metternich, chancelier de cour et d'état*, ed. Richard de Metternich (8 vols., Paris, 1880-84), VII, 382.

CHAPTER 6

THE SPRING UPRISING

1. *Allgemeine Zeitung*, March 4, 1848.
2. Adolphe de Circourt, *Souvenirs d'une mission à Berlin en 1848*, ed. Georges Bourgin (2 vols., Paris, 1908-09), I, 189-190.
3. J. Hansen, *Mevissen*, II, 353-354; Joseph Hansen, "König Friedrich Wilhelm IV. und das liberale Märzministerium der Rheinländer Camphausen und Hansemann im Jahre 1848," *Westdeutsche Zeitschrift für Geschichte und Kunst*, XXXII (1913), 185.
4. *Rudolf Virchow: Briefe an seine Eltern, 1839 bis 1864*, ed. Marie Rabl, 2nd ed. (Leipzig, 1907), pp. 143-144. Cf. *Bayerische Landbötin*, April 4, 1848; E. Kaeber, *Berlin 1848*, p. 90; V. Valentin, *Geschichte der Revolution*, I, 445; K. Haenchen, "Zur Unterwühlung Berlins," p. 114; E. Marcks, *Aufstieg des Reiches*, I, 286; P. Geissen, *Handwerkerpolitik*, p. 11; Eduard Bernstein, *Die Geschichte der Berliner Arbeiterbewegung: Ein Kapitel zur Geschichte der deutschen Sozialdemokratie* (3 vols., Berlin, 1907-10), I, 12; Wilhelm Keil, "Der 18. März 1848," *Deutschland, 1848-1948*, ed. W. Keil, p. 53; Karl Obermann, *Die deutschen Arbeiter in der Revolution von 1848*, 2nd ed. (Berlin 1953), p. 217; *Einheit und Freiheit: Die deutsche Geschichte von 1815 bis 1849 in zeitgenössischen Dokumenten*, ed. Karl Obermann (Berlin, 1950), p. 289.
5. *Bayerische Landbötin*, March 30, 1848. Cf. A. Duckwitz, *Denkwürdigkeiten*, pp. 229-230; J. Hansen, *Mevissen*, II, 353-355; Wilhelm Hüttermann, *Parteipolitisches Leben in Westfalen vom Beginn der Märzbewegung im Jahre 1848 bis zum Einsetzen der Reaktion im Jahre 1849* (Münster, 1910), pp. 13-14; Reinhard Carl Theodor Eigenbrodt, *Meine Erinnerungen aus den Jahren 1848, 1849 und 1850*, ed. Ludwig Bergsträsser (Darmstadt, 1914), p. 47; W. Ullmann, *Die hessische Gewerbepolitik*, p. 3; W. Engel, *Wirtschaftliche Kämpfe*, pp. 114-115, 136.
6. M. Quarck, *Die erste Arbeiterbewegung*, p. 19; C. Geyer, *Parteien in Sachsen*, pp. 60-61; G. Adler, *Geschichte der Arbeiterbewegung*, p. 159; H.C.M. Wendel, *Industrial Freedom*, pp. 51-52.
7. *Bayerische Landbötin*, March 30, 1848; *Rheinische Briefe*, ed. J. Hansen, I, 671; A. Thun, *Industrie am Niederrhein*, I, 113-116, 142, II, 86, 195-196; A. Sartorius von Waltershausen, *Wirtschaftsgeschichte*, p. 171; G. K. Anton, *Geschichte der Fabrikgesetzgebung*, p. 153; O. J. Hammen, "Economic and Social Factors," p. 835; M. Quarck, *Die erste Arbeiter-*

bewegung, p. 33: Konrad Repgen, *Märzbewegung und Maiwahlen des Revolutionsjahres 1848 im Rheinland* (Bonn, 1955), pp. 50-51; Jacques Droz, *Les révolutions allemandes de 1848* (Paris, 1957), pp. 212-213.

8. *Neueste Nachrichten aus dem Gebiete der Politik*, April 11, 1848. Cf. *Verhandlungen des deutschen Parlaments* (2 vols., Frankfurt am Main, 1848), II, 8, 74; V. Valentin, *Geschichte der Revolution*, I, 511; W. Schneider, *Wirtschafts- und Sozialpolitik*, p. 132.

9. *Verhandlungen des Parlaments*, II, 67, 70-71, 194-195, 330; *Verhandlungen der Nationalversammlung*, ed. F. Wigard, I, 55-56, V, 3780-3787; *Neueste Nachrichten aus dem Gebiete der Politik*, April 10, 1848; *Unter Friedrich Wilhelm IV.: Denkwürdigkeiten des Ministers Otto Freiherrn v. Manteuffel*, ed. Heinrich v. Poschinger (3 vols., Berlin, 1901), I, 12; A. Duckwitz, *Denkwürdigkeiten*, p. 230; R. v. Delbrück, *Lebenserinnerungen*, I, 222; Eberhard Gothein, *Geschichtliche Entwicklung der Rheinschiffahrt im XIX. Jahrhundert* (Leipzig, 1903), pp. 262-266; C. Eckert, *Rheinschiffahrt*, pp. 260-265; V. Valentin, *Geschichte der Revolution*, I, 512; P. Benaerts, *Les origines*, p. 326, n. 89; A. Sartorius von Waltershausen, *Wirtschaftsgeschichte*, p. 107.

10. *Verhandlungen der Nationalversammlung*, ed. F. Wigard, II, 807, 917-921, 1532-1538; *Europe by Treaty*, ed., E. Hertslet, I, 206, 270-272; W. Schneider, *Wirtschafts- und Sozialpolitik*, pp. 123-124.

11. M. Quarck, *Die erste Arbeiterbewegung*, pp. 79-83, 134; J. Kuczynski, *Short History*, p. 47; O. J. Hammen, "Economic and Social Factors," p. 835; H.C.M. Wendel, *Industrial Freedom*, pp. 51-52; *Neue Rheinische Zeitung*, February 23, 1849; G. Adler, *Geschichte der Arbeiterbewegung*, pp. 159, 197-198; E. Kaeber, *Berlin 1848*, p. 148; F. Mehring, *Geschichte der Sozialdemokratie*, I, 360; E. Barthelmess, "Sozialpolitisches," p. 122.

12. A. de Circourt, *Souvenirs*, I, 103-104.

13. *Allgemeine Zeitung*, March 13, 1848; *Bayerische Landbötin*, March 16, 1848; F. Lautenschlager, *Agrarunruhen*, pp. 2, 24-25, 42-55, 64, 69-73; V. Valentin, *Geschichte der Revolution*, I, 344-345; Franz Schnabel, "Das Land Baden und die Revolution von 1848-49," *Deutschland, 1848-1948*, ed. W. Keil, p. 65; R. Stadelmann, "Das Jahr 1848," p. 100; E. Marcks, *Männer und Zeiten*, I, 213; W. Mommsen, *Grösse und Versagen*, p. 156; K. Adam, "Stände und Berufe," p. 291.

14. *Allgemeine Zeitung*, March 16, 1848. Cf. *ibid.*, March 15, 1848; *Bayerische Landbötin*, March 16, 1848; *Freie Hessische Zeitung*, March 21, 1848; R.C.T. Eigenbrodt, *Erinnerungen*, pp. 45-50, 63-80, 313-318; [Wilhelm Heinrich Riehl], "Hessen-Darmstadt in seiner neuesten politischen Entwickelung," *Die Gegenwart: Eine encyclopädische Darstellung der neuesten Zeitgeschichte für alle Stände*, ed. August Kurtzel (12 vols., Leipzig, 1848-56), V, 486-488; S. Sugenheim, *Aufhebung der Leibeigenschaft*, pp. 459-460; E. Katz, *Landarbeiter*, p. 32; Lujo Brentano, "Familienfideikommisse und ihre Wirkungen," *Volkswirtschaftliche Zeitfragen*, XXXIII (1911), 18, n. 2; Adolphus William Ward, *Germany, 1815-1890* (3 vols., Cambridge, 1916-18), I, 372-373; A. W. Ward, "The Revolution and the Reaction in Germany and Austria (1848-9)," *The Cambridge Modern History*, ed., A. W. Ward, G. W. Prothero, and Stanley Leathes (14 vols., Cambridge, 1902-12), XI, 147; *Denkwürdigkeiten des Ministers Manteuffel*,

ed. H. v. Poschinger, I, 12; W. Hüttermann, *Parteipolitisches Leben*, pp. 12-13; K. Repgen, *Märzbewegung und Maiwahlen*, pp. 51-52; Reinhard Kaeller, *Die konservative Partei in Minden-Ravensberg: Ihre Grundlagen, Entstehung und Entwicklung bis zum Jahre 1866* (Heidelberg, 1912), p. 55.

15. *Annual Register or a View of the History and Politics of the Year 1848* (2 vols., London, 1849), I, 362.

16. *Allgemeine Zeitung*, March 12, 1848, March 15, 1848, March 16, 1848, April 13, 1848, April 17, 1848; *Bayerische Landbötin*, March 16, 1848; *Neueste Nachrichten aus dem Gebiete der Politik*, April 11, 1848, April 14, 1848; *Württembergische Jahrbücher für vaterländische Geschichte, Geographie, Statistik und Topographie* (1848), p. 10; T. Knapp, *Neue Beiträge*, I, 179, II, 177; V. Valentin, *Geschichte der Revolution*, I, 351; F. Lautenschlager, *Agrarunruhen*, p. 46; R. Stadelmann, "Das Jahr 1848," p. 100; T. Schnurre, *Die württembergischen Abgeordneten*, p. 49; E. Marcks, *Männer und Zeiten*, I, 213; W. Schneider, *Wirtschafts- und Sozialpolitik*, p. 16; M. Doeberl, *Bayern und die deutsche Frage in der Epoche des Frankfurter Parlaments* (Munich and Berlin, 1922), pp. 160-161; Sebastian Hausmann, *Die Grund-Entlastung in Bayern* (Strasbourg, 1892), p. 141; W. Engel, *Wirtschaftliche Kämpfe*, pp. 83, 95; E. Schocke, *Sachsen-Meiningen*, pp. 14-15, 24; C. Geyer, *Parteien in Sachsen*, pp. 61-62; *Einheit und Freiheit*, ed. K. Obermann, p. 311.

17. Otto von Bismarck, *Die gesammelten Werke* (15 vols., Berlin, 1924-35), XV, 18-25. Cf. Erich Marcks, *Bismarck: Eine Biographie, 1815-1851* (Stuttgart, 1951), pp. 423-432; Max Lenz, "Bismarcks Plan einer Gegenrevolution im März 1848," *Sitzungsberichte der preussischen Akademie der Wissenschaften: Philosophisch-historische Klasse* (1930), pp. 251-276.

18. O. v. Bismarck, *Werke*, XIV/I, 110. Cf. *ibid.*, XIV/I, 103; *Josef von Radowitz: Nachgelassene Briefe und Aufzeichnungen zur Geschichte der Jahre 1848-1853*, ed. Walter Möring (Stuttgart and Berlin, 1922), p. 50; A. de Circourt, *Souvenirs*, II, 500; Prussia, *Verhandlungen des am 2. April 1848 zu Berlin eröffneten zweiten vereinigten Landtages* (Berlin, [1848]), pp. 3, 17, 29, 50; E. Marcks, *Aufstieg des Reiches*, I, 284; E. Marcks, *Männer und Zeiten*, I, 213; E. Marcks, *Bismarck*, pp. 442-443; Hans Walter, *Die innere Politik des Ministers von Manteuffel und der Ursprung der Reaktion in Preussen* (Berlin, 1910), p. 75; K. Adam, "Stände und Berufe," pp. 292-293; E. Jordan, *Entstehung der konservativen Partei*, pp. 119-127; K. Reis, *Ursachen der Agrarbewegung*, pp. 3, 24-28; G. F. Knapp, *Bauern-Befreiung*, I, 218, 220; K. and F. Popiołek, "1848 in Silesia," p. 381; O. z. Stolberg-Wernigerode, *Stolberg-Wernigerode*, p. 85.

19. *Hessische Volkszeitung*, June 15, 1848; *Neue Rheinische Zeitung*, March 28, 1849; G. Hanssen, *Aufhebung der Leibeigenschaft*, pp. 144-45; [F. Soltau], "Mecklenburg in den Jahren 1848-51," *Gegenwart*, ed. A. Kurtzel, VI, 347-348; A. Werner, *Die politischen Bewegungen*, p. 92; E. Marcks, *Männer und Zeiten*, I, 213; K. and F. Popiołek, "1848 in Silesia," p. 387.

20. *Verhandlungen des Parlaments*, II, 523. Cf. *ibid.*, II, 516; Bavaria, *Verhandlungen der Kammer der Abgeordneten des Königreichs Bayern* (8 vols., Munich, 1848), I, 291; A. de Circourt, *Souvenirs*, I, 270;

A. Duckwitz, *Denkwürdigkeiten*, p. 243; E. Kaeber, *Berlin 1848*, pp. 137-138, 145; A. Sartorius von Waltershausen, *Wirtschaftsgeschichte*, pp. 153, 180; O. J. Hammen, "Economic and Social Factors," p. 837; F. Lautenschlager, *Agrarunruhen*, p. 64; K. Obermann, *Arbeiter in der Revolution*, p. 217.

21. *Allgemeine Zeitung*, March 4, 1848; Theodore S. Fay, "The Revolution of 1848 in Berlin: Personal Recollections," *Galaxy*, XVI (1873), 247-248; A. de Circourt, *Souvenirs*, I, 338; Prussia, *Gesetz-Sammlung* (1848), p. 117; *Verhandlungen des Parlaments*, II, 74-75, 189, 363; *Verhandlungen der Nationalversammlung*, ed. F. Wigard, I, 644-645, II, 902-912, III, 2255-2262; A. Sartorius von Waltershausen, *Wirtschaftsgeschichte*, p. 153; E. Jordan, *Entstehung der konservativen Partei*, pp. 127-128; V. Valentin, *Geschichte der Revolution*, I, 420; O. Reinhard, *Grundentlastung in Württemberg*, p. 49; W. Schneider, *Wirtschafts- und Sozialpolitik*, pp. 143-144; P. Albrecht, *Die volkswirtschaftlichen Fragen*, p. 63.

22. J. Hansen, *Mevissen*, II, 362. Cf. *Allgemeine Zeitung*, April 14, 1848; *Neueste Nachrichten aus dem Gebiete der Politik*, April 9, 1848; A. Bergengrün, *Hansemann*, pp. 432-434; J. Hansen, *Mevissen*, I, 538; Hans Mähl, *Die Überleitung Preussens in das konstitutionelle System durch den zweiten vereinigten Landtag* (Munich and Berlin, 1909), pp. 246-247; W. Kähler, "Handel," pp. 527-528; W. Schneider, *Wirtschafts- und Sozialpolitik*, pp. 143-144.

23. *Annual Register of 1848*, I, 363. Cf. *Allgemeine Zeitung*, March 16, 1848, March 30, 1848; J. B. Bekk, *Die Bewegung in Baden von Ende des Februar 1848 bis zur Mitte des Mai 1849* (Mannheim, 1850), pp. 142-143; E. Bernstein, *Berliner Arbeiter-Bewegung*, I, 16; *Württembergische Jahrbücher für vaterländische Geschichte, Geographie, Statistik und Topographie* (1848), pp. 11-12; W. Hüttermann, *Parteipolitisches Leben*, p. 14, n. 2; Prussia, *Verhandlungen des zweiten vereinigten Landtages*, pp. 3, 37; *Verhandlungen des Parlaments*, II, 113-114.

24. Prussia, *Gesetz-Sammlung* (1848), pp. 77-79; R. v. Delbrück, *Lebenserinnerungen*, I, 213; *Neue Preussische Zeitung*, April 13, 1849; "The American Minister in Berlin, on the Revolution of March, 1848," *American Historical Review*, XXIII (1918), 368; W. Friedensburg, *Stephan Born*, pp. 54-55; E. Barthelmess, "Sozialpolitisches," pp. 121-122; E. Kaeber, *Berlin 1848*, p. 140; A. W. Ward, "Revolution in Germany," p. 147; E. Schocke, *Sachsen-Meiningen*, pp. 24, 57; G. F. Knapp, *Bauern-Befreiung*, II, 411-421; H. Walter, *Die innere Politik*, pp. 97-98; S. Sugenheim, *Aufhebung der Leibeigenschaft*, pp. 459-461; W. H. Riehl, "Hessen-Darmstadt," p. 487; T. Knapp, *Neue Beiträge*, I, 179-181; F. Lautenschlager, *Agrarunruhen*, pp. 57-58, 79-81; [Ludwig Häusser], "Baden im Frühjahr 1848," *Gegenwart*, ed. A. Kurtzel, III, 455.

25. *Allgemeine Zeitung*, March 16, 1848; *Bayerische Landbötin*, March 16, 1848; *Hessische Volkszeitung*, June 15, 1848; A. de Circourt, *Souvenirs*, I, 103, n. 2, 105, 141-142, 188; Prussia, *Verhandlungen des zweiten vereinigten Landtages*, pp. 43, 49; B. Bauer, *Untergang des Parlaments*, p. 22; K. Adam, "Stände und Berufe," p. 291; W. Hüttermann, *Parteipolitisches Leben*, p. 14; F. Lautenschlager, *Agrarunruhen*, pp. 51-53; J. B. Bekk, *Die Bewegung in Baden*, p. 71; S. Hausmann, *Grund-Entlastung*

in Bayern, p. 141; W. H. Riehl, "Hessen-Darmstadt," p. 488; E. Schocke, *Sachsen-Meiningen*, p. 15; F. Soltau, "Mecklenburg," pp. 348-349; A. Werner, *Die politischen Bewegungen*, p. 73; E. Kaeber, *Berlin 1848*, pp. 35-51, 81, 116, 148, 173; M. Quarck, *Die erste Arbeiterbewegung*, pp. 33-35, 82-83; F. Meinecke, "The Year 1848," p. 484; L. Salvatorelli, *La rivoluzione europea*, p. 169; G. Adler, *Geschichte der Arbeiterbewegung*, p. 159; H. Rosenberg, *Weltwirtschaftskrisis*, p. 35.

26. *Aus dem Nachlass Varnhagen's von Ense: Tagebücher* (14 vols., Leipzig, Zurich, and Hamburg, 1861-70), IV, 376.

27. *Allgemeine Zeitung*, April 14, 1848; *Neue Rheinische Zeitung*, January 28, 1849; Prussia, *Gesetz-Sammlung* (1848), pp. 105-110; Prussia, *Verhandlungen des zweiten vereinigten Landtages*, pp. 22-23, 25, 43-45, 49; R. v. Delbrück, *Lebenserinnerungen*, I, 142-146, 213-216; O. v. Bismarck, *Werke*, XV, 27-29; H.C.M. Wendel, *Industrial Freedom*, pp. 66-70; A. Bergengrün, *Hansemann*, pp. 431-434, 437-448, 454-456; O. J. Hammen, "Economic and Social Factors," p. 837; A. Sartorius von Waltershausen, *Wirtschaftsgeschichte*, p. 180; E. Wolff, *Volkswirtschafts-Geschichte*, pp. 141-142; K. Adam, "Stände und Berufe," p. 297; E. Kaeber, *Berlin 1848*, p. 145; E. Jordan, *Entstehung der konservativen Partei*, pp. 127-128; W. Kähler, "Handel," pp. 527-528; H. Mähl, *Die Überleitung Preussens*, pp. 229-230.

CHAPTER 7

THE FRANKFURT PARLIAMENT

1. *Verhandlunges des Parlaments*, I, viii-xvi, 1, 5-8, 11-26, 85, 161-162, 166-169; Ulrich Freyer, *Das Vorparlament zu Frankfurt a. M. im Jahre 1848* (Greifswald, 1913), pp. 13-51, 78-145; Nanette G. Katzenstein, *Das Vorparlament* (Munich, 1922), pp. 44-88; V. Valentin, *Geschichte der Revolution*, I, 374-378, 466-501; Hans Blum, *Die deutsche Revolution, 1848-49* (Leipzig, 1898), pp. 209-221; A. Frahm, "Paulskirche," pp. 219-220; L. B. Namier, *1848: The Revolution of the Intellectuals* (London, 1946), p. 71, n. 1; Johann Gustav Droysen, *Politische Schriften*, ed. Felix Gilbert (Munich and Berlin, 1933), p. 125, n. 1; *Parteiprogramme*, ed. F. Salomon, 4th and 5th eds., I, 73, n. 1; H. v. Sybel, *Begründung des Reiches*, I, 154; S. Kan, "Predparlament i pervoie badenskoie vosstanie 1848 goda" [the preliminary parliament and the first Baden uprising of 1848], *Voprosy istorii* (1948), n. 5, pp. 78, 92. According to the minutes of the preliminary parliament the motion of the democrats that it remain in permanent session was defeated 368 to 148, but a count of the names on the roll call reveals that actually only 143 members voted in the affirmative.

2. *Verhandlungen des Parlaments*, I, 37-38, 43, 57, 162-165, 172-173, II, 46, 78-80, 91-94; *Quellensammlung zum deutschen öffentlichen Recht seit 1848*, ed. Paul Roth and Heinrich Merck (2 vols., Erlangen, 1850-52), I, 231-232; *Verhandlungen der Nationalversammlung*, ed. F. Wigard, VII,

5509; Gerhard Schilfert, *Sieg und Niederlage des demokratischen Wahl-rechts in der deutschen Revolution, 1848-49* (Berlin, 1952), pp. 86-103; U. Freyer, *Das Vorparlament*, pp. 24-25, 51- 8; N. G. Katzenstein, *Das Vorparlament*, pp. 59-65;Veit Valentin, *Die erste deutsche Nationalver-sammlung* (Munich and Berlin, 1919), pp. 5-6; J. Philippson, *Ursprung des Wahlrechts*, pp. 42-43; Paul Wentzcke, *1848: Die unvollendete deutsche Revolution* (Munich, 1938), p. 107.

3. *Verhandlungen des Parlaments*, I, x-xvi, 161-162, II, 39-40, 113-114, 150-151, 503-504; *Quellensammlung zum deutschen Recht*, ed. P. Roth und H. Merck, I, 201-205, 230-231, 312-316, 335-336; L. Salvatorelli, *La rivoluzione europea*, pp. 166-167, 175; J. Philippson, *Ursprung des Wahlrechts*, p. 44; P. Albrecht, *Die volkswirtschaftlichen Fragen*, pp. 4-5; Georg Meyer, *Das parlamentarische Wahlrecht* (Berlin, 1901), p. 178.

4. Württemberg, *Regierungs-Blatt* (1848), pp. 135-158; Hanover, *Sammlung der Gesetze* (1848), pp. 101-115; Saxony, *Verordnungsblatt* (1848), pp. 25-28, 33-34; Baden, *Regierungsblatt* (1848), pp. 61-62, 107, 129-132; Bavaria, *Gesetz-Blatt* (1848), pp. 2-7; Prussia, *Gesetz-Sammlung* (1848), pp. 94-96; *Quellensammlung zum deutschen Recht*, ed. P. Roth and H. Merck, I, 267-268, 279-280; *Verhandlungen der Nationalversammlung*, ed. F. Wigard, III, 2245; J. Philippson, *Ursprung des Wahlrechts*, pp. 48-49, 64-65, 75; G. Meyer, *Wahlrecht*, pp. 178-179; K. Biedermann, *1840-1870*, I, 286; V. Valentin, *Geschichte der Revolution*, II, 1-3; V. Valentin, *Die erste Nationalversammlung*, p. 5; Ferdinand Frensdorff, "Die Aufnahme des allgemeinen Wahlrechts in das öffentliche Recht Deutschlands," *Festgabe der Göttinger Juristen-Fakultät für Rudolf von Jhering zum fünfzigjährigen Doktor-Jubiläum am vi. August MDCCCXCII* (Leipzig, 1892), pp. 145-146; L. Salvatorelli, *La rivolu-zione europea*, p. 172; W. Mommsen, *Grösse und Versagen*, p. 74; K. Rep-gen, *Märzbewegung und Maiwahlen*, p. 139, n. 81.

5. Württemberg, *Regierungs-Blatt* (1848), pp. 135-158; Hesse-Kassel, *Sammlung von Gesetzen, Verordnungen, Ausschreiben und anderen allge-meinen Verfügungen für Kurhessen* (1848), pp. 25-28; Schleswig-Holstein, *Chronologische Sammlung der im Jahre 1848 ergangenen Gesetze, Verord-nungen und Verfügungen für die Herzogthümer Schleswig-Holstein*, pp. 75-86; Frankfurt am Main, *Gesetz- und Statuten-Sammlung der freien Stadt Frankfurt* (16 vols., Frankfurt am Main, 1817-66), VIII, 248-251; Hamburg, *Sammlung der Verordnungen der freien Hanse-Stadt Hamburg seit 1814* (1848), pp. 279-285, 299-300; Bremen, *Sammlung der Verord-nungen und Proclame des Senats der freien Hansestadt Bremen* (1848), pp. 48-52; *Verhandlungen des Parlaments*, II, 3, 66, 78-80, 91-92, 95-96, 202-203, 310; *Verhandlungen der Nationalversammlung*, ed. F. Wigard, VII, 5509; *Neue Rheinische Zeitung*, January 25, 1849; Prussia, *Steno-graphische Berichte über die Verhandlungen der durch die allerhöchste Verordnung vom 4. November 1851 einberufenen Kammern: Erste Kammer* (2 vols., Berlin, 1852), I, 295; *Württembergische Jahrbücher für vater-ländische Geschichte, Geographie, Statistik und Topographie* (1848), p. 14; *Tabellen und Nachrichten für 1849*, IV, 442-443; G. Meyer, *Wahlrecht*, p. 179; F. Frensdorff, "Aufnahme des Wahlrechts," pp. 145-146; J. Philipp-son, *Ursprung des Wahlrechts*, p. 50; L. Salvatorelli, *La rivoluzione europea*, p. 172; V. Valentin, *Die erste Nationalversammlung*, p. 5; V. Valentin,

Geschichte der Revolution, I, 86-87, II, 3; T. Schnurre, *Die württem-bergischen Abgeordneten*, pp. 2-3; E. Bernstein, *Berliner Arbeiter-Bewegung*, I, 20; K. V. Herberger, *Stellung der Konservativen*, p. 10; D. Meyer, *Das Leben in Berlin*, p. 12; V. Valentin, *Frankfurt und die Revolution*, pp. 16, n. 1, 186; M. Quarck, *Die erste Arbeiterbewegung*, p. 242; H. Pahl, *Hamburg*, pp. 20, n. 5, 23-24; K. Obermann, *Arbeiter in der Revolution*, p. 268.

6. *Bayerische Landbötin*, April 27, 1848. Cf. *Allgemeine Zeitung*, May 2, 1848; J. Philippson, *Ursprung des Wahlrechts*, p. 75; A. Frahm, "Pauls-kirche," pp. 215, 221; C. Geyer, *Parteien in Sachsen*, p. 61; K. Obermann, *Arbeiter in der Revolution*, p. 192; Rudolf Krauss, *Das sächsische Vogt-land in der Bewegung von 1848-1850* (Würzburg, 1935), p. 33; M. Klemm, *Sachsen*, p. 71; G. Schilfert, *Sieg und Niederlage*, p. 124; K. Repgen, *Märzbewegung und Maiwahlen*, p. 54.

7. *Allgemeine Zeitung*, April 30, 1848, May 1, 1848, May 2, 1848, May 9, 1848; *Bayerische Landbötin*, April 29, 1848; *Verhandlungen der Nationalversammlung*, ed. F. Wigard, VII, 5247, 5286-5287, 5307, 5509; C.F.W. Dieterici, *Handbuch der Statistik des preussischen Staats* (Berlin, 1861), p. 191; *Zeitschrift des königlich preussischen statistischen Bureaus*, I (1861), 24-25; G. v. Viebahn, *Statistik Deutschlands*, II, 180, 188; J. Müller, *Grundriss der Statistik*, III, 202; A. Frahm, "Paulskirche," pp. 215, 221; [J. Weil], "Staat und Stadt Frankfurt," *Gegenwart*, ed. A. Kurtzel, V, 386-387; "Die hessischen Wahlen zur deutschen National-versammlung in Frankfurt a. M. vom 18. April 1848," *Hessenland*, XII (1898), 105-106; H. Pahl, *Hamburg*, pp. 23-24; Percy Ernst Schramm, *Hamburg, Deutschland und die Welt: Leistung und Grenzen hanseatischen Bürgertums in der Zeit zwischen Napoleon I. und Bismarck* (Munich, 1943), p. 297; M. Klemm, *Sachsen*, p. 71; R. Krauss, *Das Vogtland*, pp. 32-33; C. Geyer, *Parteien in Sachsen*, p. 61; K. Repgen, *Märzbewegung und Maiwahlen*, pp. 141, 226.

8. Karl Demeter, "Die soziale Schichtung des deutschen Parlamentes seit 1848: Ein Spiegelbild der Strukturwandlung des Volkes," *Vierteljahr-schrift für Sozial- und Wirtschaftsgeschichte*, XXXIX (1952), 6-22; L. Rosen-baum, *Beruf und Herkunft der Abgeordneten zu den deutschen und preus-sischen Parlamenten, 1847 bis 1919* (Frankfurt am Main, 1923), pp. 53, 58, 62; G. Schilfert, *Sieg und Niederlage*, pp. 112-113, 402-405; *Hillgers Handbuch der verfassunggebenden deutschen Nationalversammlung 1919*, ed. Hermann Hillger (Berlin and Leipzig, 1919), p. 31; K. Repgen, *Märzbewegung und Maiwahlen*, p. 232; V. Valentin, *Geschichte der Revolution*, II, 11-13; L. Salvatorelli, *La rivoluzione europea*, p. 173; Wilhelm Appens, *Die Nationalversammlung zu Frankfurt a. M., 1848-49* (Jena, 1920), pp. 36-37, 41; S. Neumann, *Stufen des Konservatismus*, pp. 114, n. 9, 132, n. 7.

9. K. Biedermann, *1840-1870*, I, 290-291; [Gottfried] Eisenmann, *Die Parteyen der teutschen Reichsversammlung: Ihre Programme, Statuten und Mitglieder-Verzeichnisse* (Erlangen, 1848), pp. 8-13; *Parteiprogramme*, ed. F. Salomon, 3rd ed., I, 61-62; [Robert Heller], *Brustbilder aus der Paulskirche* (Leipzig, 1849) p. 90; V. Valentin, *Geschichte der Revolution*, II, 21; *Handbuch*, ed. H. Hillger, p. 10; L. Bergsträsser, "Parteien von 1848," pp. 193-194; W. Appens, *Die Nationalversammlung*, pp. 36, 39-40;

H. A. Strauss, *Staat, Bürger, Mensch*, p. 26, n. 29; A. de Circourt, *Souvenirs*, II, 176, n. 1.

10. Julius Fröbel, *Ein Lebenslauf: Aufzeichnungen, Erinnerungen und Bekenntnisse* (2 vols., Stuttgart, 1890-91), I, 197.

11. G. Eisenmann, *Parteyen der Reichsversammlung*, pp. 36-46; *Parteiprogramme*, ed. F. Salomon, 3rd ed., I, 67-68; K. Biedermann, *1840-1870*, I, 291; R. Heller, *Brustbilder*, pp. 67-68, 142-145, 157-161; V. Valentin, *Geschichte der Revolution*, II, 20-21, 99, 101, 157-167, 255-258; *Handbuch*, ed. H. Hillger, p. 10; G. Adler, *Geschichte der Arbeiterbewegung*, pp. 227, 231-232, 234-235, 303; L. Salvatorelli, *La rivoluzione europea*, pp. 179, 271-272; [Theodor Mundt], "Berlin in der Bewegung von 1848," *Gegenwart*, ed. A. Kurtzel, II, 578; W. Mommsen, *Grösse und Versagen*, p. 160; Wilhelm Blos, *Die deutsche Revolution* (Stuttgart, 1893), pp. 392-410, 460-462; E. Kaeber, *Berlin 1848*, p. 196; W. Appens, *Die Nationalversammlung*, pp. 40, 254-255; H. A. Strauss, *Staat, Bürger, Mensch*, p. 26, n. 29; H. Blum, *Die Revolution*, pp. 310-312.

12. *Verhandlungen der Nationalversammlung*, ed. F. Wigard, VII, 5303. Cf. G. Eisenmann, *Parteyen der Reichsversammlung*, pp. 13-32; *Parteiprogramme*, ed. F. Salomon, 3rd ed., I, 62-65; K. Biedermann, *1840-1870*, I, 291-292; A. de Circourt, *Souvenirs*, II, 176, n. 1; R. Heller, *Brustbilder*, pp. 30-36, 52-54; V. Valentin, *Geschichte der Revolution*, II, 21-23; G. Schilfert, *Sieg und Niederlage*, pp. 118-121, 406-407; *Handbuch*, ed. H. Hillger, p. 10; L. Bergsträsser, "Parteien von 1848," pp. 193, 201-202; W. E. Biermann, *Winkelblech*, I, 261; J. Droz, *Le libéralisme*, pp. 425-426; W. Appens, *Die Nationalversammlung*, pp. 36, 39-40; Karl Binding, *Der Versuch der Reichsgründung durch die Paulskirche* (Leipzig, 1892), pp. 11-12; Anton Springer, *Friedrich Christoph Dahlmann* (2 vols., Leipzig, 1870-72), II, 343; G. Erler, *Die verwaltungspolitischen Ideen*, p. 18; A. Frahm, "Paulskirche," p. 216.

13. *Verhandlungen der Nationalversammlung*, ed. F. Wigard, II, 1313. Cf. *ibid.*, II, 1293, IV, 2404, 2423, VII, 5101, 5222, 5296, 5303; Georg Beseler, *Erlebtes und Erstrebtes, 1809-1859* (Berlin, 1884), p. 59; Max Duncker, *Zur Geschichte der deutschen Reichsversammlung in Frankfurt* (Berlin, 1849), pp. 6-7; *1848: Der Vorkampf deutscher Einheit und Freiheit*, ed. Tim Klein (Ebenhausen-Munich and Leipzig, 1914), p. 112.

14. *Verhandlungen des Parlaments*, II, 221; *Verhandlungen der Nationalversammlung*, ed. F. Wigard, I, 521, 576-622, 628-638; M. Duncker, *Geschichte der Reichsversammlung*, pp. 6-7, 9; R. Haym, *Die deutsche Nationalversammlung* (3 vols., Frankfurt a. M. and Berlin, 1848-50), I, 18; G. Beseler, *Erlebtes*, p. 59; V. Valentin, *Geschichte der Revolution*, I, 28-41; *Annual Register of 1848*, I, 368; W. Appens, *Die Nationalversammlung*, p. 78.

15. *Die Verfassung des Deutschen Reiches vom Jahre 1849 mit Vorentwürfen, Gegenvorschlägen und Modifikationen bis zum Erfurter Parlament*, ed. Ludwig Bergsträsser (Bonn, 1913), pp. 72-96; H. Blum, *Die Revolution*, pp. 475-480; W. Blos, *Die Revolution*, pp. 650-657; *Verhandlungen der Nationalversammlung*, ed. F. Wigard, I, 700-701; M. Duncker, *Geschichte der Reichsversammlung*, pp. 36-37; R. Haym, *Die deutsche Nationalversammlung*, I, 51; V. Valentin, *Geschichte der Revolution*, II, 312-314; Gustav Radbruch, "Die Frankfurter Grundrechte," *Deutschland*,

1848-1948, ed. W. Keil, p. 87; Edmond Vermeil, "An Historical Paradox: The Revolution of 1848 in Germany," *Opening of an Era*, ed. F. Fejtö, p. 250; A. Whitridge, *Men in Crisis*, pp. 223-224; H. A. Strauss, *Staat, Bürger, Mensch*, p. 131; E. Barthelmess, "Sozialpolitisches," p. 115.

16. *Die Verfassung vom Jahre 1849*, ed. L. Bergsträsser, p. 72. Cf. *Verhandlungen der Nationalversammlung*, ed. F. Wigard, I, 700-701; M. Duncker, *Geschichte der Reichsversammlung*, pp. 36-37; R. Haym, *Die deutsche Nationalversammlung*, I, 51.

17. For political reforms introduced in the states of Germany in accordance with the spirit of the Fundamental Rights of the German People see V. Valentin, *Geschichte der Revolution*, II, 383-415; L. Salvatorelli, *La rivoluzione europea*, p. 184; G. Meyer, *Wahlrecht*, pp. 188-194; Prussia, *Verhandlungen der Versammlung zur Vereinbarung der preussischen Staats-Verfassung* (6 vols., Berlin, 1848), I, 1-4, 336-337, II, 589-592, 729-734; A. Tönnies, "Deutscher Adel," p. 1057; Prussia, *Gesetz-Sammlung* (1848), pp. 201-202; C. Geyer, *Parteien in Sachsen*, pp. 101, 119-121, 123; W. Kellner, *Taschenbuch*, pp. 67, 86-88, 95, 109; *Neue Rheinische Zeitung*, December 5, 1848, December 12, 1848; J. B. Bekk, *Die Bewegung in Baden*, pp. 253-254; R. Wöltge, *Die Reaktion in Hannover*, pp. 14-15; *Die deutschen Verfassungsgesetze der Gegenwart*, ed. Heinrich Albert Zachariä (Göttingen, 1855), pp. 771-776, 899-900, 955-957, 1033; E. Schocke, *Sachsen-Meiningen*, pp. 44-45; *Neue Preussische Zeitung*, January 6, 1849.

18. *Verhandlungen der Nationalversammlung*, ed. F. Wigard, VII, 5093, 5218-5559, VIII, 5652, 6069-6070, 6122-6123; *Aktenstücke und Aufzeichnungen zur Geschichte der Frankfurter Nationalversammlung aus dem Nachlass von Johann Gustav Droysen*, ed. Rudolf Hübner (Stuttgart, Berlin, and Leipzig, 1924), pp. 174, 370-405, 429-435, 760-767, 843-844; Karl Jürgens, *Zur Geschichte des deutschen Verfassungswerkes, 1848-49* (3 vols., Brunswick and Hanover, 1850-57), II, 7-8, 29-30, 456, III, 203, 262-264, 286-287: R. Haym, *Die deutsche Nationalversammlung*, II, 141-142, 191-362; Heinrich Laube, *Das erste deutsche Parlament* (3 vols., Leipzig, 1849), III, 189, 286-287, 295-296, 361-363, 378-380; Karl Biedermann, *Erinnerungen aus der Paulskirche* (Leipzig, 1849), pp. 106-108; M. Duncker, *Geschichte der Reichsversammlung*, pp. 73, 79-81, 85; *Ausgewählter Briefwechsel Rudolf Hayms*, ed. Hans Rosenberg (Stuttgart, Berlin, and Leipzig, 1930), pp. 68-69; *Max Duncker: Politischer Briefwechsel aus seinem Nachlass*, ed. Johannes Schultze (Stuttgart and Berlin, 1923), pp. 6-7; J. Hansen, *Mevissen*, I, 589-599, 608, II, 470; G. Freytag, *Karl Mathy*, p. 309; *1848*, ed. T. Klein, p. 112; Erich Brandenburg, *Untersuchungen und Aktenstücke zur Geschichte der Reichsgründung* (Leipzig, 1916), pp. 195-203; Friedrich von Raumer, *Briefe aus Frankfurt und Paris, 1848-1849* (2 vols., Leipzig, 1849), I, 170, II, 242-243; V. Valentin, *Geschichte der Revolution*, II, 366-367, 371-373; G. Schilfert, *Sieg und Niederlage*, pp. 169-186, 196-251; Heinrich von Srbik, *Deutsche Einheit: Idee und Wirklichkeit vom Heiligen Reich bis Königgrätz* (4 vols., Munich, 1935-42), I, 420-421, 433; E. Brandenburg, *Reichsgründung*, I, 267-269; H. Blum, *Die Revolution*, pp. 379-380; W. Blos, *Die Revolution*, pp. 525-526; A. Frahm, "Paulskirche," pp. 233-234; W. Mommsen, *Grösse und Versagen*, p. 152.

19. *Verhandlungen der Nationalversammlung*, ed. F. Wigard, I, 195.
20. *Die Verfassung vom Jahre 1849*, ed. L. Bergsträsser, pp. 8-31; *Verhandlungen der Nationalversammlung*, ed. F. Wigard, V, 3558-3578; A. Duckwitz, *Denkwürdigkeiten*, pp. 86, 98-102; [Johannes] Fallati, "Entwürfe zu einem Flussschifffahrts-Gesetze und zu einem Reichsgesetze über die Aufhebung der Flusszölle und die Ausgleichung für dieselbe nebst Motiven: Aus den Acten des Reichshandelsministeriums der provisorischen Centralgewalt," *Zeitschrift für die gesammte Staatswissenschaft*, VI (1850), 526-601; R. Haym, *Die deutsche Nationalversammlung*, II, 85-86; E. Barthelmess, "Sozialpolitisches," p. 115; P. Albrecht, *Die volkswirtschaftlichen Fragen*, pp. 21, 57-58; W. Schneider, *Wirtschafts- und Sozialpolitik*, pp. 126, 138-139; H. v. Festenberg-Packisch, *Geschichte*, p. 277; G. Stolper, *German Economy*, p. 27; W. Appens, *Die Nationalversammlung*, p. 42.

21. *Verhandlungen der Nationalversammlung*, ed. F. Wigard, IV, 2617-2618, V, 3239, 3334-3337, 3357, 3379, 3382, 3760; A. Duckwitz, *Denkwürdigkeiten*, pp. 92-94, 100, 269-274; W. Schneider, *Wirtschafts- und Sozialpolitik*, pp. 92-93; V. Valentin, *Geschichte der Revolution*, II, 117-118.

22. *Zollvereinsblatt*, March 22, 1848.

23. *Verhandlungen der Nationalversammlung*, ed. F. Wigard, III, 1873.

24. *Verhandlungen der Reichs-Versammlung*, ed. K. D. Hassler, V, 1, 253-257; *Verhandlungen der Nationalversammlung*, ed. F. Wigard, I, 15, II, 896-902, 1046, 1288, III, 1772, IV, 2507, 2553, 2591, VI, 4511-4512, 4623, 4670, 4749, VII, 4832, 5419, VIII, 6122, 6159, 6334; *Neue Preussische Zeitung*, January 3, 1849, January 14, 1849; W. Schneider, *Wirtschafts- und Sozialpolitik*, pp. 17, 19-21, 24; H. Pahl, *Hamburg*, pp. 31-32, 53; P. Albrecht, *Die volkswirtschaftlichen Fragen*, pp. 9-13; H. v. Festenberg-Packisch, *Geschichte*, p. 285; Ludwig Oelsner, "Die wirtschafts- und sozialpolitischen Verhandlungen des Frankfurter Parlaments," *Preussische Jahrbücher*, LXXXVII (1897), 83.

25. *Verhandlungen der Nationalversammlung*, ed. F. Wigard, III, 2215-2216, IV, 2938-2939, V, 3657-3658, VI, 4193-4223, VII, 5420, VIII, 5625, IX, 6716; *Quellensammlung zum deutschen Recht*, ed. P. Roth and H. Merck, II, 58-62; A. Duckwitz, *Denkwürdigkeiten*, pp. 77-79, 85-86, 91-94, 97-98, 264-274, 293-294; R. v. Delbrück, *Lebenserinnerungen*, I, 221; *Neue Preussische Zeitung*, July 30, 1848, August 13, 1848, September 6, 1848, November 30, 1848, December 17, 1848, March 29, 1849, July 1, 1849; W. Schneider, *Wirtschafts- und Sozialpolitik*, pp. 27-31, 50, 88-89, 92-93, 101-102; H. Pahl, *Hamburg*, pp. 54, n. 2, 75, n. 1, 101-102; W. O. Henderson, *Zollverein*, pp. 193-195; P. Albrecht, *Die volkswirtschaftlichen Fragen*, pp. 18, 21; H. v. Festenberg-Packisch, *Geschichte*, pp. 282-284; Victor Böhmert, "Deutschlands wirtschaftliche Neugestaltung," *Preussische Jahrbücher*, XVIII (1866), 278.

CHAPTER 8

THE WORKER AND THE REVOLUTION

1. Carl Schurz, *Lebenserinnerungen* (3 vols., Berlin, 1906-12), I, 168.
2. O. v. Bismarck, *Werke*, X, 140. For similar interpretations of the Revolution advanced by liberals and radicals as well as conservatives see K. Binding, *Versuch der Reichsgründung*, pp. 3-4; *Erinnerungen aus dem Leben von Unruh*, ed. H. v. Poschinger, p. 116; A. Whitridge, *Men in Crisis*, pp. 222, 234, 238; Theodor Heuss, *1848: Werk und Erbe* (Stuttgart, 1948), pp. 166-167; Monty Jacobs, "The Year 1848," *In Tyrannos*, ed. Hans J. Rehfisch (London, 1944), pp. 28, 183; A.J.P. Taylor, *German History*, p. 68; G. P. Gooch, "The Centenary of 1848 in Germany and Austria," *Contemporary Review*, CLXXIII (1948), 220; Margaret Goldsmith, "The German 'Revolution' of 1848," *Nineteenth Century and After*, CXXX (1941), 27; K. Marx, *Revolution and Counter-Revolution*, pp. 78-80, 148; Max Lenz, *Kleine historische Schriften* (Munich and Berlin, 1910), p. 346; Peter Viereck, *Metapolitics: From the Romantics to Hitler* (New York, 1941), p. 61; Theodore S. Hamerow, "History and the German Revolution of 1848," *American Historical Review*, LX (1954), 30-31, 36-39.
3. *Neue Preussische Zeitung*, October 10, 1848; *Neue Rheinische Zeitung*, April 15, 1849; V. Valentin, *Geschichte der Revolution*, II, 95-99, 256; W. Blos, *Die Revolution*, pp. 381-383; G. Adler, *Geschichte der Arbeiterbewegung*, pp. 156, 227, 231-232, 234-235; Rudolf Stadelmann, *Soziale und politische Geschichte der Revolution von 1848* (Munich, 1948), pp. 158-161; A. Meusel, "Deutsche Revolution," pp. 9-10; A. Sartorius von Waltershausen, *Wirtschaftsgeschichte*, p. 147; E. Kaeber, *Berlin 1848*, p. 162; K. V. Herberger, *Stellung der Konservativen*, p. 12; M. Quarck, *Die erste Arbeiterbewegung*, p. 74; H. Krause, *Die demokratische Partei*, p. 201; Erwin Schöttle, "1848-1948: Hundert Jahre politischer Befreiungskampf der Deutschen," *Deutschland, 1848-1948*, ed. W. Keil, p. 137; R. Stadelmann, "Das Jahr 1848," pp. 103-104; F. Meinecke, "The Year 1848," p. 488; S. B. Kan, "Rabocheie dvizhiniie v Berline v perviie nedeli martovskoi revoliutsii 1848 goda" [the workers movement in Berlin in the first weeks of the March revolution of 1848], *Izvestiia Akademii Nauk SSSR: Seriia istorii i filosofii* (1948), no. 1, p. 25.
4. Stephan Born, *Erinnerungen eines Achtundvierzigers* (Leipzig, 1898), pp. 144-145, 164-168; G. Adler, *Geschichte der Arbeiterbewegung*, pp. 157, 168-172, 303; W. Friedensburg, *Stephan Born*, pp. 97, 99; W. Blos, *Die Revolution*, pp. 386-391; E. Kaeber, *Berlin 1848*, pp. 157-163; V. Valentin, *Geschichte der Revolution*, I, 533-534, II, 56-57, 452-454; R. Stadelmann, *Soziale Geschichte von 1848*, pp. 162-164; E. Barthelmess, "Sozialpolitisches," p. 120; A. Sartorius von Waltershausen, *Wirtschaftsgeschichte*, p. 146; P. Benaerts, *Les origines*, p. 591; H.C.M. Wendel, *Industrial Freedom*, p. 56; E. Marcks, *Aufstieg des Reiches*, I, 288.
5. V. Valentin, *Geschichte der Revolution*, II, 51, 101, 256; R. Stadelmann, *Soziale Geschichte von 1848*, p. 155; E. Kaeber, *Berlin 1848*, pp. 116, 173; A. Meusel, "Deutsche Revolution," pp. 9-10; S. B. Kan,

"Rabocheie dvizhiniie v Berline," p. 25; H. Krause, *Die demokratische Partei*, p. 201; K. V. Herberger, *Stellung der Konservativen*, p. 12; M. Quarck, *Die erste Arbeiterbewegung*, pp. 74, 87; T. Mundt, "Berlin," p. 578.

6. *Verhandlungen der Nationalversammlung*, ed. F. Wigard, V, 3780-3782; E. Gothein, *Rheinschiffahrt*, pp. 262-263; V. Valentin, *Geschichte der Revolution*, I, 512; K. Obermann, *Arbeiter in der Revolution*, pp. 232-238; G. Adler, *Geschichte der Arbeiterbewegung*, p. 191; E. Barthelmess, "Sozialpolitisches," p. 119; M. Quarck, *Die erste Arbeiterbewegung*, p. 134; W. Blos, *Die Revolution*, pp. 383-384; *Bayerische Landbötin*, August 5, 1848; *Neue Preussische Zeitung*, July 28, 1848; W. E. Biermann, *Winkelblech*, II, 119-121; V. Böhmert, "Deutschlands Neugestaltung," p. 274; V. Böhmert, *Freiheit der Arbeit*, p. 168; [Albert] Schäffle, "Vorschläge zu einer gemeinsamen Ordnung der Gewerbebefugnisse und Heimathrechtsverhältnisse in Deutschland nach den Grundsätzen der Gewerbefreiheit und der Freizügigkeit," *Deutsche Vierteljahrs-Schrift*, XXII (1859), no. 1, p. 227; G. Schmoller, *Geschichte der Kleingewerbe*, p. 85.

7. *Bayerische Landbötin*, June 27, October 28, 1848; *Hessische Volkszeitung*, June 20, June 21, 1848; *Neue Preussische Zeitung*, October 10, 1848, January 19, January 21, 1849; T. Schnurre, *Die württembergischen Abgeordneten*, pp. 8-9; P. Albrecht, *Die volkswirtschaftlichen Fragen*, p. 42; H. Waentig, "Die gewerbepolitischen Anschauungen," p. 18; J. Wilden, "Handwerk," *Handwörterbuch der Staatswissenschaften*, 4th ed.; H. Schlüter, "Beiträge zur Geschichte," p. 84; J. Kuczynski, *Short History*, pp. 37-38; A. Werner, *Die politischen Bewegungen*, p. 77; W. E. Biermann, *Winkelblech*, II, 75-77; Report on the Meeting of the Master Artisans of the Duchy of Brunswick in Wolfenbüttel, July 9, 1848, *Akten des Frankfurter Handwerker-Kongresses* (Stadtarchiv Frankfurt am Main); E. Schocke, *Sachsen-Meiningen*, pp. 60-61.

8. *Offener Brief an alle Innungsgenossen Deutschlands so wie zugleich an alle Bürger und Hausväter. Von zweiundzwanzig Innungen zu Leipzig* (Leipzig, 1848), p. 3.

9. *Ibid.*, p. 7. Cf. *Neue Preussische Zeitung*, January 21, 1849; H. Waentig, "Die gewerbepolitischen Anschauungen," p. 18; P. Albrecht, *Die volkswirtschaftlichen Fragen*, p. 42; H. Schlüter, "Beiträge zur Geschichte," p. 84; J. Kuczynski, *Short History*, pp. 37-38; W. E. Biermann, *Winkelblech*, II, 33; A. Schäffle, "Vorschläge," pp. 223-224; G. Schmoller, *Geschichte der Kleingewerbe*, p. 84; A. Sartorius von Waltershausen, *Wirtschaftsgeschichte*, p. 139.

10. *Verhandlungen der ersten Abgeordneten-Versammlung des norddeutsche Handwerker- und Gewerbestandes zu Hamburg, den 2.-6. Juni 1848* (Hamburg, 1848), pp. iii-viii, 18, 20-21, 31-48, 51-56; *Allgemeine Zeitung*, June 9, June 10, June 11, 1848; *Neue Rheinische Zeitung*, June 6, 1848; Proclamation of the Elders of the Principal Guilds of Danzig, July 5, 1848, *Akten des Frankfurter Handwerker-Kongresses* (Stadtarchiv Frankfurt am Main); *Verhandlungen der Nationalversammlung*, ed. F. Wigard, I, 321; W. E. Biermann, *Winkelblech*, II, 49-73; G. Adler, *Geschichte der Arbeiterbewegung*, pp. 165-166; W. Blos, *Die Revolution*, pp. 378-379; H. Waentig, "Die gewerbepolitischen Anschauungen," p. 19; A. Sartorius von Waltershausen, *Wirtschaftsgeschichte*, pp. 139-140;

A. Schäffle, "Vorschläge," p. 224; P. Albrecht, *Die volkswirtschaftlichen Fragen*, pp. 42-43; G. Schmoller, *Geschichte der Kleingewerbe*, p. 84; J. H. Clapham, *Economic Development*, p. 323.

11. *Verhandlungen des norddeutschen Gewerbestandes*, p. 56.

12. The minutes of the German Handicraft and Artisan Congress were published by the secretary under the title *Verhandlungen des ersten deutschen Handwerker- und Gewerbe-Congresses gehalten zu Frankfurt a. M. vom 14. Juli bis 18. August 1848*, ed. G. Schirges (Darmstadt, 1848). Detailed accounts of the sessions appeared in such contemporary newspapers as *Allgemeine Zeitung*, July 20, July 21, July 25, July 26, August 10, August 18, 1848; *Neue Münchner Zeitung*, July 22, July 25, July 26, July 28, July 29, August 1, August 2, August 4, August 5, August 11, August 16, August 18, 1848; *Bayerische Landbötin*, July 27, July 29, August 1, August 3, August 5, August 8, August 11, August 17, August 19, August 24, 1848; *Neue Preussische Zeitung*, July 28, August 8, August 20, 1848. Descriptions may also be found in W. E. Biermann, *Winkelblech*, II, 93-117; A. Schäffle, "Vorschläge," pp. 225-226; W. Blos, *Die Revolution*, pp. 379-381; J. Kaizl, *Kampf um Gewerbereform*, pp. 30-31; K. Obermann, *Arbeiter in der Revolution*, pp. 240-242; E. Barthelmess, "Sozialpolitisches," p. 119; H. Schlüter, "Beiträge zur Geschichte," p. 85; L. Salvatorelli, *La rivoluzione europea*, p. 222; G. Kölzsch, *Die Entwicklung der Gewerbefreiheit in Deutschland* (Greifswald, 1920), p. 34; J. Kuczynski, *Short History*, p. 38; A. Sartorius von Waltershausen, *Wirtschaftsgeschichte*, pp. 139-140; H. Pahl, *Hamburg*, p. 184; A. Köttgen, "Gewerbegesetzgebung: Die Gewerbegesetzgebung in Deutschland," *Handwörterbuch der Staatswissenschaften*, 4th ed.; G. Albrecht, "Handwerk," *Wörterbuch der Volkswirtschaft*, 4th ed.; V. Valentin, *Geschichte der Revolution*, II, 102-103.

13. *Entwurf einer allgemeinen Handwerker- und Gewerbe-Ordnung für Deutschland berathen und beschlossen von dem deutschen Handerwerker- und Gewerbe-Congress zu Frankfurt am Main in den Monaten Juli und August 1848* ([Frankfurt am Main], 1848), p. 6.

14. *Ibid.*, pp. 3, 5-6.

15. *Ibid.*, pp. 7-22; *Verhandlungen der Nationalversammlung*, ed. F. Wigard, II, 1046, III, 1711; H. Waentig, "Die gewerbepolitischen Anschauungen," p. 19; P. Albrecht, *Die volkswirtschaftlichen Fragen*, p. 43; E. v. Philippovich, *Entwicklung der Ideen*, p. 39; G. Schmoller, *Geschichte der Kleingewerbe*, pp. 84-85; A. Sartorius von Waltershausen, *Wirtschaftsgeschichte*, pp. 139-140.

16. *Verhandlungen des Gewerbe-Congresses*, ed. G. Schirges, p. 256.

17. *Verhandlungen der Nationalversammlung*, ed. F. Wigard, III, 1658, VI, 4671, 4718, VII, 4982, 5091-5092, 5264; V. Valentin, *Geschichte der Revolution*, II, 430; V. Böhmert, *Freiheit der Arbeit*, pp. 171-173; V. Böhmert, "Deutschlands Neugestaltung," p. 274.

18. The minutes of the General German Labor Congress were never published, but its resolutions and commentary on the industrial code of the German Handicraft and Artisan Congress appear in W. E. Biermann, *Winkelblech*, II, 441-474. For general accounts of its activities see the following: *Allgemeine Zeitung*, June 10, 1848; *Neue Preussische Zeitung* July 29, 1848; *Neue Münchner Zeitung*, August 2, 1848; *Bayerische*

Landbötin, August 3, 1848; *Verhandlungen der Nationalversammlung*, ed. F. Wigard, II, 1287; W. E. Biermann, *Winkelblech*, II, 270-285; G. Adler, *Geschichte der Arbeiterbewegung*, pp. 166-168; H. Schlüter, "Beiträge zur Geschichte," p. 123; A. Schäffle, "Vorschläge," pp. 226-227; H. Waentig, "Die gewerbepolitischen Anschauungen," p. 21; W. Blos, *Die Revolution*, pp. 384-386; M. Quarck, *Die erste Arbeiterbewegung*, pp. 144-148; K. Obermann, *Arbeiter in der Revolution*, pp. 242-245; V. Valentin, *Geschichte der Revolution*, II, 103-104; J. H. Clapham, *Economic Development*, pp. 323-324; A. Sartorius von Waltershausen, *Wirtschaftsgeschichte*, p. 140; E. Marcks, *Aufstieg des Reiches*, I, 285.

19. *Verhandlungen der Nationalversammlung*, ed. F. Wigard, I, 450, 717, II, 1094, III, 1594, 1685-1686, 1711, 2003, 2006, 2095, 2315, IV, 2711, 2799, 2871, 2940, 3021-3022, 3249, V, 3581, VI, 4247, 4777, VII, 4833, 4982, 5264-5265, 5419-5420, IX, 6362-6364; V. Böhmert, *Freiheit der Arbeit*, pp. 166-168; V. Böhmert, "Deutschlands Neugestaltung," pp. 273-274; W. E. Biermann, *Winkelblech*, II, 80-90, 122-134, 136-137; A. Schäffle, "Vorschläge," p. 228.

20. Petition of the Brunswick Weavers Guild to the German Handicraft and Artisan Congress, *Akten des Frankfurter Handwerker-Kongresses* (*Stadtarchiv* Frankfurt am Main).

21. *Verhandlungen der Nationalversammlung*, ed. F. Wigard, III, 2316, 2343, IV, 2711. Cf. *ibid.*, III, 1711, 2263, 2315, IV, 2383-2384, 2799, 2842-2843, 2871, 2940, 3021-3022, 3104-3106, V, 3581-3582, VI, 4187, 4247, 4719, VII, 4833, 4982, 5265, 5420, VIII, 5704, 6224; W. E. Biermann, *Winkelblech*, II, 134, 136-137; V. Böhmert, *Freiheit der Arbeit*, pp. 166-168; V. Böhmert, "Deutschlands Neugestaltung," p. 273; H. Waentig, "Die gewerbepolitischen Anschauungen," p. 20.

22. Hanover, *Sammlung der Gesetze* (1847), pp. 215-257, (1848), pp. 156-158; *Verhandlungen der Reichs-Versammlung*, ed. K. D. Hassler, II, 271; *Neue Rheinische Zeitung*, June 4, 1848; V. Böhmert, *Freiheit der Arbeit*, pp. 262-263; W. E. Biermann, *Winkelblech*, II, 186-187; H. Waentig, "Die gewerbepolitischen Anschauungen," p. 22; J. Kaizl, *Kampf um Gewerbereform*, p. 33.

23. Prussia, *Gesetz-Sammlung* (1848), pp. 228-230; Prussia, *Verhandlungen der Versammlung* (1848), III, 830-831, IV, 1245, 1301-1302, 1509-1512, V, 1562-1564, 1767-1771, 1779-1782; *Verhandlungen der Reichs-Versammlung*, ed. K. D. Hassler, II, 872; R. v. Delbrück, *Lebenserinnerungen*, I, 219; G. K. Anton, *Geschichte der Fabrikgesetzgebung*, pp. 153-154; A. Thun, *Industrie am Niederrhein*, I, 116; K. V. Herberger, *Stellung der Konservativen*, p. 37; A. Zimmermann, *Geschichte der Handelspolitik*, pp. 393-394; P. Geissen, *Handwerkerpolitik*, p. 28.

24. Prussia, *Verhandlungen der Versammlung* (1848), I, 88.

25. Bavaria, *Regierungs-Blatt* (1848), pp. 785-790; *Verhandlungen der Nationalversammlung*, ed. F. Wigard, V, 3780-3787; *Rheinurkunden*, I, 494, 496; R. v. Delbrück, *Lebenserinnerungen*, I, 222; G. Ziegler, *Gewerbegesetz von 1868*, p. 28; P. Benaerts, *Les origines*, p. 553; W. Ullmann, *Die hessische Gewerbepolitik*, pp. 41, 44, 50; P. Möslein, *Gewerbegesetzgebung*, p. 55; W. Engel, *Wirtschaftliche Kämpfe*, pp. 114-115; E. Gothein, *Rheinschiffahrt*, pp. 264-266; C. Eckert, *Rheinschiffahrt*, pp. 263-265.

26. *Zollvereinsblatt*, August 2, 1848. Cf. *Verhandlungen der National-versammlung*, ed. F. Wigard, II, 856, IV, 2404, VII, 5101, 5109, 51'4, 5222, 5246, 5296, VIII, 5664, IX, 6362-6380; *Verhandlungen der Reichs-Versammlung*, ed. K. D. Hassler, II, 899, IV, 145-163; *Verhandlungen des Parlaments*, II, 515-516; A. Duckwitz, *Denkwürdigkeiten*, pp. 243-245.

27. *Verhandlungen der Nationalversammlung*, ed. F. Wigard, II, 866. Cf. *Die Verfassung vom Jahre 1849*, ed. L. Bergsträsser, pp. 72-73, 83; *Verhandlungen der Nationalversammlung*, ed. F. Wigard, I, 682-700, II, 1075-1076, III, 2304, V, 3894-3897, VI, 4172; *Die Verhandlungen des Verfassungs-Ausschusses der deutschen Nationalversammlung*, ed. Johann Gustav Droysen (Leipzig, 1849) pp. 14-15; V. Valentin, *Geschichte der Revolution*, II, 312-313; W. Schneider, *Wirtschafts- und Sozialpolitik*, pp. 40-41.

28. The report on an industrial code prepared by the economic committee of the Frankfurt Parliament appears in *Verhandlungen der Reichs-Versammlung*, ed. K. D. Hassler, II, 853-946. See also *Verhandlungen der National-versammlung*, ed. F. Wigard, II, 1076-1082, VI, 4224, VII, 5422-5423; W. E. Biermann, *Winkelblech*, II, 136, 160-181; P. Albrecht, *Die volks-wirtschaftlichen Fragen*, pp. 44-45; H. Waentig, "Die gewerbepolitischen Anschauungen," p. 21; W. Schneider, *Wirtschafts- und Sozialpolitik*, p. 34; L. Oelsner, "Die sozialpolitischen Verhandlungen," p. 88.

29. *Verhandlungen der Reichs-Versammlung*, ed. K. D. Hassler, IV, 146; *Verhandlungen des Parlaments*, II, 515; J. Fröbel, *Ein Lebenslauf*, 200-201, 263-264; K. Marx, *Revolution and Counter-Revolution*, p. 23; S. Born, *Erinnerungen*, pp. 136-137, 145-147; M. Quarck, *Die erste Arbeiter-bewegung*, pp. 74, 87, 310; P. Benaerts, *Les origines*, p. 591.

CHAPTER 9

THE PEASANT AND THE REVOLUTION

1. W. H. Riehl, *Die bürgerliche Gesellschaft*, 10th ed. (Stuttgart and Berlin, 1907), p. 41. Cf. *Verhandlungen der Nationalversammlung*, ed. F. Wigard, IV, 2443; W. Conze, "Wirkungen der Agrarreformen," p. 12; M. L. Hansen, "Revolutions of 1848," p. 650; K. Adam, "Stände und Berufe," pp. 293-294, 300; W. Mommsen, *Grösse und Versagen*, p. 156.

2. Württemberg, *Verhandlungen der württembergischen Kammer der Abgeordneten auf dem Landtage von 1848* (Stuttgart, 1848), p. 175.

3. *Verhandlungen der Nationalversammlung*, ed. F. Wigard, II, 1046, III, 1772, 1819, 2238, IV, 2394, 2402, 2502, VII, 4923-4924. Cf. *ibid.*, I, 244, 387, 623, II, 830-831, 1042-1043, 1094, 1286, 1538, 1540, III, 1594, 2096, 2193, IV, 2388-2403, 2426, 2504, 2842-2843, V, 3359, VI, 4188, 4225, VII, 4833, 4922-4924, 5294, VIII, 5660, 5705, 6119; W. Schneider, *Wirtschafts- und Sozialpolitik*, p. 62; Hermann Wagener, *Erlebtes: Meine Memoiren aus der Zeit von 1848 bis 1866 und von 1873 bis jetzt*, 2nd ed. (2 vols., Berlin, 1884), I, 28; H. Walter, *Die innere Politik*, p. 75; L. Brentano, *Aufsätze*, p. 257; K. Adam, "Stände und Berufe," p. 291.

NOTES FOR CHAPTER 9

4. *Verhandlungen der Nationalversammlung*, ed. F. Wigard, IV, 2388-2389, 2417; Baden, *Verhandlungen der Stände-Versammlung des Grossherzogthums Baden in den Jahren 1847-49 enthaltend die Protokolle der zweiten Kammer nebst deren Beilagen* (10 vols., Karlsruhe, [n. d.]), VIII, 33; *Neue Rheinische Zeitung*, September 2, 1848, March 28, 1849; F. Lautenschlager, *Agrarunruhen*, pp. 26-27; B. Moll, *Die Landarbeiterfrage*, p. 28; M. Doeberl, *Bayern*, pp. 160-161; Prussia, *Verhandlungen des zweiten vereinigten Landtages*, p. 29; E. Jordan, *Entstehung der konservativen Partei*, pp. 119-127; G. F. Knapp, *Bauern-Befreiung*, I, 218, II, 420-421, 423-425.

5. *Neue Rheinische Zeitung*, September 16, 1848.
6. *Quellensammlung zum deutschen Recht*, ed. P. Roth and H. Merck, II, 127.
7. *Verhandlungen der Nationalversammlung*, ed. F. Wigard, IV, 2549.
8. *Ibid.*, IV, 2417.
9. *Ibid.*, IV, 2402, 2404, 2423, VII, 5101, 5222, 5296; *Verhandlungen der Reichs-Versammlung*, ed. K. D. Hassler, IV, 199; *Die Verfassung vom Jahre 1849*, ed. L. Bergsträsser, p. 86; R. Haym, *Die deutsche Nationalversammlung*, I, 65-66.

10. Württemberg, *Verhandlungen der Kammer der Abgeordneten* (1848), pp. 229-230. Cf. *Verhandlungen der Nationalversammlung*, ed. F. Wigard, IV, 2404; *Verhandlungen der Reichs-Versammlung*, ed. K. D. Hassler, IV, 199; R. Haym, *Die deutsche Nationalversammlung*, I, 66; O. v. Bismarck, *Werke*, XV, 28-29; T. Knapp, *Neue Beiträge*, II, 177.

11. Baden, *Regierungsblatt* (1848), pp. 47, 107-108; Baden, *Verhandlungen der zweiten Kammer* (1847-49), III, 150-151, 257-263; Baden, *Verhandlungen der Stände-Versammlung des Grossherzogthums Baden in den Jahren 1847-49 enthaltend die Protokolle der ersten Kammer mit deren Beilagen* (3 vols., Karlsruhe, [n. d.]), I, 207, 260-271; F. Lautenschlager, *Agrarunruhen*, pp. 57-58, 70-73, 79-92; J. B. Bekk, *Die Bewegung in Baden*, pp. 76, 78; L. Häusser, "Baden," p. 455; G. v. Viebahn, *Statistik Deutschlands*, II, 588; "Ablösungsgesetze," p. 214; K. Lamprecht, *Deutsche Geschichte*, IX, 238; W. Schneider, *Wirtschafts- und Sozialpolitik*, p. 15.

12. Württemberg, *Regierungs-Blatt* (1848), pp. 98-99, 165-171, 173-174, 252; Württemberg, *Verhandlungen der württembergischen Kammer der Standesherren auf dem ersten ordentlichen Landtage des Jahres 1848* (Stuttgart, [1848]), pp. 39, 44-51, 57-74; Württemberg, *Verhandlungen der Kammer der Abgeordneten* (1848), pp. 214-248; *Württembergische Jahrbücher für vaterländische Geschichte, Geographie, Statistik und Topographie* (1848), p. 10; T. Knapp, *Neue Beiträge*, I, 166, 173-174, 179-182; *Verhandlungen der Nationalversammlung*, ed. F. Wigard, V, 2398-2399; O. Reinhard, *Grundentlastung in Württemberg*, pp. 50, 107; "Ablösungsgesetze," pp. 210-217; S. Sugenheim, *Aufhebung der Leibeigenschaft*, p. 460; G. v. Viebahn, *Statistik Deutschlands*, II, 587; A. Sartorius von Waltershausen, *Wirtschaftsgeschichte*, p. 137.

13. Bavaria, *Gesetz-Blatt* (1848), pp. 98-118, 130-134; Bavaria, *Verhandlungen der Kammer der Abgeordneten* (1848), I, 110-126, II, 199, VI, 204-207; Bavaria, *Verhandlungen der Kammer der Reichsräthe des Königreichs Bayern* (5 vols., Munich, 1848), III, 5-6, 369, V, 295; *Verhandlungen der Nationalversammlung*, ed. F. Wigard, IV, 2396, VII, 4923;

S. Hausmann, *Grund-Entlastung in Bayern*, pp. 141-161; "Ablösungs-gesetze," pp. 209-210, 215-216; G. v. Viebahn, *Statistik Deutschlands*, II, 586-587; M. Doeberl, *Bayern*, pp. 160-161; K. Lamprecht, *Deutsche Geschichte*, IX, 243-244; W. Schneider, *Wirtschafts- und Sozialpolitik*, pp. 59-60; [Edmund von Berg], "Das Jagdwesen," *Gegenwart*, ed. A. Kurtzel, II, 233; O. v. Nell-Breuning, "Rentenbanken," *Staatslexikon*, 5th ed.; Fr. Schulte, "Rentenbanken," *Handwörterbuch der Staatswissenschaften*, 4th ed.; Carl Johannes Fuchs, "Bauernbefreiung," *Wörterbuch der Volkswirtschaft*, 4th ed.

14. Hesse-Darmstadt, *Regierungsblatt* (1848), pp. 67-69, 209-212, 237-241, 317-318; Nassau, *Verordnungsblatt des Herzogthums Nassau* (1848), pp. 315-318: Hesse-Kassel, *Sammlung von Gesetzen* (1848), pp. 67-74; *Bayerische Landbötin*, March 16, 1848; *Verhandlungen der Nationalver-sammlung*, ed. F. Wigard, VII, 4923; "Ablösungsgesetze," pp. 208, 214-216; W. H. Riehl, "Hessen-Darmstadt," p. 486; S. Sugenheim, *Aufhebung der Leibeigenschaft*, pp. 459-460; E. Katz, *Landarbeiter*, pp. 24-25, 27; E. v. Berg, "Jagdwesen," p. 234; G. v. Viebahn, *Statistik Deutschlands*, II, 595.

15. Saxony, *Verordnungsblatt* (1848), pp. 295-302; Hanover, *Sammlung der Gesetze* (1848), pp. 206-207, 215-220; Brunswick, *Gesetz- und Ver-ordnungs-Sammlung für die herzoglich braunschweigischen Lande* (1848), pp. 147-153; Saxe-Meiningen, *Sammlung der landesherrlichen Verordnun-gen im Herzogthume Sachsen-Meiningen* (26 vols., Meiningen, 1829-1921), IX, 53-54, 101-106, 149-150; Saxe-Weimar, *Sammlung gross-herzogl. S. Weimar-Eisenachischer Gesetze, Verordnungen und Circular-befehle in chronologischer Ordnung* (17 vols., Eisenach and Jena, 1828-68), X, 29-103, 130-140, 186-189; Saxe Altenburg, *Gesetz-Sammlung für das Herzogthum Altenburg* (1849), pp. 15-18, 37-41, 59-60; Schwarz-burg-Rudolstadt, *Gesetzsammlung für das Fürstenthum Schwarzburg-Rudolstadt* (1849), pp. 87-108; *Neue Preussische Zeitung*, November 11, 1848, January 4, February 9, March 1, 1849; *Neue Rheinische Zeitung*, December 5, 1848; "Ablösungsgesetze," pp. 207-208; S. Sugenheim, *Auf-hebung der Leibeigenschaft*, pp. 460-461; G. v. Viebahn, *Statistik Deutsch-lands*, II, 589-590; E. Schocke, *Sachsen-Meiningen*, pp. 24, 48, 57; O. H. Brandt, *Sachsen-Altenburg*, p. 140; E. v. Berg, "Jagdwesen," pp. 234-235; A. Sartorius von Waltershausen, *Wirtschaftsgeschichte*, p. 137.

16. *Neue Rheinische Zeitung*, March 28, 1849; V. Valentin, *Geschichte der Revolution*, II, 390-392; F. Soltau, "Mecklenburg," pp. 347-348; A. Werner, *Die politischen Bewegungen*, p. 92; G. Hanssen, *Aufhebung der Leibeigenschaft*, pp. 144-145, 192.

17. Prussia, *Gesetz-Sammlung* (1848), pp. 201-202, 276-279, 343-344; Prussia, *Verhandlungen der Versammlung* (1848), I, 88, 242-244, 336-337, 455; II, 481-486, 510-511, 513-517, 570-583, 609, III, 889-892, IV, 1277-1300, 1326, 1343-1344, 1376-1391, 1405-1414, 1423-1436, 1451-1467, 1471-1488, 1504-1509, V, 1548-1560, 1565-1578, 1634-1647, 1650-1660, 1702-1712, 1723-1727, 1771-1776, 1789-1791, 1795-1802, 1823-1842, VI, 2018-2022; G. F. Knapp, *Bauern-Befreiung*, I, 219-220, II, 411-423; H. Walter, *Die innere Politik*, pp. 80, 84-85, 90-92, 97-99, 137-138; C. Bornhak, *Geschichte des Verwaltungsrechts*, III, 247-249;

K. Reis, *Ursachen der Agrarbewegung*, p. 3; S. Neumann, *Stufen des Konservatismus*, p. 114.

18. *Die Verfassung vom Jahre 1849*, ed. L. Bergsträsser, pp. 74, 87-91, 94; *Verhandlungen der Nationalversammlung*, ed. F. Wigard, II, 1291-1347, III, 2289-2290, IV, 2377-2381, 2387-2425, 2438-2463, 2536-2539, 2573, V, 3897-3935, VI, 4258-4272, 4281-4283, VII, 4294-4295, 5100-5120, 5127-5146, 5168-5173, VIII, 5604-5608, 5635-5636; *Verhandlungen des Verfassungs-Ausschusses*, ed. J. G. Droysen, p. 39; S. Neumann, *Stufen des Konservatismus*, p. 23; W. Schneider, *Wirtschafts- und Sozialpolitik*, p. 72; A. Sartorius von Waltershausen, *Wirtschaftsgeschichte*, pp. 137-138.

19. *Verhandlungen der Nationalversammlung*, ed. F. Wigard, II, 1293.

20. *Die Verfassung vom Jahre 1849*, ed. L. Bergsträsser, pp. 86-87, 89; *Verhandlungen der Nationalversammlung*, ed. F. Wigard, I, 691-693, II, 1312, III, 2325-2339, IV, 2539-2551, 2558-2571, V, 3426, VI, 4136, 4252-4258, 4279, 4283-4292; *Neue Münchner Zeitung*, November 16, 1848; L. Brentano, "Familienfideikommisse," pp. 25-26; P. Albrecht, *Die volkswirtschaftlichen Fragen*, pp. 34-37.

21. *Verhandlungen der Nationalversammlung*, ed. F. Wigard, IV, 2543.

22. *Ibid.*, IV, 2404.

23. *Die Verfassung vom Jahre 1849*, ed. L. Bergsträsser, pp. 86, 88, 90; *Verhandlungen der Nationalversammlung*, ed. F. Wigard, III, 2325-2339, IV, 2377-2381, 2387-2426, 2438-2463, 2539-2552, 2558-2571, V, 3887, VI, 4252, 4272-4278, 4293; *Verhandlungen der Reichs-Versammlung*, ed. K. D. Hassler, IV, 199; R. Haym, *Die deutsche Nationalversammlung*, I, 65-66.

24. C. Bornhak, *Geschichte des Verwaltungsrechts*, III, 223, 225; H. Rosenberg, *Weltwirtschaftskrisis*, p. 17; E. Marcks, *Aufstieg des Reiches*, I, 284; E. Marcks, *Männer und Zeiten*, I, 213; E. Marcks, *Bismarck*, p. 442; *Neue Rheinische Zeitung*, July 30, 1848; *Verhandlungen der Nationalversammlung*, ed. F. Wigard, II, 1295; Prussia, *Verhandlungen des zweiten vereinigten Landtages*, p. 44.

CHAPTER 10

THE FALL OF LIBERALISM

1. Paul Hassel, *Joseph Maria v. Radowitz* (Berlin, 1905), p. 574.

2. *Ibid.*, pp. 577-578.

3. *Ibid.*, p. 588. Cf. W. Früh, *Radowitz*, pp. 86-87, 89-90, 99-100; *Radowitz: Briefe und Aufzeichnungen*, ed. W. Möring, pp. 48, 50; M. Quarck, *Die erste Arbeiterbewegung*, p. 74; H. Mähl, *Die Überleitung Preussens*, pp. 196-197; H. Goetting, "Radowitz," pp. 107-108; F. Meinecke, *Radowitz*, p. 531.

4. P. Hassel, *Radowitz*, p. 538.

5. *Denkwürdigkeiten aus dem Leben Leopold von Gerlachs, Generals der Infanterie und General-Adjutanten König Friedrich Wilhelms IV.* (2 vols., Berlin, 1891-92), I, 153.

6. O. v. Bismarck, *Werke*, VII, 14.

7. E. Kaeber, *Berlin 1848*, p. 182; E. Marcks, *Bismarck*, pp. 456, 547; V. Valentin, *Geschichte der Revolution*, II, 232-233; H. Sacher, "Konservative Parteien," *Staatslexikon*, 5th ed.; H. v. Petersdorff, "Hermann Wagener," *Allgemeine deutsche Biographie*.

8. The minutes of the "Junker Parliament" were published in the *Neue Preussische Zeitung*, August 20, August 22, August 23, August 24, 1848. For the activities of the Association for the Protection of Property and the Advancement of the Welfare of All Classes see E. Marcks, *Bismarck*, pp. 462-464; V. Valentin, *Geschichte der Revolution*, II, 233-235; E. Kaeber, *Berlin 1848*, pp. 182-183; Herman v. Petersdorff, *Kleist-Retzow: Ein Lebensbild* (Stuttgart and Berlin, 1907), pp. 125-134; Herman von Petersdorff, "Kleist-Retzow," *Deutscher Aufstieg*, ed. H. v. Arnim and G. v. Below, pp. 126-127; Herman v. Petersdorff, "Bülow-Cummerow," *ibid.*, p. 46; L. Salvatorelli, *La rivoluzione europea*, pp. 222-223; H. Walter, *Die innere Politik*, pp. 30-31; *Parteiprogramme*, ed. F. Salomon, 4th and 5th eds., I, 88, n. 1, 92, n. 2; S. Neumann, *Stufen des Konservatismus*, p. 114.

9. *Neue Preussische Zeitung*, August 22, 1848.

10. *Neue Preussische Zeitung*, August 27, 1848; *Parteiprogramme*, ed. F. Salomon, 4th and 5th eds., I, 92; P. Albrecht, *Die volkswirtschaftlichen Fragen*, p. 7: *Ernst Ludwig von Gerlach: Aufzeichnungen aus seinem Leben und Wirken, 1795-1877* (2 vols., Schwerin, 1903), I, 541; G. Lüttke, *Die politischen Anschauungen*, pp. 35, 37-38; E. Marcks, *Bismarck*, pp. 456, 547-548; E. Kaeber, *Berlin 1848*, p. 183; V. Valentin, *Geschichte der Revolution*, II, 229; H. Wagener, *Erlebtes*, I, 21; E. Brandenburg, *Reichsgründung*, I, 295.

11. *Neue Preussische Zeitung*, August 27, 1848; *Parteiprogramme*, ed. F. Salomon, 4th and 5th eds., I, 92; *Ernst Ludwig von Gerlach: Aufzeichnungen*, I, 244; W. Früh, *Radowitz*, pp. 99-100; O. v. Bismarck, *Werke*, VII, 13-14, XIV/1, 111-112; E. Marcks, *Bismarck*, p. 547; Friedrich Meinecke, *Weltbürgertum und Nationalstaat: Studien zur Genesis des deutschen Nationalstaates*, 6th ed. (Munich and Berlin, 1922), pp. 439-440.

12. Prussia, *Gesetz-Sammlung* (1848), pp. 289-310; E. Kaeber, *Berlin 1848*, pp. 81, 83, 99-102, 116, 168-173, 192; V. Valentin, *Geschichte der Revolution*, II, 48-51, 70-71, 164-166, 255-258; W. Blos, *Die Revolution*, pp. 324-331, 408-409, 460-461; H. Blum, *Die Revolution*, pp. 314-315, 344-346; *Radowitz: Briefe und Aufzeichnungen*, ed. W. Möring, p. 48; F. Meinecke, "The Year 1848," p. 484; F. Meinecke, *Weltbürgertum und Nationalstaat*, p. 388; E. Bernstein, *Berliner Arbeiter-Bewegung*, I, 16; H. Rosenberg, *Weltwirtschaftskrisis*, p. 35; G. Adler, *Geschichte der Arbeiterbewegung*, p. 159.

13. *Neue Rheinische Zeitung*, October 21, October 22, 1848; *Neue Preussische Zeitung*, October 18, 1848; *Neue Münchner Zeitung*, October 17, October 21, 1848; *Bayerische Landbötin*, October 21, October 24, October 26, 1848; V. Valentin, *Geschichte der Revolution*, II, 252-254; W. Blos, *Die Revolution*, pp. 458-459; E. Kaeber, *Berlin 1848*, p. 120; H. Blum, *Die Revolution*, p. 352; J. Droz, *Les révolutions allemandes*, pp. 382-384.

14. *Neue Preussische Zeitung*, October 18, 1848.

15. *Revolutionsbriefe 1848: Ungedrucktes aus dem Nachlass König Friedrich Wilhelms IV. von Preussen*, ed. Karl Haenchen (Leipzig, 1930), p. 165. Cf. O. v. Bismarck, *Werke*, xv, 35; *König Friedrich Wilhelms IV. Briefwechsel mit Ludolf Camphausen*, ed. Erich Brandenburg (Berlin, 1906), p. 174; *Memoirs of Baron Stockmar by His Son Baron E. von Stockmar*, ed. F. Max Müller (2 vols., London, 1872), ii, 270; *Christian Carl Josias Freiherr von Bunsen: Aus seinen Briefen und nach eigener Erinnerung geschildert von seiner Witwe*, ed. Friedrich Nippold (3 vols., Leipzig, 1868-71), ii, 453, 464-470; E. Brandenburg, *Untersuchungen und Aktenstücke*, pp. 119-120, 124; J. Hansen, *Mevissen*, i, 575-576; *Denkwürdigkeiten Leopold von Gerlachs*, i, 185; H. Laube, *Das erste Parlament*, ii, 123-124; V. Valentin, *Geschichte der Revolution*, ii, 137; G. P. Gooch, "The Centenary of 1848," p. 225.

16. V. Valentin, *Geschichte der Revolution*, ii, 238-271; E. Marcks, *Aufstieg des Reiches*, i, 320-325; E. Brandenburg, *Reichsgründung*, i, 238-244; E. Brandenburg, *Untersuchungen und Aktenstücke*, pp. 124, 130, 133; E. Kaeber, *Berlin 1848*, pp. 174-175, 188, 190, 192, 200-204; H. Walter, *Die innere Politik*, pp. 36-37; K. Biedermann, *1840-1870*, i, 395; H. v. Petersdorff, *Friedrich Wilhelm der Vierte*, p. 110; J. Hansen, "Das politische Leben," pp. 726-728; *Annual Register of 1848*, i, 390-391; F. Meinecke, *Weltbürgertum und Nationalstaat*, p. 388; W. Appens, *Die Nationalversammlung*, p. 330; G. P. Gooch, "The Centenary of 1848," p. 225.

17. *Neue Preussische Zeitung*, November 12, 1848; *Kaiser Wilhelms I. Weimarer Briefe*, ed. Johannes Schultze (2 vols., Stuttgart, Berlin, and Leipzig, 1924), i, 187; *Neue Münchner Zeitung*, November 14, 1848; *Bayerische Landbötin*, November 18, 1848; *Verhandlungen der Nationalversammlung*, ed. F. Wigard, v, 3292.

18. *Neue Rheinische Zeitung*, November 26, 1848.

19. *Neue Preussische Zeitung*, November 13, 1848; *Neue Münchner Zeitung*, November 14, 1848; *Bayerische Landbötin*, November 18, December 14, 1848; *Neue Rheinische Zeitung*, December 8, 1848; *Johann Gustav Droysen: Briefwechsel*, ed. Rudolf Hübner (2 vols., Stuttgart, Berlin, and Leipzig, 1929), i, 480, 496; *Denkwürdigkeiten Leopold von Gerlachs*, i, 239, 257; O. v. Bismarck, *Werke*, xiv/i, 117; *Annual Register of 1848*, i, 393-394; J. Hansen, *Mevissen*, ii, 442-443; Theodore S. Fay, *The Three Germanys* (2 vols., New York, 1889), ii, 970, 972; R. Stadelmann, "Das Jahr 1848," p. 108; H.C.M. Wendel, *Industrial Freedom*, pp. 50-51; L. Salvatorelli, *La rivoluzione europea*, p. 281; H. Walter, *Die innere Politik*, pp. 36-37; Leopold von Ranke, *Sämmtliche Werke* (54 vols., Leipzig, 1867-90), xlix-l, 612.

20. The text of the Prussian constitution of December 5, 1848, appears in Prussia, *Gesetz-Sammlung* (1848), pp. 375-391. Representative interpretations of its significance may be found in the following: *Neue Rheinische Zeitung*, December 9, 1848; *Neue Preussische Zeitung*, December 9, 1848; V. Valentin, *Geschichte der Revolution*, ii, 290-293; E. Brandenburg, *Reichsgründung*, i, 251-253; E. Marcks, *Aufstieg des Reiches*, i, 325; W. Blos, *Die Revolution*, pp. 473-474; H. Blum, *Die Revolution*, p. 357; H. Walter, *Die innere Politik*, p. 45; A. W. Ward, *Germany*, i, 483;

S. Neumann, *Stufen des Konservatismus*, p. 117; H. v. Sybel, *Begründung des Reiches*, 1, 256.

21. Prussia, *Gesetz-Sammlung* (1848), 392-397, 399-400; *Denkwürdigkeiten des Ministers Manteuffel*, ed. H. v. Poschinger, 1, 67; *Neue Rheinische Zeitung*, December 15, 1848; *Neue Preussische Zeitung*, December 22, December 30, 1848; *Neue Münchner Zeitung*, December 23, 1848; Felix Bamberg, "David Justus Ludwig Hansemann," *Allgemeine deutsche Biographie*; A. Bergengrün, *Hansemann*, pp. 589-591; J. Hansen, *Mevissen*, 1, 608; *Nachlass Varnhagen's von Ense*, v, 362; H. Walter, *Die innere Politik*, p. 60; Wilhelm Otto Vollrath, *Der parlamentarische Kampf um das preussische Dreiklassenwahlrecht* (Borna-Leipzig, 1931), p. 2; V. Valentin, *Geschichte der Revolution*, 11, 293; G. Meyer, *Wahlrecht*, p. 189.

22. Prussia, *Gesetz-Sammlung* (1848), pp. 380, 388, 392-394, 427-441, (1849), pp. 1-13; H. Walter, *Die innere Politik*, pp. 45, 80-81, 85-86, 99-100, 137-138; *Denkwürdigkeiten Leopold von Gerlachs*, 1, 390-392; B. Bauer, *Untergang des Parlaments*, p. 206; *Denkwürdigkeiten des Ministers Manteuffel*, ed. H. v. Poschinger, 1, 60-62, 67; O. z. Stolberg-Wernigerode, *Stolberg-Wernigerode*, pp. 86-87; F. Meinecke, *Weltbürgertum und Nationalstaat*, pp. 439-440; H. v. Petersdorff, *Kleist-Retzow*, p. 160; V. Valentin, *Geschichte der Revolution*, 11, 345; S. Neumann, *Stufen des Konservatismus*, p. 117; G. F. Knapp, *Bauern-Befreiung*, 1, 221, 11, 423-428; C. Bornhak, *Geschichte des Verwaltungsrechts*, 111, 225, 249; J. Conrad, "Grossgrundbesitz in Ostpreussen," p. 838; T.v.d. Goltz, *Geschichte*, 11, 151; H. Preuss, *Junkerfrage*, p. 69; L. W. Muncy, *The Junker*, p. 24.

23. *Neue Preussische Zeitung*, January 19, January 21, January 28, 1849; *Neue Rheinische Zeitung*, December 8, 1848, February 3, February 4, 1849; *Allgemeine Zeitung*, January 15, January 25, February 6, 1849; *Reden, Proklamationen, Botschaften, Erlasse und Ordres Sr. Majestät des Königs Friedrich Wilhelm IV. vom Schlusse des vereinigten ständischen Ausschusses, am 6. März 1848, bis zur Enthüllungs-Feier des Denkmals Friedrich des Grossen, am 31. Mai 1851* (Berlin, 1851), p. 48; *Verhandlungen der Reichs-Versammlung*, ed. K. D. Hassler, 11, 872; *Denkwürdigkeiten des Ministers Manteuffel*, ed. H. v. Poschinger, 1, 70; H. Krause, *Die demokratische Partei*, p. 201; V. Böhmert, *Freiheit der Arbeit*, pp. 217-218; W. E. Biermann, *Winkelblech*, 11, 182; B. Bauer, *Untergang des Parlaments*, pp. 210-212; Alexander Bergengrün, *Staatsminister August Freiherr von der Heydt* (Leipzig, 1908), pp. 205-206; R. Stadelmann, *Soziale Geschichte von 1848*, pp. 171-172; H. Waentig, "Die gewerbepolitischen Anschauungen," p. 22; K. V. Herberger, *Stellung der Konservativen*, pp. 30, 37; P. Geissen, *Handwerkerpolitik*, pp. 28-29, 47-48; G. Schmoller, *Geschichte der Kleingewerbe*, pp. 85-87; Hugo Roehl, *Beiträge zur preussischen Handwerkerpolitik vom allgemeinen Landrecht bis zur allgemeinen Gewerbeordnung von 1845* (Leipzig, 1900), p. 274.

24. *Denkwürdigkeiten Leopold von Gerlachs*, 1, 300-301; *Erinnerungen aus dem Leben von Unruh*, ed. H. v. Poschinger, p. 123; J. Hansen, *Mevissen*, 11, 462-463; O. v. Bismarck, *Werke*, xiv/1, 122-124; *Annual Register or a View of the History and Politics of the Year 1849* (2 vols., London, 1850), 1, 344; V. Valentin, *Geschichte der Revolution*, 11, 345-346;

Paul Matter, *La Prusse et la révolution de 1848* (Paris, 1903), p. 236; L. Salvatorelli, *La rivoluzione europea*, p. 301; H. Walter, *Die innere Politik*, p. 49.

25. *Neue Rheinische Zeitung*, February 4, 1849.

26. Prussia, *Gesetz-Sammlung* (1849), pp. 93-124; *Neue Rheinische Zeitung*, February 3, February 4, 1849; *Allgemeine Zeitung*, February 6, 1849; P. Geissen, *Handwerkerpolitik*, pp. 28-40, 46-49, 52-56; H. Waentig, "Die gewerbepolitischen Anschauungen," p. 22; V. Böhmert, *Freiheit der Arbeit*, pp. 217-218; R. Stadelmann, *Soziale Geschichte von 1848*, pp. 171-172; W. E. Biermann, *Winkelblech*, II, 182; G. K. Anton, *Geschichte der Fabrikgesetzgebung*, pp. 154-156; A. Thun, "Beiträge," p. 69; K. V. Herberger, *Stellung der Konservativen*, pp. 37-38; William Harbutt Dawson, *Bismarck and State Socialism* (London, 1890), pp. 87-88; H.C.M. Wendel, *Industrial Freedom*, p. 59; G. Schmoller, *Geschichte der Kleingewerbe*, p. 85; W. Schneider, *Wirtschafts- und Sozialpolitik*, p. 11; H. Roehl, *Beiträge zur Handwerkerpolitik*, p. 274.

27. Prussia, *Stenographische Berichte über die Verhandlungen der durch das allerhöchste Patent vom 5. Dezember 1848 einberufenen Kammern: Zweite Kammer* (Berlin, 1849), pp. 1, 617-618, 708-720; *Neue Rheinische Zeitung*, March 1, 1849; *Annual Register of 1849*, I, 345; *Denkwürdigkeiten Leopold von Gerlachs*, I, 390-392; H. Walter, *Die innere Politik*, pp. 99-103; G. F. Knapp, *Bauern-Befreiung*, I, 221-223; O. z. Stolberg-Wernigerode, *Stolberg-Wernigerode*, pp. 86-87.

28. Württemberg, *Regierungs-Blatt* (1849), pp. 181-206, 269-271, 313-315, 466-470, 480-485; Nassau, *Verordnungsblatt* (1849), pp. 137-141; Hesse-Darmstadt, *Regierungsblatt* (1849), pp. 205-211; Schwarzburg-Rudolstadt, *Gesetzsammlung* (1849), pp. 87-108; Saxe-Altenburg, *Gesetz-Sammlung* (1849), pp. 215-216; Saxe-Meiningen, *Sammlung der Verordnungen* (1849), pp. 227-238; T. Knapp, *Neue Beiträge*, I, 181-182; G. v. Viebahn, *Statistik Deutschlands*, II, 587, 594; O. Reinhard, *Grundentlastung in Württemberg*, p. 107; "Ablösungsgesetze," pp. 210-215; E. Schocke, *Sachsen-Meiningen*, pp. 57-59; O. H. Brandt, *Sachsen-Altenburg*, p. 145.

29. Prussia, *Gesetz-Sammlung* (1849), pp. 93-124; Nassau, *Verordnungsblatt* (1849), pp. 63-67; Saxe-Gotha, *Gesetzsammlung für das Herzogthum Gotha* (1849), pp. 375-385, 387-397, 401-422; *Neue Rheinische Zeitung*, May 16, 1849; *Neue Preussische Zeitung*, December 31, 1848; R. v. Delbrück, *Lebenserinnerungen*, I, 226-229; P. Möslein, *Gewerbegesetzgebung*, pp. 55, 57-58; W. E. Biermann, *Winkelblech*, II, 181-182, 187-188.

30. V. Valentin, *Geschichte der Revolution*, II, 372-382; W. Blos, *Die Revolution*, pp. 520-533; H. Blum, *Die Revolution*, pp. 380-392; E. Brandenburg, *Reichsgründung*, I, 275-280; E. Marcks, *Aufstieg des Reiches*, I, 309-319; H. v. Sybel, *Begründung des Reiches*, I, 303-319; Otto Hintze, *Die Hohenzollern und ihr Werk: Fünfhundert Jahre vaterländischer Geschichte* (Berlin, 1915), pp. 544-546; T. S. Fay, *The Three Germanys*, II, 981-984; *Verhandlungen der Nationalversammlung*, ed. F. Wigard, VIII, 6084-6093; *Aus dem Briefwechsel Friedrich Wilhelms IV. mit Bunsen*, ed. Leopold von Ranke (Leipzig, 1873), p. 233; J. G. Legge, *Rhyme and Revolution*, pp. 516-517; J. Hansen, *Mevissen*, II, 470; Kurt

Schauer, *Der Einzelne und die Gemeinschaft: Vom Geschäftsverfahren des Frankfurter Parlaments* (Frankfurt am Main, 1923), p. 67.

31. *Neue Rheinische Zeitung*, May 12, 1849. Cf. V. Valentin, *Geschichte der Revolution*, II, 471-475, 479-489, 493-496, 509-540; W. Blos, *Die Revolution*, pp. 534-600; Wilhelm Blos, *Der Untergang des Frankfurter Parlaments* (Frankfurt am Main, 1924), p. 10; H. Blum, *Die Revolution*, pp. 393-464; E. Brandenburg, *Reichsgründung*, I, 282-283; Erich Brandenburg, *Die deutsche Revolution 1848* (Leipzig, 1912), pp. 99-102; E. Marcks, *Aufstieg des Reiches*, I, 319-320; A. W. Ward, *Germany*, I, 493-495; A. W. Ward, "Revolution in Germany," p. 219; B. Bauer, *Untergang des Parlaments*, pp. 292-293; C. Geyer, *Parteien in Sachsen*, pp. 179, 210-211; *Neue Rheinische Zeitung*, May 12, 1849; *Neue Preussische Zeitung*, May 13, 1849; *Allgemeine Zeitung*, May 24, 1849; C. Schurz, *Lebenserinnerungen*, I, 193, 195-196; *Kaiser Wilhelms Briefe*, ed. J. Schultze, I, 207; M. Doeberl, *Bayern*, p. 196; A. Höfle, *Gewerbeordnung der Pfalz*, p. 22; J. A. Hawgood, "1848 in Central Europe," p. 322; E. Schöttle, "1848-1948," p. 137; A. Markow, *Wachstum der Bevölkerung*, p. 28; J. Kaizl, *Kampf um Gewerbereform*, p. 143; G. v. Viebahn, *Statistik Deutschlands*, I, 349, II, 147, 161.

32. O. v. Bismarck, *Werke*, XIV/I, 160.

CHAPTER 11

THE CONSERVATIVE FIFTIES

1. H. v. Sybel, *Begründung des Reiches*, I, 321-428, II, 3-136; Heinrich Friedjung, *Österreich von 1848 bis 1860* (2 vols., Stuttgart and Berlin, 1908-12), II, 1-134; H. v. Srbik, *Deutsche Einheit*, II, 17-22; E. Marcks, *Aufstieg des Reiches*, I, 320-358; E. Brandenburg, *Reichsgründung*, I, 298-339; A. W. Ward, *Germany*, I, 502-538; O. Hintze, *Die Hohenzollern*, pp. 547-557.

2. R. v. Delbrück, *Lebenserinnerungen*, I, 273-349; W. O. Henderson, *Zollverein*, pp. 202-225; A. Zimmermann, *Geschichte der Handelspolitik*, pp. 364-384; H. v. Festenberg-Packisch, *Geschichte*, pp. 307-327; Sommaruga, "Karl Ludwig Freiherr von Bruck," *Allgemeine deutsche Biographie*; H. v. Sybel, *Begründung des Reiches*, II, 155-167; H. v. Srbik, *Deutsche Einheit*, II, 189-196; E. Brandenburg, *Reichsgründung*, I, 364-366; E. Marcks, *Aufstieg des Reiches*, I, 411-417; A. W. Ward, *Germany*, II, 3-5; O. Hintze, *Die Hohenzollern*, p. 557; E. Denis, *La fondation de l'empire*, p. 98.

3. Prussia, *Stenographische Berichte über die Verhandlungen der durch die allerhöchste Verordnung vom 2. November 1850 einberufenen Kammern: Zweite Kammer* (2 vols., Berlin, 1851), I, 44.

4. *Kaiser Wilhelms Briefe*, ed. J. Schultze, I, 238.

5. O. v. Bismarck, *Werke*, XIV/I, 179-180.

6. V. Valentin, *Geschichte der Revolution*, II, 534-544; H. Blum, *Die Revolution*, pp. 463-464; *Erinnerungen aus dem Leben von Unruh*, ed. H. v. Poschinger, pp. 135-143, 170-173; H. v. Sybel, *Begründung des*

Reiches, II, 109-113, 150-153; H. v. Srbik, *Deutsche Einheit,* II, 186-188; E. Brandenburg, *Reichsgründung,* I, 363-364; E. Marcks, *Aufstieg des Reiches,* I, 359-361; *Verfassungsgesetze,* ed. H. A. Zachariä, pp. 47-50; T. Knapp, *Neue Beiträge,* I, 183; H. A. Strauss, *Staat, Bürger, Mensch,* p. 130.

7. Richard Charmatz, *Österreichs innere Geschichte von 1848 bis 1907* (2 vols., Leipzig, 1909), I, 16-36; Josef Redlich, *Das österreichische Staats- und Reichsproblem: Geschichtliche Darstellung der inneren Politik der Habsburgischen Monarchie von 1848 bis zum Untergang des Reiches* (2 vols., Leipzig, 1920-26), I, 382-459; Viktor Bibl, *Der Zerfall Österreichs* (2 vols., Vienna, Berlin, Leipzig, and Munich, 1922-24), I, 227-239; H. Friedjung, *Österreich,* II, 171-209, 244-263, 494-508; H. v. Srbik, *Deutsche Einheit,* II, 123-133, 145-159; H. v. Sybel, *Begründung des Reiches,* II, 103-104; E. Brandenburg, *Reichsgründung,* I, 343-350; E. Marcks, *Aufstieg des Reiches,* I, 361-369.

8 A. Bernstein, *Revolutions- und Reaktions-Geschichte Preussens und Deutschlands von den Märztagen bis zur neuesten Zeit* (3 vols., Berlin, 1882), II, 22-243; H. v. Sybel, *Begründung des Reiches,* II, 104-109; C. Bornhak, *Geschichte des Verwaltungsrechts,* III, 252-263; H. Heffter, *Selbstverwaltung,* pp. 327-343; E. Brandenburg, *Reichsgründung,* I, 350-363; E. Marcks, *Aufstieg des Reiches,* I, 369-378; H. v. Srbik, *Deutsche Einheit,* II, 160-165; O. Hintze, *Die Hohenzollern,* pp. 548-549, 558-560; H. Walter, *Die innere Politik,* pp. 122, 128-129, 154; W. Zimmermann, *Entstehung der Selbstverwaltung,* pp. 18-19, 21; Ludolf Parisius, *Deutschlands politische Parteien und das Ministerium Bismarck: Ein Beitrag zur vaterländischen Geschichte* (Berlin, 1878), pp. 19-20; Friedrich Thimme, "Ferdinand Otto Wilhelm Henning von Westphalen," *Allgemeine deutsche Biographie;* S. Neumann, *Stufen des Konservatismus,* p. 23; G. Meyer, *Wahlrecht,* pp. 194-195, 249; J. Conrad, "Fideikommisse," p. 273; J. Conrad, "Grossgrundbesitz in Ostpreussen," p. 834.

9. H. v. Sybel, *Begründung des Reiches,* II, 113-136, 168-169; H. Heffter, *Selbstverwaltung,* pp. 343-349; G. Meyer, *Wahlrecht,* pp. 196-205; E. Brandenburg, *Reichsgründung,* I, 363-364; E. Marcks, *Aufstieg des Reiches,* I, 381-386; *Verfassungsgesetze,* ed. H. A. Zachariä, pp. 775, 899-900, 955-957; W. Kellner, *Taschenbuch,* pp. 67-102; R. Wöltge, *Die Reaktion in Hannover,* p. 14.

10. G. v. Viebahn, *Statistik Deutschlands,* II, 365, 371, 407-409, 421, 487-489; J. Kuczynski, *Short History,* pp. 15, 69-70, 72; J. Kuczynski, *Bewegung der Wirtschaft,* pp. 198-199; W. Sombart, *Die deutsche Volkswirtschaft,* pp. 183, 521; G. Schmoller, *Geschichte der Kleingewerbe,* pp. 162-163, 399, 478; H. Rosenberg, *Weltwirtschaftskrisis,* pp. 130-137; G. Stolper, *German Economy,* pp. 25, 47; L. Pohle, *Entwicklung des Wirtschaftslebens,* p. 14; E. Denis, *La fondation de l'empire,* p. 99; Hans Rothfels, "1848: One Hundred Years After," *Journal of Modern History,* XX (1948), 297.

11. P. Benaerts, *Les origines,* pp. 131-136; J. Müller, *Grundriss der Statistik,* III, 17; G. Stolper, *German Economy,* p. 38; W. Sombart, *Kapitalismus,* III, 377; A. M. Carr-Saunders, *Population* (London, 1925), p. 76.

12. *Zeitschrift des königlich preussischen statistischen Bureaus*, XIII (1873), 2-3; G. v. Viebahn, *Statistik Deutschlands*, II, 241, 247; M. L. Hansen, "Revolutions of 1848," pp. 632-634, 657-658; P. Benaerts, *Les origines*, pp. 132, 139; A. Markow, *Wachstum der Bevölkerung*, pp. 162, 199; A. J. May, "The United States," pp. 221-222; J. Kuczynski, *Short History*, p. 49; H. v. Treitschke, *Deutsche Geschichte*, V, 491; G. Stolper, *German Economy*, p. 39; J. Kaizl, *Kampf um Gewerbereform*, p. 168; E. Katz, *Landarbeiter*, pp. 31, 35, 37; A. Nebel, *Arbeiterverhältnisse*, p. 15.

13. J. Kuczynski, *Short History*, pp. 28, 60, 151, 153; J. Kuczynski, *Labour Conditions*, p. 95; J. Kuczynski, *Bewegung der Wirtschaft*, pp. 197, 199; A. Sartorius von Waltershausen, *Wirtschaftsgeschichte*, p. 92; P. Benaerts, *Les origines*, p. 598.

14. *Zeitschrift des königlich preussischen statistischen Bureaus*, VI (1866), 70; *ibid.*, XI (1871), 243; F. Kühnert, "Schlachtvieh- und Fleischpreise," pp. 379-380; P. Benaerts, *Les origines*, p. 598; J. Kuczynski, *Short History*, pp. 32, 63; T.v.d. Goltz, *Vorlesungen*, pp. 44-45; E. Jordan, *Entstehung der konservativen Partei*, p. 110; J. Kaizl, *Kampf um Gewerbereform*, p. 142; A. Zimmermann, *Blüthe und Verfall*, p. 474; E. Katz, *Landarbeiter*, p. 37; G. Schmoller, *Geschichte der Kleingewerbe*, p. 429.

15. Prussia, *Verhandlungen der Kammern: Erste Kammer* (1851-52), I, 295; Prussia, *Stenographische Berichte über die Verhandlungen der durch die allerhöchste Verordnung vom 29. Oktober 1853 einberufenen Kammern: Erste Kammer* (2 vols., Berlin, 1854), II, 553; *Neue Preussische Zeitung*, September 21, 1848; *Tabellen und Nachrichten für 1855*, p. 197; K. V. Herberger, *Stellung der Konservativen*, pp. 10, 56; A. Zimmermann, *Blüthe und Verfall*, p. 468; H. Lehmann, "Die Textilindustrie," *Rheinprovinz*, ed. J. Hansen, I, 395; A. Höfle, *Gewerbeordnung der Pfalz*, p. 23.

16. L. v. Ranke, *Werke*, XLIX-L, 597-598. Cf. K. V. Herberger, *Stellung der Konservativen*, pp. 48, 74; Hermann Wagener, *Die kleine aber mächtige Partei* (Berlin, 1885), p. 9; H. v. Petersdorff, "Wagener," p. 170; H. Goetting, "Huber," pp. 79-81; Franz Hahne, "Lagarde als Politiker," *Deutscher Aufstieg*, ed. H. v. Arnim and G. v. Below, p. 290; G. Schilfert, *Sieg und Niederlage*, pp. 157-158.

17. J. v. Radowitz, *Gesammelte Schriften* (5 vols., Berlin, 1852-53), IV, 265-266.

18. *Denkwürdigkeiten des Ministers Manteuffel*, ed. H. v. Poschinger, II, 241, 322, III, 107; *Preussens auswärtige Politik, 1850 bis 1858: Unveröffentlichte Dokumente aus dem Nachlasse des Ministerpräsidenten Otto Frhrn. v. Manteuffel*, ed. Heinrich v. Poschinger (3 vols., Berlin, 1902), I, 141; Karl Enax, *Otto von Manteuffel und die Reaktion in Preussen* (Dresden, 1907), pp. 11-12, 19, 50, 53, 56-57; P. Geissen, *Handwerkerpolitik*, p. 10; H. Walter, *Die innere Politik*, pp. 149-150; E. Denis, *La fondation de l'empire*, p. 98; H. Heffter, *Selbstverwaltung*, p. 328; J. v. Radowitz, *Schriften*, IV, 211, 265-266; W. Früh, *Radowitz*, pp. 101, 117, 120-121; F. Meinecke, *Radowitz*, p. 531; H. Goetting, "Radowitz," pp. 107-108; O. v. Bismarck, *Werke*, XIV/1, 223; E. Marcks, *Bismarck*, pp. 547-548; H. v. Petersdorff, *Friedrich Wilhelm der Vierte*, pp. 9, 60; H. Wagener, *Die Politik Friedrich Wilhelm IV.*, p. 25.

19. *Parteiprogramme*, ed. F. Salomon, 1st ed., I, 33.

20. *Denkwürdigkeiten des Ministers Manteuffel*, ed. H. v. Poschinger, I, 70, II, 231; *Denkwürdigkeiten Leopold von Gerlachs*, I, 639; *Ernst Ludwig von Gerlach: Aufzeichnungen*, I, 541; G. Lüttke, *Die politischen Anschauungen*, pp. 34-35, 37-38; H. Delbrück, *Erinnerungen*, p. 215; H. v. Petersdorff, *Kleist-Retzow*, p. 265; F. Tönnies, "Deutscher Adel," pp. 1044, 1060-1061; K. V. Herberger, *Stellung der Konservativen*, pp. 30, 74; P. Geissen, *Handwerkerpolitik*, p. 12.

21. *Zeitschrift des königlich preussischen statistischen Bureaus*, II (1862), 101, 112; *ibid.*, VII (1867), 240-242; *Statistisches Handbuch für den preussischen Staat*, IV (1903), 649; *Mittheilungen des statistischen Bureau's in Berlin*, III (1850), 87-88, 91, 185; *Neue Preussische Zeitung*, July 20, July 24, 1849; O. v. Bismarck, *Werke*, XIV/I, 129; *Parteiprogramme*, ed. F. Salomon, 4th and 5th eds., I, 179; L. Parisius, *Deutschlands Parteien*, pp. 16, 19-20, 22; G. Schilfert, *Sieg und Niederlage*, p. 408; F. Meinecke, *Radowitz*, pp. 309-310; W. O. Vollrath, *Der parlamentarische Kampf*, p. 14.

22. *Neue Preussische Zeitung*, July 15, 1849; *Denkwürdigkeiten Leopold von Gerlachs*, I, 281-282; O. v. Bismarck, *Werke*, X, 356-357; G. Schilfert, *Sieg und Niederlage*, pp. 259, 286, 306; Friedrich Thimme, "Ferdinand Otto Wilhelm Henning von Westphalen," *Allgemeine deutsche Biographie*; Georg von Below, *Das parlamentarische Wahlrecht in Deutschland* (Berlin, 1909), pp. 3-5; L. Parisius, *Deutschlands Parteien*, pp. 19-20; Eugene N. Anderson, *The Social and Political Conflict in Prussia, 1858-1864* (Lincoln, 1954), pp. 270-271.

23. Prussia, *Gesetz-Sammlung* (1849), pp. 205-210; *Denkwürdigkeiten des Ministers Manteuffel*, ed. H. v. Poschinger, I, 67; J. Hansen, *Mevissen*, I, 608, II, 491-492; *Friedrich Wilhelms IV. Briefwechsel mit Camphausen*, ed. E. Brandenburg, p. 203; Felix Bamberg, "David Justus Ludwig Hansemann," *Allgemeine deutsche Biographie*; A. Bergengrün, *Hansemann*, p. 623; A. Wolfstieg, "Wer ist der 'Vater' des Dreiklassenwahlrechts in Preussen?", *Preussische Jahrbücher*, CLXIV (1916), 349-355; Anna Caspary, *Ludolf Camphausens Leben* (Stuttgart and Berlin, 1902), pp. 321, 341; J. Hansen, "Friedrich Wilhelm IV. und das Märzministerium," p. 189; J. Philippson, *Ursprung des Wahlrechts*, p. 20; G. Schilfert, *Sieg und Niederlage*, pp. 150, 167, 252-287; W. O. Vollrath, *Der parlamentarische Kampf*, pp. 3-4; F. Frensdorff, "Aufnahme des Wahlrechts," pp. 177-179; G. Meyer, *Wahlrecht*, pp. 257-258; H. Walter, *Die innere Politik*, p. 64.

24. J. Hansen, *Mevissen*, II, 488.

25. H. Heffter, *Selbstverwaltung*, pp. 349-372; E. Brandenburg, *Reichsgründung*, I, 368-374; E. Marcks, *Aufstieg des Reiches*, I, 386-410; H. v. Srbik, *Deutsche Einheit*, II, 297-307; L. Parisius, *Deutschlands Parteien*, pp. 16, 19-20, 22; *Duncker: Politischer Briefwechsel*, ed. J. Schultze, pp. 35-36; F. Meinecke, *Radowitz*, pp. 309-310.

26. Friedrich Engels, "Für Republik zu sterben!", *Neue Rheinische Zeitung: Politisch-ökonomische Revue* (1850), no. 3, p. 79. Cf. Franz Mehring, *Karl Marx: Geschichte seines Lebens*, 4th ed. (Leipzig, 1923), pp. 197-201, 206-212; G. Mayer, *Friedrich Engels*, I, 362-372; G. Adler, *Geschichte der Arbeiterbewegung*, pp. 252-253, 255-256.

CHAPTER 12

THE ECONOMICS OF REACTION

1. *Preussens auswärtige Politik*, ed. H. v. Poschinger, I, 141.
2. *Denkwürdigkeiten des Ministers Manteuffel*, ed. H. v. Poschinger, I, 70, II, 241, III, 107; *Ernst Ludwig von Gerlach: Aufzeichnungen*, I, 541; *Parteiprogramme*, ed. F. Salomon, 1st ed., I, 23-24; K. Enax, *Manteuffel*, pp. 53, 56-57; E. Denis, *La fondation de l'empire*, p. 98; G. Lüttke, *Die politischen Anschauungen*, pp. 34-35, 37-38; H. Delbrück, *Erinnerungen*, p. 215; E. Marcks, *Bismarck*, p. 547; O. z. Stolberg-Wernigerode, *Stolberg-Wernigerode*, p. 86; H. v. Petersdorff, *Kleist-Retzow*, pp. 160, 265.
3. *Denkwürdigkeiten des Ministers Manteuffel*, ed. H. v. Poschinger, I, 163, II, 241, 322, III, 107; *Denkwürdigkeiten Leopold von Gerlachs*, I, 390-392; O. z. Stolberg-Wernigerode, *Stolberg-Wernigerode*, pp. 86-87; H. v. Petersdorff, *Kleist-Retzow*, p. 160; G. F. Knapp, *Bauern-Befreiung*, I, 221-223; H. Walter, *Die innere Politik*, pp. 99-103; Prussia, *Verhandlungen der Kammern: Zweite Kammer* (1849), pp. 617-618; Prussia, *Stenographische Berichte über die Verhandlungen der durch die allerhöchste Verordnung vom 30. Mai 1849 einberufenen zweiten Kammer* (5 vols., Berlin, 1849-50), I, 28, III, 1286-1677, IV, 1991-2211, V, 2755-2769; Prussia, *Verhandlungen der Kammern: Erste Kammer* (1849-50), IV, 1957-1958, V, 2453-2837.
4. Prussia, *Gesetz-Sammlung* (1850), pp. 77-128; *Neue Preussische Zeitung*, September 16, 1849; *Tabellen und Nachrichten für 1849*, IV, 550-551; G. F. Knapp, *Bauern-Befreiung*, I, 221-273; H. Walter, *Die innere Politik*, pp. 103-110, 112, 156; G. v. Viebahn, *Statistik Deutschlands*, II, 584, 1009-1010; C.F.W. Dieterici, *Handbuch der Statistik*, p. 316; E. Wolff, *Volkswirtschafts-Geschichte*, pp. 101-102; A. Sartorius von Waltershausen, *Wirtschaftsgeschichte*, p. 137; K. Reis, *Ursachsen der Agrarbewegung*, p. 8; L. Brentano, *Aufsätze*, pp. 257-258; W. Kellner, *Taschenbuch*, p. 34; S. Sugenheim, *Aufhebung der Leibeigenschaft*, pp. 473-475; C. Bornhak, *Geschichte des Verwaltungsrechts*, III, 248-249; O. v. Nell-Breuning, "Rentenbanken," *Staatslexikon*, 5th ed.; J. Kuczynski, *Bewegung der Wirtschaft*, p. 41.
5. Saxony, *Verordnungsblatt* (1851), pp. 129-138; Hanover, *Sammlung der Gesetze* (1851), pp. 11-12; Saxe-Altenburg, *Gesetz-Sammlung* (1851), pp. 23-32; Schwarzburg-Rudolstadt, *Gesetzsammlung* (1856), pp. 5-41; Saxe-Weimar, *Sammlung grossherzogl. Gesetze*, X, 296-297, 302-303; "Ablösungsgesetze," pp. 207-208; S. Sugenheim, *Aufhebung der Leibeigenschaft*, pp. 462-464; G. v. Viebahn, *Statistik Deutschlands*, II, 589-595; O. H. Brandt, *Sachsen-Altenburg*, pp. 145-146, 150; E. Schocke, *Sachsen-Meiningen*, pp. 57-59; W. Kellner, *Taschenbuch*, pp. 28-33.
6. Hesse-Kassel, *Sammlung von Gesetzen* (1849), p. 25, (1850), pp. 29-30.
7. *Zeitschrift des königlich preussischen statistischen Bureaus*, V (1865), 8-9; *Preussische Statistik*, V (1864), 21; *Neue Preussische Zeitung*, September 16, 1849; E. Jordan, *Entstehung der konservativen Partei*, pp. 27-28; F. Gutmann, "Bauernbefreiung," *Handwörterbuch der Staatswissenschaften*,

4th ed.; G. v. Viebahn, *Statistik Deutschlands*, II, 560, 562-564, 584-585, 1010; J. Kuczynski, *Bewegung der Wirtschaft*, p. 41; S. Sugenheim, *Aufhebung der Leibeigenschaft*, pp. 474-475; W. Kellner, *Taschenbuch*, p. 34; H. Walter, *Die innere Politik*, p. 112; L. Pohle, *Entwicklung des Wirtschaftslebens*, p. 35; W. Sombart, *Kapitalismus*, III, 335-336; W. Sombart, *Die deutsche Volkswirtschaft*, p. 518; Herbert Heaton, *Economic History of Europe* (New York and London, 1936), p. 461.

8. Prussia, *Gesetz-Sammlung* (1852), p. 319, (1853), pp. 181, 238-239, (1856), p. 353; H. Walter, *Die innere Politik*, pp. 128-129, 154; J. Conrad, "Grossgrundbesitz in Ostpreussen," p. 838; J. Conrad, "Fideikommisse," p. 273; C. v. Dietz, "Fideikommisse," *Handwörterbuch der Staatswissenschaften*, 4th ed.; C. Bornhak, *Geschichte des Verwaltungsrechts*, III, 247, 249-250, 255; G. Meyer, *Wahlrecht*, p. 249; H. Preuss, *Junkerfrage*, pp. 69-71; F. Schnabel, *Deutsche Geschichte*, II, 297; W. Zimmermann, *Entstehung der Selbstverwaltung*, pp. 18-19, 21; S. Neumann, *Stufen des Konservatismus*, p. 23.

9. J. Conrad, "Latifundien," pp. 140-145, 150-152, 164-166; J. Conrad, "Grossgrundbesitz in Ostpreussen," pp. 831, 844; J. Conrad, "Fideikommisse," pp. 293, 296; G. v. Viebahn, *Statistik Deutschlands*, II, 1019; W. Sombart, *Die deutsche Volkswirtschaft*, p. 520; W. Sombart, *Kapitalismus*, III, 335; E. v. Philippovich, *Entwicklung der Ideen*, pp. 100-101; S. Neumann, *Stufen des Konservatismus*, p. 40; L. Brentano, "Familienfideikommisse," p. 21; L. W. Muncy, *The Junker*, p. 85; F. Tönnies, "Deutscher Adel," p. 1053; Max Weber, *Gesammelte Aufsätze zur Soziologie und Sozialpolitik* (Tübingen, 1924), p. 328.

10. *Zeitschrift des königlich preussischen statistischen Bureaus*, V (1865), 5-9; *ibid.*, XIII (1873), 25; *Tabellen und Nachrichten für 1849*, V, 550-551, 908-909; *Tabellen und Nachrichten für 1855*, pp. 197-201; *Preussische Statistik*, V (1864), 21; *Neue Preussische Zeitung*, September 16, 1849; G. v. Viebahn, *Statistik Deutschlands*, II, 560, 562-564, 584-585, 589-593, 595; J. Conrad, "Latifundien," pp. 134-135; M. Sering, *Die innere Kolonisation*, pp. 63, 296-297; E. Jordan, *Entstehung der konservativen Partei*, pp. 28, 39; G. F. Knapp, *Bauern-Befreiung*, I, 257-258; G. F. Knapp, *Landarbeiter*, p. 83; G. F. Knapp, *Grundherrschaft*, p. 71; M. Sering, *Deutsche Agrarpolitik*, p. 29; W. Sombart, *Kapitalismus*, III, 335-336; W. Sombart, *Die deutsche Volkswirtschaft*, pp. 52, 518; A. Sartorius von Walterhausen, *Wirtschaftsgeschichte*, p. 124; T.v.d. Goltz, *Geschichte*, II, 189-190; F. Gutmann, "Bauernbefreiung," *Handwörterbuch der Staatswissenschaften*, 4th ed.; W. Wittich, *Grundherrschaft*, p. 446; W. Kellner, *Taschenbuch*, p. 34; E. Katz, *Landarbeiter*, pp. 31-32, 40-42; S. Sugenheim, *Aufhebung der Leibeigenschaft*, pp. 474-475; H. Walter, *Die innere Politik*, p. 112; L. Brentano, *Aufsätze*, pp. 257-258; J. Kuczynski, *Bewegung der Wirtschaft*, p. 41; L. Pohle, *Entwicklung des Wirtschaftslebens*, p. 35; W. Bowden, M. Karpovich, and A. P. Usher, *Economic History*, pp. 275, 277, 281; H. Heaton, *Economic History*, p. 461; Carl Johannes Fuchs, "Bauernbefreiung," *Wörterbuch der Volkswirtschaft*, 4th ed.; W. Conze, "Wirkungen der Agrarreformen," pp. 16-17, 42-43; F. Schnabel, *Deutsche Geschichte*, II, 294; Alexander Gerschenkron, *Bread and Democracy in Germany* (Berkeley and Los Angeles, 1943), p. 23, n. 2.

11. *Denkwürdigkeiten Leopold von Gerlachs*, I, 639.

12. O. v. Bismarck, *Werke*, x, 52; H. v. Petersdorff, *Kleist-Retzow*, p. 267; *Ernst Ludwig von Gerlach: Aufzeichnungen*, I, 541; H. Wagener, *Die kleine Partei*, p. 12.

13. O. v. Bismarck, *Werke*, x, 49. Cf. Prussia, *Verhandlungen der Kammern: Zweite Kammer* (1849-50), II, 744-745, 747-748, 754-755, 767-769, 779-781; *Parteiprogramme*, ed. F. Salomon, 1st ed., I, 33-34; H. Wagener, *Die kleine Partei*, p. 9; P. Geissen, *Handwerkerpolitik*, pp. 12, 41-45; G. Lüttke, *Die politischen Anschauungen*, pp. 35, 37-38; E. Marcks, *Bismarck*, pp. 547-548; K. Enax, *Manteuffel*, p. 53; K. V. Herberger, *Stellung der Konservativen*, p. 30; Karl Braun, "Das Zwangs-Zölibat für Mittellose in Deutschland," *Vierteljahrschrift für Volkswirtschaft und Kulturgeschichte*, v (1867), no. 4, p. 29.

14. Prussia, *Gesetz-Sammlung* (1854), pp. 138-139; R. v. Delbrück, *Lebenserinnerungen*, I, 226-229; A. Bergengrün, *Heydt*, p. 208; V. Böhmert, *Freiheit der Arbeit*, pp. 223-225; P. Geissen, *Handwerkerpolitik*, pp. 37, 45, 50-51, 55-58; K. V. Herberger, *Stellung der Konservativen*, pp. 6, 30-31, 37-38, 74; F. Schnabel, *Deutsche Geschichte*, III, 426.

15. Prussia, *Stenographische Berichte über die Verhandlungen der durch die allerhöchste Verordnung vom 29. Oktober 1853 einberufenen Kammern: Zweite Kammer* (2 vols., Berlin, 1854), II, 787.

16. Hanover, *Sammlung der Gesetze* (1848), pp. 156-158; Nassau, *Verordnungsblatt* (1849), pp. 63-67; Saxe-Gotha, *Gesetzsammlung* (1849), pp. 375-385, 387-397, 401-422, (1851), pp. 9-11; W. E. Biermann, *Winkelblech*, II, 181-182, 186-188; P. Benaerts, *Les origines*, p. 554; P. Möslein, *Gewerbegesetzgebung*, pp. 55, 57-58; V. Valentin, *Frankfurt und die Revolution*, pp. 113-114; M. Quarck, *Die erste Arbeiterbewegung*, p. 98; L. Grambow, *Die Freihandelspartei*, p. 20; J. Kaizl, *Kampf um Gewerbereform*, p. 33.

17. Bavaria, *Regierungs-Blatt* (1848), pp. 785-790, (1853), pp. 1863-2026; J. Kaizl, *Kampf um Gewerbereform*, pp. 48, 105-119; G. Ziegler, *Gewerbegesetz von 1868*, pp. 26-29; P. Benaerts, *Les origines*, p. 553; G. Schmoller, *Geschichte der Kleingewerbe*, p. 121; W. Schneider, *Wirtschafts- und Sozialpolitik*, p. 12; G. Kölzsch, *Entwicklung der Gewerbefreiheit*, p. 37.

18. Saxony, *Verordnungsblatt* (1834), pp. 449-456; Prussia, *Gesetz-Sammlung* (1843), pp. 5-7; Hanover, *Sammlung der Gesetze* (1851), pp. 63-92; Württemberg, *Regierungs-Blatt* (1852), pp. 105-111; *Die Verfassung vom Jahre 1849*, ed. L. Bergsträsser, p. 73; L. Grambow, *Die Freihandelspartei*, pp. 36-37, 40-41; K. V. Herberger, *Stellung der Konservativen*, p. 62; K. Adam, "Stände und Berufe," p. 286; G. Lüttke, *Die politischen Anschauungen*, p. 35; O. Loening, "Freizügigkeit," *Handwörterbuch der Staatswissenschaften*, 4th ed.; M. Lichter, "Freizügigkeit," *Staatslexikon*, 5th ed.

19. Württemberg, *Regierungs-Blatt* (1852), pp. 105-111; Hesse-Darmstadt, *Regierungsblatt* (1852), pp. 233-234; K. Braun, "Zwangs-Zölibat," pp. 3-12, 28-29; J. Kaizl, *Kampf um Gewerbereform*, pp. 149, 153; K. V. Herberger, *Stellung der Konservativen*, pp. 62-63.

20. Prussia, *Gesetz-Sammlung* (1849), pp. 93-124, (1853), pp. 729-730, (1855), pp. 311-315; P. Geissen, *Handwerkerpolitik*, p. 37; K. V. Herberger, *Stellung der Konservativen*, pp. 57-60; L. Grambow, *Die Frei-*

handelspartei, pp. 36-37, 40-41; B. Laum, "Armenwesen: Geschichte der öffentlichen Armenpflege," *Handwörterbuch der Staatswissenschaften,* 4th ed.; F. Diefenbach, "Armenwesen: Armengesetzgebung und Armenpolizei in Deutschland," *Handwörterbuch der Staatswissenschaften,* 4th ed.; Franz Riss, "Armenfürsorge," *Staatslexikon,* 5th ed.

21. Prussia, *Gesetz-Sammlung* (1837), p. 19, (1849), pp. 93-110; Prussia, *Verhandlungen der Versammlung* (1848), v, 1779-1782; R. v. Delbrück, *Lebenserinnerungen,* I, 226-229; A. Thun, "Beiträge," pp. 67, 93; A. Thun, *Industrie am Niederrhein,* II, 196.

22. Prussia, *Gesetz-Sammlung* (1839), pp. 156-158; A. Thun, "Beiträge," pp. 61, 82, 94; K. V. Herberger, *Stellung der Konservativen,* p. 50; G. K. Anton, *Geschichte der Fabrikgesetzgebung,* p. 92; G. Albrecht, "Arbeiterschutz," *Wörterbuch der Volkswirtschaft,* 4th ed.; L. Brentano, "Reform der Fabrikgesetzgebung," p. 177.

23. Prussia, *Stenographische Berichte über die Verhandlungen der durch die allerhöchste Verordnung vom 13. November 1852 einberufenen Kammern: Erste Kammer* (2 vols., Berlin, 1853), II, 1108. Cf. *ibid.,* II, 1107-1110; Prussia, *Stenographische Berichte über die Verhandlungen der durch die allerhöchste Verordnung vom 13. November 1852 einberufenen Kammern: Zweite Kammer* (3 vols., Berlin, 1853), III, 1452-1471; K. V. Herberger, *Stellung der Konservativen,* pp. 50-51; G. K. Anton, *Geschichte der Fabrikgesetzgebung,* p. 95; A. Thun, "Beiträge," p. 61.

24. Prussia, *Gesetz-Sammlung* (1853), pp. 225-227; G. K. Anton, *Geschichte der Fabrikgesetzgebung,* pp. 83, n. 1, 108; A. Thun, "Beiträge," pp. 79, 93; K. V. Herberger, *Stellung der Konservativen,* pp. 51, 74; J. Kuczynski, *Short History,* p. 98; A. Bergengrün, *Heydt,* p. 213.

25. *Denkwürdigkeiten des Ministers Manteuffel,* ed. H. v. Poschinger, II, 241.

CHAPTER 13

THE NEW ERA

1. H. v. Sybel, *Begründung des Reiches,* II, 170-370; A. Bernstein, *Reaktions-Geschichte,* II, 243-260, III, 3-130; H. v. Srbik, *Deutsche Einheit,* II, 204-411, III, 3-25; J. Redlich, *Staats- und Reichsproblem,* I, 460-553; V. Bibl, *Der Zerfall Österreichs,* II, 227-275; H. Friedjung, *Österreich,* II, 229-243; R. Charmatz, *Österreichs Geschichte,* I, 34-47; E. Brandenburg, *Reichsgründung,* I, 379-417; E. Marcks, *Aufstieg des Reiches,* I, 421-474; A. W. Ward, *Germany,* II, 7-51; Johannes Ziekursch, *Politische Geschichte des neuen deutschen Kaiserreiches: Die Reichsgründung,* 2nd ed. (Frankfurt am Main, 1932), pp. 7-28; Erich Marcks, *Kaiser Wilhelm I.,* 9th ed. (Berlin, 1943), pp. 123-157; O. Hintze, *Die Hohenzollern,* pp. 562-567; *Parteiprogramme,* ed. F. Salomon, 4th and 5th eds., I, 179; *Zeitschrift des königlich preussischen statistischen Bureaus,* II (1862), 112; L. Parisius, *Deutschlands Parteien,* p. 16; A. Thun, "Beiträge," p. 93.

2. G. Schmoller, *Geschichte der Kleingewerbe*, pp. 71, 94-95, 105-106, 110-112, 124-137, 145-147, 162-163, 399, 478, 631, 665; *Zeitschrift des königlich preussischen statistischen Bureaus*, I, (1861), 50-52; W. Sombart, *Kapitalismus*, III, 340-343; P. Benaerts, *Les origines*, p. 394; J. Kaizl, *Kampf um Gewerbereform*, pp. 170-171; A. Höfle, *Gewerbeordnung der Pfalz*, pp. 31, 39; K. V. Herberger, *Stellung der Konservativen*, pp. 4, 6; L. Pohle, *Entwicklung des Wirtschaftslebens*, p. 14.

3. Prussia, *Gesetz-Sammlung* (1849), pp. 93-124, (1854), pp. 138-139; H. Waentig, "Die gewerbepolitischen Anschauungen," pp. 23-24; P. Geissen, *Handwerkerpolitik*, pp. 56-58; A. Bergengrün, *Heydt*, pp. 207-208; W. E. Biermann, *Winkelblech*, II, 183; L. Grambow, *Die Freihandelspartei*, p. 20; G. Albrecht, "Handwerks- und Gewerbekammern," *Wörterbuch der Volkswirtschaft*, 4th ed.

4. Prussia, *Stenographische Berichte über die Verhandlungen der durch die allerhöchste Verordnung vom 2. November 1850 einberufenen Kammern: Erste Kammer* (2 vols., Berlin, 1851), II, 1404-1405, 1412; Prussia, *Verhandlungen der Kammern: Erste Kammer* (1852-53), II, 821-823; Prussia, *Verhandlungen der Kammern: Zweite Kammer* (1852-53), III, 1105-1112; Prussia, *Sammlung sämmtlicher Drucksachen der zweiten Kammer aus der ersten Session der III. Legislatur-Periode, 1852 bis 1853* (8 vols., Berlin, 1853), VI, no. 275, pp. 1-17; Prussia, *Stenographische Berichte über die Verhandlungen der durch die allerhöchste Verordnung vom 12. November 1855 einberufenen beiden Häuser des Landtages: Haus der Abgeordneten* (3 vols., Berlin, 1856), II, 720-729; Prussia, *Sammlung sämmtlicher Drucksachen des Hauses der Abgeordneten aus der ersten Session der IV. Legislatur-Periode, 1855 bis 1856* (6 vols., Berlin, 1856), III, no. 155, pp. 1-17; K. V. Herberger, *Stellung der Konservativen*, pp. 3, 5-6, 31-32; V. Böhmert, *Freiheit der Arbeit*, pp. 225-230; P. Geissen, *Handwerkerpolitik*, pp. 13-14; H. Waentig, "Die gewerbepolitischen Anschauungen," p. 24; W. E. Biermann, *Winkelblech*, II, 186; J. Wilden, "Handwerk," *Handwörterbuch der Staatswissenschaften*, 4th ed.; G. Albrecht, "Handwerk," *Wörterbuch der Volkswirtschaft*, 4th ed.

5. Prussia, *Sammlung sämmtlicher Drucksachen des Hauses der Abgeordneten* (1855-56), III, no. 155, p. 8.

6. *Parteiprogramme*, ed. F. Salomon, 1st ed., I, 43-44.

7. K. V. Herberger, *Stellung der Konservativen*, pp. 6-7, 31; V. Böhmert, *Freiheit der Arbeit*, pp. 223-225; H. Waentig, "Die gewerbepolitischen Anschauungen," pp. 24-25; J. Wilden, "Handwerk," *Handwörterbuch der Staatswissenschaften*, 4th ed.; G. Albrecht, "Handwerk," *Wörterbuch der Volkswirtschaft*, 4th ed.

8. *Parteiprogramme*, ed. F. Salomon, 1st ed., I, 51. Cf. K. V. Herberger, *Stellung der Konservativen*, pp. 3, 31-32, 37-38; F. Tönnies, "Deutscher Adel," p. 1044.

9. Austria, *Reichs-Gesetz-Blatt für das Kaiserthum Oesterreich* (1859), pp. 619-650, (1860), pp. 336-338; P. Benaerts, *Les origines*, p. 553; G. Kölzsch, *Entwicklung der Gewerbefreiheit*, p. 36; G. Schmoller, *Geschichte der Kleingewerbe*, p. 109; V. Valentin, *Frankfurt und die Revolution*, p. 515; L. Grambow, *Die Freihandelspartei*, pp. 20, 33; P. Möslein, *Gewerbegesetzgebung*, pp. 49-52; V. Böhmert, *Freiheit der Arbeit*, pp. 230-239; H. Waentig, "Die gewerbepolitischen Anschauungen," p. 31;

J. Kaizl, *Kampf um Gewerbereform*, p. 34; G. Ziegler, *Gewerbegesetz von 1868*, p. 34.

10. Nassau, *Verordnungsblatt* (1860), pp. 99-102; Saxony, *Verordnungsblatt* (1861), pp. 187-217; Württemberg, *Regierungs-Blatt* (1862), pp. 67-86; Baden, *Regierungsblatt* (1862), pp. 409-416; G. Kölzsch, *Entwicklung der Gewerbefreiheit*, pp. 35-38; P. Möslein, *Gewerbegesetzgebung*, pp. 49-52, 68-88; G. Schmoller, *Geschichte der Kleingewerbe*, pp. 109, 151; G. v. Viebahn, *Statistik Deutschlands*, II, 545; H. Waentig, "Die gewerbepolitischen Anschauungen," p. 31; J. Kaizl, *Kampf um Gewerbereform*, p. 34; G. Ziegler, *Gewerbegesetz von 1868*, p. 34; L. Grambow, *Die Freihandelspartei*, p. 33; M. Biermer, "Handwerk: Moderne Bestrebungen," *Wörterbuch der Volkswirtschaft*, 2nd ed.

11. Hesse-Darmstadt, *Regierungsblatt* (1864), pp. 9-11, (1866), pp. 93-94; Bavaria, *Regierungs-Blatt* (1862), pp. 713-870; Bavaria, *Gesetz-Blatt* (1868), pp. 309-328; Prussia, *Gesetz-Sammlung* (1861), pp. 441-445, 749-753; G. Kölzsch, *Entwicklung der Gewerbefreiheit*, pp. 35, 37-39; W. Ullmann, *Die hessische Gewerbepolitik*, pp. 75-76; G. Ziegler, *Gewerbegesetz von 1868*, pp. 29-33, 41-49; J. Kaizl, *Kampf um Gewerbereform*, pp. 34, 48; G. Schmoller, *Geschichte der Kleingewerbe*, p. 121; H. Waentig, "Die gewerbepolitischen Anschauungen," p. 31; L. Grambow, *Die Freihandelspartei*, pp. 34-35; V. Böhmert, "Deutschlands Neugestaltung," p. 292; A. Köttgen, "Gewerbegesetzgebung: Die Gewerbegesetzgebung in Deutschland," *Handwörterbuch der Staatswissenschaften*, 4th ed.; G. Albrecht, "Handwerk," *Wörterbuch der Volkswirtschaft*, 4th ed.

12. O. v. Bismarck, *Werke*, X, 47-55.

13. *Ibid.*, XII, 194.

14. *Ibid.*, XIV/1, 223. Cf. *ibid.*, X, 38, XIV/1, 160, XV, 28; E. Marcks, *Bismarck*, pp. 442, 547-548.

15. O. v. Bismarck, *Werke*, XIV/1, 302.

16. *Jacob Burckhardts Briefe an seinen Freund Friedrich von Preen, 1864-1893* (Stuttgart and Berlin, 1922), p. 51. Cf. Arthur Rosenberg, *Die Entstehung der Deutschen Republik, 1871-1918* (Berlin, 1928), p. 13; E. N. Anderson, *Conflict in Prussia*, pp. 442-443; Otto Pflanze, "Bismarck and German Nationalism," *American Historical Review*, LX (1955), 554-555.

17. O. v. Bismarck, *Werke*, XIII, 563. Cf. *ibid.*, XIII, 448, 459.

18. Germany, *Bundes-Gesetzblatt des Norddeutschen Bundes* (1868), pp. 406-407, (1869), pp. 245-282; G. Kölzsch, *Entwicklung der Gewerbefreiheit*, pp. 39-51; H. Waentig, "Die gewerbepolitischen Anschauungen," pp. 32-33; L. Brentano, "Reform der Fabrikgesetzgebung," p. 184; A. Thun, "Beiträge," pp. 62, 67-68; J. Kaizl, *Kampf um Gewerbereform*, pp. 34, 137, n. 1; W. Sombart, *Die deutsche Volkswirtschaft*, p. 130; G. Ziegler, *Gewerbegesetz von 1868*, p. 51; W. Schneider, *Wirtschafts- und Sozialpolitik*, p. 12; J. Kuczynski, *Short History*, p. 99; E. v. Philippovich, *Entwicklung der Ideen*, p. 7; P. Möslein, *Gewerbegesetzgebung*, p. 70; W. Wygodzinski, *Wandlungen der Volkswirtschaft*, p. 75; J. Wilden, "Handwerk," *Handwörterbuch der Staatswissenschaften*, 4th ed.; A. Köttgen, "Gewerbegesetzgebung: Die Gewerbegesetzgebung in Deutschland," *ibid.*; G. Albrecht, "Handwerk," *Wörterbuch der Volkswirtschaft*, 4th ed.

19. Germany, *Bundes-Gesetzblatt* (1867), pp. 1-24, 55-58, 137-144, (1869) pp. 379-381; G. Ziegler, *Gewerbegesetz von 1868*, p. 51; H. Waentig, "Die gewerbepolitischen Anschauungen," p. 32; G. Stolper, *German Economy*, pp. 27, 33, 61; J. H. Clapham, *Economic Development*, p. 397; W. Sombart, *Die deutsche Volkswirtschaft*, p. 130; W. O. Henderson, *Zollverein*, p. 310; E. v. Philippovich, *Entwicklung der Ideen*, p. 8; H. Neisser, "Ausfuhrzölle, Ausfuhrverbote, Ausfuhrregelung," *Handwörterbuch der Staatswissenschaften*, 4th ed.

20. Germany, *Bundes-Gesetzblatt* (1868), pp. 473-478; Germany, *Reichs-Gesetzblatt* (1871), pp. 404-406, (1873), pp. 233-240; G. Stolper, *German Economy*, pp. 31-34; A. Sartorius von Waltershausen, *Wirtschaftsgeschichte*, p. 177; W. Sombart, *Die deutsche Volkswirtschaft*, p. 128; W. O. Henderson, *Zollverein*, pp. 139-140; W. Schneider, *Wirtschafts- und Sozialpolitik*, p. 140; J. H. Clapham, *Economic Development*, p. 125; Plato, "Mass- und Gewichtswesen," *Handwörterbuch der Staatswissenschaften*, 4th ed.

21. Germany, *Bundes-Gesetzblatt* (1867), p. 328; Germany, *Reichs-Gesetzblatt* (1873), pp. 164-165; *Europe by Treaty*, ed. E. Hertslet, I, 93; II, 1250-1265; III, 1847-1852, 1875-1876; *Rheinurkunden*, II, 80-106; W. Schneider, *Wirtschafts- und Sozialpolitik*, pp. 133-134, 137-138; G. Stolper, *German Economy*, pp. 28, 71-74, 76; C.F.W. Dieterici, *Handbuch der Statistik*, p. 579; L. Pohle, *Entwicklung des Wirtschaftslebens*, p. 116; Richard Büchner, "Wasserstrassenabgaben," *Handwörterbuch der Staatswissenschaften*, 4th ed.; A. F. Napp-Zinn, "Post," *Wörterbuch der Volkswirtschaft*, 4th ed.; A. F. Napp-Zinn, "Internationalisierung von Flüssen," *ibid.*

22. Johann Peter Eckermann, *Gespräche mit Goethe in den letzten Jahren seines Lebens*, ed. H. H. Houben (Leipzig, 1925), pp. 558-559.

CHAPTER 14

THE ROAD TO UNIFICATION

1. Johann Wolfgang von Goethe, *Faust: A Tragedy*, trans. Bayard Taylor (2 vols., Boston, 1871), I, 68-69. Cf. *Goethes Werke* (55 vols., Weimar, 1887-1918), XIV, 62-63.

2. W. Mommsen, *Grösse und Versagen*, p. 215. Cf. T. S. Hamerow, "History and the Revolution," pp. 27-44.

INDEX

Act of Confederation, 4, 7, 54, 56, 105, 164

Adolf, Duke of Nassau, 108

agrarian problem, 38-40; under enlightened despotism, 41-44; in the French Revolution and the Napoleonic Era, 44-47; in the Restoration, 47-55; in the Revolution of 1848, 163-72; in the Reaction, 180, 187-88, 190-91, 219-27. *See also* peasantry

Ahrens, Heinrich, 168

Alexandra Feodorovna, Empress of Russia, 183

Altenstein, Karl von, 24

Anneke, Fritz, 139

Arnim, Achim von, 69

Arnim-Boitzenburg, Count Adolf von, 100-01

artisan movement: in the Restoration, 30-35; in the Revolution of 1848, 102-06, 140-50, 155; in the reaction, 243-44; in the new era, 245. *See also* handicraft system

Assembly of Delegates of the North German Handicraft and Industrial Class, 143-44

Association for the Protection of Property and the Advancement of the Welfare of All Classes, 178-79

Auerswald, Alfred von, 92, 101-02

Auerswald, General Hans von, 181

Auerswald, Rudolf von, 183, 240

Bach, Baron Alexander von, 204

Bakunin, Mikhail, 193

Bamberger, Ludwig, 253

Banfield, Thomas C., 18, 53

Bassermann, Friedrich, 89

Beck, Karl, 8

Beckerath, Hermann von, 92, 184, 193, 216, 228

Bethmann-Hollweg, Moritz von, 240

Beust, Friedrich von, 239

Biedermann, Karl, 63

Bismarck, Otto von, 109-10, 116, 125, 138, 177, 179, 183, 189, 195, 203, 213, 215, 228, 239, 248-55, 260

Blum, Robert, 173

Bodelschwingh-Velmede, Ernst von, 100

Bonin, Gustav von, 184

Born, Stephan, 67, 139, 204

Borsig, August, 5

Brandenburg, Count Friedrich Wilhelm von, 185, 201, 215, 222

Brentano, Lorenz, 126, 193

Bruck, Baron Karl von, 135, 202

Bucher, Lothar, 216

Buchsweiler, Saul, 125

Büchner, Karl, 57

Bülow-Cummerow, Ernst von, 179, 215, 220

Bunsen, Baron Christian von, 171

Buol-Schauenstein, Count Karl von, 204, 239

Burckhardt, Jacob, 251

Burke, Edmund, 68

Camphausen, Ludolf, 9, 63, 92, 101, 183, 228

Camphausen, Otto, 9

Cavour, Count Camillo di, 203

Central Society for the Welfare of the Working Classes, 73

child labor, 18-19, 234-36

Circourt, Adolphe de, 100, 107

Cobden, Richard, 13

commerce, *see* industry and commerce

Commercial and Industrial Union, 10-11

conservatism, 68-73

constitution of Germany (March 28, 1849), 130-33, 169-70

constitution of Prussia (December 5, 1848), 186-87

constitutionalism, *see* liberalism

counterrevolution, 177-95

Dalwigk, Reinhard von, 239

Degenkolb, Karl, 235